7, 25, 18
₱ 19.99

POP CULTURE
NEW YORK CITY

The Ultimate
Location Finder

Bob Egan
Maps by Jim Egan

APPLAUSE
THEATRE & CINEMA BOOKS

An Imprint of Hal Leonard LLC

Published in 2018 by Applause Theatre & Cinema Books
An Imprint of Hal Leonard LLC
7777 West Bluemound Road
Milwaukee, WI 53213

Trade Book Division Editorial Offices
33 Plymouth St., Montclair, NJ 07042

Printed in the United States of America

Book design by John J. Flannery

Maps by Jim Egan

Library of Congress Cataloging-in-Publication Data

Names: Egan, Bob, author. | Egan, Jim, (Cartographer)
Title: Pop culture New York City : the ultimate location finder / Bob Egan ;
  maps by Jim Egan.
Description: Milwaukee, WI : Applause Theatre & Cinema Books logo, an imprint
  of Hal Leonard LLC, 2018. | Includes bibliographical references.
Identifiers: LCCN 2018012777 | ISBN 9781495093159
Subjects: LCSH: Popular culture--New York (State)--New York--Guidebooks. |
  New York (N.Y.)--Social life and customs--Guidebooks. | New York
  (N.Y.)--Guidebooks.
Classification: LCC F128.18 .E33 2018 | DDC 917.47/10444--dc23
LC record available at https://lccn.loc.gov/2018012777

www.applausebooks.com

CONTENTS

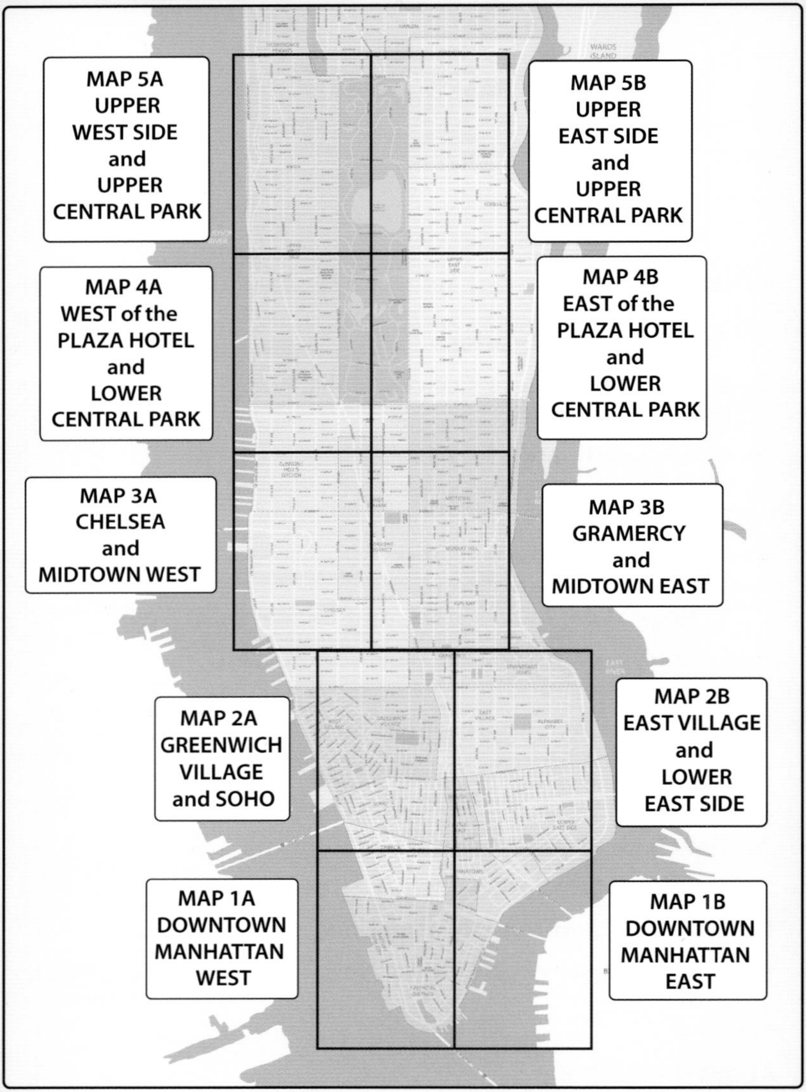

MAP 5A
UPPER
WEST SIDE
and
UPPER
CENTRAL PARK

MAP 5B
UPPER
EAST SIDE
and
UPPER
CENTRAL PARK

MAP 4A
WEST of the
PLAZA HOTEL
and
LOWER
CENTRAL PARK

MAP 4B
EAST of the
PLAZA HOTEL
and
LOWER
CENTRAL PARK

MAP 3A
CHELSEA
and
MIDTOWN WEST

MAP 3B
GRAMERCY
and
MIDTOWN EAST

MAP 2A
GREENWICH
VILLAGE
and SOHO

MAP 2B
EAST VILLAGE
and
LOWER
EAST SIDE

MAP 1A
DOWNTOWN
MANHATTAN
WEST

MAP 1B
DOWNTOWN
MANHATTAN
EAST

**Guide to
Manhattan Maps**

INTRODUCTION

NEW YORK CITY is the pop culture capital of the world. Books and magazines are written about it, and it's where movies are filmed, TV shows are taped, stars are photographed, art is made, music is created and performed, and legendary sports events played. And it's natural that visitors to New York (and New Yorkers themselves) would want see exactly where all these things took place—to go behind the scenes to the exact locations where pop cultural history was made.

With over one hundred colorful and detailed neighborhood maps, this guide gives you the locations and addresses of thousands of famous pop culture spots: where famous movies and TV shows were filmed, where movie and rock stars have lived, where iconic record album covers were photographed, where novels took place, and a lot more.

It's the guidebook that begins where most other guidebooks end. It's chock full of all the famous places you've seen in movies and on TV, read about in magazines, and always wanted to see in person.

I put the book together in map form so that wherever you are in New York, you can look at up to ten maps of that neighborhood. Each one focuses on a different pop cultural aspect (movies, music, art, celebrities, etc.) so you and your friends and family can tour the city by your main interests.

Welcome to New York City. There are cool things to see everywhere. You just have to know where to look. I hope this helps.

Bob Egan
New York City

MOVIE AND TV LOCATIONS

OVER TWO HUNDRED OF THE BEST-KNOWN MOVIES FEATURING NEW YORK CITY

*The locations for these movies
are shown on the neighborhood maps.*

A Chorus Line (**1985**)
Across 110th Street (**1972**)
Addicted to Love (**1997**)
After Hours (**1985**)
Almost Famous (**2000**)
American Psycho (**2000**)
An Affair to Remember (**1957**)
An Unmarried Woman (**1978**)
Angel Heart (**1987**)
Annie (**1982**)
Annie Hall (**1977**)
The April Fools (**1969**)
The Apartment (**1960**)
Arthur (**1981**)
As Good as It Gets (**1997**)
The Avengers (**2012**)
August Rush (**2007**)
Autumn in New York (**2001**)

Barefoot in the Park (**1967**)
Basquiat (**1996**)
Batteries Not Included (**1987**)
Bed of Roses (**1996**)
Big (**1988**)
The Big Broadcast (**1932**)
Big Business (**1988**)
Big Daddy (**1999**)

Birdman (**2014**)
Black Caesar (**1973**)
Black Swan (**2010**)
Blue Valentine (**2010**)
Bonfire of the Vanities (**1990**)
Boomerang (**1992**)
Breakfast at Tiffany's (**1961**)
Brewster's Millions (**1985**)
Bride Wars (**2009**)
Bright Lights, Big City (**1988**)
Brighton Beach Memoirs (**1986**)
Broadway Danny Rose (**1984**)
The Butcher's Wife (**1991**)

Carlito's Way (**1993**)
Center Stage (**2000**)
Chelsea Girls (**1966**)
Children of Men (**2006**)
City Hall (**1996**)
The Clock (**1945**)
Cloverfield (**2008**)
Cocktail (**1988**)
Coming to America (**1988**)
Coogan's Bluff (**1968**)
The Cotton Club (**1984**)
Cotton Comes to Harlem (**1970**)
The Cowboy Way (**1994**)

Crocodile Dundee (**1986**)
Crocodile Dundee II (**1988**)
Crooklyn (**1994**)
Crossing Delancey (**1988**)
Cruel Intentions (**1999**)

The Day After Tomorrow (**2004**)
Death Wish (**1974**)
Deceived (**1991**)
Desperately Seeking Susan (**1985**)
The Devil Wears Prada (**2006**)
Devil's Advocate (**1997**)
Die Hard with a Vengeance (**1995**)
Do the Right Thing (**1989**)
Dog Day Afternoon (**1975**)
Donnie Brasco (**1997**)
Dressed to Kill (**1980**)

Eat Pray Love (**2010**)
Elf (**2003**)
Empire **by Andy Warhol** (**1964**)
Enchanted (**2007**)
Escape from New York (**1981**)
Eternal Sunshine of the Spotless Mind (**2004**)
Eyewitness (**1981**)

Factory Girl (**2006**)
The Family Man (**2000**)
The First Wives Club (**1996**)
The Fisher King (**1991**)
For Love or Money (**1993**)
Fort Apache, The Bronx (**1981**)
Frankie and Johnny (**1991**)
The French Connection (**1971**)
The Freshman (**1990**)
Friends with Benefits (**2011**)
Funny Girl (**1968**)

Ghost (**1990**)
Ghostbusters (**1984**)
Ghostbusters II (**1989**)
The Godfather (**1972**)
The Godfather, Part II (**1974**)
The Godfather, Part III (**1990**)

Going the Distance (**2010**)
Godzilla (**1998**)
The Goodbye Girl (**1977**)
Goodfellas (**1980**)
The Great Gatsby (**1974**)
Great Expectations (**1998**)
Green Card (**1990**)

Hair (**1979**)
Hannah and Her Sisters (**1986**)
Hell Up in Harlem (**1973**)
Hitch (**2005**)
Home Alone 2: Lost in New York (**1992**)
The House on Carroll Street (**1988**)
How to Lose a Guy in 10 Days (**2003**)
Hudson Hawk (**1991**)
Husbands and Wives (**1992**)

I Am Legend (**2007**)
The Immigrant (**1917**)
Independence Day (**1996**)
Inside Llewyn Davis (**2013**)
Inside Man (**2006**)
The International (**2009**)
The Interpreter (**2005**)
It Could Happen to You (**1994**)
It Happened in Brooklyn (**1947**)

Joe Versus the Volcano (**1990**)
Johnny Dangerously (**1984**)
Julie & Julia (**2009**)
Jungle 2 Jungle (**1997**)
Just My Luck (**2006**)

Kids (**1995**)
King Kong (**1933**)
King Kong (**1976**)
The King of Comedy (**1982**)
Kinsey (**2004**)
Klute (**1971**)
Kramer vs. Kramer (**1979**)

The Last Action Hero (**1993**)
Last Exit to Brooklyn (**1989**)
Legal Eagles (**1986**)

Leon: The Professional (**1994**)
Limitless (**2011**)
Little Fugitive (**1953**)
Little Manhattan (**2005**)
The Lords of Flatbush (**1974**)
Love Affair (**1994**)
Love Story (**1970**)

Made (**2001**)
Maid in Manhattan (**2002**)
Malcolm X (**1992**)
Man on a Ledge (**2012**)
Man on a Wire (**2008**)
Manchurian Candidate (**1962**)
Manhattan (**1979**)
Manhattan Murder Mystery (**1993**)
Marathon Man (**1976**)
Marty (**1955**)
Mean Streets (**1973**)
Men in Black (**1997**)
Men in Black II (**2002**)
Mickey Blue Eyes (**1999**)
Midnight Cowboy (**1969**)
Mighty Aphrodite (**1995**)
Miracle on 34th Street (**1947**)
Mirage (**1965**)
Miss Congeniality (**2000**)
Mo' Better Blues (**1990**)
Mona Lisa Smile (**2003**)
Money Pit (**1986**)
Money Train (**1995**)
Moonstruck (**1987**)
Moscow on the Hudson (**1984**)
The Muppets Take Manhattan (**1984**)
My Dinner with Andre (**1981**)
My Favorite Year (**1982**)

The Naked City (**1948**)
The Nanny Diaries (**2007**)
National Treasure (**2004**)
Network (**1976**)
New Jack City (**1991**)
New Year's Eve (**2011**)
New York Stories/Life Lessons (**1989**)
Next Stop, Greenwich Village (**1976**)

Night at the Museum (**2006**)
Nighthawks (**1981**)
9 1/2 Weeks (**1986**)
North by Northwest (**1959**)

On the Town (**1949**)
Once Upon a Time in America (**1984**)
One Fine Day (**1996**)
The Other Guys (**2010**)

The Paper (**1994**)
A Perfect Murder (**1998**)
The Pick-Up Artist (**1987**)
Pitch Perfect (**2012**)
Planet of the Apes (**1968**)
Plaza Suite (**1971**)
The Prince of Central Park (**2000**)
Prince of Tides (**1991**)
Prizzi's Honor (**1985**)
The Producers (**1968**)
The Producers (**2005**)

Queens Logic (**1991**)

Radio Days (**1987**)
Raging Bull (**1980**)
Regarding Henry (**1991**)
Remember Me (**2010**)
Rent (**2005**)
Report to the Commissioner (**1975**)
Requiem for a Dream (**2000**)
Revolutionary Road (**2008**)
Romancing the Stone (**1984**)
Rosemary's Baby (**1968**)
The Rose (**1979**)
The Royal Tenenbaums (**2001**)
Rumble in the Bronx (**1995**)

Sabrina (*1954, 1995*)
The Saint of Fort Washington (**1993**)
Saturday Night Fever (**1977**)
Scent of a Woman (**1992**)
School of Rock (**2003**)
Searching for Bobby Fischer (**1993**)
Serendipity (**2001**)

*Serpico (*1973**)**
The Seven Year Itch (**1955**)
Sex and the City: The Movie (**2008**)
Shaft (**1971**)
Shaft (**2000**)
She Devil (**1989**)
She's Gotta Have It (**1986**)
She's the One (**1996**)
Sid and Nancy (**1986**)
The Siege (**1998**)
Single White Female (**1992**)
Six Degrees of Separation (**1993**)
Sleepers (**1996**)
Sleepless in Seattle (**1993**)
Sliver (**1993**)
Smithereens (**1982**)
Small Time Crooks (**2000**)
Sophie's Choice (**1982**)
Spider-Man (**2002**)
Spider-Man 2 (**2004**)
Spider-Man 3 (**2007**)
Spike of Bensonhurst (**1988**)
Splash (**1984**)
The Squid and the Whale (**2005**)
Straight Out of Brooklyn (**1991**)
Summer of Sam (**1999**)
The Sunshine Boys (**1975**)
Superman (**1978**)
The Sweet Smell of Success (**1957**)

Taxi Driver (**1976**)
Teenage Mutant Ninja Turtles (**1990**)
The Terminal (**2004**)
The Thomas Crown Affair (**1999**)
13 Going on 30 (**2004**)
Three Days of the Condor (**1975**)

Three of Hearts (**1993**)
Titanic (**1997**)
Tootsie (**1982**)
Trading Places (**1983**)
Transformers (**2007**)
A Tree Grows in Brooklyn (**1945**)
Turbulence (**1997**)
The Turning Point (**1977**)
12 Angry Men (**1957**)
25th Hour (**2002**)
28 Days (**2000**)
2 Days in New York (**2012**)

An Unmarried Woman (**1978**)

Vanilla Sky (**2001**)
Vanya on 42nd Street (**1994**)

Wait Until Dark (**1967**)
Wall Street (**1987**)
The Walk (**2015**)
The Warriors (**1979**)
The Way We Were (**1973**)
Weekend at Bernie's (**1989**)
West Side Story (**1961**)
Whatever Works (**2009**)
When Harry Met Sally (**1989**)
The Wiz (**1978**)
The Wolf of Wall Street (**2013**)
Wolfen (**1981**)
Working Girl (**1988**)

X-Men (**2000**)

You've Got Mail (**1998**)

MOVIE AND TV LOCATIONS ON THE MAPS

Addicted to Love: 35 Wooster and Grand Street

The April Fools: 56 Beaver Street at South William Street. Delmonico's.

As Good as It Gets: 31–33 West 12th Street between 5th and 6th Avenues

Barefoot in the Park: 111 Waverly Place between 5th and 6th Avenues

Basquiat: 177 Prince Street at Thompson Street (closed). Restaurant scene.

Batteries Not Included: 373 East 8th Street between Avenues C and D (approximately). Demolished.

Big: 83 Grand Street between Greene Street and Wooster Street. Josh Baskin's apartment.

Big Daddy: 340 West Broadway at Grand (Felix Restaurant), 16 Mercer Street at Howard Street. Sonny Koufax's apartment.

Breakfast at Tiffany's: 169 East 71st Street between 3rd Avenue and Lexington Avenue. Holly's apartment.

The Cosby Show (TV): 10 St. Luke's Place between 7th Avenue South and Hudson Street

Cruel Intentions: 2 East 79th Street near 5th Avenue

Crossing Delancey: 35 Essex Street between Hester and Grand. Guss' Pickles.

Desperately Seeking Susan: 29 St. Mark's Place between 2nd and 3rd Avenues (approximately)

Die Hard with a Vengeance: 33 Liberty Street between William and Nassau. Federal Reserve Bank.

Eat Pray Love: 244 East 5th Street between 2nd and 3rd Avenues

The Family Man: 14 Washington Mews near MacDougal Street

Friends (TV): 90 Bedford Street at Grove Street. The friends' apartment and Central Perk.

Ghost: 102 Prince between Green and Mercer. Their apartment.

Ghostbusters: 55 Central Park West at West 66th Street (Dana Barrett's apartment), Broadway at 58th Street (Stay Puft Man), 14 North Moore Street at Varick Street (Hook & Ladder 8)

Godfather 2: East 6th Street between Avenue A and Avenue B. Entire block.

The Goodbye Girl: 170 West 78th Street and Amsterdam Avenue

Great Expectations: Near East 10th Street and Avenue A. Center of Tompkins Square Park.

I Am Legend: 11 Washington Square North between 5th Avenue and University Place

Inside Man: 20 Exchange Place between Beaver and Hanover Streets

The Interpreter: 128 East 10th Street at Stuyvesant Street

I Love Lucy (TV): 623 East 68th Street. Would be in the river.

Made: 310 West Broadway between Grand and Canal Streets. SoHo Grand Hotel.

Magnolia Bakery: 401 Bleecker Street at West 11th Street

Marathon Man: 141 East 76th Street, northwest corner at Lexington Avenue. Staircase.

Municipal Building (City Hall Park) 1
- *Ghostbusters* (as City Hall)
- *Devil's Advocate*
- *Great Expectations*
- *Crocodile Dundee*

The Odeon
- *Life Lessons*
- *Bright Lights, Big City*

Caroline in the City (Caroline's apt.)

Surrogate's Courthouse
- *Great Expectations* (as the Met)
- *The Devil Wears Prada* (as a museum)

Tweed Courthouse
- *Kramer vs. Kramer*
- *The Verdict* (interiors)
- *Law and Order* (TV)
- *Law and Order* (courtrooms) (TV)

City Hall
- *City Hall*
- *It Could Happen to You*
- *Spin City* (TV)

Woolworth Building
- *Enchanted*
- *The Great Gatsby* (2013)
- *Ugly Betty* (TV)

World Financial Center
- *Bonfire of the Vanities*
- *Boomerang*

World Trade Center (The Twin Towers)
- *Home Alone 2*
- *Trading Places*
- *King Kong* (1976)
- *Superman*
- *Escape From NY*
- *The Wiz*
- *The Walk*
- *25th Hour*
- *Man on a Wire*
- *Three Days of the Condor*

140 Broadway
- *Klute*
- *An Unmarried Woman*

Trinity Church
- *The Great Gatsby*
- *National Treasure*

Federal Hall
- *Ghostbusters*
- *Kramer vs. Kramer*
- *Ghost*

New York Stock Exchange
- *Wall Street*

Ellis Island
- *The Godfather: Part II*
- *Hitch*
- *The Immigrant*

Statue of Liberty, Liberty Isalnd
- *Titanic*
- *Ghostbusters II*
- *Splash*
- *Escape from NY*
- *Cloverfield*
- *Children of Men*
- *Planet of the Apes*
- *Working Girl*
- *Superman*
- *Funny Girl*
- *On the Town*
- *An American Tale*
- *National Treasure*
- *The Day After Tomorrow*
- *Remo Williams*
- *X-Men*
- *Saboteur*

The Siege

The Apartment

Wall Street

Die Hard with a Vengeance

Inside Man

Sabrina

The April Fools

Battery Park Promenade
- *Desperately Seeking Susan*
- *Mirage*
- *Men in Black*
- *Wall Street*
- *She's the One*
- *Friends with Benefits*

National Museum of the American Indian (U. S. Custom House)
- *Ghostbusters II* (as Museum of Art)
- *Working Girl*

Staten Island Ferry
- *Working Girl*
- *Titanic*
- *Jungle 2 Jungle*
- *Ghostbusters II*
- *Escape from New York*

FINANCIAL DISTRICT

CHERRY ST

4

HENRY ST   PARK ROW   PIKE ST

CATHERINE ST

MADISON ST

MONROE ST

ST JAMES PL

AVE OF THE FINEST

MANHATTAN BRIDGE

New York Country Courthouse
- *Miracle on 34th Street*
- *Regarding Henry*
- *Legal Eagles*
- *The Godfather*
- *Shaft* (2000)
- *The Devil's Advocate*
- *12 Angry Men*
- *Green Card*
- *Cagney and Lacy* (TV)
- *Law and Order* (TV)
- *Kojak* (TV)

A

U.S. Court of Appeals
Night Court (TV)

Manhattan Bridge
- *The Cowboy Way*
- *Blue Valentine*
- *How to Lose a Guy in 10 Days*
- *Ghostbusters*

BROOKLYN BRIDGE

Brooklyn Bridge
- *I Am Legend*
- *Hudson Hawk*
- *The Wiz*
- *Sex and the City: The Movie*
- *Transformers*
- *Limitless*
- *If I Fell*
- *The French Connection*
- *The Siege*
- *On the Town*
- *It Happened in Brooklyn*
- *Sophie's Choice*
- *Mo' Better Blues*
- *Sex and the City* (TV)

B

GOLD ST

BEEKMAN ST

The Paper

Annie Hall

PEARL ST

PINE ST

WATER ST

FRONT ST

FRANKLIN DELANO ROOSEVELT DR

OLD SLIP

C

BROOKLYN

D

1B

TUNNEL

Mean Streets: Mulberry at Prince Street. Door to graveyard of Old St. Patrick's.

1980s MTV Studios: 1515 Broadway between 44th and 45th Streets

The Naked City: Williamsburg Bridge. Chase scene.

The Odd Couple **(TV):** 1049 Park Avenue between 86 and 87th Streets

The Paper: 127 John Street between Pearl and Water Streets

A Perfect Murder: 180 Prince between Sullivan and Thompson Streets. Raoul's restaurant.

Raging Bull: 1 Clarkson Street at Varick Street. Carmine Street Pool.

Romancing the Stone: 495 West End Avenue between 83rd and 84th Streets

Rhoda **(TV):** 332 East 84th Street between 1st and 2nd Avenues

Sabrina **(1954):** 30 Broad Street at Exchange Place

Seinfeld: 321 West 90th Street between West End Avenue and Riverside. George Costanza's apartment.

Serpico: 5–7 Minetta Lane between Minetta and Bleecker Streets

Sex and the City: 403 West 13th Street at 9th Avenue. Samantha's apartment.

The Seven Year Itch: 590 Lexington Avenue at 52nd Street (the subway grate/ Marilyn's white dress), 164 East 61st Street between 3rd and Lexington Avenues (Marilyn's apartment)

The Siege: 1 Liberty Plaza. At Broadway and Liberty.

Six Degrees of Separation: 828 Broadway at 12th Street (Strand bookstore), 860 Fifth Avenue between 67th and 68th Street

Sliver: 211 Madison Avenue between East 35th and 36th Streets. Morgan Court.

Smithereens: 54 Greene Street between Grand and Broome Streets

Summer of Sam: 315 Bowery between 1st and 2nd Streets. Was CBGB, now a clothing store.

Superman: 240 Central Park South between 7th Avenue and Broadway. Lois Lane's apartment.

Taxi **(TV):** 534 Hudson Street at Charles Street. Former Dover Garage.

That Girl **(TV):** FDR Drive between 78th and 79th Streets. Ann Marie's apartment.

30 Rock **(TV):** 160 West 88th at Riverside Drive. Liz Lemon's apartment.

Wait Until Dark: 5 St. Luke's Place between 7th Avenue South and Hudson Street

Wall Street: 222 Broadway between Fulton and Ann Streets

The Warriors **(poster):** Riverside Drive and West 97th Street. Dinosaur Playground.

When Harry Met Sally: 205 East Houston Street at Ludlow Street. Katz's Deli.

Whatever Works: 137 East Houston Street between Forsyth and Eldridge Streets. Yonah Schimmel Bakery.

Wild Style: East River Park Amphitheater, near FDR Drive and Cherry Street

Will and Grace **(TV):** 155 Riverside Drive at 88th Street. Will's apartment.

LOCATIONS WHERE MULTIPLE MOVIES HAVE BEEN FILMED

See the names of movies filmed at these places on the maps.

Alice in Wonderland Statue: Central Park, west of 75th Street
American Museum of Natural History: Central Park West and 79th Street
The Ansonia: 2109 Broadway between 73rd and 74th Streets
The Apthorp: 2211 Broadway between 78th and 79th Streets
The Arcade: Central Park
Balto Statue: Central Park
Battery Park Promenade: Battery Park
Ben's Pizza: 177 Spring Street, northeast corner at Thompson
Belvedere Castle: Central Park
Bergdorf Goodman: 754 Fifth Avenue at West 58th Street
Bethesda Fountain: Central Park
Bethesda Terrace/Steps: Central Park
Bleecker Street Cinema: 144 Bleecker Street between LaGuardia and Thompson Streets. Replaced.
Bloomingdale's: 1000 3rd Avenue between 59th and 60th Streets
Bow Bridge: Central Park
The Brill Building: 1619 Broadway, northwest corner at 49th Street
Brooklyn Bridge: East River
Bryant Park: Sixth Avenue between 40th and 42nd Streets
Café Des Artists: 1 West 67th Street at Central Park West. Closed.
Cafe Lalo: 201 West 83rd Street between Broadway and Amsterdam Avenue
Cafe Luxembourg: 200 West 70th Street
Caffe Reggio: 119 MacDougal Street between Minetta and West 3rd Street
The Carnegie Deli (former): 854 7th Avenue between 54th and 55th Streets
Carnegie Mansion: 2 East 91st Street, northeast corner at 5th Avenue
The Carousel: Central Park
Central Park Reservoir Track: Central Park, 86th to 96th Streets
Central Park Zoo: Central Park
The Chelsea Hotel: 222 West 23rd Street between 7th and 8th Avenues
Cherry Hill: Central Park
Chess and Checkers House: Central Park
The Chrysler Building: 405 Lexington between 42nd and 43rd Streets
City Hall: Broadway at Murray Street
Columbus Circle: 59th Street and 8th Avenue
Columbia University: 116th Street and Broadway
Conservatory Water: Central Park. Model boat pond.
Crosby Street: 104 Prince Street between Greene and Mercer Streets
The Daily News Building: 220 East 42nd Street between 2nd and 3rd Avenues
The Dairy: Central Park
The Dakota: 1 West 72nd Street at Central Park West
Dean & Deluca: 560 Broadway at Prince Street

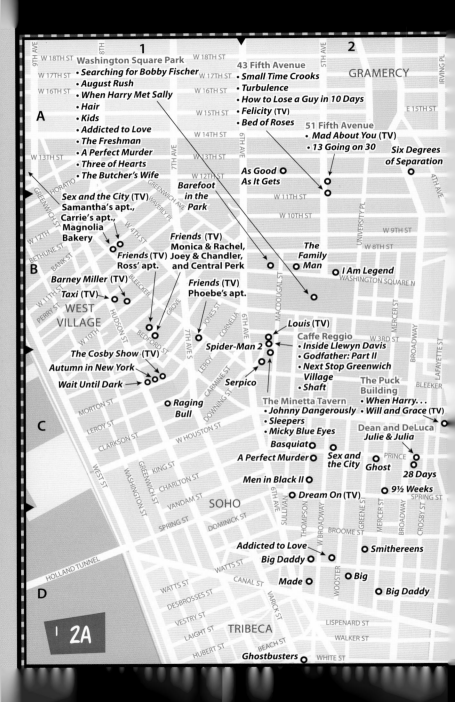

1

Washington Square Park
- *Searching for Bobby Fischer*
- *August Rush*
- *When Harry Met Sally*
- *Hair*
- *Kids*
- *Addicted to Love*
- *The Freshman*
- *A Perfect Murder*
- *Three of Hearts*
- *The Butcher's Wife*

Sex and the City (TV)
Samantha's apt.,
Carrie's apt.,
Magnolia
Bakery

Friends (TV)
Ross' apt.

*Barefoot
in the
Park*

Friends (TV)
Monica & Rachel,
Joey & Chandler,
and Central Perk

Barney Miller (TV)
Taxi (TV)

Friends (TV)
Phoebe's apt.

**WEST
VILLAGE**

The Cosby Show (TV)
Autumn in New York
Wait Until Dark

Spider-Man 2

Serpico

*Raging
Bull*

Basquiat
A Perfect Murder

Men in Black II

SOHO

Addicted to Love
Big Daddy

Made

TRIBECA

Ghostbusters

2

GRAMERCY

43 Fifth Avenue
- *Small Time Crooks*
- *Turbulence*
- *How to Lose a Guy in 10 Days*
- *Felicity* (TV)
- *Bed of Roses*

51 Fifth Avenue
- *Mad About You* (TV)
- *13 Going on 30*

*Six Degrees
of Separation*

*As Good
As It Gets*

*The
Family
Man*

I Am Legend
WASHINGTON SQUARE N

Louis (TV)
Caffe Reggio
- *Inside Llewyn Davis*
- *Godfather: Part II*
- *Next Stop Greenwich
  Village*
- *Shaft*

**The Puck
Building**
- *When Harry. . .*
- *Will and Grace* (TV)

Dean and DeLuca
Julie & Julia

The Minetta Tavern
- *Johnny Dangerously*
- *Sleepers*
- *Micky Blue Eyes*

*Sex and
the City*

Ghost

28 Days

9½ Weeks

Dream On (TV)

Smithereens

Big

Big Daddy

2A

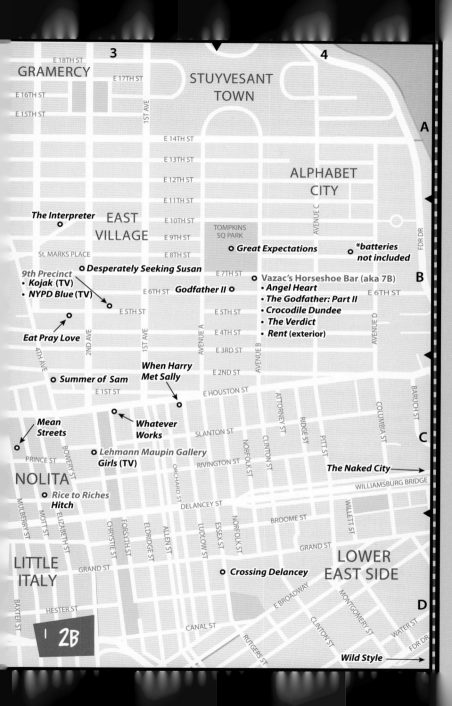

3 **4**

GRAMERCY

E 18TH ST
E 17TH ST
E 16TH ST
E 15TH ST

1ST AVE

STUYVESANT
TOWN

E 14TH ST
E 13TH ST
E 12TH ST
E 11TH ST

ALPHABET
CITY

AVENUE C

FDR DR

A

The Interpreter

EAST
VILLAGE

E 10TH ST
E 9TH ST
E 8TH ST

ST. MARKS PLACE

TOMPKINS
SQ PARK

Great Expectations

***batteries
not included**

○ Desperately Seeking Susan

E 7TH ST

Vazac's Horseshoe Bar (aka 7B)

9th Precinct
• **Kojak (TV)**
• **NYPD Blue (TV)**

E 6TH ST

Godfather II ○

E 5TH ST

• **Angel Heart**
• **The Godfather: Part II**
• **Crocodile Dundee**
• **The Verdict**
• **Rent (exterior)**

E 6TH ST

AVENUE D

B

Eat Pray Love

2ND AVE

1ST AVE

E 4TH ST
E 3RD ST

AVENUE A

AVENUE B

4TH AVE

**When Harry
Met Sally**

E 2ND ST

Summer of Sam

E 1ST ST

E HOUSTON ST

ATTORNEY ST

RIDGE ST

PITT ST

COLUMBIA ST

BARUCH ST

**Mean
Streets**

*Whatever
Works*

SLANTON ST

C

BOWERY ST

○ Lehmann Maupin Gallery
Girls (TV)

ORCHARD ST

RIVINGTON ST

NORFOLK ST

CLINTON ST

The Naked City →

PRINCE ST

WILLIAMSBURG BRIDGE

NOLITA

Rice to Riches
Hitch

MULBERRY ST

MOTT ST

ELIZABETH ST

CHRYSTIE ST

FORSYTH ST

ELDRIDGE ST

ALLEN ST

LUDLOW ST

ESSEX ST

NORFOLK ST

DELANCEY ST

BROOME ST

GRAND ST

WILLETT ST

LOWER
EAST SIDE

LITTLE
ITALY

BAXTER ST

GRAND ST

HESTER ST

○ Crossing Delancey

E BROADWAY

MONTGOMERY ST

WATER ST

FDR DR

D

2B

CANAL ST

RUTGERS ST

CLINTON ST

Wild Style →

Delmonico's: 56 Beaver Street at South William Street
Hotel Edison: 228 West 47th Street between Broadway and 8th Avenue
Elaine's: 1703 2nd Avenue between 88th and 89th Streets. Closed.
Ellen's Stardust Diner: 1650 Broadway, southeast corner at 51st Street
Ellis Island: New York Harbor
The Empire State Building: 350 Fifth Avenue between 33rd and 34th Streets
FAO Schwartz (moved): 767 Fifth Avenue, northeast corner at 58th Street
Federal Hall: 26 Wall Street at Broad Street
Federal Reserve Bank: 33 Liberty Street between William and Nassau Streets
Felix Restaurant: 340 West Broadway at Grand Street
51 Fifth Avenue: 51 Fifth Avenue, southeast corner at 12th Street
59th Street Entrance: Central Park
Flatiron Building: 175 Fifth Avenue at 23rd Street
4 East 74th Street: Between Fifth Avenue and Madison Avenue
The Four Seasons (moved): 9 East 52nd Street between Park and Lexington
    Avenues
Frank Campbell Funeral Home: 1076 Madison Avenue at 81st Street
The Fred French Building: 551 Fifth Avenue, northeast corner at 45th Street
The Golf Club at Chelsea Piers: 59 Chelsea Piers at 19th Street
Grand Army Plaza: 59th Street and 8th Avenue
Grand Central Terminal: 89 East 42nd Street between Vanderbilt and Park
    Avenue
The Great Lawn: Central Park
Greyshot Arch: Central Park
The Guggenheim Museum: 1071 Fifth Avenue between 88th and 89th Streets
Guss' Pickle: 35 Essex Street between Hester and Grand Streets
The Half King: 505 West 23rd Street between 10th and 11th Avenues
Hans Christian Andersen Statue: Central Park
Harlem Meer: Central Park
Heckscher Ballfields: Central Park
The High Line (park): Gansevoort Street to 34th Street, near 10th Avenue
Hook & Ladder 8: 14 North Moore Street at Varick Street
Intrepid Sea, Air & Space Museum: Pier 86, 46th Street and 12th Avenue
Jacqueline Kennedy Onassis Reservoir: Central Park
J. G. Melon: 1291 Third Avenue and, northeast corner at 74th Street
Joe's Pizza (moved): 233 Bleecker Street at Carmine Street
Katz's Delicatessen: 205 East Houston at Ludlow Street
The Lake: Central Park
Lexington Candy Shop: 1226 Lexington Avenue at 83rd Street
Lincoln Center: 62nd and Columbus Avenue
Loeb Boathouse: Central Park
Macy's/Herald Square: 151 West 34th Street between Broadway and 7th
    Avenue
The Mall: Central Park
Manhattan Bridge: East River

Mark Hellinger Theater: 237 West 51st Street between 7th and 8th Avenues
The Metropolitan Life Building: Madison Avenue at 23rd Street
Metropolitan Museum of Art: 1000 Fifth Avenue at 82nd Street
Minetta Tavern: 113 MacDougal Street at Minetta Lane
Morgan Court: 211 Madison between 35th and 36th Streets
Municipal Building (City Hall Park): 1 Centre Street at Chambers Street
Museum of Modern Art: 11 West 53rd Street between 5th and 6th Avenues
National Museum of the American Indian (U.S. Custom House): 1 Bowling
    Green between State Street and Whitehall Street
Naumburg Bandshell: Central Park
New York County Courthouse: 60 Centre Street at Pearl Street
The New York Public Library: 476 Fifth Avenue between 40th and 42nd Streets
New York Stock Exchange: 11 Wall Street
North Gate House: Central Park, on the reservoir
The Obelisk: Central Park
The Odeon: 145 West Broadway at Thomas Street
1 Liberty Plaza: Liberty Street and Broadway
140 Broadway: Between Liberty and Cedar Streets
127 John Street: Between Pearl and Water Streets
Pershing Square: 90 East 42nd Street at Park Avenue
The Pierre Hotel: 2 East 61st Street at Fifth Avenue
Pine Branch Arch: Central Park
The Plaza Hotel: 768 Fifth Avenue between 58th and 59th Streets
The Port Authority Bus Terminal: 625 8th Avenue between 40th and 42nd
    Streets
P.S. 6: 45 East 81st Street at Madison Avenue
The Puck Building: 295 Lafayette Street at Houston Street
Radio City Music Hall: 1260 Avenue of the Americas, northeast corner at
    50th Street
The Ramble: Central Park
Rice to Riches: 37 Spring Street near Mott Street
Rivera School Playground: 220 East 110th Street between 2nd and 3rd
    Avenues
Rockefeller Center Ice Rink/Summer Garden: Rockefeller Plaza between
    49th and 50th Streets
The Roosevelt Hotel: 45 East 45th Street at Madison Avenue
Roosevelt Island Tram: Entrance at East 59th Street and 2nd Avenue
The Russian Tea Room: 150 West 57th Street between 6th and 7th Avenues
Sardi's: 234 West 44th Street between 7th and 8th Avenues
Serendipity 3: 225 East 60th Street between 2nd and 3rd Avenues
Shakespeare & Co.: 2259 Broadway at 81st Street, second floor. Closed.
The Sheep Meadow: Central Park
Smith & Wollensky: 797 Third Avenue at 49th Street
Street Regis Hotel: 2 East 55th Street between Fifth Avenue and Madison
    Avenue

1

2

W 50TH ST

W 49TH ST

W 48TH ST

The Brill Building
The Sweet Smell of Success

Time/Life Building
1271 6th Avenue
Mad Men (TV)
Sterling Cooper Draper Pryce

Taxi Driver (poster)

W 47TH ST

Hotel Edison
The Godfather
1980s MTV Studios

The Intrepid (museum)
I Am Legend

W 46TH ST

A

W 45TH ST

W 44TH ST

Sardi's
The Muppets Take Manhattan

11TH AVE

10TH AVE

W 43RD ST

Times Square
• *Shaft*
• *Birdman*
• *New Year's Eve*
• *Vanilla Sky*
• *Enchanted*
• *Just My Luck*
• *Center Stage*
• *Friends with Benefits*
• *The Last Action Hero*
• *Report to the Commissioner*
• *Dick Clark's New Year's Rockin' Eve* (TV)

7TH AVE

BROADWAY

W 42ND ST

The Port Authority Bus Terminal (two buildings)
• *Frankie and Johnny*
• *Cocktail*
• *Desperately Seeking Susan*

W 41ST ST

W 40TH ST

W 39TH ST

B

9TH AVE

8TH AVE

BROADWAY

HELL'S KITCHEN

W 37TH ST

11TH AVE

10TH AVE

W 35TH ST

W 34TH ST

Macy's/Herald Square
Miracle on 34th Street

JOE DIMAGGIO HWY

W 33RD ST

PENN STATION

W 32ND ST

C

W 31ST ST

11TH AVE

10TH AVE

9TH AVE

8TH AVE

7TH AVE

W 30TH ST

W 29TH ST

W 28TH ST

12TH AVE

W 27TH ST

W 27TH ST

W 26TH ST

CHELSEA

W 25ND ST

W 24TH ST

The Half King (Bar)
Going the Distance

W 23RD ST

D

W 22ND ST

The Chelsea Hotel
• *9½ Weeks*
• *Chelsea Girls*
• *Leon: the Professional*
• *Sid and Nancy*

W 21ST ST

3A

The Golf Club at Chelsea Piers
The Other Guys

W 20TH ST

W 19TH ST

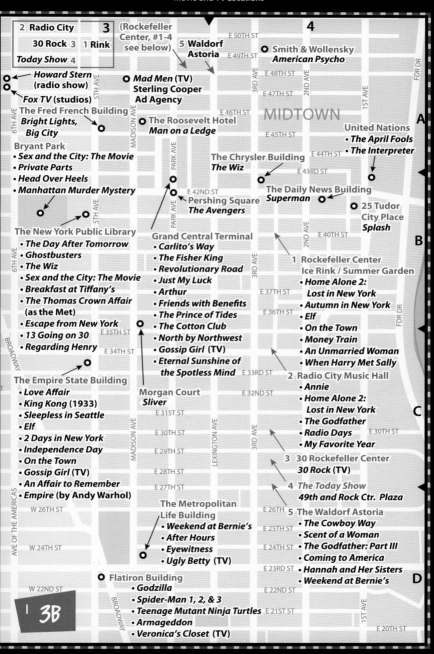

2 Radio City	**3**
30 Rock 3	1 Rink
Today Show 4	

(Rockefeller Center, #1-4 see below)

4

E 50TH ST

5 **Waldorf Astoria**
E 49TH ST

Howard Stern (radio show)

Fox TV (studios)

Mad Men (TV) Sterling Cooper Ad Agency

E 48TH ST

E 47TH ST

☉ **Smith & Wollensky** *American Psycho*

MIDTOWN

The Fred French Building
Bright Lights, Big City

E 46TH ST

The Roosevelt Hotel *Man on a Ledge*

E 45TH ST

A

United Nations
• *The April Fools*
• *The Interpreter*

Bryant Park
• *Sex and the City: The Movie*
• *Private Parts*
• *Head Over Heels*
• *Manhattan Murder Mystery*

The Chrysler Building
The Wiz

E 44TH ST

E 43RD ST

E 42ND ST

Pershing Square
The Avengers

The Daily News Building
Superman ☉

B

☉ 25 **Tudor City Place**
Splash

The New York Public Library
• *The Day After Tomorrow*
• *Ghostbusters*
• *The Wiz*
• *Sex and the City: The Movie*
• *Breakfast at Tiffany's*
• *The Thomas Crown Affair* (as the Met)
• *Escape from New York*
• *13 Going on 30*
• *Regarding Henry*

E 40TH ST

Grand Central Terminal
• *Carlito's Way*
• *The Fisher King*
• *Revolutionary Road*
• *Just My Luck*
• *Arthur*
• *Friends with Benefits*
• *The Prince of Tides*
• *The Cotton Club*
• *North by Northwest*
• *Gossip Girl* (TV)
• *Eternal Sunshine of the Spotless Mind*

E 37TH ST

E 36TH ST

E 35TH ST

E 34TH ST

E 33RD ST

1 **Rockefeller Center**
Ice Rink / Summer Garden
• *Home Alone 2: Lost in New York*
• *Autumn in New York*
• *Elf*
• *On the Town*
• *Money Train*
• *An Unmarried Woman*
• *When Harry Met Sally*

2 **Radio City Music Hall**
• *Annie*
• *Home Alone 2: Lost in New York*
• *The Godfather*
• *Radio Days*
• *My Favorite Year*

C

The Empire State Building
• *Love Affair*
• *King Kong* (1933)
• *Sleepless in Seattle*
• *Elf*
• *2 Days in New York*
• *Independence Day*
• *On the Town*
• *Gossip Girl* (TV)
• *An Affair to Remember*
• *Empire* (by Andy Warhol)

Morgan Court
Sliver

E 32ND ST

E 31ST ST

E 30TH ST

E 29TH ST

E 28TH ST

E 27TH ST

3 **30 Rockefeller Center**
30 Rock (TV)

4 *The Today Show*
49th and Rock Ctr. Plaza

The Metropolitan Life Building
• *Weekend at Bernie's*
• *After Hours*
• *Eyewitness*
• *Ugly Betty* (TV)

E 26TH

E 25TH ST

E 24TH ST

E 23RD ST

5 **The Waldorf Astoria**
• *The Cowboy Way*
• *Scent of a Woman*
• *The Godfather: Part III*
• *Coming to America*
• *Hannah and Her Sisters*
• *Weekend at Bernie's*

D

☉ **Flatiron Building**
• *Godzilla*
• *Spider-Man 1, 2, & 3*
• *Teenage Mutant Ninja Turtles*
• *Armageddon*
• *Veronica's Closet* (TV)

E 22ND ST

E 21ST ST

E 20TH ST

3B

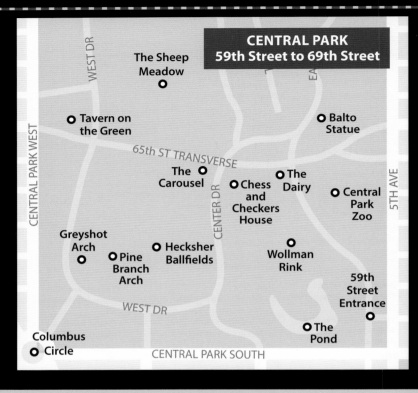

CENTRAL PARK
59th Street to 69th Street

WEST DR

The Sheep Meadow

Tavern on the Green

Balto Statue

CENTRAL PARK WEST

65th ST TRANSVERSE

The Carousel

CENTER DR

Chess and Checkers House

The Dairy

Central Park Zoo

5TH AVE

Greyshot Arch

Pine Branch Arch

Hecksher Ballfields

Wollman Rink

59th Street Entrance

Columbus Circle

WEST DR

The Pond

CENTRAL PARK SOUTH

CENTRAL PARK FROM 59TH STREET TO 69TH STREET

Balto Statue
• *Six Degrees of Separation*

Central Park Zoo
• *Oliver's Story*

Columbus Circle
• *Look Who's Talking Too*
• *Ghostbusters*
• *Taxi Driver*
• *Teenage Mutant Ninja Turtles II*

59th Street Entrance
• *Manhattan (Carriage Ride)*

Greyshot Arch
• *Hair*

Hecksher Ballfields
• *Mr. Popper's Penguins*

Pine Branch Arch
• *Leon: the Professional*
• *Elf*

The Carousel
• *Now You See Me*
• *The Producers* (1968)
• *The Spanish Prisoner*

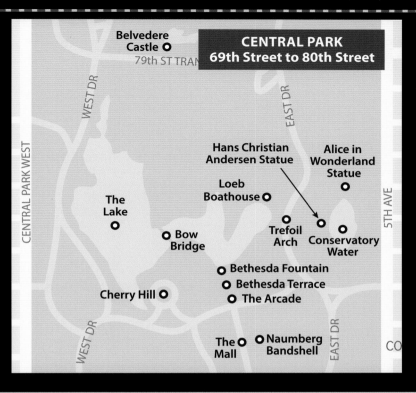

CENTRAL PARK
69th Street to 80th Street

Belvedere Castle O
79th ST TRAN

WEST DR

EAST DR

CENTRAL PARK WEST

Hans Christian Andersen Statue

Alice in Wonderland Statue O

Loeb Boathouse O

The Lake O

O Bow Bridge

5TH AVE

O Trefoil Arch

O Conservatory Water

O Bethesda Fountain
O Bethesda Terrace
O The Arcade

Cherry Hill O

WEST DR

The O Mall

O Naumberg Bandshell

EAST DR

CO

• Up the Sandbox
• I'm Not Rappaport

The Dairy
• Portrait of Jennie
• Independence Day

The Sheep Meadow
• Look Who's Talking Too
• It Could Happen to You
• The Fisher King
• Wall Street
• The Manchurian Candidate
• Antz

Tavern on the Green
• Ghostbusters

• The Out-of-Towners (1999)
• Heartburn
• Portrait of Jeannie
• Alfie (2004)
• New York Stories
• Made
• Wall Street
• Misery

Wollman Rink
• Love Story
• Oliver's Story
• Serendipity
• Carnal Knowledge
• Stepmom
• The January Man

CENTRAL PARK FROM 69TH STREET TO 80TH STREET

Alice in Wonderland Statue
- *Oliver's Story*
- *Remember Me*
- *Key Exchange*
- *The Mirror Has Two Faces*

Bethesda Fountain
- *Manhattan Murder Mystery*
- *It Could Happen to You*
- *Home Alone 2*
- *Annie Hall*
- *Staying Alive*
- *Enchanted*
- *Godspell*
- *Ransom*
- *The Avengers*
- *Keeping the Faith*
- *The Way We Were*
- *27 Dresses*
- *The Producers (1968)*
- *One Fine Day*
- *The Producers (2005)*
- *Deconstructing Harry*
- *Fools Rush In*

Bow Bridge
- *Autumn in New York*
- *Cafe Society*
- *Uptown Girls*
- *The World of Henry Orient*
- *Manhattan*

Bethesda Terrace/Steps
- *27 Dresses*
- *The Avengers*
- *Delivery Man*
- *Elf*
- *Godspell*
- *It Should Happen to You*
- *Manchurian Candidate*
- *Mr. Deeds*
- *One Fine Day*
- *The Prisoner of Second Avenue*
- *Ransom*

Cherry Hill
- *Passion of Mind*
- *The Mirror Has Two Faces*
- *Cruel Intentions*

Staten Island Ferry: Battery Park Esplanade
Strand Bookstore: 828 Broadway at 12th Street
Statue of Liberty: Liberty Island
Surrogate's Courthouse: 31 Chambers Street
Tavern on the Green: Central Park
30 Broad Street: Near Exchange Place
Tiffany & Company: 727 Fifth Avenue, southeast corner at 57th Street
Times Square: 46th Street and Broadway
Tony Dapolito Recreation Center: 1 Clarkson Street at Varick Street
Trefoil Arch: Central Park
Trinity Church: 75 Broadway at Wall Street
Tweed Courthouse: 52 Chambers Street
20 Exchange Place: Between William and Hanover Streets
21 Club: 21 West 52nd Street between 5th and 6th Avenues
25 Tudor City Place: Between 41st and 42nd Streets

Conservatory Water
(The Model Boat Pond)
- *Breakfast at Tiffany's*
- *Stuart Little*
- *Oliver's Story*
- *Key Exchange*
- *Little Manhattan*
- *F/X*
- *The Object of My Affection*
- *The World of Henry Orient*

Loeb Boathouse
- *When Harry Met Sally*
- *Sex and the City*

Hans Christian Andersen Statue
- *I'm Not Rapport*

Trefoil Arch
- *Still of the Night*
- *You Don't Mess With the Zohan*
- *The Out-of-Towners (1970)*

The Arcade
- *Home Alone 2: Lost in New York*

Naumberg Bandshell
- *Breakfast at Tiffany's*
- *Hair*
- *I'm Not Rapport*
- *The Lonely Guy*
- *Mighty Aphrodite*

The Lake
- *Autumn in New York*
- *Annie Hall*
- *The Way We Were*
- *Anger Management*
- *The Producers (1968)*

The Mall
- *Big Daddy*
- *Kramer vs. Kramer*
- *Enchanted*
- *Vanilla Sky*
- *The Producers (2005)*
- *Get Him to the Greek*
- *When in Rome*
- *One Fine Day*
- *Little Murders*
- *Maid in Manhattan*
- *When in Rome*

2 Broadway: Between Stone and Beaver Streets
222 Broadway: Between Fulton and Ann Streets
Vazac's Horseshoe Bar (aka 7B): 108 Avenue B at East 7th Street
Vesuvio Bakery: 160 Prince Street between Thompson Street and West Broadway
The Waldorf Astoria: 301 Park Avenue between 49th and 50th Streets
Washington Square Park: Washington Square North and 5th Avenue
Whitney Museum (old): 945 Madison Avenue
Wollman Rink: Central Park
Woolworth Building: 233 Broadway between Barclay Street and Park Place
World Financial Center: West Street at Vesey Street
World Trade Center (The Twin Towers): Greenwich and West Streets
Yonah Schimmel Knish Bakery: 137 East Houston Street at Forsyth Street
Zabar's: 2245 Broadway, northwest corner at 80th Street

FAMOUS NYC MOVIE POSTER LOCATIONS

Annie Hall: Pier 16 near South Street Seaport
Taxi Driver: Eighth Avenue between 46th and 47th Streets
Manhattan: Sutton Square at East 58th Street
Breakfast at Tiffany's: 727 Fifth Avenue at 57th Street
Midnight Cowboy: 1414 Sixth Avenue at 58th Street. The "I'm Walkin' Here" poster.
The Warriors: Riverside Drive at West 97th Street. Dinosaur Playground.
Death Wish: Steps at Riverside Drive and 124th Street

TV SITCOM AND TV DRAMA LOCATIONS: WHERE THE CHARACTERS LIVE, WORK, AND PLAY

82nd Street–113th Street (Map 1–5)

The Jeffersons: 185 East 85th Street between Lexington and 3rd Avenues. The deluxe apartment in the sky.
The Odd Couple: 1049 Park Avenue at 87th Street. Oscar and Felix's apartment.
Rhoda: 332 East 84th Street between 1st and 2nd Avenues. Rhoda's apartment.
Seinfeld: 321 West 90th Street. George Costanza's apartment.
Seinfeld: Tom's Restaurant, 2880 Broadway, northeast corner at 112th Street. Monk's Café exterior.
30 Rock: 160 Riverside Drive, northeast corner at West 88th Street. Liz Lemon's apartment.
Will and Grace: 155 Riverside Drive, southeast corner at 88th Street. Will's apartment.

51st Street–81st Street (Map 1–4)

Diff'rent Strokes: 900 Park Avenue, northwest corner at East 79th Street. Mr. Drummond's home.
I Love Lucy: 623 East 68th Street. Lucy and Desi Ricardo's apartment; address would put it in the East River.
Murder, She Wrote: 941 West 60th Street, Apartment 4-B, at Amsterdam, northeast corner. Jessica's apartment.
The Nanny: 7 East 75th Street between Fifth and Madison Avenues. Sheffield family apartment.
Seinfeld: 129 West 81st Street between Amsterdam and Columbus Avenues. Jerry: Apartment 5A, Kramer: Apartment 5B. Also the real address where Jerry Seinfeld and Larry David lived during the early standup years. The building exterior was filmed at 757 South New Hampshire Avenue, Los Angeles.
Seinfeld: 16 West 75th Street, Apartment 2G, between Columbus and Central Park West. Elaine Benes' apartment.
That Girl: FDR Drive between 78th and 79th Streets. Ann Marie's apartment.

***The Late Show with Stephen Colbert**, **The Late Show with David Letterman** (former), and **The Ed Sullivan Show** (The Beatles, 1964):* The Ed Sullivan Theater, 1697 Broadway between 53rd and 54th Streets

The Apprentice: 725 Fifth Avenue, northeast corner at 56th Street. Trump Tower.

How I Met Your Mother: McGee's Pub, 240 West 55th Street between Broadway and 8th Avenue. Inspired MacLaren's Pub.

Seinfeld: The Original Soup Man, 259-A West 55th Street. Inspired the "Soup Nazi" episode.

19th Street–50th Street (Map 1–3)

Dick Clark's New Year's Rockin' Eve: Times Square, 7th Avenue and West 45th Street

1980s MTV Studios: 1515 Broadway between 44th and 45th Streets

Fox News: Fox TV Studios, 1221 Avenue of the Americas between 48th and 49th Streets

Howard Stern Radio Show: 1221 Avenue of the Americas between 48th and 49th Streets. Sirius Radio.

The Today Show: Southwest corner at 49th Street and Rockefeller Plaza. The *Today Show* Studios.

NBC News**, **Dateline**, **Saturday Night Live**, **The Tonight Show with Jimmy Fallon**, **Late Night with Conan O'Brien** (former), **30 Rock: 30 Rockefeller Center, Rockefeller Plaza between 49th and 50th Streets

Veronica's Closet: The Flatiron Building, 175 Fifth Avenue at 23rd Street. Veronica Chase's office.

Ugly Betty: Metropolitan Life North Building, 11 Madison Avenue between 24th and 25th Streets. *Mode* magazine.

White Street–18th Street (Map 1–2)

Barney Miller: 233 West 10th Street between Hudson and Bleecker Streets. 6th Precinct (as fictional 12th Precinct).

The Cosby Show: 10 St. Luke's Place. The Huxtables' townhouse, supposedly 10 Stigwood Avenue, Brooklyn Heights.

Dream On: 196 Spring Street at Sullivan Street. Martin Tupper's apartment.

Felicity: 43 Fifth Avenue at 11th Street. Dorm.

Friends: 90 Bedford Street at Grove Street, 5th floor. Monica's, Rachel's, Chandler's, and Joey's apartments; aka 495 Grove #20 in later seasons.

Friends: 90 Bedford Street at Grove Street. Central Perk.

Friends: 19–21 Grove Street at Bedford Street. Ross and "naked guy" apartment building.

Friends: 5 Morton Street between Bleecker and 7th Avenue South. Phoebe's apartment.

Kate & Allie: Somewhere on Bank Street. Their apartment.

Kojak: 321 East 5th Street between 1st and 2nd Avenues. 9th Precinct house (police station).

Louie: 117 MacDougal Street near West 3rd Street. Comedy Cellar.

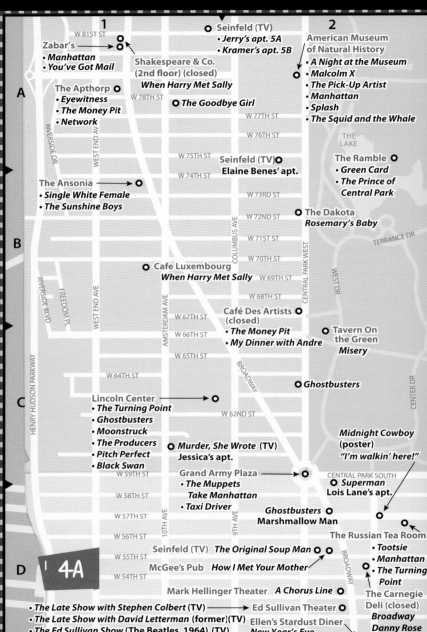

1

W 81ST ST

Zabar's ──→
• *Manhattan*
• *You've Got Mail*

Seinfeld (TV)
• *Jerry's apt. 5A*
• *Kramer's apt. 5B*

**Shakespeare & Co.
(2nd floor) (closed)**
When Harry Met Sally

The Apthorp
• *Eyewitness*
• *The Money Pit*
• *Network*

W 78TH ST

A

○ *The Goodbye Girl*

W 77TH ST

W 76TH ST

W 75TH ST

W 74TH ST

Seinfeld (TV)○
Elaine Benes' apt.

The Ansonia ──→ ○
• *Single White Female*
• *The Sunshine Boys*

W 73RD ST

W 72ND ST

2

**American Museum
of Natural History**
• *A Night at the Museum*
○ • *Malcolm X*
• *The Pick-Up Artist*
• *Manhattan*
• *Splash*
• *The Squid and the Whale*

THE
LAKE

The Ramble ○
• *Green Card*
• *The Prince of
Central Park*

TERRANCE DR

○ **The Dakota**
Rosemary's Baby

B

W 71ST ST

W 70TH ST

○ **Cafe Luxembourg**
When Harry Met Sally W 69TH ST

W 68TH ST

Café Des Artists ○
(closed)
• *The Money Pit*
• *My Dinner with Andre*

W 67TH ST

W 66TH ST

W 65TH ST

W 64TH ST

○ **Tavern On
the Green**
Misery

○ *Ghostbusters*

Lincoln Center ──→ ○
• *The Turning Point*
• *Ghostbusters*
• *Moonstruck*
• *The Producers*
• *Pitch Perfect*
• *Black Swan*

C

W 62ND ST

**Midnight Cowboy
(poster)**
"I'm walkin' here!"

○ **Murder, She Wrote** (TV)
Jessica's apt.

Grand Army Plaza ──→ ○
• *The Muppets
Take Manhattan*
• *Taxi Driver*

W 59TH ST

CENTRAL PARK SOUTH
○ **Superman**
Lois Lane's apt.

W 58TH ST

Ghostbusters ○
Marshmallow Man

D

4A

W 57TH ST

W 56TH ST

Seinfeld (TV) **The Original Soup Man** ○ ○

McGee's Pub *How I Met Your Mother*

W 55TH ST

W 54TH ST

The Russian Tea Room
• *Tootsie*
• *Manhattan*
• *The Turning
Point*

**The Carnegie
Deli (closed)**
*Broadway
Danny Rose*

Mark Hellinger Theater *A Chorus Line* ○

• **The Late Show with Stephen Colbert** (TV) ──→ **Ed Sullivan Theater** ○
• **The Late Show with David Letterman** (former)(TV) **Ellen's Stardust Diner**
• **The Ed Sullivan Show** (The Beatles, 1964) (TV) *New Year's Eve*

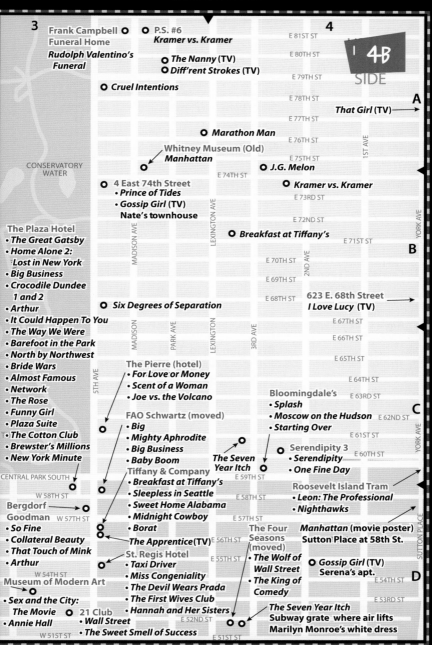

3

Frank Campbell Funeral Home
Rudolph Valentino's Funeral

P.S. #6
Kramer vs. Kramer

The Nanny **(TV)**
Diff'rent Strokes **(TV)**

Cruel Intentions

4

4B
SIDE

E 81ST ST
E 80TH ST
E 79TH ST
E 78TH ST
E 77TH ST

That Girl **(TV)** →

A

Marathon Man

Whitney Museum (Old) Manhattan

J.G. Melon

E 76TH ST
E 75TH ST
E 74TH ST

CONSERVATORY WATER

4 East 74th Street
• *Prince of Tides*
• *Gossip Girl* **(TV)**
Nate's townhouse

Kramer vs. Kramer

E 73RD ST
E 72ND ST

The Plaza Hotel
• *The Great Gatsby*
• *Home Alone 2: Lost in New York*
• *Big Business*
• *Crocodile Dundee 1 and 2*
• *Arthur*
• *It Could Happen To You*
• *The Way We Were*
• *Barefoot in the Park*
• *North by Northwest*
• *Bride Wars*
• *Almost Famous*
• *Network*
• *The Rose*
• *Funny Girl*
• *Plaza Suite*
• *The Cotton Club*
• *Brewster's Millions*
• *New York Minute*

Breakfast at Tiffany's

E 71ST ST

B

E 70TH ST
E 69TH ST
E 68TH ST

623 E. 68th Street
I Love Lucy **(TV)** →

Six Degrees of Separation

E 67TH ST
E 66TH ST
E 65TH ST

The Pierre (hotel)
• *For Love or Money*
• *Scent of a Woman*
• *Joe vs. the Volcano*

FAO Schwartz (moved)
• *Big*
• *Mighty Aphrodite*
• *Big Business*
• *Baby Boom*

Tiffany & Company
• *Breakfast at Tiffany's*
• *Sleepless in Seattle*
• *Sweet Home Alabama*
• *Midnight Cowboy*
• *Borat*
• *The Apprentice* **(TV)**

Bloomingdale's
• *Splash*
• *Moscow on the Hudson*
• *Starting Over*

Serendipity 3
• *Serendipity*
• *One Fine Day*

Roosevelt Island Tram →
• *Leon: The Professional*
• *Nighthawks*

E 64TH ST
E 63RD ST
E 62ND ST
E 61ST ST
E 60TH ST
E 59TH ST

The Seven Year Itch

C

CENTRAL PARK SOUTH

W 58TH ST

Bergdorf Goodman →
• *So Fine*
• *Collateral Beauty*
• *That Touch of Mink*
• *Arthur*

W 57TH ST

Museum of Modern Art
• *Sex and the City: The Movie*
• *Annie Hall*

W 54TH ST

St. Regis Hotel
• *Taxi Driver*
• *Miss Congeniality*
• *The Devil Wears Prada*
• *The First Wives Club*
• *Hannah and Her Sisters*

21 Club
• *Wall Street*
• *The Sweet Smell of Success*

E 58TH ST
E 57TH ST

The Four Seasons (moved)
• *The Wolf of Wall Street*
• *The King of Comedy*

Manhattan (movie poster)
Sutton Place at 58th St.

Gossip Girl **(TV)**
Serena's apt.

E 56TH ST
E 55TH ST
E 54TH ST
E 53RD ST

D

The Seven Year Itch
Subway grate where air lifts
Marilyn Monroe's white dress

W 51ST ST
E 52ND ST
E 51ST ST

MADISON AVE
PARK AVE
LEXINGTON AVE
3RD AVE
2ND AVE
1ST AVE
YORK AVE
5TH AVE
SUTTON PLACE

Mad About You: 51 Fifth Avenue at 12th Street. The Buchmans' apartment.
NYPD Blue: 321 East 5th Street between 1st and 2nd Avenues. 9th Precinct (police station).
Sesame Street: 123 Avenue B at East 8th Street. Original conceived location.
Sex and the City: 64 Perry Street between Bleecker and West 4th Streets. Carrie's apartment.
Sex and the City: 401 Bleecker Street at West 11th Street. Magnolia Bakery.
Sex and the City: 403 West 13th Street at 9th Avenue. Samantha's apartment.
Taxi: 534 Hudson Street, southeast corner at Charles Street (demolished 1998). Sunshine Cab Company.
Will and Grace: The Puck Building, 295 Lafayette Street at Houston Street. Grace's studio.

Ferry Street–White Street (Map 1–1)
Caroline in the City: 168 Duane Street between Hudson and Greenwich Streets. Caroline's apartment.
Spin City: City Hall, Murray Street and Broadway
Cagney and Lacy, Law and Order, Kojak: 60 Centre Street at Pearl Street. New York County Courthouse.
Law and Order: Tweed Courthouse, 52 Chambers Street at Elk Street. Courtrooms
Night Court: U.S. Court of Appeals, Centre Street at Pearl Street

Brooklyn (Map 1–6)
The Honeymooners: 328 Chauncey Street, earlier #728. In Bedford Stuyvesant, though said to be in Bensonhurst; was also Jackie Gleason's childhood home address.
The Patty Duke Show: 8 Remsen Street, Brooklyn. No townhouse there today.
Welcome Back, Kotter: 1601 80th Street at 16th Avenue, Brooklyn. Based on New Utrecht High School.
Everybody Hates Chris: Decatur Street, Bedford-Stuyvesant, Brooklyn. Fictional Corleone High School.

Bronx (Map 1–6)
The Goldbergs: 1038 East Tremont Avenue at Boston Road. 1950s TV show.

Queens (Map 1–6)
All in the Family: Exterior filmed at 89–70 Cooper Avenue, Glendale, Queens, to represent 704 Hauser Street, Astoria, Queens. The Bunkers' house.
Dear John: Rego Park, Queens. Judd Hirsch's apartment.
The King of Queens: 3121 Aberdeen Street, Rego Park, Queens. The Heffernan's house. Actually, the house in the credits is at 519 Longview Avenue in Cliffside Park, New Jersey.
Rescue Me: 38–49 9th Street at 40th Avenue, Long Island City, Queens
Seinfeld: 22–37 37th Street, Astoria, Queens. Frank and Estelle Costanza's House.

SPOTLIGHT ON FIVE CULT TV SHOW LOCATIONS

Sex and the City (1998–2004)
Carrie's apartment: 64 Perry Street between Bleecker Street and West 4th Street, representing her stated address of 245 East 73rd Street between Park and Madison Avenues

Magnolia Bakery: 401 Bleecker Street at West 11th Street

Samantha's Apartment: 403 West 13th Street at 9th Avenue

Seinfeld (1989–1998)
Monk's Café: Tom's Restaurant, 2880 Broadway at 112th Street

The Apartment Building of Jerry, Kramer, and Newman: 129 West 81st between Amsterdam and Columbus. This is where Jerry and Larry David lived during their early standup years; the building exterior is 757 South New Hampshire Avenue, Los Angeles.

Soup Nazi: The Original Soup Man, 259–A West 55th Street, near 8th Avenue

Elaine Benes' Apartment: 16 West 75th Street, Apartment 2G. She also lived at 78 West 86th Street, Apartment 3E and at 448 Central Park West at 105th Street.

George Costanza's Apartment: 321 West 90th Street

Frank and Estelle Costanza's House: 22–37 37th Street, Astoria, Queens

Gossip Girl (2007–2012)
Nate Archibald's Townhouse: 4 East 74th Street

Blair Waldorf's Apartment: 1136 5th Avenue

Serena van der Woodsen's Apartment: 300 East 55th Street at 2nd Avenue

New York Palace Hotel: 455 Madison Avenue between 50th and 51st Streets. Including Gilt Restaurant. Also the Van der Woodsen's home, aka "Serena's Lair."

Museum of the City of New York: 1220 Fifth Avenue between 103rd and 104th Streets

Nightingale-Bamford School: 20 East 92nd Street between 5th and Madison Avenues. The showrunner went to school here.

St. Jude School for Boys Steps: The Synod School for Boys, 75 East 93rd Street at Park Avenue

Other *Gossip Girls* Locations, Not on Map
The Campbell Apartment: 89 East 42nd Street, in Grand Central. Closed.

Central Park: Bethesda Terrace/The Arcade (wedding): in Central Park at 72nd Street

Cooper Hewitt Museum (wedding): 2 East 91st Street at Fifth Avenue

Columbia University: Broadway and 116th Street, Upper West Side

Dan Humphrey's Loft: 455 Water Street, Apartment #6, at Hudson Avenue, Dumbo, Brooklyn

Dylan's Candy Bar: 1011 Third Avenue at East 60th Street

Empire Hotel: 44 West 63rd Street at Broadway, Upper West Side
Grand Central: 89 East 42nd Street at Park Avenue. Serena's arrival, tracks 27–28.
Henri Bendel (*Breakfast at Tiffany's* scene): 712 Fifth Avenue at 56th Street
Metropolitan Museum of Art Steps: 1000 Fifth Avenue at 82nd Street
Plaza Hotel Fountain (photo shoot): 768 Fifth Avenue at 59th Street

Mad Men (2007–2015)
Sterling Cooper Advertising Agency: 405 Madison Avenue between 47th and 48th Streets (fictional building)
Sterling Cooper Draper Pryce offices (Don's new agency): The Time/Life Building, 1271 Sixth Avenue, 37th floor

Other *Mad Men* Locations, Not on Map
Grand Central Oyster Bar: 89 East 42nd Street at Park Avenue
P.J. Clarke's: 915 Third Avenue between 55th and 56th Streets
The Pierre Hotel: 2 East 61st Street at 5th Avenue
The Roosevelt Hotel: 45 East 45th Street at Madison Avenue
Sardi's: 234 West 44th Street between 7th and 8th Avenues

Girls (2012–2017)
Lehmann Maupin Gallery: 201 Chrystie Street, Lower East Side. Where Marnie works.

Other *Girls* Locations, Not on Map
Adam (Adam Driver)'s apartment: St. John's Place in Prospect Heights
Babycakes: 248 Broome Street between Ludlow Street and Orchard Street, Lower East Side
Cafe Grumpy: 193 Meserole Avenue at Diamond Street, Greenpoint
The Foundry: 42–38 9th Street, Long Island City. Jessa's wedding.
The Jane Hotel: 113 Jane Street at West Street, West Village. Book party.
Jessa (Jemima Kirke) and Shoshanna's apartment , season 1: "On Elizabeth near Broome" in Nolita
Hannah (Lena Dunham) and Marnie's apartment: 102 India Street, Greenpoint, Brooklyn
The Sorry Wall: North 5th Street and Kent Avenue, Williamsburg
Tom and Jerry's 288 Bar: 288 Elizabeth Street at East Houston Street, East Village
Vesuvius Playground: Thompson Street between Prince and Spring, Soho
Shoshanna (Zosia Mamet)'s university: New York University, East of Washington Square Park, Greenwich Village

WHERE TO SEE LIVE AND TAPED TV SHOWS AND NEWSCASTS IN MANHATTAN

These shows are very popular, so email for tickets in advance.
Check show websites for standby tickets.

The Daily Show with Trevor Noah (Comedy Central)
Tickets: showclix.com
Location: 733 Eleventh Avenue between West 51st and 52nd Streets
Schedule: Tapes Monday through Thursday, 6 p.m. to 7:15 p.m.

The Dr. Oz Show (syndicated)
Tickets: Online, plus standby available
Location: 320 West 66th Street between West End Avenue and Freedom
   Place
Schedule: Tapes two times a day, three times a week, at 10 a.m. and 3 p.m.

Good Morning America (ABC)
Tickets: Website
Location: Times Square, Broadway at West 44th Street
Schedule: Tapes Monday–Friday, 7 to 9 a.m.

Inside the Actors Studio (Bravo) (James Lipton)
Tickets: Day of show, at Michael Schimmel Center for the Arts
Location: Michael Schimmel Center for the Arts, Pace University, 3 Spruce
   Street between William and Gold Streets
Schedule: Varies. See schimmel.pace.edu

Last Week Tonight with John Oliver (HBO)
Tickets: lastweektickets.com
Location: The CBS Broadcast Center, 528 West 57th Street between Tenth
   and Eleventh Avenues
Schedule: Tapes Sundays at 6:15.

Late Night with Seth Myers (NBC)
Tickets: Website. For rehearsal, go to the shop at NBC Studios ("30 Rock") at
   12:30 p.m.
Location: Studio 8G, Rockefeller Plaza between Fifth and Sixth Avenues and
   West 49th and 50th Streets
Schedule: Tapes Monday–Thursday at 6:30 p.m.

The Late Show with Stephen Colbert (CBS)
Tickets: Website
Location: 1697 Broadway between West 53rd and 54th Streets
Schedule: Tapes Monday–Friday 5:30 p.m.

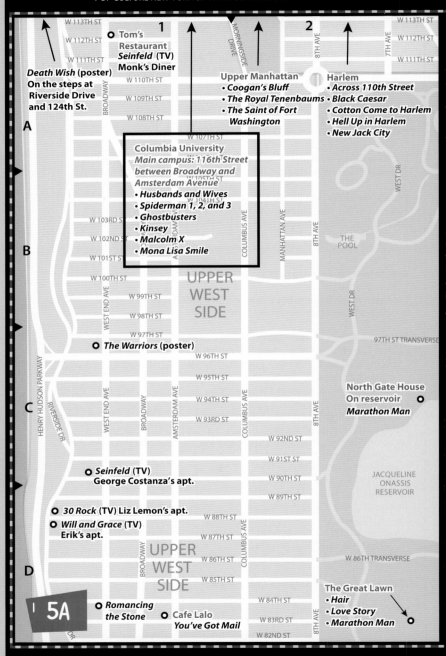

1

2

W 113TH ST
W 112TH ST
W 111TH ST

O **Tom's Restaurant**
Seinfeld (TV)
Monk's Diner

MORNINGSIDE DRIVE

8TH AVE
7TH AVE

Death Wish (poster)
On the steps at
Riverside Drive
and 124th St.

W 110TH ST
W 109TH ST
W 108TH ST

BROADWAY

Upper Manhattan
• *Coogan's Bluff*
• *The Royal Tenenbaums*
• *The Saint of Fort Washington*

Harlem
• *Across 110th Street*
• *Black Caesar*
• *Cotton Come to Harlem*
• *Hell Up in Harlem*
• *New Jack City*

A

W 107TH ST

Columbia University
Main campus: 116th Street
between Broadway and
Amsterdam Avenue
• *Husbands and Wives*
• *Spiderman 1, 2, and 3*
• *Ghostbusters*
• *Kinsey*
• *Malcolm X*
• *Mona Lisa Smile*

W 105TH ST
W 104TH ST

COLUMBUS AVE

MANHATTAN AVE

8TH AVE

WEST DR

W 103RD ST
W 102ND ST
W 101ST ST

AMSTERDAM AVE

THE POOL

B

W 100TH ST
W 99TH ST
W 98TH ST
W 97TH ST

WEST END AVE

UPPER WEST SIDE

WEST DR

97TH ST TRANSVERSE

O **The Warriors (poster)**

W 96TH ST
W 95TH ST
W 94TH ST
W 93RD ST

HENRY HUDSON PARKWAY
RIVERSIDE DR

WEST END AVE

BROADWAY

AMSTERDAM AVE

COLUMBUS AVE

8TH AVE

North Gate House
On reservoir O
Marathon Man

C

W 92ND ST
W 91ST ST
W 90TH ST
W 89TH ST

JACQUELINE ONASSIS RESERVOIR

O *Seinfeld* (TV)
George Costanza's apt.

O *30 Rock* (TV) **Liz Lemon's apt.**
O *Will and Grace* (TV)
Erik's apt.

W 88TH ST
W 87TH ST
W 86TH ST
W 85TH ST

BROADWAY

COLUMBUS AVE

UPPER WEST SIDE

W 86TH TRANSVERSE

D

| 5A

O *Romancing the Stone*
O **Cafe Lalo**
You've Got Mail

W 84TH ST
W 83RD ST
W 82ND ST

8TH AVE

DR

The Great Lawn
• *Hair*
• *Love Story*
• *Marathon Man* O

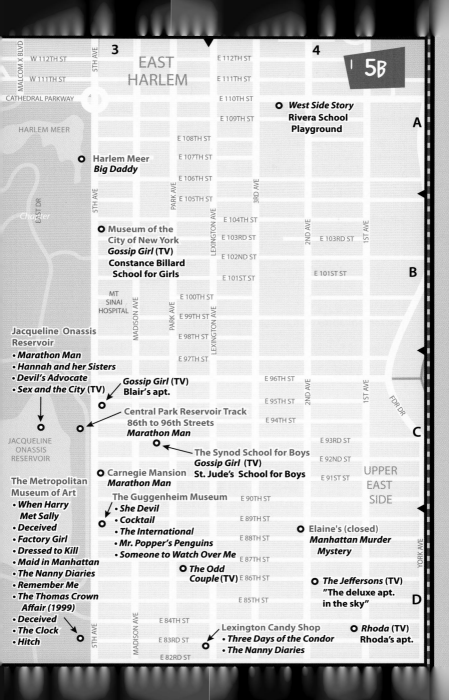

3

EAST HARLEM

5B

W 112TH ST
W 111TH ST
CATHEDRAL PARKWAY

HARLEM MEER

E 112TH ST
E 111TH ST
E 110TH ST
E 109TH ST

4

○ *West Side Story*
Rivera School Playground

A

E 108TH ST
E 107TH ST
E 106TH ST
E 105TH ST

○ Harlem Meer
Big Daddy

○ Museum of the City of New York
Gossip Girl **(TV)**
Constance Billard School for Girls

E 104TH ST
E 103RD ST
E 102ND ST
E 101ST ST

E 103RD ST
E 101ST ST

B

MT SINAI HOSPITAL

E 100TH ST
E 99TH ST
E 98TH ST
E 97TH ST

Jacqueline Onassis Reservoir
• *Marathon Man*
• *Hannah and her Sisters*
• *Devil's Advocate*
• *Sex and the City* (TV)

Gossip Girl **(TV)**
Blair's apt.

○

Central Park Reservoir Track
86th to 96th Streets
Marathon Man

○

E 96TH ST
E 95TH ST
E 94TH ST

C

○
JACQUELINE ONASSIS RESERVOIR

○

The Synod School for Boys
Gossip Girl **(TV)**
St. Jude's School for Boys

E 93RD ST
E 92ND ST
E 91ST ST

UPPER EAST SIDE

The Metropolitan Museum of Art
• *When Harry Met Sally*
• *Deceived*
• *Factory Girl*
• *Dressed to Kill*
• *Maid in Manhattan*
• *The Nanny Diaries*
• *Remember Me*
• *The Thomas Crown Affair (1999)*
• *Deceived*
• *The Clock*
• *Hitch*

○ Carnegie Mansion
Marathon Man

The Guggenheim Museum
• *She Devil*
• *Cocktail*
• *The International*
• *Mr. Popper's Penguins*
• *Someone to Watch Over Me*

E 90TH ST
E 89TH ST
E 88TH ST
E 87TH ST

○

○ Elaine's (closed)
Manhattan Murder Mystery

○ *The Odd Couple* **(TV)**

E 86TH ST
E 85TH ST

○ *The Jeffersons* **(TV)**
"The deluxe apt. in the sky"

D

○

Lexington Candy Shop
• *Three Days of the Condor*
• *The Nanny Diaries*

E 84TH ST
E 83RD ST
E 82RD ST

○

○ *Rhoda* **(TV)**
Rhoda's apt.

Live with Kelly (syndicated)
Tickets: Website
Location: 7 Lincoln Square, Columbus and West 67th Street
Schedule: Tapes weekdays 9–10 a.m.

The Rachael Ray Show (syndicated)
Tickets: rachaelrayshow.com
Location: Chelsea Television Studios, 221 West 26th Street between Seventh
    and Eighth Avenues
Schedule: Tapes Tuesday–Thursday at 11 a.m., 2:30 p.m., and 4:15 p.m.

Saturday Night Live (NBC)
Tickets: snltickets@nbcuni.com
Standby Tickets: 7 a.m. West 49th Street at 30 Rockefeller Center, day of taping
Location: 30 Rockefeller Plaza between Fifth and Sixth Avenues and West
    49th and 50th Streets
Schedule: 7:15 p.m. for 8:00 p.m. dress rehearsal/10:45 p.m. for 11:30 p.m.
    show

The Tonight Show with Jimmy Fallon (NBC)
Tickets: nbc.com/the-tonight-show
Location: 30 Rockefeller Plaza: 49th Street between 5th and 6th Avenues

The View (ABC)
Location: ABC Television Studios, "57 West 66th Street"/320 West 66th
    Street

The Wendy Williams Show (syndicated BET)
Tickets: wendyshow.com
Location: Chelsea Television Studios, 221 West 26th Street between 7th and
    8th Avenues

WHERE TO SEE LIVE TV
THROUGH THE STUDIO WINDOW
Check schedules online.

ABC News: 7th Avenue and West 44th Street, 2nd floor, in Times Square
CBS This Morning: 524 West 57th Street between 10th and 11th Avenue
Fox TV: 6th Avenue and West 48th Street
Good Morning America (NBC): 49th Street between 5th and 6th Avenues, in
    Rockefeller Center
Today (NBC): West 48th Street and Rockefeller Plaza. 30 Rockefeller Plaza be-
    tween Fifth and Sixth Avenues, enter at West 48th Street. Tapes Monday
    to Friday 7 to 11 a.m., Saturday 7 to 9 a.m., and Sunday 8 to 9 a.m.
WABC-TV Studios: Columbus Avenue and West 66th Street

HEADQUARTERS OF TV NETWORKS
AND THEIR NEWS DIVISIONS IN MANHATTAN

ABC News/Good Morning America: 1500 Broadway at 44th Street
WABC-TV: 47 West 66th at Columbus Avenue
CBS Evening News: 524 West 57th between 10th and 11th Avenues
CBS Headquarters: 51 West 52nd Street at 6th Avenue. "Black Rock" building.
FOX News/News Corp.: 1211 Avenue of the Americas between 47th and
48th Streets
NBC News/NBC Headquarters: 30 Rockefeller Plaza, Rockefeller Center
NBC Universal National Headquarters: The Comcast Building (formerly the
GE Building) in Rockefeller Center. NBC also owns Universal Studios.
Home Box Office (HBO) Main Office: 1100 6th Avenue at 42nd Street.
Owned by Time Warner.
Time Warner Inc.: Time Warner Center, 10 Columbus Circle, 59th Street and
8th Avenue. Time Warner owns HBO, Turner, the CW, Warner Bros. CNN,
and DC Comics.

The Bronx

- *A Beautiful Mind (2001)*
- *A Bronx Tale (1993)*
- *Awake (2007)*
- *Awakenings (1990)*
- *The Catered Affair (1956)*
- *City Island (2009)*
- *Finding Forester (2000)*
- *Fort Apache: The Bronx (1981)*
- *The Godfather (1972)*
- *I Like It Like That (1994)*
- *Kinsey (2004)*
- *Long Day's Journey into Night (1962)*
- *Lost in Yonkers (1993)*
- *Marty (1955)*
- *Rumble In the Bronx (1995)*
- *Summer of Sam (1999)*
- *The Verdict (1982)*
- *True Love (1989)*
- *The Wanderers (1979)*
- *Wolfen (1981)*
- *The Goldbergs (TV)*

Staten Island

- *A Beautiful Mind (2001)*
- *Big Fan (2009)*
- *The Book of Daniel (2005)*
- *Diggers (2006)*
- *Donnie Brasco (1997)*
- *Easy Money (1983)*
- *The Education of Max Bickford (2001)*
- *Fur (2006)*
- *The Godfather (1972)*
- *Grace Quigley (1984)*
- *How to Lose a Guy in 10 Days (2003)*
- *Kinsey (2004)*
- *Little Children (2006)*
- *Mr. Popper's Penguins (2011)*
- *Neighbors (1981)*
- *Salt (2010)*
- *Saturday Night Fever (1977)*
- *School of Rock (2003)*
- *Shamus (1973)*
- *The Siege (1998)*
- *Sisters (1973)*
- *Sorry, Wrong Number (1948)*
- *Splendor in the Grass (1961)*
- *Staten Island (2008)*
- *That Kind of Woman (1959)*
- *Trainwreck (2015)*
- *War of the Worlds (2005)*
- *Who's That Knocking at My Door? (1968)*
- *Working Girl (1988)*
- *You Don't Know Jack (2010)*
- *Grounded for Life (2001–2005)* **(TV)**

Staten Island

6A

Upper Manhattan
- *Coogan's Bluff (1968)* (The Cloisters)
- *The Royal Tenenbaums (2001)*
  (339 Convent Avenue at West 144th Street)
- *The Saint of Fort Washington (1993)*

The Bronx

Harlem
- *Across 110th Street (1972)*
- *Black Caesar (1973)*
- *Cotton Come to Harlem (1970)*
- *Hell Up in Harlem (1973)*
- *New Jack City (1991)*

Manhattan

Queens
- *A Guide to Recognizing Your Saints (2006)*
- *Captain America: Civil War (2016)*
- *Chop Shop (2007)*
- *Coming to America (1988)*
- *Empire State (2013)*
- *Now You See Me (2013)*
- *Queens Logic (1991)*
- *Secretariat (2010)*
- *The Terminal (2004)*
- *All in the Family (TV)*
- *Dear John (TV)*
- *Rescue Me (TV)*
- *The King of Queens (TV)*

Queens

Brooklyn
- *Annie Hall (1977)*
- *Brighton Beach Memoirs (1986)*
- *Crooklyn (1994)*
- *The Departed (2006)*
- *Do the Right Thing (1989)*
- *Dog Day Afternoon (1975)*
- *Eat Pray Love (2010)*
- *French Connection (1971)*
- *Goodfellas (1990)*
- *He Got Game (1998)*
- *The House on Carroll Street (1988)*
- *Last Exit to Brooklyn (1989)*
- *The Little Fugitive (1953)*
- *Little Manhattan (2005)*
- *Lords of Flatbush (1974)*
- *Moonstruck (1987)*
- *New Year's Eve (2011)*
- *Once Upon a Time in America (1984)*
- *Prizzi's Honor (1985)*
- *Requiem for a Dream (2000)*
- *Saturday Night Fever (1977)*
- *She's Gotta Have It (1986)*
- *Sophie's Choice (1982)*
- *Spike of Bensonhurst (1988)*
- *Straight Out of Brooklyn (1991)*
- *Summer of Sam (1999)*
- *A Tree Grows in Brooklyn (1945)*
- *The Warriors (1979)*
- *Everybody Hates Chris (TV)*
- *The Honeymooners (TV)*
- *The Patty Duke Show (TV)*
- *Welcome Back, Kotter (TV)*

Brooklyn

6B

BROADWAY THEATERS, CONCERT HALLS, AND COMEDY CLUBS

BROADWAY THEATERS

THE TERMS "BROADWAY," "Off-Broadway," and "Off-Off-Broadway" came about because of union payment schedules. The bigger the theater, the bigger the hourly pay, because there's more to do. Broadway: 500 seats and up (to the largest, with 1935 seats); Off-Broadway: 100–499 seats; and Off-Off-Broadway: up to ninety-nine seats.

There are usually about forty Broadway theaters in any given year, located in and around Times Square or Lincoln Center. In general, musicals play in the larger theaters.

Here they are in order of size and with the famous musicals or plays they are known for hosting. These listings also show the year built and other information.

Gershwin Theater (1972): 222 West 51st Street. *Show Boat.* Originally the Uris Theater. Contains The American Theater Hall of Fame, available to ticket holders. 1,933 seats.

Lyric Theater (1998): 213 West 42nd Street. *42nd Street.* Originally the Ford Center for Performing Arts. 1,930 seats.

New Amsterdam Theater (1903): 214 West 42nd Street. *The Lion King.* First Disney lease on 42nd Street. 1,801 seats.

Broadway Theater (1924): 1681 Broadway at 53rd Street. *Miss Saigon.* Originally a movie theater. 1,761 seats.

Palace Theater (1913): 1554 Broadway at 46th Street. *Beauty and the Beast.* To "play the Palace" meant "hit the pinnacle of show biz success." 1,743 seats.

St. James Theater (1927): 246 West 44th Street. *Hello Dolly!* Originally Ehrlanger's Theater. 1,710 seats.

Minskoff Theater (1973): 200 West 45th Street. *Sunset Boulevard.* Located inside One Astor Plaza, an office tower that replaced the Astor Hotel in 1972. 1,710 seats.

Marquis Theater (1886): 1535 Broadway at 45th Street. *Me and My Girl.* Located in the Marriott Hotel. 1,615 seats.

Majestic Theater (1927): 247 West 44th Street. *The Phantom of the Opera. Phantom* is the longest running Broadway show in history. 1,609 seats.

Lunt-Fontanne Theater (1910): 205 West 46th Street. *Ziegfeld Follies of 1918.* Named for married actors Alfred Lunt and Lynn Fontanne. 1,509 seats.

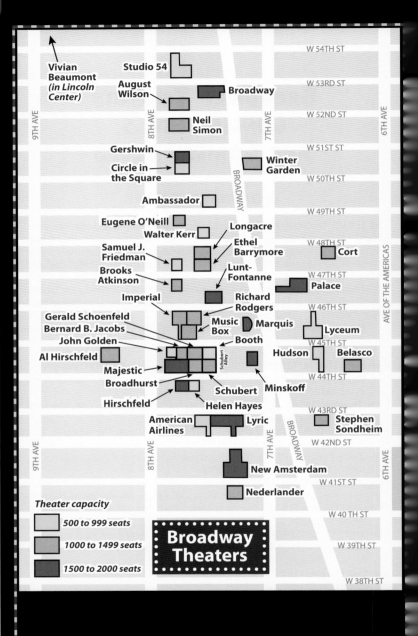

Winter Garden Theater (1911): 1634 Broadway at 51st Street. *Cats*. *Cats* played for eighteen years. The theater was originally built in 1896 to hold horses for auction. 1,498 seats.

Shubert Theater (1913): 225 West 44th Street. *The Third Party*. *A Chorus Line* played here from 1975 to 1990. 1,468 seats.

Al Hirschfeld Theater (1924): 302 West 45th Street. *Man of La Mancha*. The name changed from the Martin Beck Theater in 2003 to honor Hirschfeld, the famed Broadway caricaturist. 1,437 seats.

Imperial Theater (1923): 249 West 45th Street. *Les Misérables*. "*Les Miz*" ran here for sixteen years. 1,435 seats.

Neil Simon Theater (1927): 250 West 52nd Street. *Wings Over Europe*. Renamed from the Alvin Theater in 1983. 1,428 seats.

Richard Rodgers Theater (1925): 226 West 46th Street. *L'Illusionniste*. Holds the record with the most Tony-winning Best Plays and Best Musicals, with eleven awards. 1,380 seats.

Nederlander Theater (1921): 208 West 41st Street. *Mei Lanfang*. Mei Lanfang was a 1930s Chinese opera legend. 1,232 seats.

August Wilson Theater (1925): 245 West 52nd Street. *Jersey Boys*. Was the Virginia Theater from 1981 to 2005. 1,222 seats.

Broadhurst Theater (1917): 235 West 44th Street. *Amadeus*. Jerry Seinfeld's 2015 HBO special was filmed here. 1,218 seats.

Ambassador Theater (1921): 219 West 49th Street. *Chicago* (revival). From the 1930s to the 1950s this was the Dumont TV Studio. 1,120 seats.

Brooks Atkinson Theater (1926): 256 West 47th Street. *Same Time, Next Year*. Originally the Mansfield Theater, until 1960. 1,109 seats.

Eugene O'Neill Theater (1925): 230 West 49th Street. *Tobacco Road*. Originally the Forrest Theater, then the Coronet Theater. 1,108 seats.

Vivian Beaumont Theater (1965): 150 West 65th Street. *Contact*. Located in Lincoln Center. 1,105 seats.

Cort Theater (1912): 138 West 48th Street. *The Inner Man*. *The Merv Griffin Show* shot here from 1969–1972. 1,102 seats.

Bernard B. Jacobs Theater (1927): 242 West 45th Street. *Grease*. Hosted the musical *Once* in 2012. 1,101 seats.

Ethel Barrymore Theater (1928): 243 West 47th Street. *I Love My Wife*. The theater has had the same name since opening. 1,096 seats.

Longacre Theater (1913): 220 West 48th Street. *Maria Rosa*. To raise money for his theater ventures, the owner sold Babe Ruth from the Red Sox to the Yankees. Named for Longacre Square, the original name of Times Square. 1,095 seats.

Gerald Schoenfeld Theater (1917): 236 West 45th Street. *Jekyll & Hyde*. Originally named the Plymouth Theater. 1,093 seats.

Stephen Sondheim Theater (1918): 124 West 43rd Street. *Urinetown: The Musical*. Originally Henry Miller's Theater with 950 seats. Was the Xenon disco in the late '70s. Everything but the front facade was completely rebuilt in 2004 during construction of the neighboring Bank of America tower. 1,055 seats.

Belasco Theater (1907): 111 West 44th Street. *Hedwig and the Angry Inch.* Marlon Brando's first big success was in a 1946 play here. 1,040 seats.

Music Box Theater (1921): 239 West 45th Street. *Deathtrap.* Designed to accommodate Irving Berlin's *Music Box Revue.* 1,025 seats.

Hudson Theater (1903): 139–141 West 44th Street. *State of the Union.* Was the Savoy nightclub in the 1980s. 970 seats.

Walter Kerr Theater (1921): 219 West 48th Street. *Proof.* A TV studio from 1943–1965. Renamed for the celebrated theater critic in 1990. 947 seats.

Lyceum Theater (1903): 149 West 45th Street. *Born Yesterday.* One of the three oldest surviving theaters; others are the Hudson and the New Amsterdam, both also from 1903. 943 seats.

Studio 54 Theater (1927): 254 West 54th Street. *Cabaret.* Built as an opera house. Was the famed Studio 54 disco from 1977 to 1991. 922 seats.

Booth Theater (1913): 222 West 45th Street. *Prunella.* Named for the famous actor Edwin Booth, brother of John Wilkes Booth. 806 seats.

John Golden Theater (1927): 252 West 45th Street. *Avenue Q.* The exterior was used in the movie *All About Eve.* 805 seats.

Circle in the Square Theater (1972): 235 West 50th Street. *20th Annual Putnam County Spelling Bee.* Seats surround the stage. 776 seats.

American Airlines Theater (1918): 227 West 42nd Street. *The Royal Family.* From the 1930s to 2000 it was a 42nd Street movie theater; the modern entrance masks an old historic theater. 740 seats.

Samuel J. Friedman Theater (1925): 261 West 47th Street. *Hair.* Vacant from the 1980s–1990s, restored in early 2000s. 650 seats.

Helen Hayes Theater (1912): 240 West 44th Street. *Gemini.* Originally called The Little Theater, as it had only 299 seats. Expanded but still the smallest Broadway theater. TV's *American Bandstand* was shot here from 1958–1960 as *The Dick Clark Saturday Night Beech-Nut Show.* 597 seats.

NEW YORK CITY CONCERT HALLS
(By Number of Seats)

Madison Square Garden: 4 Penn Plaza, 32nd Street and 7th Avenue. 20,789 seats.

Barclays Center: 620 Atlantic Avenue, Fort Green/Prospect Heights, Brooklyn. 18,103 seats.

Radio City Music Hall: 1260 6th Avenue at West 50th Street. 6,015 seats.

The Theater at Madison Square Garden: 4 Penn Plaza, 32nd Street and 7th Avenue. 5,500 seats.

Metropolitan Opera House: 30 Lincoln Center Plaza at 63rd Street. 3,794 seats.

Kings Theater: 1027 Flatbush Avenue, Flatbush, Brooklyn. 3,676 seats.

United Palace Theater: 4140 Broadway at 175th Street, Washington Heights. 3,293 seats.

Terminal 5: 610 West 56th Street, west of 11th Avenue. 3,000 seats.

BAM (Brooklyn Academy of Music): 30 Lafayette Avenue, Fort Green, Brooklyn. 2,983 seats.

Beacon Theater: 2121 Broadway at 74th Street. 2,894 seats.

St. George Theater: 35 Hyatt Street, St. George, Staten Island. 2,876 seats.

Carnegie Hall: 881 7th Avenue at 57th Street. 2,804 seats.

New York City Center: 131 West 55th Street between 6th and 7th Avenues. 2,750 seats.

David Geffen Hall: 10 Lincoln Center Plaza at 64th Street. Formerly Philharmonic Hall (1962–1973), and then Avery Fisher Hall (1973–2015). 2,738 seats.

David Koch Theater: 20 Lincoln Center Plaza at 62nd Street. Formerly the New York State Theater. 2,563 seats.

Hammerstein Ballroom (in the Manhattan Center): 311 West 34th Street between 8th and 9th Avenues. 2,200 seats.

PlayStation Theater: 1515 Broadway at 44th Street. 2,100 seats.

The Riverside Church (Nave): 490 Riverside Drive at 120th Street. 1,900 seats.

Apollo Theater: 253 West 125th Street. 1,506 seats.

St. Ann's Warehouse: 45 Water Street, Dumbo, Brooklyn. 1,500 seats.

The Town Hall: 123 West 43rd Street between 6th and 7th Avenues. 1,495 seats.

Rose Theater (Jazz at Lincoln Center): 10 Columbus Circle at West 60th Street. 1,233 seats.

Vivian Beaumont Theater: 150 West 65th Street at Lincoln Center. 1,200 seats.

Alice Tully Hall: 1941 Broadway at Lincoln Center. 1,087 seats.

Irving Plaza: 17 Irving Place at East 15th Street. 1,025 seats.

Skirball Center for the Performing Arts (NYU): 566 LaGuardia Place at West 4th Street. 850 seats.

B.B. King's Blues Club: 237 West 42nd Street between 7th and 8th Avenues. 550 seats.

The Gramercy Theater: 127 East 23rd Street at Lexington Avenue. 499 seats.

Joyce Theater: 175 8th Avenue at West 19th Street. 472 seats.

Merkin Concert Hall: 129 West 67th Street between Amsterdam and Broadway. 449 seats.

Ed Sullivan Theater: 1697 Broadway between 53rd and 54th Streets. 400 seats.

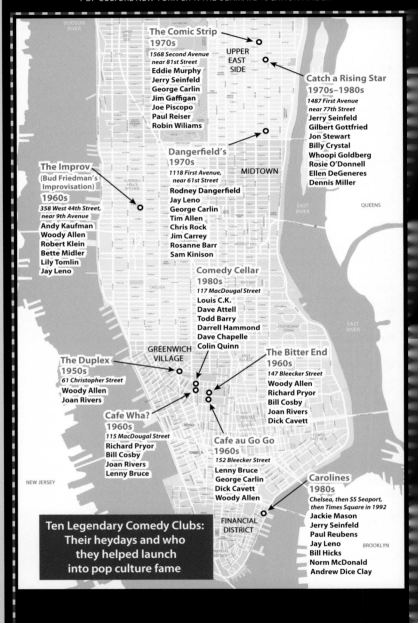

The Comic Strip
1970s
1568 Second Avenue near 81st Street
Eddie Murphy
Jerry Seinfeld
George Carlin
Jim Gaffigan
Joe Piscopo
Paul Reiser
Robin Wiliams

UPPER EAST SIDE

Catch a Rising Star
1970s–1980s
1487 First Avenue near 77th Street
Jerry Seinfeld
Gilbert Gottfried
Jon Stewart
Billy Crystal
Whoopi Goldberg
Rosie O'Donnell
Ellen DeGeneres
Dennis Miller

Dangerfield's
1970s
1118 First Avenue, near 61st Street
Rodney Dangerfield
Jay Leno
George Carlin
Tim Allen
Chris Rock
Jim Carrey
Rosanne Barr
Sam Kinison

MIDTOWN

The Improv
(Bud Friedman's Improvisation)
1960s
358 West 44th Street, near 9th Avenue
Andy Kaufman
Woody Allen
Robert Klein
Bette Midler
Lily Tomlin
Jay Leno

Comedy Cellar
1980s
117 MacDougal Street
Louis C.K.
Dave Attell
Todd Barry
Darrell Hammond
Dave Chapelle
Colin Quinn

GREENWICH VILLAGE

The Bitter End
1960s
147 Bleecker Street
Woody Allen
Richard Pryor
Bill Cosby
Joan Rivers
Dick Cavett

The Duplex
1950s
61 Christopher Street
Woody Allen
Joan Rivers

Cafe Wha?
1960s
115 MacDougal Street
Richard Pryor
Bill Cosby
Joan Rivers
Lenny Bruce

Cafe au Go Go
1960s
152 Bleecker Street
Lenny Bruce
George Carlin
Dick Cavett
Woody Allen

Carolines
1980s
Chelsea, then SS Seaport, then Times Square in 1992
Jackie Mason
Jerry Seinfeld
Paul Reubens
Jay Leno
Bill Hicks
Norm McDonald
Andrew Dice Clay

NEW JERSEY

FINANCIAL DISTRICT

BROOKLYN

QUEENS

**Ten Legendary Comedy Clubs:
Their heydays and who
they helped launch
into pop culture fame**

3

Music Landmarks, Jazz Clubs, Rock 'n' Roll Hangouts, and Album Cover Locations

FAMOUS NYC MUSIC VENUES, PAST AND PRESENT

The Big Band/Swing Era, 1900–1950

Cafe Society: 1 Sheridan Square at Barrow Street

The Cotton Club: Lenox Avenue and 142nd Street (1923–1935), Times Square, 200 West 48th Street at Broadway (1936–1940)

Copacabana: 10 East 60th Street between 5th Avenue and Madison Avenue (1940–1992)

Latin Quarter: 1580 Broadway between 47th and 48th Streets (1942–1970s)

The Stork Club: 3 East 53rd Street between 5th Avenue and Madison Avenue (1929–1965)

Paradise Cabaret: 1619 Broadway at 49th Street, second floor (1930s)

Hurricane: 1619 Broadway at 49th Street, second floor (1940–1944)

Zanzibar: 1619 Broadway at 49th Street, second floor (1944–1948)

Bop City: 1619 Broadway at 49th Street, second floor (1949–1951)

Jimmy Ryan's: 53 West 52nd Street (1940–1962), 154 West 54th Street (1962–1983). Dixieland jazz.

El Morocco: 154 East 54th between 3rd and Lexington Avenues (1930s–1950s)

The Rainbow Room: 30 Rockefeller Plaza, 65th floor, near 49th Street and 6th Avenue (1934–2009)

Famous 1950s Rock 'n' Roll Venues

American Bandstand Theater: 240 West 44th Street between 7th and 8th Avenues. Was the Little Theater, now the Helen Hayes.

Apollo Theater: 253 West 125th Street, Harlem

Brooklyn Paramount Theater: Flatbush Avenue at DeKalb Avenue, Brooklyn. Alan Freed's rock and roll shows. Now a Long Island University gymnasium.

Fox Theater: 20 Flatbush Avenue at Fulton Street, Brooklyn. Alan Freed's rock and roll shows. Demolished.

The Paramount: 1501 Broadway at 43rd Street, Times Square. Now the Hard Rock Cafe.

Iconic Music Clubs from Folk to Punk

Greenwich Village Folk Music Clubs and Venues, circa 1955–1965

The Bitter End: 147 Bleecker Street between Thompson Street and LaGuardia Place

Cafe Bizarre: 106 West 3rd Street between MacDougal and Sullivan Streets

Cafe Figaro: 186 Bleecker Street at MacDougal Street

Cafe Wha?: 115 MacDougal Street at Minetta Lane

The Cock 'n' Bull: 147 Bleecker Street between Thompson Street and LaGuardia Place. Closed in 1961 and became The Bitter End.

The Commons/Fat Black Pussycat: 11–13 Minetta Street between Minetta Lane and Bleecker Street. Other end was 105 MacDougal Street.

The Dugout: 145 Bleecker Street between Thompson Street and LaGuardia Place

The Gaslight Cafe: 116 MacDougal Street between Bleecker Street and West 3rd Street

Gerde's Folk City: 11 West 4th Street at Mercer Street. Previously 11 West 3rd Street at Mercer Street (1952–1956), 11 West 4th Street at Mercer Street (1956–1969), 130 West 3rd Street at 6th Avenue (1969–1986).

The Night Owl Cafe: 118 West 3rd Street between MacDougal Street and Sixth Avenue

The Village Gate: 160 Bleecker Street at Thompson Street

The Village Vanguard: 178 Seventh Avenue South at Waverly Place

The Limelight: 71 Seventh Avenue South between Grove and Barrow Streets

The Other End: 147 Bleecker Street between Thompson Street and LaGuardia Place

The White Horse Tavern: 567 Hudson Street at West 11th Street

Other Folk–Era Places

The Kettle of Fish (bar/restaurant): 114 MacDougal Street

Mills Tavern (bar): 167 Bleecker Street between Sullivan and Thompson Streets

Tin Angel (restaurant): 145 Bleecker Street between Thompson Street and LaGuardia Place

Alan Block's Sandal Shop: 171 West 4th Street between Sixth Avenue and Jones Street

Izzy Young's Folklore Center: 110 MacDougal Street between Minetta Lane and Bleecker Street

Cafe Feenjon: 105 MacDougal Street between Bleecker Street and Minetta Lane. It came after The Fat Black Pussycat.

Famous 1950s and 1960s Folk Music Concert Halls: Larger Venues

Carnegie Hall: 145 West 57th Street and 7th Avenue/881 7th Avenue

New York City Center: 131 West 55th Street between 6th and 7th Avenues

Philharmonic Hall: 132 West 65th Street. Now David Geffen Hall/Lincoln Center.

The Town Hall: 123 West 43rd Street at Sixth Avenue

Famous Rock Clubs, Venues, and Arenas, circa 1965–1980s

The Beacon Theater: 2124 Broadway between 74th and 75th Streets

The Bottom Line: 15 West 4th Street at Mercer Street

Cafe au Go Go: 152 Bleecker Street, basement, between Thompson Street and LaGuardia Place

Cheetah: 53rd Street between Broadway and 7th Avenue

The Dom: 19–23 St. Mark's Place between 2nd and 3rd Avenues

The Electric Circus: 19–23 St. Mark's Place between 2nd and 3rd Avenues (1967–1971)

Fillmore East: 105 2nd Avenue between 6th and 7th Streets

The Garrick Theater: 152 Bleecker Street between Thompson Street and LaGuardia Place

Kenny's Castaways: Uptown (1967–1976); 157 Bleecker Street (1976–2012)

Lone Star Cafe: 61 Fifth Avenue at 13th Street

Lone Star Roadhouse: 240 West 52nd Street between 7th and 8th Avenues

Madison Square Garden: 4 Penn Plaza, 32nd Street and 7th Avenue

Max's Kansas City: 213 Park Avenue South between 17th and 18th Streets

The Mercer Arts Center: 240 Mercer Street at 3rd Street (in the back of Broadway Central Hotel)

Ondine: 308 East 59th Street between 1st and 2nd Avenues. (Discotheque, 1960s–1970s.)

The Palladium: 126 East 14th Street between 3rd and 4th Avenues. Formerly the Academy of Music, now an NYU dorm.

The Peppermint Lounge: Knickerbocker Hotel, 128 West 45th Street between 6th and 7th Avenues (1958–1965). Later became G.G. Barnum's PL. Reopened in 1982 at 100 5th Avenue. Discotheque.

The Ritz: 125 East 11th Street. Now Webster Hall.

The Saint: 105 2nd Avenue between 6th and 7th Streets. Discotheque, 1970s.

Steve Paul's The Scene: 301 West 46th Street at 8th Avenue

Studio 54: 254 West 54th Street between Broadway and 8th Avenue. Discotheque, 1960s–1970s.

Trude Heller's: 418 Sixth Avenue at 9th Street

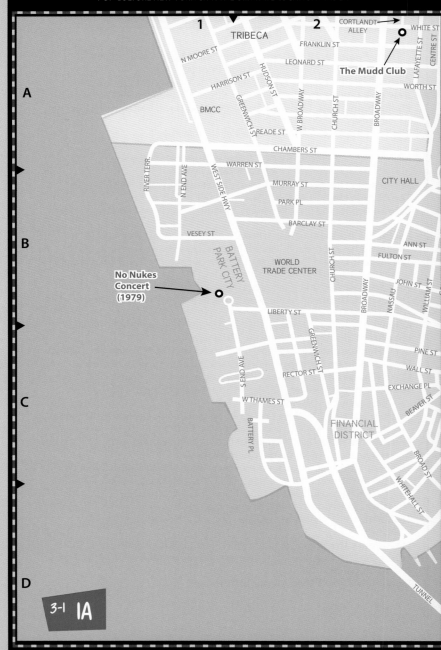

1

2

TRIBECA

CORTLANDT-ALLEY

WHITE ST

N MOORE ST

FRANKLIN ST

LAFAYETTE ST

CENTRE ST

HUDSON ST

LEONARD ST

The Mudd Club

HARRISON ST

GREENWICH ST

W BROADWAY

CHURCH ST

BROADWAY

WORTH ST

A

BMCC

READE ST

CHAMBERS ST

RIVER TERR.

N END AVE

WEST SIDE HWY

WARREN ST

MURRAY ST

PARK PL

CITY HALL

B

VESEY ST

BATTERY PARK CITY

BARCLAY ST

WORLD TRADE CENTER

CHURCH ST

ANN ST

FULTON ST

No Nukes Concert (1979)

LIBERTY ST

GREENWICH ST

BROADWAY

NASSAU

JOHN ST

WILLIAM ST

PINE ST

WALL ST

S END AVE

RECTOR ST

EXCHANGE PL

BEAVER ST

C

W THAMES ST

BATTERY PL

FINANCIAL DISTRICT

BROAD ST

WHITEHALL ST

D

3-1 IA

TUNNEL

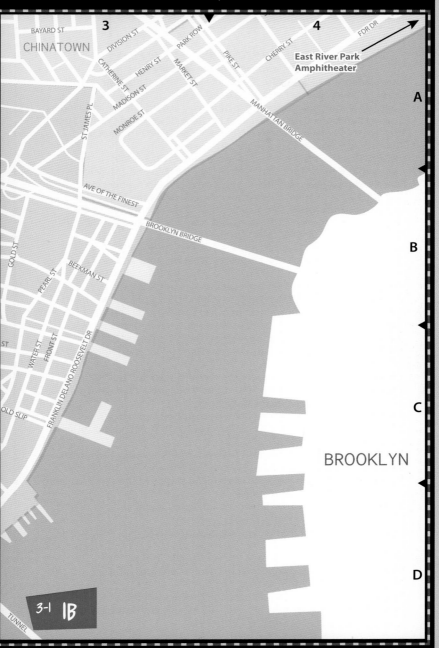

Famous 1970s–1980s Mostly Punk and New Wave Venues

The Academy: 234 West 43rd Street between 7th and 8th Avenues

Area: 157 Hudson Street at Laight Street

Bond's International Casino: 1526 Broadway at 45th Street, Times Square

Bowery Ballroom: 6 Delancey Street between Bowery and Christie Streets

Brownies: 169 Avenue A between East 10th and East 11th Streets

The Cat Club: 76 East 13th Street at 4th Avenue

CBGB: 315 Bowery at the end of Bleecker Street (1973–2006)

Coney Island High: 15 St. Mark's Place between 2nd and 3rd Avenues

Danceteria: 30 West 21st Street between 5th and 6th Avenues (1979–1988)

Fez: 380 Lafayette Street at Great Jones Street, under the Time Cafe

Great Gildersleeves: 331 Bowery between 2nd and 3rd Streets

Hurrah: 36 West 62nd Street, southwest corner at Broadway (1976–1980)

Irving Plaza: 17 Irving Place at 15th Street

King Tut's Wah Wah Hut: 112 Avenue A at East 7th Street

The Knitting Factory: 47 East Houston Street between Mulberry and Mott Streets

The Limelight: 47 West 20th Street at 6th Avenue (1983–1990s)

Lismar Lounge: 41 First Avenue between East 2nd and East 3rd Streets

Luna Lounge: 171 Ludlow Street between East Houston and Stanton Streets

The Marquee: 547 West 21st Street between 10th and 11th Avenues

Maxwell's: 1039 Washington Street, Hoboken, New Jersey

The Mercury Lounge: 217 East Houston Street between Ludlow and Essex Streets

The Mudd Club: 77 White Street between Broadway and Lafayette Street

The Palladium: 140 East 14th Street between 3rd and 4th Avenues (1976–1995). Formerly the Academy of Music.

Paradise Garage: 84 King Street between Hudson and Varick Streets

The Peppermint Lounge: 100 5th Avenue at 15th Street, previously at 45th Street

The Pyramid Club: 101 Avenue A between East 6th and East 7th Streets

Save the Robots: 25 Avenue B between East 2nd and East 3rd Streets

Tramps: 125 East 15th Street between Irving Place and Third Avenue; later moved to 51 West 21st Street

Trax: 100 West 72nd Street, basement, between Columbus Avenue and Broadway

The Tunnel: 220 12th Avenue between West 27th and West 28th Streets (1986–2001)

Wetlands Preserve: 161 Hudson Street at Laight Street

White Columns: 325 Spring Street between Washington and Greenwich Streets

The World: 254 East 2nd Street between Avenues B and C

Xenon: 124 West 43rd Street between 6th Avenue and Broadway, in the former Henry Miller Theater (1978–1984)

Large 1960s–1990s Venues

Carnegie Hall: 145 West 57th Street and 7th Avenue/881 7th Avenue
Central Park, Wollman Rink: Rheingold Music Festival (1966–1967)
Central Park, Wollman Rink: Schaefer Music Festival (1967–1976)
Central Park, Bandshell: SummerStage (1986–1990)
Central Park, Rumsey Playfield: SummerStage (1990–present)
Central Park, Sheep Meadow: Last show in 1979
Central Park, The Great Lawn:
>Elton John: September 13, 1980
>Simon & Garfunkel (reunion concert): September 19, 1981
>Diana Ross: July 21, 1983
>Paul Simon: August 15, 1991
>Garth Brooks: August 7, 1991
>Dave Matthews: September 25, 2003
>Bon Jovi: July 12, 2008
>The Black Eyed Peas: September 30, 2011

Pier 84: West 44th Street and the Hudson River (Dr. Pepper Music Festival, later Miller Time Concerts, 1981–1988)
Madison Square Garden: 4 Penn Plaza, 32nd Street and 7th Avenue
Metropolitan Opera House: Lincoln Center at Broadway and 64th Street
Radio City Music Hall: 1260 Avenue of the Americas at West 50th Street
Shea Stadium: 126th Street and Roosevelt Avenue, Queens
Nassau Coliseum: 1255 Hempstead Turnpike, Uniondale, NY
Forest Hills Tennis Stadium: 1 Tennis Place, Forest Hills, Queens
Barclays Center: 620 Atlantic Avenue, Brooklyn. Opened 2012.
Brendan Byrne Arena (1981–1996)/Continental Airlines Arena (1996–2007): East Rutherford, New Jersey
Battery Park City Landfill: No Nukes Concert, 1979. 200,000 people.

Famous 1970s–1980s Disco and Dance Venues

Cheetah: 310 West 52nd Street and Broadway
Studio 54: 254 West 54th Street between Broadway and 8th Avenue
Heartbreak: 179 Varick Street between Charlton and King Streets
Roxy: 515 West 18th Street between 10th and 11th Avenues. Went from roller disco to hip hop venue. Closed in 2007.
Roseland Ballroom: 239 West 52nd Street between Broadway and 8th Avenue
S.O.B.'s (Sounds of Brazil): 204 Varick Street at West Houston Street (1982–present)
The Tunnel: 220 12th Avenue between 27th and 28th Streets (1986–2001)
Regine's: 502 Park Avenue at 59th Street (1976–1991)
Le Club: 416 East 55th Street between 1st Avenue and Sutton Place. Opened in 1960.
Arthur: 154 East 54th Street between 3rd and Lexington Avenues. Opened in 1965.
Salvation: 1 Sheridan Square at Barrow Street. Opened in 1969.

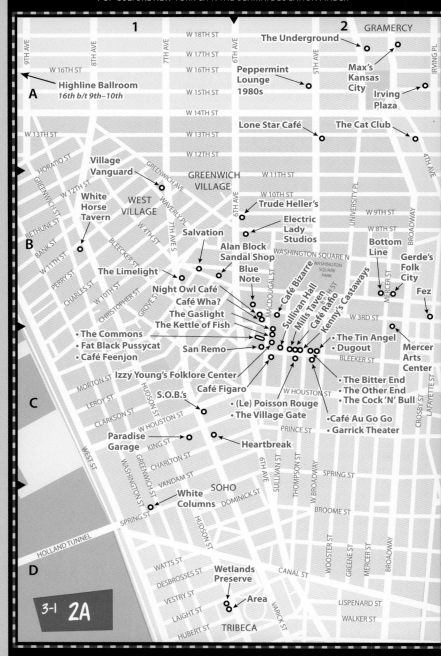

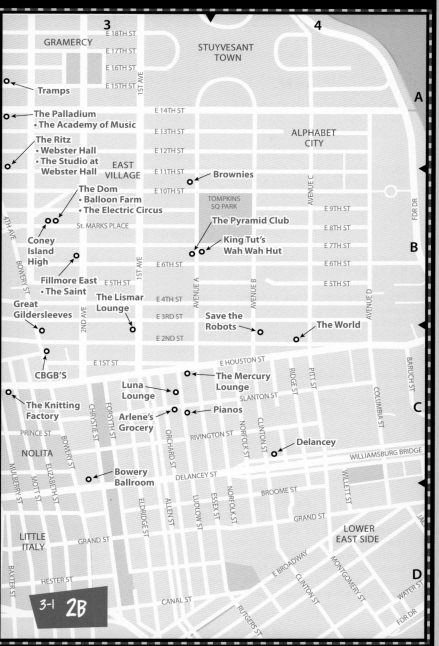

Sanctuary: 407 West 43rd Street between 9th and 10th Avenues. Opened in 1970.
Le Jardin: 110 West 43rd Street between 6th and 7th Avenues, in Hotel Diplomat
The Underground: 860 Broadway at 17th Street
2001 Odyssey: 802 64th Street, Brooklyn (was the club 1978 in *Saturday Night Fever*)

Famous 1970s–1980s Hip Hop Venues and Locations
1520 Sedgewick Avenue, the Bronx: Birthplace of hip hop.
Tramps: 51 West 21st Street between 5th and 6th Avenues
The Tunnel: 220 12th Avenue between West 27th and West 28th Streets (1986–2001)

Famous Post–1980s Rock Clubs, Venues, and Arenas: Manhattan
Arlene's Grocery: 95 Stanton Street between Orchard and Ludlow Streets
B.B. King's Blues Club & Grill: 237 West 42nd Street between 7th and 8th Avenues
The Blue Note Jazz Club: 131 West 3rd Street. Since 1981.
Bowery Ballroom: 6 Delancey Street between Bowery and Christie Streets
The Delancey: 168 Delancey Street between Clinton and Attorney Streets
Pianos: 158 Ludlow Street between Stanton and Rivington Streets
The Gramercy Theater: 127 East 23rd Street between Park and Lexington Avenues
Hammerstein Ballroom: 311 West 34th Street between 8th and 9th Avenues
Highline Ballroom: 431 West 16th Street between 9th and 10th Avenues
PlayStation Theater: 1515 Broadway at West 44th Street. Was Nokia Theater (2005–2010), Best Buy Theater (2010–2015). Became PlayStation Theater in 2015.
Le Poisson Rouge: 158 Bleecker Street between Sullivan and Thompson Streets
The Studio at Webster Hall: 125 East 11th Street between 3rd and 4th Avenues
Sullivan Hall: 214 Sullivan Street between Bleecker and West 3rd Streets
Terminal 5: 610 West 56th Street between 11th and 12th Avenues

Famous Post–1980s Rock Clubs, Venues and Arenas: Brooklyn
Littlefield: 635 Sackett Street, Gowanus, Brooklyn
The Bell House: 149 7th Street, Gowanus, Brooklyn
Knitting Factory: 361 Metropolitan Avenue, Williamsburg, Brooklyn
Music Hall of Williamsburg 66 North 6th Street, Williamsburg, Brooklyn
Union Hall: 702 Union Street, Park Slope, Brooklyn
Street Ann's Warehouse: 38 Water Street, Dumbo, Brooklyn

Famous 1950s–1960s Rock–Related Buildings

The Brill Building: 1619 Broadway at 49th Street. Entire building of record-producing companies.

Ed Sullivan Theater: 1695 Broadway between 53rd and 54th Streets. The Beatles, Rolling Stones, and Elvis famously performed here.

Pythian Temple: 135 West 70th Street between Broadway and Columbus Avenue. The first rock song was recorded here in 1955: "Rock Around the Clock" by Bill Haley and the Comets.

The Hard Rock Café: 221 West 57th Street between 7th Avenue and Broadway

Strawberry Fields: Central Park West and 72nd Street entrance

The Dakota: 1 West 42nd Street at Central Park West

The Chelsea Hotel: 222 West 23rd Street between 7th and 8th Avenues

FAMOUS RECORDING STUDIOS AND THE SONGS RECORDED THERE

A&R Studio 1: 112 West 48th Street between 6th and 7th Avenues; later 700 Seventh Avenue, 322 West 48th Street. "The Girl from Ipanema," Stan Getz/Astrid Gilberto (1964); "Brown Eyed Girl," Van Morrison (1967); "I Dig Rock and Roll Music," Peter, Paul and Mary, (1967).

Atlantic Records: 234 West 56th between Broadway and 8th Avenue; later 11 West 60th and 1841 Broadway

Bell Sound: 237 West 54th Street. "Walk on By," Dionne Warwick (1964); "Raindrops Keep Falling on My Head," B.J. Thomas (1969); "Rock and Roll All Nite," Kiss (1975). Later became The Hit Factory.

Columbia Studio A: 799 Seventh Avenue at 52nd Street. "Homeward Bound," Simon and Garfunkel (1966); "Summer in the City," the Lovin' Spoonful (1966). Later, as A&R Studio 2: "A Simple Twist of Fate," Bob Dylan (1975); "The Weight," The Band (1968).

Columbia Studio B: 49 East 52nd Street. "Piece of my Heart," Janis Joplin/Big Brother and the Holding Company (1968); "The Only Living Boy in New York," Simon and Garfunkel (1970).

Columbia 30th Street Studios ("The Church"): 207 East 30th Street between 2nd and 3rd Avenues. *Kind of Blue*, Miles Davis; Duke Ellington; Dizzy Gillespie; Thelonious Monk; Dave Brubeck.

Electric Lady Studio: 52 West 8th at Sixth Avenue. "Superstition," Stevie Wonder (1972); "Fame," David Bowie (1975); "Say It Ain't So," Weezer (1995).

The Hit Factory: 237 West 54th between Broadway and 8th Avenue (1975–1991). "Sir Duke," Stevie Wonder (1976). Later, at 421 West 54th Street between 9th and 10th Avenues (1991–2005), Bruce Springsteen, Madonna, John Lennon, 50 Cent.

Mira Studios: 145 West 47th between 6th and 7th Avenues. "Remember (Walking in the Sand)," The Shangri-Las; "Society's Child," Janis Ian.

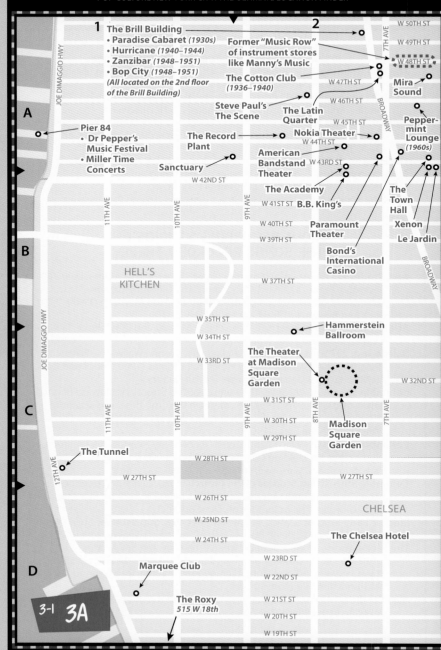

1

W 50TH ST
W 49TH ST
W 48TH ST

2

The Brill Building
• **Paradise Cabaret** *(1930s)*
• **Hurricane** *(1940–1944)*
• **Zanzibar** *(1948–1951)*
• **Bop City** *(1948–1951)*
(All located on the 2nd floor of the Brill Building)

Former "Music Row" of instrument stores like Manny's Music

The Cotton Club *(1936–1940)*

W 47TH ST

Mira Sound

Steve Paul's The Scene

W 46TH ST

The Latin Quarter

W 45TH ST

Peppermint Lounge *(1960s)*

A

Pier 84
• **Dr Pepper's Music Festival**
• **Miller Time Concerts**

The Record Plant

Nokia Theater

W 44TH ST

Sanctuary

W 43RD ST

American Bandstand Theater

The Academy

B.B. King's

W 41ST ST

W 40TH ST

W 39TH ST

Paramount Theater

The Town Hall

Xenon

Le Jardin

Bond's International Casino

W 42ND ST

11TH AVE
10TH AVE
9TH AVE

B

HELL'S KITCHEN

W 37TH ST

BROADWAY

W 35TH ST
W 34TH ST

Hammerstein Ballroom

W 33RD ST

The Theater at Madison Square Garden

W 32ND ST

C

11TH AVE
10TH AVE
9TH AVE
8TH AVE
7TH AVE

W 31ST ST
W 30TH ST
W 29TH ST

Madison Square Garden

JOE DIMAGGIO HWY

12TH AVE

The Tunnel

W 28TH ST
W 27TH ST

W 27TH ST

W 26TH ST

CHELSEA

W 25ND ST

W 24TH ST

The Chelsea Hotel

W 23RD ST

D

Marquee Club

W 22ND ST

3-1 3A

The Roxy
515 W 18th

W 21ST ST
W 20TH ST
W 19TH ST

3

4

The Rainbow Room

ROCKEFELLER
CENTER

Radio City
Music Hall

The first
A&R Studios

MIDTOWN

RCA Studios
(1953-1968)

A

B

Columbia Records
30th Street Studios

C

RCA Studios
(Elvis recorded here)

The Gramercy
Theater

D

The
Limelight

Tramps

Danceteria

3-1 3B

E 50TH ST
E 49TH ST
E 48TH ST
E 47TH ST
E 46TH ST
E 45TH ST
E 44TH ST
E 43RD ST
E 42ND ST
E 41ST ST
E 40TH ST
E 37TH ST
E 36TH ST
E 35TH ST
E 34TH ST
E 33RD ST
E 32ND ST
E 31ST ST
E 30TH ST
E 29TH ST
E 28TH ST
E 27TH ST
E 26TH ST
E 25TH ST
E 24TH ST
E 23RD ST
E 22ND ST
E 21
E 20T

W 26TH ST
W 25ND ST
W 24TH ST
W 23RD ST
W 22ND ST
W 21ST ST
W 20TH ST

5TH AVE
MADISON AVE
PARK AVE
3RD AVE
2ND AVE
1ST AVE
FDR DR
6TH AVE
LEXINGTON AVE
BROADWAY
AVE OF THE AMERICAS
E 30TH ST

Media Sound: 311 West 57th Street between 8th and 9th Avenues. Jimi Hendrix, Billy Joel, John Lennon, the Rolling Stones, Aerosmith, Stevie Wonder, Frank Sinatra, Barbra Streisand.

The Power Station: 441 West 53rd between 9th and 10th Streets. "Hungry Heart," Bruce Springsteen (1980); "Let's Dance," David Bowie (1983); "Like a Virgin," Madonna (1984). Now Avatar.

RCA Studios: 55 East 24th Street. Elvis: "Hound Dog," "Blue Suede Shoes," "Don't Be Cruel" in Studio A at 55 East 24th. At 110 West 44th Street (1953–1968): Louis Armstrong, Perry Como, Harry Belafonte.

The Record Plant: 321 West 44th between 8th and 9th Avenues. *Electric Ladyland,* Jimi Hendrix (1968); "Walk This Way," Aerosmith (1975), "School's Out," Alice Cooper (1972); "(Just Like) Starting Over," John Lennon (1980).

USED RECORD STORES
Manhattan

A-1 Record Shop: 439 East 6th Street near Avenue A, East Village. a1record-shop.com

Academy Records & CDs: 12 West 18th Street near 5th Avenue, Greenwich Village. (212) 242-3000. academy-records.com

Academy Records: 415 East 12th Street near 1st Avenue, East Village. (212) 780-9166. academy-records.com. Classical and jazz.

Downtown Music Gallery: 13 Monroe Street between Christie and Market Streets, Chinatown, East. (212) 473-0043

Generation Records: 210 Thompson Street near Bleecker Street, Greenwich Village. (212) 254-1100. facebook.com/generationrecords

Good Records NYC: 218 East 5th Street near 3rd Avenue, East Village. goodrecordsnyc.com

House of Oldies: 35 Carmine Street near Bleecker Street, Greenwich Village. (212) 243-0500. houseofoldies.com

In Living Stereo: 2 Great Jones Street at Broadway, Noho

Jazz Record Center: 236 West 26th Street, 8th floor, Room 804, near 8th Avenue, Chelsea. (212) 675-4480. jazzrecordcenter.com

Record Runner: 5 Jones Street near West 4th Street, Greenwich Village. (212) 255-4280. recordrunnerusa.com

Turntable Lab: 84 East 10th Street between 3rd and 4th Avenues. (212) 677-0675

Westsider Records: 233 West 72nd Street near Broadway, Upper West Side. (212) 874-1588. westsiderbooks.com/recordstore

Brooklyn

Almost Ready: 135 Huntington Street, Carroll Gardens

Black Gold Records: 461 Court Street near Luquer Street, Carroll Gardens. blackgoldbrooklyn.com

Human Head Records: 168 Johnson Avenue near Avenue of Puerto Rico, Bushwick. humanheadnyc.com

Material World: 184 Noll Street, Bushwick

Music Matters: 413 7th Avenue, Park Slope

Norton Record Shop: 595 Washington Avenue between Pacific and Dean Streets, Prospect Heights. nortonrecords.com

Permanent Records: 159 20th Street #1B at 4th Avenue, South Slope. permanentrecords.info

Record Shop: 360 Van Brunt Street between Wolcott and Sullivan Streets, Red Hook

Rough Trade NYC: 64 North 9th Street near Kent Avenue, Williamsburg. roughtrade.com

Superior Elevation: 100 White Street, Bushwick

The Thing: 1001 Manhattan Avenue near Huron Street, Greenpoint. facebook.com/the-thing-vinyl-sales

Queens

Hifi Records & Café: 23–19 Steinway Street between 23rd Avenue and 23rd Road, Astoria. hifi-records.com

The Bronx

Moodies Records and Tapes: 3976 White Plains Road, Bronx

Staten Island

Majors Records & Video: 12 Barrett Avenue, Staten Island. majorrecordsny.com

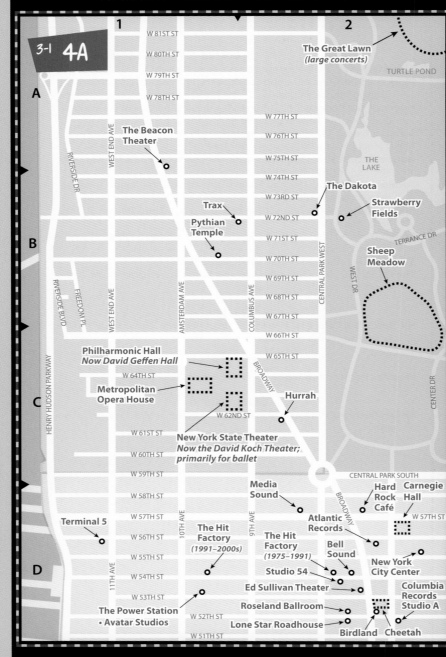

3-1 4A

1

W 81ST ST
W 80TH ST
W 79TH ST
W 78TH ST

2

The Great Lawn
(large concerts)

TURTLE POND

A

WEST END AVE

The Beacon
Theater

RIVERSIDE DR

W 77TH ST
W 76TH ST
W 75TH ST
W 74TH ST
W 73RD ST

THE
LAKE

The Dakota

Strawberry
Fields

Trax

Pythian
Temple

W 72ND ST
W 71ST ST

TERRANCE DR

B

RIVERSIDE BLVD

FREEDOM PL

WEST END AVE

AMSTERDAM AVE

COLUMBUS AVE

W 70TH ST
W 69TH ST
W 68TH ST
W 67TH ST
W 66TH ST
W 65TH ST

CENTRAL PARK WEST

WEST DR

Sheep
Meadow

Philharmonic Hall
Now David Geffen Hall

W 64TH ST

Metropolitan
Opera House

W 62ND ST

New York State Theater
*Now the David Koch Theater;
primarily for ballet*

BROADWAY

Hurrah

C

HENRY HUDSON PARKWAY

W 61ST ST
W 60TH ST
W 59TH ST
W 58TH ST

CENTER DR

CENTRAL PARK SOUTH

Media
Sound

Hard
Rock
Café

Carnegie
Hall

Terminal 5

W 57TH ST

10TH AVE

9TH AVE

Atlantic
Records

BROADWAY

W 57TH ST

The Hit
Factory
(1991–2000s)

The Hit
Factory
(1975–1991)

Bell
Sound

Studio 54

New York
City Center

D

11TH AVE

W 56TH ST
W 55TH ST
W 54TH ST
W 53RD ST

Ed Sullivan Theater

The Power Station
• Avatar Studios

W 52ND ST

Roseland Ballroom

Lone Star Roadhouse

W 51ST ST

Birdland

Columbia
Records
Studio A

Cheetah

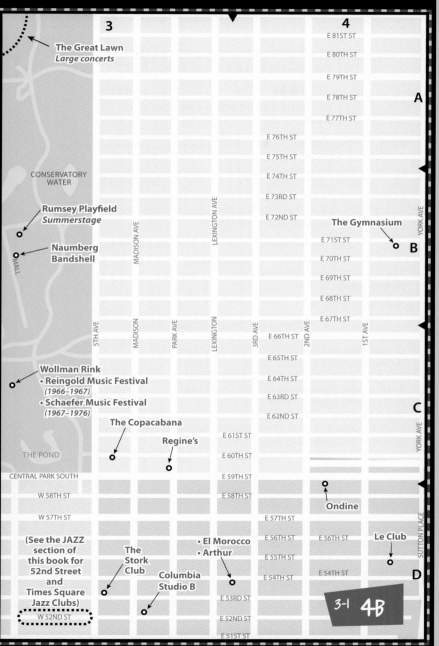

3

4

E 81ST ST

E 80TH ST

E 79TH ST

The Great Lawn
Large concerts

E 78TH ST

A

E 77TH ST

E 76TH ST

E 75TH ST

CONSERVATORY
WATER

E 74TH ST

E 73RD ST

E 72ND ST

Rumsey Playfield
Summerstage

The Gymnasium

E 71ST ST

B

Naumberg
Bandshell

E 70TH ST

E 69TH ST

E 68TH ST

E 67TH ST

E 66TH ST

E 65TH ST

Wollman Rink
• **Reingold Music Festival**
(1966–1967)
• **Schaefer Music Festival**
(1967–1976)

E 64TH ST

E 63RD ST

E 62ND ST

C

The Copacabana

E 61ST ST

Regine's

E 60TH ST

THE POND

E 59TH ST

CENTRAL PARK SOUTH

E 58TH ST

W 58TH ST

W 57TH ST

E 57TH ST

Ondine

(See the JAZZ
section of
this book for
52nd Street
and
Times Square
Jazz Clubs)

• **El Morocco**
• **Arthur**

E 56TH ST   E 56TH ST

Le Club

The
Stork
Club

E 55TH ST

E 54TH ST   E 54TH ST

D

Columbia
Studio B

E 53RD ST

3-1 **4B**

W 52ND ST

E 52ND ST

E 51ST ST

MADISON AVE · LEXINGTON AVE · YORK AVE · MALL · 5TH AVE · MADISON · PARK AVE · LEXINGTON · 3RD AVE · 2ND AVE · 1ST AVE · YORK AVE · SUTTON PLACE

LEGENDARY MANHATTAN JAZZ CLUB LOCATIONS FROM THE GOLDEN ERA OF NYC JAZZ CLUBS, 1930–1950

52nd Street and Times Square
(Addresses as of around 1944–1947)

FIFTY-SECOND STREET between 5th Avenue and Broadway was known as "Swing Street," or just "The Street," from the 1940s to 1960s. After prohibition ended in 1933, the center of jazz activity slowly moved downtown to the Times Square area. Most of the clubs on 52nd Street were located in the bottom floors of four- to five-story tenement buildings and were usually about twenty feet wide and sixty feet deep. As rents went up, it was easy for them to relocate quickly just by moving the chairs, tables, and small stage.

52nd Street, North Side, 5th Avenue to 6th Avenue
Jazz Clubs

The Onyx: 55 West 52nd Street
Jimmy Ryan's: 53 West 52nd Street
Tondelayo's: Swing Street, north side

Other 52nd Street Establishments

Tony's Restaurant: 59 West 52nd Street
Orchard Room Restaurant: 57 West 52nd Street
Ha-Ha Club: 51 West 52nd Street
Eugene's Luncheonette: 51 West 52nd Street
Swiss Chalet Restaurant: 45 West 52nd Street
Follies Restaurant: 39 West 52nd Street
Alton Liquors: 35 West 52nd Street
Leon & Eddie's: 33 West 52nd Street. Burlesque club with some jazz.
House of Ballantine Liquors: 23 West 52nd Street
21 Club: 21 West 52nd Street. Originally Jack and Charlie's 21 Club.

52nd Street, South Side, 5th Avenue to 6th Avenue
Jazz Clubs

3 Deuces: 72 West 52nd Street
Club Downbeat: 66 West 52nd Street
Club Carousel: 66 West 52nd Street
Yacht Club (later Downbeat): 66 West 52nd Street
Club Samoa: 62 West 52nd Street. Burlesque club.
Famous Door: 56 West 52nd Street
Spotlight: 56 West 52nd Street

Other 52nd Street Establishments

Chez Lina Restaurant: 70 West 52nd Street
Chez Remy Restaurant: 64 West 52nd Street
Johnny's Tavern: 60 West 52nd Street
Michael Riley's Restaurant: 58 West 52nd Street
Club Nocturne: 56 West 52nd Street
Drama Bookshop: 48 West 52nd Street

52nd Street, 6th Avenue to 7th Avenue
Jazz Clubs

Kelly's Stables: 137 West 52nd Street between 6th and 7th Avenues
Hickory House: 144 West 52nd Street between 6th and 7th Avenues

Times Square North: Broadway and 7th Avenue between 46th and 54th Streets from South to North

Arcadia Ballroom: 1680–1688 Broadway, southeast corner at 53rd Street
Band Box: Broadway between West 52nd and West 53rd Streets, east side of street
Birdland: 1678 Broadway between West 52nd and West 53rd Streets.
Iridium Jazz Club: 1650 Broadway between 50th and 51st Streets, east side. Formerly 63rd and 8th Avenue (1994–2001).
Zanzibar: 1619 Broadway (1944–1949), northwest corner of Broadway and 49th Street
Bop City: 1619 Broadway (1949–1965), northwest corner of Broadway and 49th Street
Latin Quarter: 1580 Broadway between 47th and 48th Streets
Royal Roost: 1574 Broadway, northwest corner at 47th street. Also known as "the Metropolitan Bopera House."
Metropole Café: 725 7th Avenue between 46th and 47th Streets

Further South from Times Square

Buddy's Place: 133 West 33rd Street between 6th and 7th Avenues

East of Fifth Avenue

The Embers: 161 East 54th Street between Lexington and Third Avenues
Basin Street East: 137 East 48th Street, northeast corner at Lexington Avenue

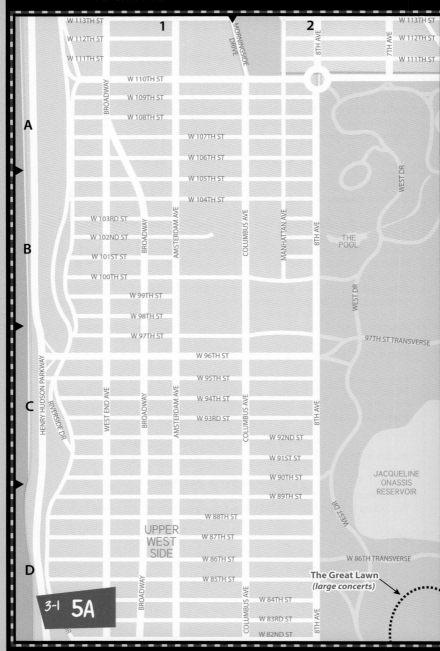

The Great Lawn
(large concerts)

3-1 5A

3

W 112TH ST

W 111TH ST

CATHEDRAL PARKWAY

5TH AVE

EAST
HARLEM

E 112TH ST

E 111TH ST

E 110TH ST

E 109TH ST

4

A

A Great Day In Harlem (1958)
**Famous photo by Art Kane of
57 Jazz Musicians on steps
17 East 126th Street**

HARLEM MEER

E 108TH ST

E 107TH ST

E 106TH ST

E 105TH ST

EAST DR

MADISON AVE

PARK AVE

LEXINGTON AVE

E 104TH ST

E 103RD ST

E 102ND ST

3RD AVE

2ND AVE

E 103RD ST

1ST AVE

**East Meadow
(Concerts have
been held here)**

5TH AVE

E 101ST ST

E 100TH ST

E 101ST ST

B

MT
SINAI
HOSPITAL

E 99TH ST

E 98TH ST

E 97TH ST

MADISON AVE

PARK AVE

LEXINGTON AVE

E 96TH ST

E 95TH ST

E 94TH ST

2ND AVE

1ST AVE

FDR DR

C

E 93RD ST

E 92ND ST

UPPER
EAST
SIDE

JACQUELINE
ONASSIS
RESERVOIR

E 91ST ST

E 90TH ST

E 89TH ST

E 88TH ST

E 87TH ST

E 86TH ST

E 85TH ST

YORK AVE

D

**The Great Lawn
(large concerts)**

E 84TH ST

E 83RD ST

E 82RD ST

3-1 **5B**

61

Harlem Jazz Clubs, Restaurants, and Ballrooms
from the 1920s–1940s
New York's original Swing Street was 133rd Street, often called just "the Street."

Alamo Club (1915–1925): 253 West 125th Street between 7th and 8th Avenues, basement. AKA Alamo Cafe, Jimmy Durante.

Alhambra Ballroom (1929–1945): 2116 Adam Clayton Powell Jr. Boulevard (7th Avenue) at 126th Street. Built in 1903 for vaudeville. An upstairs ballroom was opened in 1929 (closed in the 1960s) and featured jazz performers like Bessie Smith and Billie Holiday. AKA "the Harlem Alhambra."

The Apollo Theater: 253 West 125th Street between 7th and 8th Avenues

Baby Grand Cafe (1945–1965): 319 West 125th Street between St. Nicholas and 8th Avenues. Address from 1964 phone book. AKA Club Baby Grand.

Bank's Club: 133rd Street

Barbeque Club: 169 West 133rd Street. Restaurant above The Nest, established in 1923.

Barron's Club: 198 West 134th Street at 7th Avenue, basement. Duke Ellington played here in the 1920s.

Basement Brownies (1930–1935): 152 West 133rd Street between 6th and 7th Avenues

Brittwood Bar: 594 Lenox Avenue at 141st Street, next to the Savoy Ballroom

Capitol Palace: 575 Lenox Avenue at 139th Street

Clark Monroe's Uptown House: 198 West 134th Street between Lenox Avenue and Adam Clayton Powell Boulevard (7th Avenue). The building still stands.

Club Harlem: 145th Street and 7th Avenue

Connie's Inn (1923–1934): 2221 7th Avenue at 131st Street, basement. 131st Street and 7th Avenue was "The Corner." Connie was Conrad Immerman, a Lithuanian. Unlike the Cotton Club, it wasn't whites only.

Cotton Club: 644 Lenox Avenue and 142nd Street, northeast corner

Count Basie's Lounge (1955–1964): 2245 7th Avenue, northeast corner at 132nd Street. The building still stands.

Covan's: 148 West 133rd between 6th and 7th Avenues. AKA Covan's Morocco Club.

Dickie Wells' Shim Sham Club (1932–1942): 169 West 133rd Street (in the same space as The Nest)

Edith's Clam House: 146 West 133rd Street between 6th and 7th Avenues. AKA Harry Hansberry's Clam House or just The Clam House.

Gee Haw Stables: 113 West 132nd Street between Lenox and 7th Avenues. The after-hours club was so-named because there was a sculpted horse's head at the entrance. Much of Art Tatum's *God is in the House* LP was recorded here on a tape recorder in 1941.

Golden Gate Ballroom (1939–1950): 640 Lenox Avenue at West 142nd Street

(Harry Hansberry's) Clam House (1928): 146 West 133rd Street between Lenox and 7th Avenues

Harlem Opera House: 209 West 125th Street at 7th Avenue

Havana San Juan: 138th Street and Broadway

Herman's Inn: 2493 Seventh Avenue between 144th and 145th Streets

Hoofers: 2235 7th Avenue, in the basement of the Lafayette Theater/Dancers Bojangles Robinson

Hot Cha: 2280 7th Avenue at 134th Street, northwest corner. Where Billie Holiday stayed. AKA Hot Cha Bar and Grill, Club Hot Cha.

Lafayette Theater: 2227 7th Avenue. The Rhythm Club that was under the Lafayette became the Hoofer's Club.

Lenox Lounge: 288 Lenox Avenue between 124th and 125th Streets. The Zebra Room was inside. From 1939.

Lincoln Theater (1909–1964): 58 West 135th Street between 6th and 7th Avenues

Mexico's: 154 West 133rd Street between 6th and 7th Avenues, basement

Minton's Playhouse: 206 West 118th Street at St. Nicholas Avenue, southeast corner. Jazz club and bar located on the first floor of the Cecil Hotel (1938–1974, reopened 2006).

The Nest (1923–1932): 169 West 133rd Street, basement. Men played in bird outfits and sang "Where do the young birds go? To the Nest!" Later the Rhythm Club and upstairs, The Barbeque Club.

The Palace Ballroom: 280 West 155th Street at 8th Avenue. AKA the Rockland Palace Ballroom, originally the State Palace Ballroom.

The Plantation Club: 80–82 West 126th Street between 5th and Lenox Avenues

Pod's and Jerry's (1928–1948): 168 West 133rd Street between 6th and 7th Avenues. Officially the Patagonia, later The Log Cabin. A cabaret and jazz club. The "log cabin" front is still there.

Happy Rhone's Radium Club (1920–1925): 654 Lenox Avenue between 143rd and 144th Streets

Reuben's: 242 West 30th Street between 7th and 8th Avenues. A small piano club. Art Tatum played here. Owned by Reuben Harris, who played along with two whiskbrooms over a folded newspaper.

Renaissance Ballroom (1915–1964): 150 West 138th Street between Lenox and 7th Avenues

The Rhythm Club: 169 West 133rd Street. Later moved to 168 West 132nd Street (1932), and then was later taken over by the Hoofer's Club. Previously the Nest.

St. Nick's Jazz Pub: 773 St. Nicholas Avenue. Since 1940.

Savoy Ballroom (1926–1958): 596 Lenox Avenue between West 140th and West 141st Streets

Showman's Bar/Showman's Jazz Club: 375 West 125th Street. Originally located next to the Apollo Theater at 267 West 125th Street, where it was a hangout for the performers. Moved three times in forty-two years.

Small's Paradise (1925–1980s): 2294 1/2 Seventh Avenue at 135th Street, at southwest corner. Later became Big Wilt's Small's Paradise, now an International House of Pancakes. AKA Ed Small's Paradise.

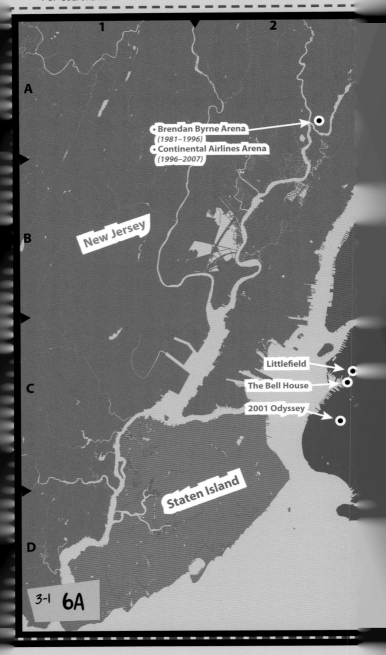

1   2

A

• Brendan Byrne Arena
  (1981–1996)
• Continental Airlines Arena
  (1996–2007)

New Jersey

B

Littlefield

The Bell House

2001 Odyssey

C

Staten Island

D

3-1 6A

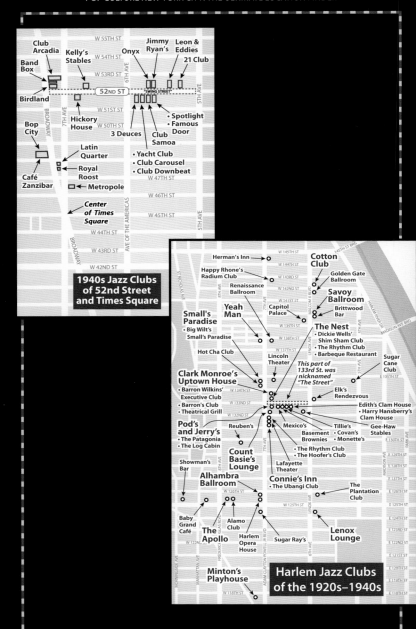

1940s Jazz Clubs of 52nd Street and Times Square

Club Arcadia
Kelly's Stables
Onyx
Jimmy Ryan's
Leon & Eddies
21 Club
Band Box
Birdland
Bop City
Hickory House
Spotlight
Famous
Door
3 Deuces
Club Samoa
Latin Quarter
Yacht Club
Club Carousel
Club Downbeat
Royal Roost
Café Zanzibar
Metropole
Center of Times Square

Harlem Jazz Clubs of the 1920s–1940s

Herman's Inn
Cotton Club
Happy Rhone's Radium Club
Golden Gate Ballroom
Renaissance Ballroom
Savoy Ballroom
Small's Paradise
Yeah Man
Capitol Palace
Brittwood Bar
• Big Wilt's Small's Paradise
The Nest
• Dickie Wells'
Shim Sham Club
• The Rhythm Club
• Barbeque Restaurant
Hot Cha Club
Lincoln Theater
Sugar Cane Club
Clark Monroe's Uptown House
This part of 133rd St. was nicknamed "The Street"
• Barron Wilkins' Executive Club
• Barron's Club
• Theatrical Grill
Elk's Rendezvous
Edith's Clam House
• Harry Hansberry's Clam House
Pod's and Jerry's
Reuben's
Mexico's
Tillie's
Gee-Haw Stables
• The Patagonia
• The Log Cabin
Basement Brownies
• Covan's
• Monette's
Count Basie's Lounge
• The Rhythm Club
• The Hoofer's Club
Showman's Bar
Lafayette Theater
Alhambra Ballroom
Connie's Inn
• The Ubangi Club
The Plantation Club
Baby Grand Café
The Apollo
Alamo Club
Harlem Opera House
Sugar Ray's
Lenox Lounge
Minton's Playhouse

W 55TH ST
W 54TH ST
6TH AVE
W 53RD ST
52ND ST
SWING STREET
5TH AVE
W 51ST ST
BROADWAY
7TH AVE
W 50TH ST
W 47TH ST
W 46TH ST
W 45TH ST
AVE OF THE AMERICAS
W 44TH ST
W 43RD ST
BROADWAY
W 42ND ST

W 145TH ST
145TH ST BRG
W 144TH ST
ST. NICHOLAS AVE
W 143RD ST
MALCOLM X BLVD
W 142ND ST
HARLEM RIVER DR
W 141ST ST
W 139TH ST
MADISON AVE BRG
W 138TH ST
LENOX AVE
W 137TH ST
5TH AVE
E 135TH ST
W 134TH ST
W 133RD ST
W 132ND ST
PARK AVE
7TH AVE
E 130TH ST
8TH AVE
MADISON AVE
E 129TH ST
E 128TH ST
W 126TH ST
E 127TH ST
E 126TH ST
E 125TH ST
W 125TH ST
LENOX AVE
E 124TH ST
FREDERICK DOUGLAS BLVD
E 123RD ST
ADAM CLAYTON POWELL JR BLVD
8TH AVE
E 122ND ST
W 122ND ST
E 121ST ST
MORNINGSIDE AVE
MANHATTAN AVE
E 120TH ST
E 119TH ST
W 118TH ST
E 118TH ST

Greenwich Village
Jazz Clubs from
1930s to Today

Snookie's Sugar Bowl: A luncheonette in Harlem during the 1950s–1960s.

Sugar Cane Club (1917–1925): 2212 5th Avenue at 135th Street, entrance through narrow underground passage. AKA Small's Sugar Cane Club.

Sugar Ray's: 2074 7th Avenue between 123rd and 124th Streets. Owned by boxer Sugar Ray Robinson.

Theatrical Grill: 198 West 134th Street. Clark Monroe opened the Uptown House in the 1930s at 198 West 134th Street in Harlem, in a building that formerly held Barron's Club, where Duke Ellington worked early in the 1920s, and the Theatrical Grill.

Tillie's (opened in 1926): 148 West 133rd Street. Chicken, waffles, and jazz. Later, it was Monette's Supper Club, where legend has it that John Hammond first heard seventeen-year-old Billie Holiday. Since 2006, Bill's Place, a small jazz club.

The Ubangi Club (1934–1937): 2221 7th Avenue at 131st Street. The Ubangi Club was opened in 1934 by Gladys Bentley, a famous lesbian singer who sang in tux and tails. Her club took over the space that had been occupied by Connie's Inn from 1923 to 1934. Both clubs were in the basement.

The Yeah Man (1925–1960): 2350 7th Avenue at 138th Street

Greenwich Village (1930s–Today)

Arthur's Tavern: 57 Grove between 7th Avenue South and Bedford Street

Blue Note Jazz Club: 131 West 3rd Street between 6th Avenue and MacDougal Street

Bradley's: 70 University Place between East 10th and East 11th Streets

Cafe au Go Go: 152 Bleecker Street between Thompson and LaGuardia Streets

Café Bohemia: 15 Barrow Street between West 4th Street and Bleecker Street

Cafe Society: 1 Sheridan Square, corner of Barrow Street and Waverly Place, basement

Cinderella Jazz Club (1930s–1950s): 82 West 3rd Street between Sullivan and Thompson Streets

The Cookery (1969–1984): 21 University Place and 8th Street

Eddie Condon's (1945): 47 West 3rd between Mercer and Greene Streets. Later moved uptown.

Fat Tuesdays: 190 Third Avenue at 17th Street, downstairs

Five Spot: 5 Cooper Square, Third Avenue between East 4th and East 5th Streets, at the north end of the Bowery. The club was here from 1956 to 1962, when the building it was in was demolished for an apartment building. In 1962 it moved about four blocks north to 2 St. Mark's Place at Third Avenue until 1967. Later it was the Two Saints but closed in January 1976.

Half Note: 289 Hudson Street, southwest corner at Spring Street. Later moved to West 3rd Street.

The Music Box (1950–1972): 121 West 3rd Street between MacDougal Street and 6th Avenue

Open Door: 55 West Third Street at West Broadway, northeast corner. Now called LaGuardia Place.

Seventh Avenue South: 21 Seventh Avenue South near Leroy. Run by the Brecker Brothers from 1977–1986.

Slugs (mid 1960s–1972): 242 East 3rd Street between Avenues B and C.

Small's Jazz Club: 183 West 10th Street between 7th Avenue South and West 4th Street

Sweet Basil Jazz Club (1974–2000): 88 Seventh Avenue South between Bleecker and Grove Streets

The Village Gate: 158 Bleecker Street between Sullivan and Thompson Streets. Now Le Poisson Rouge.

Village Vanguard: 178 Seventh Avenue South between Perry and West 11th Streets, downstairs.

Upper West Side:

Smoke: 2751 Broadway between 105th and 106th Streets, West side. Previously a jazz club called *Augie's.*

NEW YORK CITY ALBUM COVER LOCATIONS

BELOW IS AN ALPHABETICAL LIST of album covers listed by artist, with exact addresses of where the covers were shot and grid positions so you can find them on the maps.

The albums listed have had PopSpots made of them. Find The PopSpots Guide on the main PopSpots site (popspotsnyc.com) or on the PopSpots Facebook page (facebook.com/PopSpotsNYC-193602670694020). For many of these, a web search for "popspotsnyc.com + album name" often shows the PopSpot as one of the first results.

Ryan Adams, "Lucky Now" (45 single, 2011): 309 East 9th Street between 1st and 2nd Avenues (Map 2B/Grid 3B)

Eric Anderson, *Avalanche* (1969): Mercer and Spring Streets, Soho (Map 2A/ Grid 2C)

Aztec Two-Step, *Aztec Two-Step* (1972): 14–16 Gay Street between Christopher Street and Waverly Place (Map 2A/Grid 1B)

Babs Gonzales, *Tales of Manhattan* (1959): West 45th Street and Broadway (Map 3A/Grid 2A)

The Beastie Boys, *Paul's Boutique* (1989): Corner of Ludlow and Rivington Streets (Map 2B/Grid 3C)

The Beau Brummels, *Volume 2* (1965): The Arcade, Central Park, 72nd Street (Map 4B/Grid 3B)

Harry Belafonte, *Streets I Have Walked* (1963): Bethesda Terrace, inside Central Park at 72nd Street (Map 4B/Grid 3B)

Ruben Blades, *y Seis del Solar* (1985): 112–114 East 17th Street between Park Avenue South and Irving Place (Map 2A/Grid 2A)

Blondie, *Autoamerican* (1980): 300 Mercer Street at Waverly Place (Map 2A/Grid 2B)

The Blues Project, *Live at the Cafe Au Go Go* (1966): Bleecker Street near Thompson Street (Map 2A/Grid 2C)

The Boomtown Rats, *Ratrospective* (1983): Met Steps, 83rd Street and Fifth Avenue (Map 4B/Grid 3A)

Pat Boone, *Pat Boone* (1957): 116th Street and Broadway, Columbia University (Map 5A/Grid 1B)

The Brecker Brothers, *Straphangin'* (1981): City Hall Subway Station (private), Center and Chambers Streets (Map 1A/Grid 2B)

The BT Express, *Do It 'Til You're Satisfied* (1974): LIRR, Nostrand Avenue Station (Map 6B/Brooklyn)

Roy Buchanan, *Loading Zone* (1977): Pete's Tavern, 129 East 18th Street at Irving Place (Map 2A/Grid 2A)

Bunky and Jake, *Bunky and Jake* (1968): Commerce Street at Barrow Street. Back cover by Peter Strongwater. (Map 2A/Grid 2C)

Gary Burton, *Gary Burton Quartet in Concert* (1968): Carnegie Hall, 57th Street and 7th Avenue (Map 4A/Grid 2D)

Gary Burton, *New Vibe Man in Town* (1961): Corner of Gramercy Park East and East 21st Street (Map 3B/Grid 4D)

Donald Byrd, *Byrd in Flight* (1960): Bethesda Steps, Central Park, 72nd Street (Map 4B/Grid 3B)

Cashman & West, *Moondog Serenade* (1973): Cop Cot, Central Park, 60th Street (Map 4A/Grid 2C)

Judy Collins, *Sings Dylan Just Like a Woman* (1993): Vestry and Greenwich Streets (Map 2A/Grid 1D)

Willie Colon, *Cosa Nuestra* (1970): Bike path along the East River, just north of the Manhattan side of the Brooklyn Bridge (Map 2A/Grid 1D)

John Coltrane, *Coltrane Live at the Village Vanguard Again!* (1966): 178 7th Avenue South at Waverly Place. Photo by Charles Stewart. (Map 2A/Grid 1B)

Larry Coryell, *Live at the Village Gate* (1971): Bleecker Street at Thompson Street (Map 2A/Grid 2C)

Country Joe McDonald, *The Collected Country Joe and the Fish* (1987): 23rd Street and 6th Avenue (Map 3A/Grid 2D)

The Cramps, *Smell of Female* (1983): Peppermint Lounge, 128 West 45th Street between 6th and 7th Avenues (Map 3A/Grid 2A)

Bobby Darin, *Inside Out* (1967): 4 Gramercy Park West between East 20th and East 21st Streets (Map 3B/Grid 3D)

Miles Davis, *Workin' with the Miles Davis Quintet* (1959): 447 West 50th Street near 10th Avenue (Map 3A/Grid 1A)

Detroit Emeralds, *You Want It, You Got It* (1972): 17 Beekman Place, which is the east end of 50th Street near FDR Drive (Map 3B/Grid 4A)

Bo Diddley, *Have Guitar, Will Travel* (1960): 368 Livingston Street at Flatbush Avenue, Brooklyn (Map 6B/Brooklyn)

Dion & the Belmonts, *Cigars, Acapella, Candy* (1972): Arthur Avenue, Belmont, Bronx (Map 6B/Bronx)

Dion & the Belmonts, *Together Again* (1967): Gapstow Bridge, Central Park, 62nd Street (Map 4B/Grid 3C)

The Doors, *Strange Days* (1967): Sniffen Court, 150–158 East 36th Street between Lexington and 3rd Avenues. Photo by Joel Brodsky. (Map 3B/Grid 4B)

Bob Dylan, *Another Side of Bob Dylan* (1964): 52nd Street and Broadway. Photo by Sandy Speiser. (Map 4A/Grid 2D)

Bob Dylan, *Blonde on Blonde* (1966): 375 West Street at Morton Street. Photo by Jerry Schatzberg. (Map 2A/Grid 1C)

Bob Dylan, *Bob Dylan's American Journey* (2004): Roof of 901 Broadway at East 20th Street. Custom compilation CD. Photographer of the 1963 photo unknown. (Map 3B/Grid 3D)

Bob Dylan, *Chronicles* (2005): Roof, 901 Broadway at East 20th Street. Paperback edition. Photographer of the 1963 photo unknown. (Map 3B/Grid 3D)

Bob Dylan, *Freewheelin'* (1963): Jones and West 4th Streets (Map 2A/Grid 1B)

Bob Dylan, *Highway 61 Revisited* (1965): 4 Gramercy Park West between East 20th and East 21st Streets (Map 3B/Grid 3D)

Bob Dylan, "I Want You" (45 single, 1966): Jacob Street near the Brooklyn Bridge. Now demolished. (Map 1B/Grid 3B)

Bob Dylan, *Modern Times* (2006): 59th Street and Central Park West. 1947 photo by Ted Kroner. (Map 4A/Grid 2C)

Ramblin' Jack Elliott, *Jack Elliott Sings the Songs of Woody Guthrie* (1960): Washington Square Park, Center/west side (Map 2A/Grid 1B)

Booker Ervin, *The Blues Book* (1964): 16 Minetta Lane at Minetta Street (Map 2A/Grid 2B)

Mimi and Richard Farina, *Celebrations for a Grey Day* (1965): Eaglevale Arch, West 77th Street and Central Park West. Photo by Kenneth Van Sickle. (Map 4A/Grid 2A)

The Fifth Avenue Band, *The Fifth Avenue Band* (1969): Delmonico's Restaurant, 56 Beaver Street at South William Street (Map 1A/Grid 2C)

Foghat, *Fool for the City* (1975): 232 East 11th Street between 2nd and 3rd Avenues (Map 2B/Grid 3A)

The Four Tops *Changing Times* (1970): 4 Gramercy Park West between East 20th and East 21st Streets (Map 3B/Grid 3D)

Peter Frampton, *Breaking All The Rules* (1981): Fifth Avenue and 31st Street (Map 3B/Grid 3C)

Red Garland, *Red in Bluesville* (1959): 446 West 50th Street near 10th Avenue (Map 3A/Grid 1A)

Dexter Gordon, *Doin' Allright* **(1961):** 59th Street and Fifth Avenue (Map 4B/Grid 3C)

Herbie Hancock, *Inventions & Dimensions* **(1964):** West 41st Street and Madison Avenue (Map 3B/Grid 3B)

P.J. Harvey, *Stories from the City, Stories from the Sea* **(2000):** Times Square, 7th Avenue and 47th Street (Map 3A/Grid 2A)

Joe Henderson, *Page One* **(1963):** David Geffen Hall, Lincoln Center, 65th Street between Broadway and Amsterdam (Map 4A/Grid 1C)

Herman's Hermits, *The Best of Herman's Hermits* **(1965):** The Bandshell, inside Central Park at 70th Street (Map 4B/Grid 3B)

The Impressions, *The Young Mods' Forgotten Story* **(1969):** East 108th Street and Park Avenue (Map 5B/Grid 3A)

Tommy James and the Shondells, *The Very Best of Tommy James and the Shondells* **(1969):** The Cloisters, 99 Margaret Corbin Drive (Map 5A/Grid 2A)

The James Gang, *Live in Concert* **(1971):** Carnegie Hall, 57th Street and 7th Avenue (Map 4A/Grid 2D)

Thad Jones, *The Magnificent Thad Jones* **(1956):** Broadway and West 47th Street (Map 3A/Grid 2A)

Billy Joel, *An Innocent Man* **(1983):** 142 Mercer Street near Prince Street. Front and back covers. (Map 2A/Grid 2C)

Billy Joel, *52nd Street* **(1978):** 52nd Street and 7th Avenue, southeast corner. Photo by Jim Houghton. (Map 4A/Grid 2D)

Billy Joel, *The Stranger* **(1977):** 511 9th Avenue between 38th and 39th Streets. Demolished. (Map 3A/Grid 2B)

Billy Joel, *Turnstiles* **(1976):** Uptown Astor Place subway station, Astor Place at 8th Street (Map 2B/Grid 3B)

Kiss, *Dressed to Kill* **(1975):** West 23rd Street and 8th Avenue. Photo by Bob Gruen. (Map 3A/Grid 2D)

James Last, *Goodtimes* **(1972):** The Pond, Central Park, 61st Street. Back cover. (Map 4B/Grid 3C)

Cyndi Lauper, *A Night to Remember* **(1989):** Plymouth Street at Pearl Street, Brooklyn (Map 6B/Brooklyn)

Cyndi Lauper, *She's So Unusual* **(1983):** Henderson Walk, Coney Island (Map 6B/Brooklyn)

Led Zeppelin, *Physical Graffiti* **(1975):** 96–98 St. Mark's Place between First Avenue and Avenue A (Map 2B/Grid 3B)

John Lennon & Yoko Ono, *Double Fantasy* **(1980):** 72nd Street and Central Park West. Back cover. (Map 4A/Grid 2B)

John Lennon & Yoko Ono, *Milk and Honey* **(1984):** The Lake, Central Park, 72nd Street (Map 4A/Grid 2B)

John Lennon & Yoko Ono, "Watching the Wheels" (45 single, 1980): The Dakota, 72nd and Central Park West (Map 4A/Grid 2B)

Avril Lavigne, *Let Go* **(2002):** 415 Broadway at Canal Street (Map 2A/Grid 2D)

LL Cool J, *BAD (Bigger and Deffer)* (1987): Andrew Jackson High School, 207-01 116th Avenue (Map 6B/Grid 4C)

The Lovin' Spoonful, "Daydream" (45 single, 1966): Central Park, 62nd Street near 7th Avenue (Map 4A/Grid 2C)

The Lovin' Spoonful, *Daydream* CD (1966): Alice in Wonderland Statue at the Levin Playground, in Central Park at East 77th Street and Fifth Avenue. Back cover. (Map 4B/Grid 3A)

Manhattan Transfer, *Manhattan Transfer* (1975): 159 2nd Avenue, 10th Street entrance. Back cover. (Map 2B/Grid 3B)

Hugh Masekela, *Hugh Masekela's Next Album* (1966): Times Square, West 44th Street and Broadway (Map 3A/Grid 2A)

Johnny Mathis, *Johnny's Greatest Hits* (1958): 48th Street between 1st Avenue and FDR Drive. Photo by Norman Menard. (Map 3B/Grid 4A)

Chad Mitchell, *Chad Mitchell Himself* (1966): Gapstow Bridge, Central Park, 62nd Street (Map 4B/Grid 3C)

Joni Mitchell, *Songs to a Seagull* (1967): 169 Mercer Street between Houston and Prince Streets. Back cover. (Map 2A/Grid 2C)

Van Morrison, *Too Long in Exile* (1993): 246 Pearl Street between Fulton and John Streets (Map 1B/Grid 3C)

Morris Nanton, *Something We've Got* (1961): 271 West 126th Street at Frederick Douglass Boulevard (Map 5A/Grid 2A)

Fred Neil, *Bleecker and MacDougal* (1965): Intersection of Bleecker Street and MacDougal Street (Map 2A/Grid 2C)

New Swing Sextet, *Swinging' Along* (1969): Bryant Park, West 41st Street and 6th Avenue. Photo by Charles Stewart. (Map 3B/Grid 3B)

New York Dolls, *The New York Dolls* (1973): Gem Spa, 131 2nd Avenue at St. Mark's Place. Back cover photo by Toshi Matsuo. (Map 2B/Grid 3B)

Phil Ochs, *All the News That's Fit to Sing* (1964): Next to the Washington Square arch, Phil facing east. Balconies of 2 Fifth Avenue reflected in water. (Map 2A/Grid 2B)

Phil Ochs, *I Ain't Marching Anymore* (1965): West Third Street and Sullivan Street (Map 2A/Grid 2B)

Yoko Ono, *Season of Glass* (1981): The Dakota, 72nd Street and Central Park West (Map 4A/Grid 2B)

Buck Owens, *Carnegie Hall Concert* (1966): Carnegie Hall, 57th Street and 7th Avenue (Map 4A/Grid 2D)

Peter, Paul and Mary, *Album 1700* (1967): 70 Bedford Street between Commerce and Morton Streets (Map 2A/Grid 1C)

Peter, Paul and Mary, *The Best of Peter, Paul and Mary* (1970): 70 Bedford Street between Commerce and Morton Streets (Map 2A/Grid 1C)

Peter, Paul and Mary, *Peter, Paul and Mary* (1962): The Bitter End, 147 Bleecker Street near LaGuardia Place (Map 2A/Grid 2C)

Ramones, "I Want to Be Your Boyfriend" (45 single, 1976): Inscope Arch, Central Park, 62nd Street (Map 4B/Grid 3C)

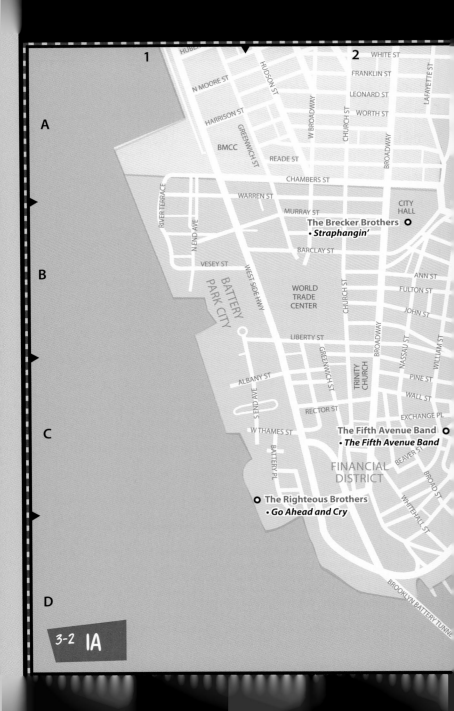

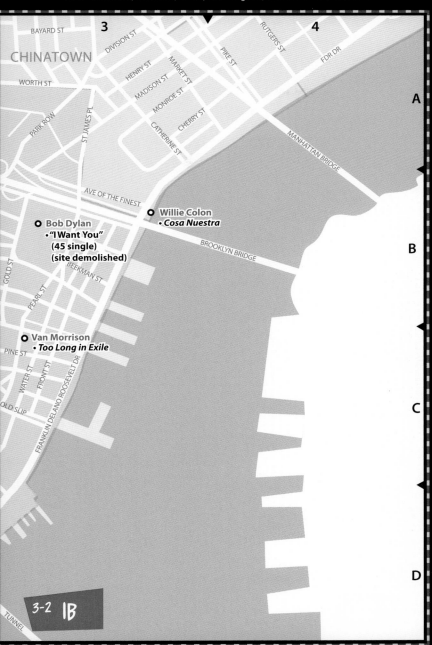

BAYARD ST

3

DIVISION ST

RUTGERS ST

4

PIKE ST

FDR DR

CHINATOWN

HENRY ST

MARKET ST

MADISON ST

WORTH ST

MONROE ST

CHERRY ST

PARK ROW

ST JAMES PL

CATHERINE ST

MANHATTAN BRIDGE

A

AVE OF THE FINEST

○ **Willie Colon**
• *Cosa Nuestra*

○ **Bob Dylan**
• "I Want You"
(45 single)
(site demolished)

BROOKLYN BRIDGE

B

GOLD ST

BEEKMAN ST

PEARL ST

○ **Van Morrison**
• *Too Long in Exile*

PINE ST

WATER ST

FRONT ST

FRANKLIN DELANO ROOSEVELT DR

OLD SLIP

C

D

3-2 **1B**

TUNNEL

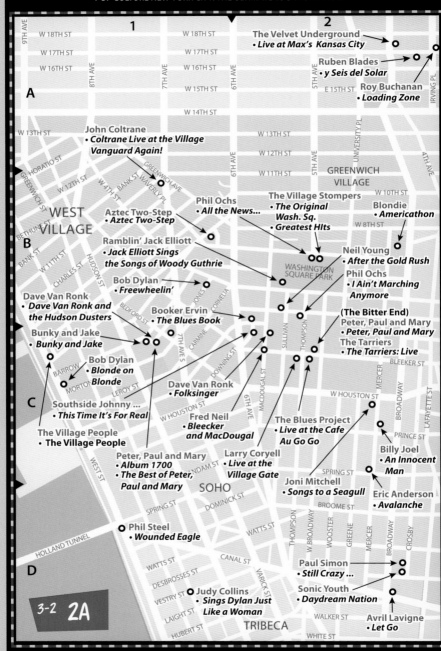

1

2

W 18TH ST

W 17TH ST

W 16TH ST

W 15TH ST

W 14TH ST

9TH AVE

8TH AVE

7TH AVE

6TH AVE

5TH AVE

E 15TH ST

IRVING PL

A

The Velvet Underground
• *Live at Max's Kansas City*

Ruben Blades
• *y Seis del Solar*

Roy Buchanan
• *Loading Zone*

W 13TH ST

HORATIO ST

GREENWICH ST

John Coltrane
• *Coltrane Live at the Village Vanguard Again!*

GREENWICH AVE

BANK ST

WAVERLY PL

W 4TH ST

W 12TH ST

W 13TH ST

W 12TH ST

W 11TH ST

5TH AVE

UNIVERSITY PL

GREENWICH VILLAGE

W 10TH ST

4TH AVE

WEST VILLAGE

Aztec Two-Step
• *Aztec Two-Step*

Phil Ochs
• *All the News...*

The Village Stompers
• *The Original Wash. Sq.*
• *Greatest Hits*

Blondie
• *Americathon*

W 8TH ST

B

BETHUNE ST

BANK ST

W 11TH ST

CHARLES ST

HUDSON ST

Ramblin' Jack Elliott
• *Jack Elliott Sings the Songs of Woody Guthrie*

Bob Dylan
• *Freewheelin'*

JONES ST

CORNELIA

WASHINGTON SQUARE PARK

Neil Young
• *After the Gold Rush*

Phil Ochs
• *I Ain't Marching Anymore*

Dave Van Ronk
• *Dave Van Ronk and the Hudson Dusters*

BEDFORD ST

Booker Ervin
• *The Blues Book*

SULLIVAN

THOMPSON

(The Bitter End)
Peter, Paul and Mary
• *Peter, Paul and Mary*

The Tarriers
• *The Tarriers: Live*

Bunky and Jake
• *Bunky and Jake*

7TH AVE S

CARMINE

DOWNING ST

BLEEKER ST

MERCER

BROADWAY

LAFAYETTE ST

BARROW

MORTON

LEROY ST

Bob Dylan
• *Blonde on Blonde*

Dave Van Ronk
• *Folksinger*

C

Southside Johnny ...
• *This Time It's For Real*

W HOUSTON ST

6TH AVE

MACDOUGAL ST

W HOUSTON ST

PRINCE ST

The Village People
• *The Village People*

WEST ST

Fred Neil
• *Bleecker and MacDougal*

The Blues Project
• *Live at the Cafe Au Go Go*

Billy Joel
• *An Innocent Man*

Peter, Paul and Mary
• *Album 1700*
• *The Best of Peter, Paul and Mary*

Larry Coryell
• *Live at the Village Gate*

Joni Mitchell
• *Songs to a Seagull*

SPRING ST

Eric Anderson
• *Avalanche*

VANDAM ST

SOHO

DOMINICK ST

BROOME ST

THOMPSON

W BROADWAY

WOOSTER

GREENE

MERCER

BROADWAY

CROSBY

SPRING ST

WATTS ST

Phil Steel
• *Wounded Eagle*

HOLLAND TUNNEL

WATTS ST

CANAL ST

VARICK ST

D

DESBROSSES ST

Paul Simon
• *Still Crazy ...*

Sonic Youth
• *Daydream Nation*

3-2 2A

VESTRY ST

LAIGHT ST

HUBERT ST

Judy Collins
• *Sings Dylan Just Like a Woman*

WALKER ST

WHITE ST

TRIBECA

Avril Lavigne
• *Let Go*

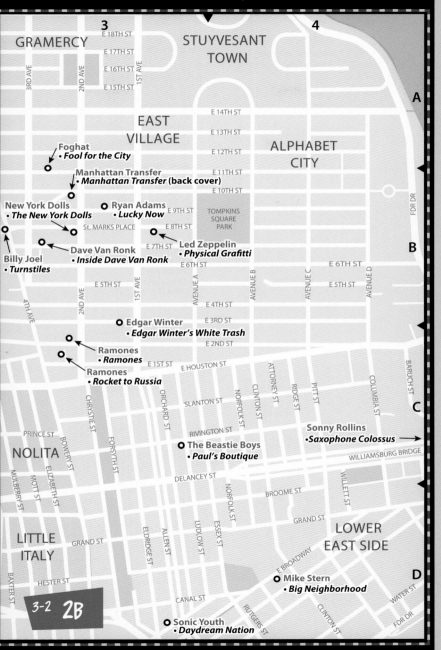

3 E 18TH ST   **4**

GRAMERCY

E 17TH ST

E 16TH ST

E 15TH ST

STUYVESANT
TOWN

3RD AVE

2ND AVE

1ST AVE

A

EAST
VILLAGE

E 14TH ST

E 13TH ST

E 12TH ST

ALPHABET
CITY

Foghat
• **Fool for the City**

Manhattan Transfer
• **Manhattan Transfer (back cover)**

E 11TH ST

E 10TH ST

New York Dolls
• **The New York Dolls**

Ryan Adams
• **Lucky Now**

E 9TH ST

TOMPKINS
SQUARE
PARK

St. MARKS PLACE

E 8TH ST

Dave Van Ronk
• **Inside Dave Van Ronk**

E 7TH ST

Led Zeppelin
• **Physical Grafitti**

B

Billy Joel
• **Turnstiles**

E 6TH ST

E 6TH ST

4TH AVE

2ND AVE

1ST AVE

E 5TH ST

AVENUE A

AVENUE B

AVENUE C

AVENUE D

E 5TH ST

E 4TH ST

Edgar Winter
• **Edgar Winter's White Trash**

E 3RD ST

E 2ND ST

Ramones
• **Ramones**

Ramones
• **Rocket to Russia**

E 1ST ST

E HOUSTON ST

ATTORNEY ST

CLINTON ST

RIDGE ST

PITT ST

COLUMBIA ST

BARUCH ST

C

CHRYSTIE ST

ORCHARD ST

SLANTON ST

NORFOLK ST

PRINCE ST

RIVINGTON ST

Sonny Rollins
•**Saxophone Colossus** →

NOLITA

BOWERY ST

FORSYTH ST

ELIZABETH ST

The Beastie Boys
• **Paul's Boutique**

WILLIAMSBURG BRIDGE

DELANCEY ST

NORFOLK ST

BROOME ST

WILLETT ST

MULBERRY ST

MOTT ST

GRAND ST

LITTLE
ITALY

GRAND ST

ELDRIDGE ST

ALLEN ST

LUDLOW ST

ESSEX ST

BROOME ST

GRAND ST

LOWER
EAST SIDE

BAXTER ST

HESTER ST

E BROADWAY

Mike Stern
• **Big Neighborhood**

WATER ST

D

3-2 **2B**

CANAL ST

RUTGERS ST

CLINTON ST

FDR DR

Sonic Youth
• **Daydream Nation**

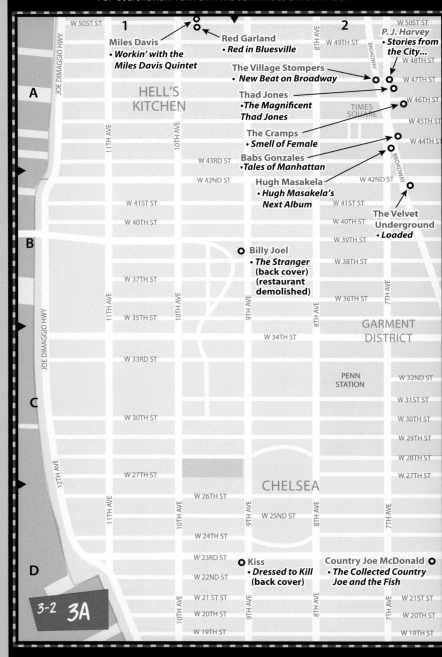

1

Miles Davis
• *Workin' with the Miles Davis Quintet*

Red Garland
• *Red in Bluesville*

The Village Stompers
• *New Beat on Broadway*

Thad Jones
• *The Magnificent Thad Jones*

The Cramps
• *Smell of Female*

Babs Gonzales
• *Tales of Manhattan*

Hugh Masakela
• *Hugh Masakela's Next Album*

Billy Joel
• *The Stranger* (back cover) (restaurant demolished)

Kiss
• *Dressed to Kill* (back cover)

2

P. J. Harvey
• *Stories from the City...*

The Velvet Underground
• *Loaded*

Country Joe McDonald
• *The Collected Country Joe and the Fish*

W 50ST ST
W 49TH ST
W 48TH ST
W 47TH ST
W 46TH ST
W 45TH ST
W 44TH ST
W 43RD ST
W 42ND ST
W 41ST ST
W 40TH ST
W 39TH ST
W 38TH ST
W 37TH ST
W 36TH ST
W 35TH ST
W 34TH ST
W 33RD ST
W 32ND ST
W 31ST ST
W 30TH ST
W 29TH ST
W 28TH ST
W 27TH ST
W 26TH ST
W 25ND ST
W 24TH ST
W 23RD ST
W 22ND ST
W 21 ST ST
W 20TH ST
W 19TH ST

HELL'S KITCHEN

TIMES SQUARE

GARMENT DISTRICT

PENN STATION

CHELSEA

JOE DIMAGGIO HWY
12TH AVE
11TH AVE
10TH AVE
9TH AVE
8TH AVE
7TH AVE
BROADWAY

3-2 3A

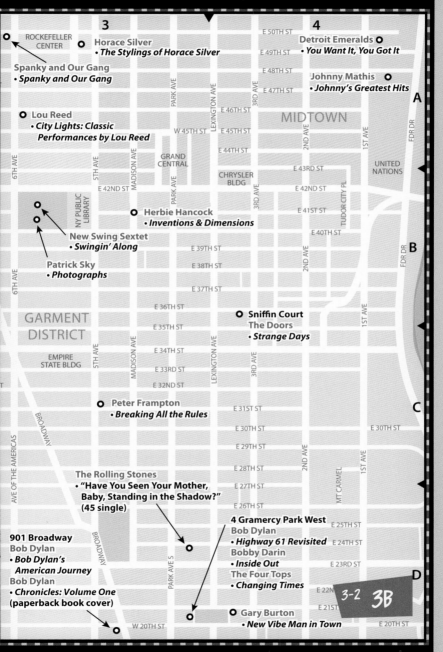

3

ROCKEFELLER CENTER

Horace Silver
• *The Stylings of Horace Silver*

Spanky and Our Gang
• *Spanky and Our Gang*

Lou Reed
• *City Lights: Classic Performances by Lou Reed*

Herbie Hancock
• *Inventions & Dimensions*

New Swing Sextet
• *Swingin' Along*

Patrick Sky
• *Photographs*

6TH AVE

5TH AVE

MADISON AVE

PARK AVE

NY PUBLIC LIBRARY

GRAND CENTRAL

CHRYSLER BLDG

E 42ND ST

GARMENT DISTRICT

EMPIRE STATE BLDG

5TH AVE

MADISON AVE

BROADWAY

AVE OF THE AMERICAS

E 50TH ST
E 49TH ST
E 48TH ST
E 47TH ST
E 46TH ST
W 45TH ST
E 45TH ST
E 44TH ST
E 43RD ST
E 41ST ST
E 40TH ST
E 39TH ST
E 38TH ST
E 37TH ST
E 36TH ST
E 35TH ST
E 34TH ST
E 33RD ST
E 32ND ST
E 31ST ST
E 30TH ST
E 29TH ST
E 28TH ST
E 27TH ST
E 26TH ST
E 25TH ST
E 24TH ST
E 23RD ST
E 22N
E 21ST
E 20TH ST

LEXINGTON AVE

3RD AVE

2ND AVE

1ST AVE

FDR DR

MIDTOWN

UNITED NATIONS

TUDOR CITY PL

FDR DR

4

Detroit Emeralds
• *You Want It, You Got It*

Johnny Mathis
• *Johnny's Greatest Hits*

A

B

Sniffin Court
The Doors
• *Strange Days*

C

Peter Frampton
• *Breaking All the Rules*

The Rolling Stones
• "Have You Seen Your Mother, Baby, Standing in the Shadow?" (45 single)

901 Broadway
Bob Dylan
• *Bob Dylan's American Journey*
Bob Dylan
• *Chronicles: Volume One* (paperback book cover)

4 Gramercy Park West
Bob Dylan
• *Highway 61 Revisited*
Bobby Darin
• *Inside Out*
The Four Tops
• *Changing Times*

MT CARMEL

1ST AVE

2ND AVE

PARK AVE S

BROADWAY

W 20TH ST

Gary Burton
• *New Vibe Man in Town*

D

3-2 **3B**

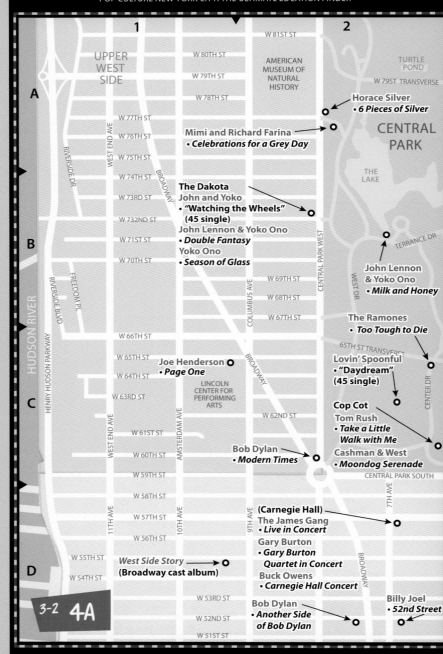

1

2

UPPER
WEST
SIDE

W 81ST ST

W 80TH ST

W 79TH ST

W 78TH ST

AMERICAN
MUSEUM OF
NATURAL
HISTORY

TURTLE
POND

W 79ST TRANSVERSE

A

Horace Silver
• 6 Pieces of Silver

CENTRAL
PARK

W 77TH ST

W 76TH ST

W 75TH ST

W 74TH ST

W 73RD ST

W 732ND ST

W 71ST ST

W 70TH ST

Mimi and Richard Farina
• Celebrations for a Grey Day

THE
LAKE

The Dakota
John and Yoko
• "Watching the Wheels"
(45 single)
John Lennon & Yoko Ono
• Double Fantasy
Yoko Ono
• Season of Glass

B

TERRANCE DR

John Lennon
& Yoko Ono
• Milk and Honey

W 69TH ST

W 68TH ST

W 67TH ST

The Ramones
• Too Tough to Die

W 66TH ST

W 65TH ST

W 64TH ST

W 63RD ST

Joe Henderson
• Page One

LINCOLN
CENTER FOR
PERFORMING
ARTS

65TH ST TRANSVERSE

Lovin' Spoonful
• "Daydream"
(45 single)

W 62ND ST

C

Cop Cot

Tom Rush
• Take a Little
Walk with Me

W 61ST ST

W 60TH ST

W 59TH ST

Bob Dylan
• Modern Times

Cashman & West
• Moondog Serenade

CENTRAL PARK SOUTH

W 58TH ST

W 57TH ST

W 56TH ST

(Carnegie Hall)
The James Gang
• Live in Concert

W 55TH ST

W 54TH ST

West Side Story
(Broadway cast album)

Gary Burton
• Gary Burton
Quartet in Concert
Buck Owens
• Carnegie Hall Concert

D

3-2 **4A**

W 53RD ST

W 52ND ST

W 51ST ST

Bob Dylan
• Another Side
of Bob Dylan

Billy Joel
• 52nd Street

RIVERSIDE DR

WEST END AVE

BROADWAY

CENTRAL PARK WEST

COLUMBUS AVE

WEST DR

CENTER DR

HUDSON RIVER

RIVERSIDE BLVD

FREEDOM PL

HENRY HUDSON PARKWAY

WEST END AVE

AMSTERDAM AVE

BROADWAY

11TH AVE

10TH AVE

9TH AVE

7TH AVE

BROADWAY

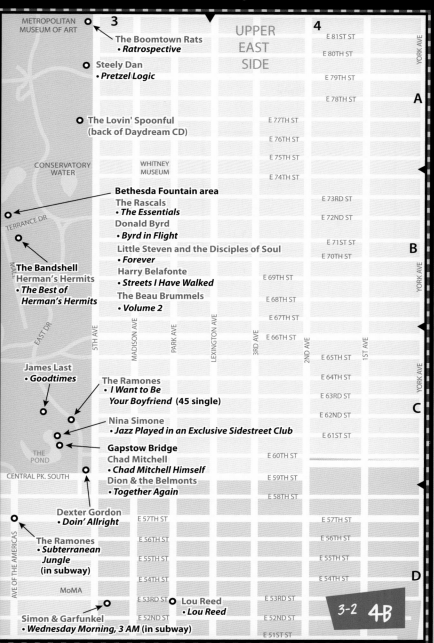

METROPOLITAN
MUSEUM OF ART

3

UPPER
EAST
SIDE

4

E 81ST ST
E 80TH ST

YORK AVE

The Boomtown Rats
• *Ratrospective*

E 79TH ST

E 78TH ST

A

Steely Dan
• *Pretzel Logic*

E 77TH ST

The Lovin' Spoonful
(back of Daydream CD)

E 76TH ST

E 75TH ST

CONSERVATORY
WATER

WHITNEY
MUSEUM

E 74TH ST

Bethesda Fountain area

E 73RD ST

The Rascals
• *The Essentials*

E 72ND ST

TERRANCE DR

Donald Byrd
• *Byrd in Flight*

E 71ST ST

Little Steven and the Disciples of Soul
• *Forever*

E 70TH ST

B

The Bandshell
Herman's Hermits
• *The Best of Herman's Hermits*

Harry Belafonte
• *Streets I Have Walked*

E 69TH ST

The Beau Brummels
• *Volume 2*

E 68TH ST

E 67TH ST

EAST DR

5TH AVE

MADISON AVE

PARK AVE

LEXINGTON AVE

3RD AVE

E 66TH ST

2ND AVE

1ST AVE

YORK AVE

E 65TH ST

James Last
• *Goodtimes*

E 64TH ST

The Ramones
• *I Want to Be Your Boyfriend* (45 single)

E 63RD ST

E 62ND ST

C

Nina Simone
• *Jazz Played in an Exclusive Sidestreet Club*

E 61ST ST

THE
POND

Gapstow Bridge
Chad Mitchell
• *Chad Mitchell Himself*

E 60TH ST

CENTRAL PK. SOUTH

Dion & the Belmonts
• *Together Again*

E 59TH ST

E 58TH ST

Dexter Gordon
• *Doin' Allright*

E 57TH ST

E 57TH ST

AVE OF THE AMERICAS

The Ramones
• *Subterranean Jungle*
(in subway)

E 56TH ST

E 56TH ST

E 55TH ST

E 55TH ST

D

E 54TH ST

E 54TH ST

MoMA

E 53RD ST

Lou Reed
• *Lou Reed*

E 53RD ST

Simon & Garfunkel
• *Wednesday Morning, 3 AM* (in subway)

E 52ND ST

E 52ND ST

E 51ST ST

3-2 **4B**

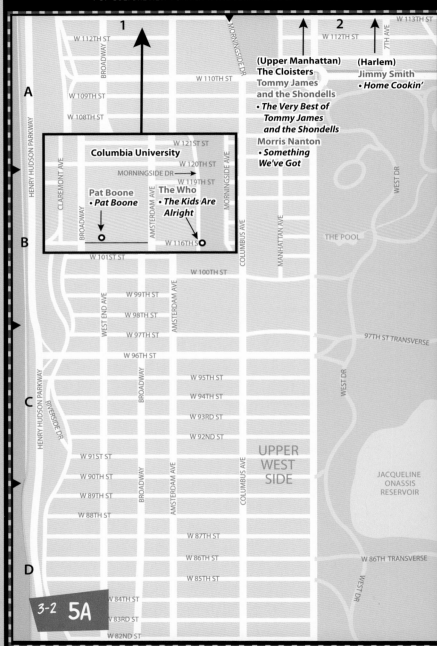

1

W 113TH ST
2
W 112TH ST
W 112TH ST
7TH AVE
W 110TH ST
MORNINGSIDE DR

A
W 109TH ST
W 108TH ST

(Upper Manhattan)
The Cloisters
Tommy James
and the Shondells
• *The Very Best of
Tommy James
and the Shondells*
Morris Nanton
• *Something
We've Got*

(Harlem)
Jimmy Smith
• *Home Cookin'*

HENRY HUDSON PARKWAY
CLAREMONT AVE
BROADWAY

W 121ST ST
Columbia University
W 120TH ST
MORNINGSIDE DR →
W 119TH ST
AMSTERDAM AVE
MORNINGSIDE AVE
COLUMBUS AVE
MANHATTAN AVE
WEST DR
THE POOL

Pat Boone
• *Pat Boone*

The Who
• *The Kids Are
Alright*

B
W 116TH ST
W 101ST ST
W 100TH ST

W 99TH ST
WEST END AVE
W 98TH ST
AMSTERDAM AVE
W 97TH ST
W 96TH ST

97TH ST TRANSVERSE

BROADWAY
W 95TH ST
W 94TH ST
W 93RD ST
W 92ND ST

WEST DR

C
HENRY HUDSON PARKWAY
RIVERSIDE DR
W 91ST ST
W 90TH ST
BROADWAY
AMSTERDAM AVE
W 89TH ST
W 88TH ST
COLUMBUS AVE

UPPER
WEST
SIDE

JACQUELINE
ONASSIS
RESERVOIR

W 87TH ST
W 86TH ST
W 86TH TRANSVERSE
WEST DR

D
W 85TH ST

3-2 **5A**
W 84TH ST
W 83RD ST
W 82ND ST

W 112TH ST

5TH AVE

E 112TH ST

E 111TH ST

2ND AVE

CATHEDRAL PARKWAY

E 110TH ST

HARLEM MEER

E 109TH ST

A

E 108TH ST

O The Impressions
• *The Young Mods' Forgotten Story*

5TH AVE

E 107TH ST

E 106TH ST

E 105TH ST

EAST DR

E 104TH ST

MADISON AVE

PARK AVE

LEXINGTON AVE

E 104TH ST

1ST AVE

E 103RD ST

E 102ND ST

B

E 101ST ST

MT
SINAI
HOSPITAL

E 100TH ST

E 99TH ST

E 99TH ST
METROPOLITAN
HOSPITAL
CENTER

E 98TH ST

97TH ST TRANSVERSE

E 97TH ST

E 97TH ST

E 96TH ST

E 95TH ST

FDR DR

O Simon and Garfunkel
• Greatest Hits (1972)
(front cover)

E 94TH ST

E 93RD ST

E 93RD ST

C

E 92ND ST

EAST DR

O Simon and Garfunkel
• *Greatest Hits (1972)*
(back cover)

E 91ST ST

2ND AVE

E 91ST ST

E 90TH ST

JACQUELINE
ONASSIS
RESERVOIR

E 89TH ST

E 89TH ST

YORKVILLE

GUGGENHEIM

E 88TH ST

LEXINGTON AVE

3RD AVE

E 87TH ST

1ST AVE

E 87TH ST

E 86TH ST

5TH AVE

MADISON AVE

E 85TH ST

D

E 84TH ST

3-2 **5B**

E 83RD ST

YORK AVE

E 82ND ST

Manhattan

Staten Island

3-2 6A

The Bronx

○ **Dion & the Belmonts**
• *Cigars, Acapella, Candy*

○ **Stray Cats**
• *Gonna Ball*

Queens

○ **Cyndi Lauper**
• *A Night to Remember*

○ **The BT Express**
• *Do It 'Til You're Satisfied*

○ **LL Cool J**
• *BAD (Bigger and Deffer)*

○ **Cyndi Lauper**
• *She's So Unusual*

○ **Bo Diddley**
• *Have Guitar, Will Travel*

Brooklyn

3-2 **6B**

Ramones, *Ramones* (1976): Albert's Garden, 16 East 2nd Street between Bowery and 2nd Avenues (Map 2B/Grid 3C)

Ramones, *Rocket to Russia* (1977): Extra Place at 1st Street (Map 2B/Grid 3C)

Ramones, *Subterranean Jungle* (1983): Sixth Avenue subway platform at 6th Avenue and 57th Street (Map 4A/Grid 2D)

Ramones, *Too Tough to Die* (1984): Playmate's Arch, Central Park, 64th Street (Map 4A/Grid 2C)

The Rascals, *The Essentials* (2002): Bethesda Fountain, Central Park, 72nd Street (Map 4B/Grid 3B)

Lou Reed, *City Lights: Classic Performances by Lou Reed* (1985): 45th Street and 6th Avenue (Map 3B/Grid 3A)

Lou Reed, *Lou Reed* (1972): 390 Park Avenue between East 53rd and 54th Streets (Map 4B/Grid 3D)

The Righteous Brothers, *Go Ahead and Cry* (1966): Battery Park Promenade (Map 1A/Grid 2C)

Rolling Stones, "Have You Seen Your Mother, Baby, Standing in the Shadow" (45 single, 1966): 124 East 24th Street between Park Avenue South and Lexington Avenue. Photo by Jerry Schatzberg. (Map 3B/Grid 3D)

Sonny Rollins, *Saxophone Colossus* (1956): The highest point of the Williamsburg Bridge (Map 2B/Grid 4C)

Tom Rush, *Take a Little Walk with Me* (1966): Cop Cot, Central Park, 60th Street (Map 4A/Grid 2C)

Horace Silver, *6 Pieces of Silver* (1957): 77th Street and Central Park West (Map 4A/Grid 2A)

Horace Silver, *The Stylings of Horace Silver* (1957): Rockefeller Center Skating Rink, West 50th Street between 5th and 6th Avenues (Map 3B/Grid 3A)

Paul Simon, *Still Crazy After All These Years* (1975): 10–12 Crosby Street at Howard Street (Map 2A/Grid 2D)

Simon and Garfunkel, *Greatest Hits* (1972): 7 East 94th Street near Fifth Avenue. Front cover. (Map 5B/Grid 3C)

Simon and Garfunkel, *Greatest Hits* (1972): Central Park Reservoir, East 91st Street near Fifth Avenue. Back cover. (Map 5B/Grid 3C)

Simon & Garfunkel, *Wednesday Morning, 3 AM* (1964): Fifth Avenue and 53rd Street (Map 4B/Grid 3D)

Nina Simone, *Jazz Played in an Exclusive Side Street Club* (1958): Gapstow Bridge, Central Park, 62nd Street (Map 4B/Grid3C)

Patrick Sky, *Photographs* (1969): Bryant Park, 6th Avenue and 40th Street (Map 3B/Grid 3B)

Jimmy Smith, *Home Cookin'* (1965): 271 West 126th Street at Frederick Douglass Boulevard (Map 5A/Grid 2A)

Sonic Youth, *Daydream Nation* (1988): Crosby Street at Howard Street. CD insert. (Map 2A/Grid 2D)

Sonic Youth, *Daydream Nation* (1988): Behind 100 Division Street, Chinatown. Album inner gatefold. (Map 2B/Grid 3D)

Southside Johnny and the Asbury Jukes, *This Time It's For Real* **(1977):** Minetta Street, between Minetta Lane and Bleecker Street (Map 2A/Grid 2C)

Spanky and Our Gang, *Spanky and Our Gang* **(1967):** 50th Street and 6th Avenue. Back cover. (Map 3B/Grid 3A)

Phil Steel, *Wounded Eagle* **(1980):** West Side Highway at Canal Street (Map 2A/Grid 1D)

Steely Dan, *Pretzel Logic* **(1974):** Fifth Avenue and 79th Street. Photo by Raeanne Rubinstein. (Map 4B/Grid 3A)

Mike Stern, *Big Neighborhood* **(2009):** 205 East Broadway between Jefferson and Clinton Streets (Map 2B/Grid 4D)

Stray Cats *Gonna Ball* **(1981):** 69–35 Astoria Boulevard, East Elmhurst, New York (Map 6B/Queens)

The Tarriers, *The Tarriers: A Live Performance Recorded at "The Bitter End"* **(1962):** The Bitter End, 147 Bleecker Street near LaGuardia Place (Map 2A/Grid 2C)

Dave Van Ronk, *Dave Van Ronk and the Hudson Dusters* **(1968):** 38 Commerce Street between Bedford and Barrow Streets (Map 2A/Grid 1C)

Dave Van Ronk, *Folksinger* **(1963):** Folklore Center, 110 MacDougal Street between Minetta Lane and Bleecker Street (Map 2A/Grid 2C)

Dave Van Ronk, *Inside Dave Van Ronk* **(1964):** McSorley's Old Ale House, 15 East 7th Street between 2nd and 3rd Avenues (Map 2B/Grid 3B)

Steve Van Zandt/Little Steven and the Disciples of Soul, *Forever* **(1982):** Central Park's Bethesda Steps at 72nd Street (Map 4B/Grid 3B)

The Velvet Underground, *Live at Max's Kansas City* **(1972):** 213 Park Avenue between East 17th and East 18th Streets (Map 2A/Grid 2A)

The Velvet Underground, *Loaded* **(1970):** Times Square, 42nd and Broadway (Map 3A/Grid 2B)

The Village People, *The Village People* **(1977):** 388 West Street at Morton Street (Map 2A/Grid 1C)

The Village Stompers, *Greatest Hits* **(1967):** The arch at Washington Square Park, Greenwich Village (Map 2A/Grid 2B)

The Village Stompers, *New Beat on Broadway* **(1964):** Broadway and West 47th Street (Map 3A/Grid 2A)

The Village Stompers, *The Original Washington Square* **(1963):** Washington Square Park Arch (Map 2A/Grid 2B)

West Side Story Soundtrack (1957): 418 West 56th between 9th and 10th Avenues. The Broadway musical. (Map 4A/Grid 1D)

The Who, *The Kids Are Alright* **(1978):** 116th Street and Morningside Drive. Movie soundtrack. (Map 5A/Grid 1B)

Edgar Winter, *Edgar Winter's White Trash* **(1971):** 88 East 3rd Street between 1st and 2nd Avenues. Photo by Alen MacWeeney. (Map 2B/Grid 3B)

Neil Young, *After the Gold Rush* **(1970):** Sullivan Street at the corner of West 3rd Street. Photo by Joel Bernstein. (Map 2A/Grid 2B)

WHERE THE CELEBRITIES LIVE: PAST OR PRESENT RESIDENCES OF ROCK STARS, MOVIE STARS, AND TV STARS

Christina Aguilera: Born in Staten Island (Map 6 West/Staten Island)
Alan Alda: 101 West 67th Street between Broadway and Columbus Avenue (Map 4 West/2B)
Woody Allen: Born in the Bronx (Map 6 East/Bronx)
Paul Anka: 721 Fifth Avenue between 56th and 57th Streets (Map 4 East/4B)
The Ansonia: 2109 Broadway at 73rd Street (Map 4 West/1B)
Judd Apatow: Born in Flushing, Queens (Map 6 East/Queens)
The Ardsley: 320 Central Park West between 91st and 92nd Streets (Map 5 West/2C)
Louis Armstrong: 34–56 107th Street between 37th and 34th Avenue, Corona, Queens. The house is now a museum (Map 6 East/Queens)
Fred Astaire: 115 Central Park West between 71st and 72nd Streets (Map 4 West/2B)
Steve Augeri: Born in Staten Island (Map 6 West/Staten Island)
Hank Azaria: 75 Central Park West at 67th Street (Map 4 West/2B)

Lauren Bacall: 1 West 72nd Street at Central Park West (Map 4 West/2B)
Kevin Bacon: 285 Central Park West at 89th Street (Map 5 West/1B)
Joan Baez: Born in Staten Island (Map 6 West/Staten Island)
Alec Baldwin: 300 Central Park West between 90th and 91st Streets (Map 5 West/2C)
Anne Bancroft: Born in the Bronx (Map 6 East/Bronx)
Antonio Banderas: 50 Central Park West at 65th Street (Map 4 West/2C)
Count Basie: 555 Edgecombe Avenue at 160th Street (Map 6 East/Upper Manhattan)
Lance Bass: 252 Seventh Avenue between 24th and 25th Streets (Map 3West/2D)
Harry Belafonte: 300 West End Avenue at 74th Street (Map 4 West/1A)
Tony Bennett: Born in Astoria, Queens (Map 6 East/Queens)
The Beresford: 211 Central Park West between 81st and 82nd Streets (Map 4 West/2A)

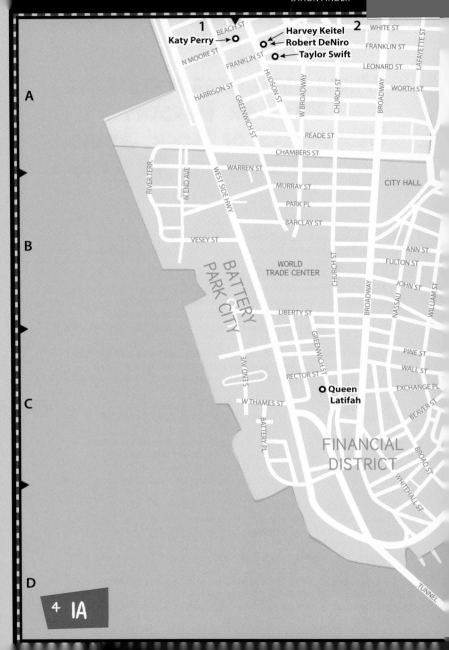

1 BEACH ST **2** WHITE ST

Katy Perry → ○

Harvey Keitel ← ○
Robert DeNiro ← ○
Taylor Swift ← ○

N MOORE ST

FRANKLIN ST

FRANKLIN ST

LEONARD ST

LAFAYETTE ST

HUDSON ST

W BROADWAY

CHURCH ST

BROADWAY

WORTH ST

A

HARRISON ST

GREENWICH ST

READE ST

CHAMBERS ST

WARREN ST

CITY HALL

RIVER TERR.

N END AVE

WEST SIDE HWY

MURRAY ST

PARK PL

BARCLAY ST

VESEY ST

B

BATTERY PARK CITY

WORLD TRADE CENTER

CHURCH ST

ANN ST

FULTON ST

JOHN ST

WILLIAM ST

NASSAU

BROADWAY

LIBERTY ST

GREENWICH ST

PINE ST

WALL ST

EXCHANGE PL

C

S END AVE

RECTOR ST

W THAMES ST

○ Queen Latifah

BEAVER ST

BROAD ST

BATTERY PL

FINANCIAL DISTRICT

WHITEHALL ST

D

⁴ IA

TUNNEL

BAYARD ST

3

CHINATOWN

DIVISION ST

4

CHERRY ST

PARK ROW

HENRY ST

CATHERINE ST

PIKE ST

H ST

MARKET ST

MADISON ST

MANHATTAN BRIDGE

A

ST JAMES PL

MONROE ST

AVE OF THE FINEST

BROOKLYN BRIDGE

B

BEEKMAN ST

PEARL ST

ST

FRANKLIN DELANO ROOSEVELT DR

WATER ST

FRONT ST

C

BROOKLYN

LD SLIP

D

4 1B

OOKLYN BATT

Milton Berle: 115 Central Park West between 71st and 72nd Streets (Map 4 West/2B)

Irving Berlin: 17 Beekman Place, east of 1st Avenue and 50th Street (Map 3 East/4A)

Leonard Bernstein: 205 West 57th Street at 7th Avenue (Map 4 West/2D), 1 West 72nd Street at Central Park West (Map 4 West/2B)

Jeff Bezos: 25 Central Park West between 62nd and 63rd Streets (Map 4A/2C)

Jessica Biel: 311 West Broadway between Canal and Grand Streets (Map 2 West/2D)

Jessica Biel: 443 Greenwich Street at Vestry Street (Map 2 West/2D)

Big Pun: Born in the Bronx (Map 6 East/Bronx)

Mary J. Blige: Born in the Bronx (Map 6 East/Bronx)

Emily Blunt: Park Slope, Brooklyn (Map 6 East/Bronx)

Humphrey Bogart: 245 West 103rd Street between Broadway and West End Avenue (Map 5 West/1B)

Jon Bon Jovi: 583 Broadway between Prince and West Houston Street (Map 2 West/2C)

Bono: 145–146 Central Park West between 74th and 75th Streets (Map 4 West/2A), 300 Central Park West between 90th and 91st Streets (Map 5 West/2C)

David Bowie: 285 Lafayette Street between Prince and West Houston Streets (Map 2 West/2C)

Ed Bradley: 285 Central Park West at 89th Street (Map 5 West/1B)

"Carrie Bradshaw": 64 Perry Street between Bleecker and West 4th Streets (Map 2 West/2A)

Tom Brady: 10 Columbus Circle at 59th and Broadway (Map 4 West/2C)

The Brentmore: 88 Central Park West between 68 and 69th Streets (Map 4 West/2B)

Adrien Brody: Born in Woodside, Queens (Map 6 East/Queens)

Jimmy Buffet: 10 Columbus Circle at 59th and Broadway (Map 4 West/2C)

Steve Buscemi: 450 5th Street, Park Slope, Brooklyn (Map 6 East/Brooklyn)

Rose Byrne: Boerum Hill, Brooklyn (Map 6 East/Brooklyn)

John Cage: 105 Bank Street between Greenwich and Washington Streets (Map 2 West/2A)

John Cale: 56 Ludlow Street between Grand and Hester Streets (Map 2 East/4D)

Bobby Cannavale: Boerum Hill, Brooklyn (Map 6 East/Brooklyn)

The Century: 25 Central Park West between 62nd and 63rd Streets (Map 4 West/2C)

David Chase: London Terrace. Between 9th and 10 Avenues and 23rd and 24th Streets (Map 3 West/1D)

Jessica Chastain: 311 West Broadway between Canal and Grand Streets (Map 2 West/2D)

The Chelsea Hotel: 222 West 23rd Street between 7th and 8th Avenues (Map 3 West/2D)

Cher: 14 East 4th Street at Broadway (Map 2 West/2C)

Dick Clark: 60 Sutton Place South between 53rd and 54th Streets (Map 4 East/4D)

Connie Chung: 1 West 72nd Street at Central Park West (Map 4 West/2B)

Adam Clayton: 300 Central Park West between 90th and 91st Streets (Map 5 West/2C)

Glenn Close: 145–146 Central Park West between 74th and 75th Streets (Map 4 West/2A), 211 Central Park West between 81st and 82nd Streets (Map 4 West/2A)

Leonard Cohen: The Chelsea Hotel, 222 West 23rd Street between 7th and 8th Avenues (Map 3 West/2D)

John Coltrane: 203 West 103rd Street at Amsterdam Avenue (Map 5 West/1B)

Judy Collins: 845 West End Avenue at 101st Street (Map 5 West/1B)

Phil Collins: 455 Central Park West between 105th and 106th Streets (Map 5 West/2A)

Sean "P. Diddy" Combs: 230 West 56th Street at Broadway (Map 4 West/2D)

Bob Costas: 15 Central Park West between 61st and 62nd Streets (Map 4 West/2C)

The Oliver Cromwell: 12 West 72nd Street between Columbus and Central Park West (Map 4 West/2B)

The Dakota: 1 West 72nd Street at Central Park West

Salvador Dali: St. Regis Hotel, 2 East 55th Street at Fifth Avenue (Map 4 East/3D)

Bobby Darin: Born in the Bronx (Map 6 East/Bronx)

Brad Davis: 61 Jane Street at Hudson Street (Map 2 West/2B)

Miles Davis: 312 West 77th Street between West End Avenue and Riverside Drive (Map 4 West/1A)

James Dean: 19 West 68th Street between Central Park West and Columbus Avenue (Map 4 West/2B)

Robert DeNiro: 15 Central Park West between 61st and 62nd Streets (Map 4 West/2C)

Robert DeNiro: 106 Hudson Street at Franklin Street (Map 1 West/2A)

Cameron Diaz: 204 West 18th Street at 7th Avenue (Map 2 West/1A)

Michael Douglas: 151 Central Park West at 75th Street (Map 4 West/2A)

Richard Dreyfuss: 241 Central Park West at 84th Street (Map 5 West/2D), 300 Central Park West between 90th and 91st Streets (Map 5 West/2C)

Faye Dunaway: 300 Central Park West between 90th and 91st Streets (Map 5 West/2C)

Lena Dunham: 145 Hicks Street, Brooklyn Heights, Brooklyn (Map 6 East/Brooklyn)

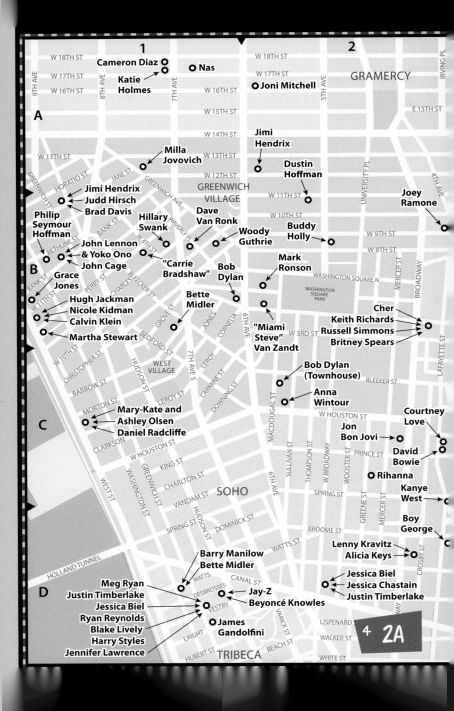

3

4

E 18TH ST

○ **Stevie Wonder**

○ **David Lee Roth**
E 17TH ST

STUYVESANT TOWN

E 16TH ST

GRAMERCY

E 15TH ST

1ST AVE

E 14TH ST

ALPHABET CITY

E 13TH ST

A

E 12TH ST

EAST VILLAGE

E 11TH ST

Charlie Parker

E 10TH ST

TOMPKINS SQ PARK

AVENUE C

E 9TH ST

○ ○ **Leadbelly**

E 8TH ST

Iggy Pop

St. MARKS PLACE

E 7TH ST

B

○ **Nora Jones**

E 6TH ST

○ **Nico**

E 6TH ST

FDR DR

4TH AVE

E 5TH ST

AVENUE A

AVENUE B

E 5TH ST

AVENUE D

○ **John Legend**

E 4TH ST

○ **Madonna**

Moby

E 3RD ST

2ND AVE

E 2ND ST

E 1ST ST

E HOUSTON ST

ATTORNEY ST

RIDGE ST

PITT ST

BARUCH ST

C

Lady Gaga ○

ORCHARD ST

SLANTON ST

NORFOLK ST

CLINTON ST

COLUMBIA ST

RIVINGTON ST

PRINCE ST

NOLITA

BOWERY ST

CHRYSTIE ST

FORSYTH ST

WILLIAMSBURG BRIDGE

ELIZABETH ST

DELANCEY ST

NORFOLK ST

BROOME ST

WILLETT ST

MOTT ST

MULBERRY ST

ELDRIDGE ST

ALLEN ST

LUDLOW ST

GRAND ST

LOWER EAST SIDE

LITTLE ITALY

GRAND ST

○ **John Cale**

Lou Reed

D

BAXTER ST

HESTER ST

ESSEX ST

E BROADWAY

MONTGOMERY ST

WATER ST

CANAL ST

CLINTON ST

RUTGERS ST

FDR DR

4 2B

Fran Drescher: Born in Kew Gardens Hills, Queens (Map 6 East/Queens)

Bob Dylan: 94 MacDougal Street between Bleecker and West Houston Streets (townhouse) (Map 2 West/2B); The Chelsea Hotel, 222 West 23rd Street between 7th and 8th Avenues (Map 3 West/2D); 161 West 4th Street (3rd floor, back) between 6th Avenue and Barrow Street. First NYC apartment. (Map 2 West/2B)

The Eldorado: 300 Central Park West between 90th and 91st Streets (Map 5 West/2C)

Duke Ellington: 935 St. Nicholas Avenue at 157th Street, Apartment 4A (Map 6 East/Harlem); 400 Central Park West between 100th and 101st Streets (Map 5 West/2B)

Mia Farrow: 135 Central Park West between 73rd and 74th Streets (Map 4 West/2B)

Jon Favreau: Born in Flushing, Queens (Map 6 East/Queens)

Tina Fey: 300 West End Avenue at 74th Street (Map 4 West/1A)

50 Cent: Born in Jamaica, Queens (Map 6 East/Queens)

Carrie Fisher: 300 Central Park West between 90th and 91st Streets (Map 5 West/2C)

Roberta Flack: 1 West 72nd Street at Central Park West (Map 4 West/2B)

Harrison Ford: 101 Central Park West between 70th and 71st Streets (Map 4 West/2B)

Michael J. Fox: 300 Central Park West between 90th and 91st Streets (Map 5 West/2C)

Lady Gaga: 176 Stanton Street between Clinton and Attorney Streets (Map 2 East/4C)

James Gandolfini: 429 Greenwich Street between Laight and Vestry Streets (Map 2 West/2D)

Greta Garbo: 450 East 52nd Street at 1st Avenue (Map 4 East/4B)

Art Garfunkel: 136–58 72nd Avenue, Kew Gardens Hills, Queens (Map 6 East/Queens)

Judy Garland: 1 West 72nd Street at Central Park West (Map 4 West/2B)

Boy George: 255 Centre Street at Broome Street (Map 2 West/2D)

George Gershwin: 316 West 103rd Street between Riverside and West End Avenue (Map 5 West/1B), 132 East 72nd Street between Park and Lexington Avenues (Map 4 East/3B)

Ira Gershwin: 125 East 72nd between Park and Lexington Avenues (Map 4 East/3B)

Paul Giamatti: 187 Hicks Street, Brooklyn Heights, Brooklyn (Map 6 East/Brooklyn)

Lilian Gish: 1 West 72nd Street at Central Park West (Map 4 West/2B)

Jeff Gordon: 15 Central Park West between 61st and 62nd Streets (Map 4 West/2C)

Elliott Gould: 320 Central Park West between 91st and 92nd Streets (Map 5 West/2C)

Grandmaster Flash: Born in the Bronx (Map 6 East/Bronx)

Cary Grant: Warwick Hotel, 65 West 54th Street at Sixth Avenue (Map 4 East/3D)

Merv Griffin: 135 Central Park West between 73rd and 74th Streets (Map 4 West/2B)

Melanie Griffith: 50 Central Park West at 65th Street (Map 4 West/2C)

Tim Gunn: London Terrace, between 9th and 10 Avenues and 23rd and 24th Streets (Map 3 West/1D)

Woody Guthrie: Almanac House, 130 West 10th Street near Greenwich Avenue (Map 2 West/2A)

Maggie Gyllenhaal: Sterling Place, Park Slope, Brooklyn (Map 6 East/Brooklyn)

Bill Hader: London Terrace, between 9th and 10 Avenues and 23rd and 24th Streets (Map 3 West/1D)

Mark Hamill: 271 Central Park West at 87th Street (Map 5 West/1B)

Jon Hamm: 40 West 67th Street between Columbus and Central Park West (Map 4 West/2C)

Harperly Hall: 41 Central Park West at 64th Street (Map 4 West/2C)

Mariska Hargitay: 45 West 84th Street between Central Park West and Columbus Avenue (Map 5 West/2D)

Debbie Harry: London Terrace, between 9th and 10 Avenues and 23rd and 24th Streets (Map 3 West/1D)

Anne Hathaway: 1 Main Street, Dumbo, Brooklyn (Map 6 East/Brooklyn)

Ethan Hawke: 247 Dean St, Boerum Hill, Brooklyn (Map 6 East/Brooklyn)

Coleman Hawkins: 555 Edgecombe Avenue at 160th Street (Map 6 East/Upper Manhattan)

Rita Hayworth: 145–146 Central Park West between 74th and 75th Streets (Map 4 West/2A)

Jimi Hendrix: 61 Jane Street at Hudson Street (Map 2 West/2B), 59 West 12th Street between 5th and 6th Avenues (Map 2 West/2A)

Katherine Hepburn: 244 East 49th between 2nd and 3rd Avenues (Map 3 East/4A)

Judd Hirsch: 61 Jane Street at Hudson Street (Map 2 West/2B)

Dustin Hoffman: 16 West 11th Street, 2nd floor (1970) (Map 2 West/2B); 145–146 Central Park West between 74th and 75th Streets (Map 4 West/2A)

Philip Seymour Hoffman: 35 Bethune between Washington and Greenwich Streets (Map 2 West/2A)

Billie Holiday: 108 West 139th Street between Malcom X Boulevard and A. C. Powell Boulevard (Map 6 East/Harlem)

Buddy Holly: 11 Fifth Avenue between 9th and 10th Streets (Map 2 West/2B)

Katie Holmes: 201 West 17th Street at 7th Avenue (Map 2 West/1A)

Lena Horne: 555 Edgecombe Avenue at 160th Street (Map 6 East/Upper Manhattan)

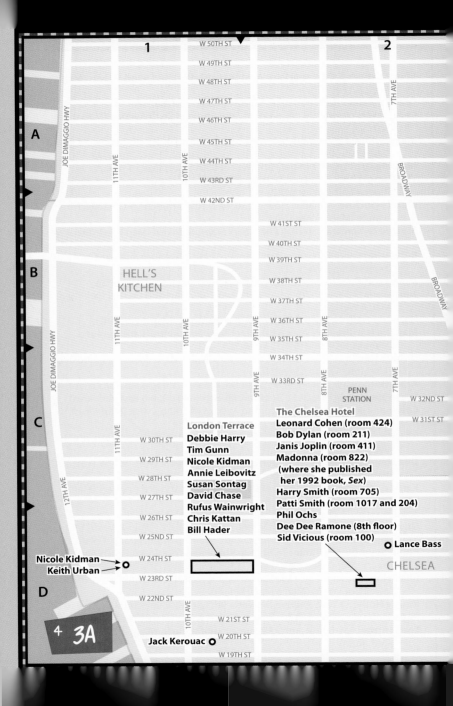

W 50TH ST
W 49TH ST
W 48TH ST
W 47TH ST
W 46TH ST
W 45TH ST
W 44TH ST
W 43RD ST
W 42ND ST

7TH AVE
BROADWAY

1 **2**

A

JOE DIMAGGIO HWY
11TH AVE
10TH AVE

W 41ST ST
W 40TH ST
W 39TH ST
W 38TH ST
W 37TH ST
W 36TH ST
W 35TH ST
W 34TH ST
W 33RD ST

BROADWAY

B

HELL'S
KITCHEN

11TH AVE
10TH AVE
9TH AVE
9TH AVE
8TH AVE

JOE DIMAGGIO HWY

PENN
STATION

7TH AVE

W 32ND ST
W 31ST ST

C

11TH AVE
12TH AVE

W 30TH ST
W 29TH ST
W 28TH ST
W 27TH ST
W 26TH ST
W 25ND ST
W 24TH ST
W 23RD ST
W 22ND ST
W 21ST ST
W 20TH ST
W 19TH ST

London Terrace
Debbie Harry
Tim Gunn
Nicole Kidman
Annie Leibovitz
Susan Sontag
David Chase
Rufus Wainwright
Chris Kattan
Bill Hader

The Chelsea Hotel
Leonard Cohen (room 424)
Bob Dylan (room 211)
Janis Joplin (room 411)
Madonna (room 822)
 (where she published
 her 1992 book, *Sex*)
Harry Smith (room 705)
Patti Smith (room 1017 and 204)
Phil Ochs
Dee Dee Ramone (8th floor)
Sid Vicious (room 100)

O Lance Bass

CHELSEA

Nicole Kidman ➔ O
Keith Urban ➔ O

D

4 **3A**

Jack Kerouac O

10TH AVE

3

ROCKEFELLER
CENTER

○ **Cole Porter**

E 50TH ST

E 49TH ST

4

Irving Berlin ○

E 48TH ST

○ ○

E 47TH ST

**Stephen
Sondheim**

**Katherine
Hepburn**

E 46TH ST

6TH AVE

5TH AVE

MADISON AVE

PARK AVE

3RD AVE

2ND AVE

1ST AVE

FDR DR

A

MIDTOWN

E 45TH ST

E 44TH ST

E 43RD ST

E 42ND ST

BRYANT
PARK

5TH AVE

PARK AVE

2ND AVE

E 40TH ST

6TH AVE

3RD AVE

B

FDR DR

E 37TH ST

E 36TH ST

E 35TH ST

E 34TH ST

E 33RD ST

E 32ND ST

BROADWAY

E 31ST ST

MADISON AVE

E 30TH ST

LEXINGTON AVE

E 29TH ST

3RD AVE

1ST AVE

C

E 30TH ST

E 28TH ST

E 27TH ST

AVE OF THE AMERICAS

W 26TH ST

○ **Jennifer Lopez**

E 26TH ST

MADISON
SQUARE
PARK

E 25TH ST

W 24TH ST

E 24TH ST

E 23RD ST

D

BROADWAY

W 22ND ST

E 22ND ST

E 21ST ST

4 **3B**

Julia Roberts ○

○ **Rufus Wainwright**

E 20TH ST

Harry Houdini: 278 West 113th Street between Frederick Douglass Boulevard and A. C. Powell Boulevard (Map 5 West/2A)

Rock Hudson: 211 Central Park West between 81st and 82nd Streets (Map 4 West/2A)

Hugh Jackman: 176 Perry Street at West Street (Map 2 West/2A)

La Toya Jackson: 106 Central Park South at 6th Avenue (Map 4 East/3D)

Jay-Z: 10 Columbus Circle at 59th Street and Broadway (Map 4 West/2C), 195 Hudson Street between Vestry and Desbrosses Streets (Map 2 West/2D)

Peter Jennings: 135 Central Park West between 73rd and 74th Streets (Map 4 West/2B)

Steve Jobs: 145–146 Central Park West between 74th and 75th Streets (Map 4 West/2A)

Billy Joel: 128 Central Park South between 6th and 7th Avenues (Map 4 West/2D), 88 Central Park West between 68 and 69th Streets (Map 4 West/2B), born in the Bronx (Map 6 East/Bronx)

Betsey Johnson: 25 Central Park West between 62nd and 63rd Streets (Map 4 West/2C)

Grace Jones: 166 Bank Street at West Street (Map 2 West/2A)

Norah Jones: 62 Cooper Square at East 7th Street (Map 2 West/2B); 172 Pacific Street, Brooklyn Heights, Brooklyn (Map 6 East/Brooklyn)

Janis Joplin: The Chelsea Hotel, 222 West 23rd Street between 7th and 8th Avenues (Map 3 West/2D)

Milla Jovovich: 100 Greenwich Avenue between West 12th and West 13th Streets (Map 2 West/2A)

Boris Karloff: 1 West 72nd Street at Central Park West (Map 4 West/2B)

Chris Kattan: London Terrace, between 9th and 10 Avenues and 23rd and 24th Streets (Map 3 West/1D)

Alicia Keys: 30 Crosby Street between Grand and Broome Streets (Map 2 West/2D)

Diane Keaton: 145–146 Central Park West between 74th and 75th Streets (Map 4 West/2A)

Garrison Keillor: 300 Central Park West between 90th and 91st Streets (Map 5 West/2C)

Harvey Keitel: 106 Hudson Street at Franklin Street (Map 1 West/2A)

Grace Kelly: 200 East 66th Street at Third Avenue (Map 4 East/4C)

Jack Kerouac: 454 West 20th Street between 9th and 10th Avenues (Map 3 West/1D)

Calvin Klein: 176 Perry Street at West Street (Map 2 West/2A), 211 Central Park West between 81st and 82nd Streets (Map 4 West/2A)

The Kenilworth: 151 Central Park West at 75th Street (Map 4 West/2A)

Nicole Kidman: London Terrace, between 9th and 10 Avenues and 23rd and 24th Streets (Map 3 West/1D); 176 Perry Street at West Street (Map 2 West/2A); 200 11th Avenue at 24th Street (Map 3 West/1D)

Beyoncé Knowles: 195 Hudson Street between Vestry and Desbrosses Streets (Map 2 West/2D), 151 East 58th Street between Lexington and 3rd Avenues (Map 4 East/4D)

John Krasinski: Park Slope, Brooklyn (Map 6 East/Brooklyn)

Lenny Kravitz: 30 Crosby Street between Grand and Broome Streets (Map 2 West/2D)

Queen Latifah: 88 Greenwich Street south of Rector Street (Map 1 West/2C)

Michael Landon: Born in Kew Gardens Hills, Queens (Map 6 East/Queens)

The Langham: 135 Central Park West between 73rd and 74th Streets (Map 4 West/2B)

Cyndi Lauper: 2207 Broadway between 78 and 79th Street/390 West End Avenue (Map 4 West/1A), born in Astoria, Queens (Map 6 East/Queens)

Ralph Lauren: Born in the Bronx (Map 6 East/Bronx)

Jennifer Lawrence: 443 Greenwich Street at Vestry Street (Map 2 West/2D)

Leadbelly: 414 East 10th Street between Avenues C and D (Map 2 East/4B)

John Legend: 52 East 4th Street between Bowery and 2nd Avenue (Map 2 West/2C)

John Leguizamo: Born in Jackson Heights, Queens (Map 6 East/Queens)

John Lennon: 1 West 72nd Street at Central Park West (Map 4 West/2B)

John Lennon and Yoko Ono: 105 Bank Street between Greenwich and Washington Streets (Map 2 West/2A)

John Lennon and May Pang: 434 East 52nd Street east of 1st Avenue (Map 4 East/4D)

Annie Leibovitz: London Terrace, between 9th and 10 Avenues and 23rd and 24th Streets (Map 3 West/1D)

LL Cool J: Born in Bay Shore, Queens (Map 6 East/Queens)

Lucy Liu: Born in Jackson Heights, Queens (Map 6 East/Queens)

Blake Lively: 443 Greenwich Street at Vestry Street (Map 2 West/2D)

Jennifer Lopez: 2210 Blackrock Avenue, Castle Hill, Bronx (Map 6 East/Bronx); 21 East 26th Street between 5th and Madison Avenues (Map 3 East/3D)

Courtney Love: 285 Lafayette Street at Jersey Street (Map 2 West/2D)

Madonna: 232 East 4th Street between Avenues A and B, 5th floor (Map 2 East/4B)

Madonna: 41 Central Park West at 64th Street (Map 4 West/2C)

Madonna: 152 East 81st Street between Lexington and 3rd Avenues (Map 4 East/4A)

The Majestic: 115 Central Park West between 71st and 72nd Streets (Map 4 West/2B)

Nicki Minaj: Jamaica, Queens (Map 6 East/Queens)

Barry Manilow: 145–146 Central Park West between 74th and 75th Streets (Map 4 West /2A), 451 Washington Street at Watts Street (Map 2 West/2D)

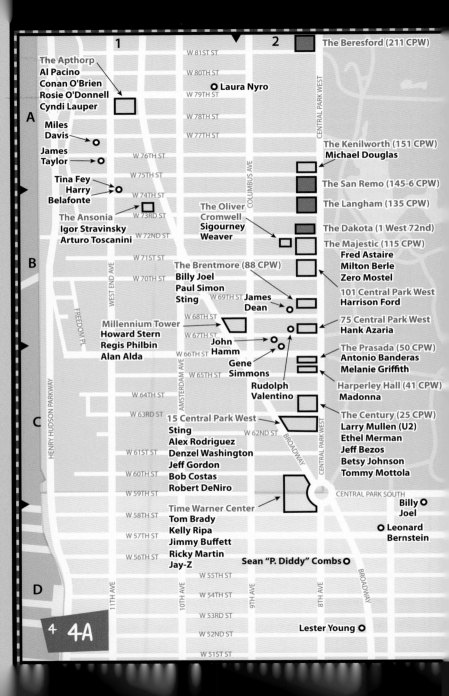

1 **2**

The Beresford (211 CPW)

W 81ST ST
W 80TH ST
W 79TH ST ○ **Laura Nyro**
W 78TH ST

The Apthorp
Al Pacino
Conan O'Brien
Rosie O'Donnell
Cyndi Lauper

CENTRAL PARK WEST

W 77TH ST

A

Miles
Davis → ○
James
Taylor → ○

W 76TH ST

The Kenilworth (151 CPW)
Michael Douglas

W 75TH ST

The San Remo (145-6 CPW)

Tina Fey
Harry
Belafonte → ○

W 74TH ST

The Langham (135 CPW)

W 73RD ST
COLUMBUS AVE

The Ansonia
Igor Stravinsky
Arturo Toscanini

W 72ND ST

The Dakota (1 West 72nd)
The Majestic (115 CPW)

The Oliver
Cromwell
Sigourney
Weaver

W 71ST ST

Fred Astaire
Milton Berle
Zero Mostel

B

WEST END AVE

W 70TH ST

The Brentmore (88 CPW)
Billy Joel
Paul Simon
Sting

W 69TH ST **James**
Dean → ○

101 Central Park West
Harrison Ford

W 68TH ST

75 Central Park West
Hank Azaria

Millennium Tower
Howard Stern
Regis Philbin
Alan Alda

W 67TH ST

John
Hamm → ○ ○

FREEDOM PL

W 66TH ST

○ ○

The Prasada (50 CPW)
Antonio Banderas
Melanie Griffith

AMSTERDAM AVE

W 65TH ST

Gene
Simmons

Rudolph
Valentino

Harperley Hall (41 CPW)
Madonna

W 64TH ST

W 63RD ST

The Century (25 CPW)
Larry Mullen (U2)
Ethel Merman
Jeff Bezos
Betsy Johnson
Tommy Mottola

HENRY HUDSON PARKWAY

C

15 Central Park West
Sting
Alex Rodriguez
Denzel Washington
Jeff Gordon
Bob Costas
Robert DeNiro

W 62ND ST
BROADWAY
CENTRAL PARK WEST

W 61ST ST

W 60TH ST

W 59TH ST

CENTRAL PARK SOUTH

Time Warner Center
Tom Brady
Kelly Ripa
Jimmy Buffett
Ricky Martin
Jay-Z

W 58TH ST

Billy ○
Joel

W 57TH ST

○ **Leonard**
Bernstein

W 56TH ST

Sean "P. Diddy" Combs ○

W 55TH ST

11TH AVE
10TH AVE
9TH AVE
8TH AVE
BROADWAY

D

W 54TH ST
W 53RD ST

4 **4A**

W 52ND ST

Lester Young ○

W 51ST ST

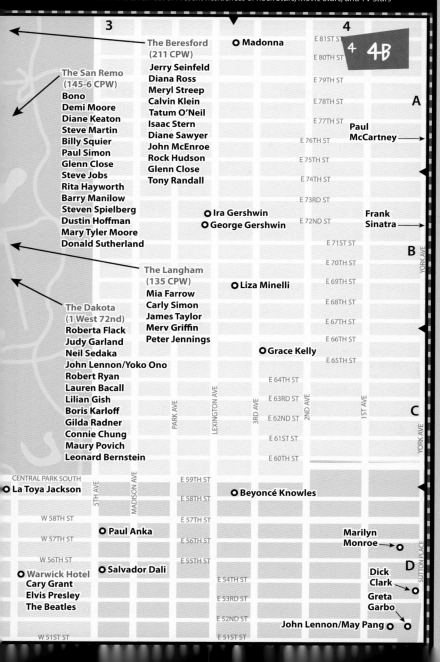

3

4

4 **4B**

The Beresford
(211 CPW)

Jerry Seinfeld
Diana Ross
Meryl Streep
Calvin Klein
Tatum O'Neil
Isaac Stern
Diane Sawyer
John McEnroe
Rock Hudson
Glenn Close
Tony Randall

The San Remo
(145-6 CPW)
Bono
Demi Moore
Diane Keaton
Steve Martin
Billy Squier
Paul Simon
Glenn Close
Steve Jobs
Rita Hayworth
Barry Manilow
Steven Spielberg
Dustin Hoffman
Mary Tyler Moore
Donald Sutherland

The Langham
(135 CPW)
Mia Farrow
Carly Simon
James Taylor
Merv Griffin
Peter Jennings

The Dakota
(1 West 72nd)
Roberta Flack
Judy Garland
Neil Sedaka
John Lennon/Yoko Ono
Robert Ryan
Lauren Bacall
Lilian Gish
Boris Karloff
Gilda Radner
Connie Chung
Maury Povich
Leonard Bernstein

O **Madonna**

E 81ST ST
E 80TH ST
E 79TH ST
E 78TH ST **A**
E 77TH ST **Paul**
E 76TH ST **McCartney** ⟶
E 75TH ST
E 74TH ST
E 73RD ST

O **Ira Gershwin**
O **George Gershwin** E 72ND ST **Frank**
Sinatra ⟶

E 71ST ST **B**
E 70TH ST
E 69TH ST
O **Liza Minelli** E 68TH ST
E 67TH ST
E 66TH ST
O **Grace Kelly** E 65TH ST
E 64TH ST
E 63RD ST
E 62ND ST **C**
E 61ST ST
E 60TH ST

CENTRAL PARK SOUTH
O **La Toya Jackson** E 59TH ST
E 58TH ST O **Beyoncé Knowles**
W 58TH ST E 57TH ST
W 57TH ST O **Paul Anka** E 56TH ST **Marilyn**
Monroe ⟶ O
W 56TH ST E 55TH ST **D**
O **Warwick Hotel** O **Salvador Dali** E 54TH ST **Dick**
Cary Grant E 53RD ST **Clark** O
Elvis Presley **Greta**
The Beatles E 52ND ST **Garbo**
John Lennon/May Pang O O
W 51ST ST E 51ST ST

PARK AVE
LEXINGTON AVE
3RD AVE
2ND AVE
1ST AVE
YORK AVE
5TH AVE
MADISON AVE
SUTTON PLACE

Ricky Martin: 10 Columbus Circle at 59th Street and Broadway (Map 4 West/2C)

Steve Martin: 145–146 Central Park West between 74th and 75th Streets (Map 4 West/2A)

The Marx Brothers: 179 East 93rd Street between Lexington and Third Avenues (Map 5 East/4C)

John McEnroe: 211 Central Park West between 81st and 82nd Streets (Map 4 West/2A)

Paul McCartney: 530 East 76th Street at FDR Drive (Map 4 East/4A)

Ethel Merman: 25 Central Park West between 62nd and 63rd Streets (Map 4 West/2C)

Bette Midler: 451 Washington Street at Watts Street (Map 2 West/2D), 36 Barrow Street near 7th Avenue (Map 2 West/2A), 1125 Fifth Avenue at 94th Street (Map 5 East/3C)

Millennium Tower: 101 West 67th Street between Broadway and Columbus Avenue (Map 4 West/2B)

Liza Minelli: 150 East 69th Street between Lexington and 3rd Avenues (Map 4 East/4B)

Joni Mitchell: 41 West 16th Street between 5th and 6th Avenues (Map 2 West/1A)

Moby: 52 East 4th Street between Bowery and 2nd Avenue (Map 2 West/2C), 300 Central Park West between 90th and 91st Streets (Map 5 West/2C)

Marilyn Monroe: 444 East 57th Street between First Avenue and Sutton Place (Map 4 East/4D)

Demi Moore: 145–146 Central Park West between 74th and 75th Streets (Map 4 West/2A)

Mary Tyler Moore: 145–146 Central Park West between 74th and 75th Streets (Map 4 West/2A)

Emily Mortimer: 152 Dean Street, Boerum Hill, Brooklyn (Map 6 East/Brooklyn)

Zero Mostel: 115 Central Park West between 71st and 72nd Streets (Map 4 West/2B)

Tommy Mottola: 25 Central Park West between 62nd and 63rd Streets (Map 4 West/2C)

Larry Mullen: 25 Central Park West between 62nd and 63rd Streets (Map 4 West/2C)

Nas: 151 West 17th Street between 6th and 7th Avenues (Map 2 West/1A)

Nico: 101 Avenue A between 6th and 7th Streets (Map 2 East/3B)

Laura Nyro: Born in the Bronx (Map 6 East/Bronx), 145 West 79th Street between Amsterdam and Columbus Avenues (Map 4 West/1A)

Conan O'Brien: 2207 Broadway between 78 and 79th Streets/390 West End Avenue (Map 4 West /1A)

Phil Ochs: The Chelsea Hotel, 222 West 23rd Street between 7th and 8th Avenues (Map 3 West/2D)

Rosie O'Donnell: 2207 Broadway between 78 and 79th Streets/390 West End Avenue (Map 4 West/1A)

Mary-Kate and Ashley Olsen: 100 Morton Street at West Street (Map 2 West/2B)

Jacqueline Kennedy Onassis: 1040 Fifth Avenue between 85th and 86th Streets (Map 5 East/3D)

Tatum O'Neal: 211 Central Park West between 81st and 82nd Streets (Map 4 West/2A)

Yoko Ono: 1 West 72nd Street at Central Park West (Map 4 West/2B), 105 Bank Street between Greenwich and Washington Streets (Map 2 West/3A)

Al Pacino: Born in the Bronx (Map 6 East/Bronx), 2207 Broadway between 78 and 79th Streets/390 West End Avenue (Map 4 West/1A)

Chazz Palminteri: Born in the Bronx (Map 6 East/Bronx)

Charlie Parker: 151 Avenue B between East 9th and East 10th Streets (Map 2 East/4B)

Katy Perry: 65 North Moore Street between Greenwich and Hudson Streets (Map 1 West/1A)

Regis Philbin: Born in the Bronx (Map 6 East/Bronx), 101 West 67th Street between Broadway and Columbus Avenue (Map 4 West/2B)

Edward Platt: Born in Staten Island. "Chief" on *Get Smart*. (Map 6 West/Staten Island

Iggy Pop: 143 Avenue B at East 9th Street. (Map 2 East/4B)

Cole Porter: Waldorf-Astoria, 100 East 50th Street at Park Avenue (Map 3 East/3A)

Maury Povich: 1 West 72nd Street at Central Park West (Map 4 West/2B)

Robin Quivers: Born in Staten Island (Map 6 West/Staten Island)

Daniel Radcliffe: 100 Morton Street at West Street (Map 2 West/2B)

Gilda Radner: 1 West 72nd Street at Central Park West (Map 4 West/2B)

Dee Dee Ramone: The Chelsea Hotel, 222 West 23rd Street between 7th and 8th Avenues (Map 3 West/2D)

Joey Ramone: 11 East 9th Street at 3rd Avenue (Map 2 West/2A)

Tony Randall: 211 Central Park West between 81st and 82nd Streets (Map 4 West/2A)

Lou Reed: 56 Ludlow Street between Grand and Hester Streets (Map 2 East/4D)

Ryan Reynolds: 443 Greenwich Street at Vestry Street (Map 2 West/2D)

Keith Richards: 14 East 4th Street at Broadway (Map 2 West/2C)

Rihanna: 92 Greene Street between Spring and Prince Streets (Map 2 West/2D)

Kelly Ripa: 10 Columbus Circle at 59th Street and Broadway (Map 4 West/2C)

Julia Roberts: 7 Gramercy Park West at Park Avenue South (Map 3 East/3D)

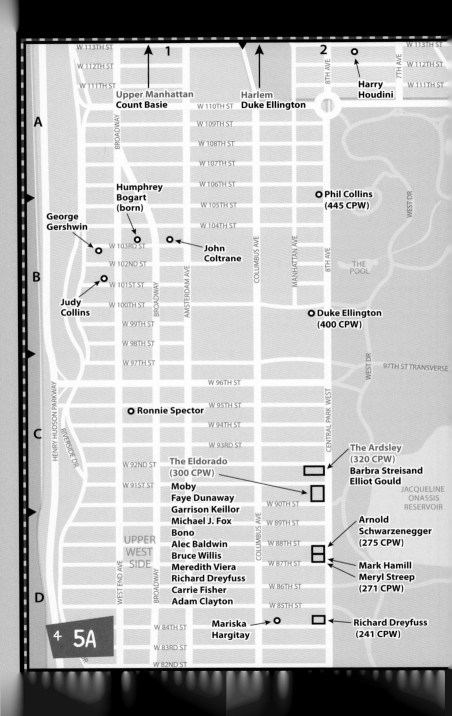

3

**EAST
HARLEM**

4

W 112TH ST

E 112TH ST

MALCOM X BLVD

5TH AVE

W 111TH ST

E 111TH ST

CATHEDRAL PARKWAY

E 110TH ST

E 109TH ST

A

FDR DR

HARLEM MEER

E 108TH ST

E 107TH ST

MADISON AVE

PARK AVE

LEXINGTON AVE

3RD AVE

2ND AVE

1ST AVE

5TH AVE

E 106TH ST

E 105TH ST

EAST DR

E 104TH ST

E 103RD ST

E 102ND ST

B

E 101ST ST

MT
SINAI
HOSPITAL

E 100TH ST

E 99TH ST

E 98TH ST

E 97TH ST

E 96TH ST

E 95TH ST

E 94TH ST

FDR DR

C

O ← **Bette
Midler**

O ← **The Marx
Brothers**

**UPPER
EAST
SIDE**

E 93RD ST

MADISON AVE

PARK AVE

LEXINGTON AVE

3RD AVE

2ND AVE

1ST AVE

5TH AVE

E 92ND ST

E 91ST ST

E 90TH ST

E 89TH ST

JACQUELINE
ONASSIS
RESERVOIR

E 88TH ST

E 87TH ST

E 86TH ST

YORK AVE

O ← **Jacqueline
Kennedy
Onassis**

E 85TH ST

D

E 84TH ST

E 83RD ST

E 82RD ST

4 **5B**

Alex Rodriguez: 15 Central Park West between 61st and 62nd Streets (Map 4 West/2C)

Ray Romano: Born in Forest Hills, Queens (Map 6 East/Queens)

Mark Ronson: 69 Washington Place between 6th Avenue and MacDougal Street (Map 2 West/2B)

Diana Ross: 211 Central Park West between 81st and 82nd Streets (Map 4 West/2A)

David Lee Roth: 305 Second Avenue at East 17th Street (Map 2 East/3A)

Kerri Russell: Boerum Hill, Brooklyn (Map 6 East/Brooklyn)

Meg Ryan: 443 Greenwich Street at Vestry Street (Map 2 West/2D)

Robert Ryan: 1 West 72nd Street at Central Park West (Map 4 West/2B)

The Street Urban: 285 Central Park West at 89th Street (Map 5 West/1B)

The San Remo: 145–146 Central Park West between 74th and 75th Streets (Map 4 West/2A)

Susan Sarandon: Born in Jackson Heights, Queens (Map 6 East/Queens)

Peter Sarsgaard: Sterling Place, Park Slope, Brooklyn (Map 6 East/Brooklyn)

Diane Sawyer: 211 Central Park West between 81st and 82nd Streets (Map 4 West/2A)

Arnold Schwarzenegger: 275 Central Park West at 88th Street (Map 5 West/1B)

Martin Scorsese: Born in Flushing, Queens (Map 6 East/Queens)

Gil Scott-Heron: Born in the Bronx (Map 6 East/Bronx)

Neil Sedaka: 1 West 72nd Street at Central Park West (Map 4 West/2B)

Carly Simon: 135 Central Park West between 73rd and 74th Streets (Map 4 West/2B)

Paul Simon: 145–146 Central Park West between 74th and 75th Streets (Map 4 West/2A); 137–62 70th Road, Kew Gardens Hills, Queens (Map 6 East/Queens), 88 Central Park West between 68 and 69th Streets (Map 4 West/2B)

Gene Simmons: 10 West 66th Street between Columbus Avenue and Central Park West (Map 4 West/2C)

Russell Simmons: 14 East 4th Street at Broadway (Map 2 West/2C)

Frank Sinatra: 530 East 72nd Street at FDR Drive (Map 4 East/3D)

Harry Smith: The Chelsea Hotel, 222 West 23rd Street between 7th and 8th Avenues (Map 3 West/2D)

Patti Smith: The Chelsea Hotel, 222 West 23rd Street between 7th and 8th Avenues (Map 3 West/2D)

Stephen Sondheim: 246 East 49th Street between 2nd and 3rd Avenues (Map 3 East/4A)

Susan Sontag: London Terrace, between 9th and 10 Avenues and 23rd and 24th Streets (Map 3 West/1D)

Britney Spears: 14 East 4th Street at Broadway (Map 2 West/2C)

Ronnie Spector: 710 West End Avenue at 95th Street (Map 5 West/1C)

Steven Spielberg: 145–146 Central Park West between 74th and 75th Streets (Map 4 West/2A)

Billy Squier: 145–146 Central Park West between 74th and 75th Streets (Maps 4 West/2A)

Jerry Seinfeld: 211 Central Park West between 81st and 82nd Streets (Map 4 West/2A)

Howard Stern: 101 West 67th Street between Broadway and Columbus Avenue (Map 4 West/2B); born or lived in Jackson Heights, Queens (Map 6 East/Queens)

Isaac Stern: 211 Central Park West between 81st and 82nd Streets (Map 4 West/2A)

Martha Stewart: 173 Perry Street at West Street (Map 2 West/2A)

Patrick Stewart: 288 7th Street, Park Slope, Brooklyn (Map 6 East/Brooklyn)

Sting: 88 Central Park West between 68th and 69th Streets (Map 4 West/2B), 15 Central Park West between 61st and 62nd Streets (Map 4 West/2C)

Igor Stravinsky: The Ansonia, 2109 Broadway at 73rd Street (Map 4 West/1B)

Barbra Streisand: 320 Central Park West between 91st and 92nd Streets (Map 5 West/2C)

Meryl Streep: 211 Central Park West between 81st and 82nd Streets (Map 4 West/2A)

Meryl Streep: 271 Central Park West at 87th Street (Map 5 West/1B)

Harry Styles: 443 Greenwich Street at Vestry Street (Map 2 West/2D)

Ed Sullivan: East 114th Street, Harlem (Map 6 East/Harlem)

Donald Sutherland: 145–146 Central Park West between 74th and 75th Streets (Map 4 West/2A)

Hillary Swank: 33 Charles Street between West 4th Street and 7th Avenue (Map 2 West/2A)

Taylor Swift: 155 Franklin Street between Hudson and Varick Streets (Map 1 West/1A)

James Taylor: 333 West End Avenue at 76th Street (Map 4 West/1A), 135 Central Park West between 73rd and 74th Street (Map 4 West/2B)

Justin Timberlake: 311 West Broadway between Canal Street and Grand Street (Map 2 West/2D), 443 Greenwich Street at Vestry Street (Map 2 West/2D)

Time Warner Center: 10 Columbus Circle at 59th and Broadway (Map 4 West/2C)

Arturo Toscanini: The Ansonia, 2109 Broadway at 73rd Street (Map 4 West/1B)

John Turturro: Park Slope, Brooklyn (Map 6 East/Brooklyn)

Steven Tyler: Born in the Bronx (Map 6 East/Bronx)

Keith Urban: 200 11th Avenue at 24th Street (Map 3 West/1D)

Rudolph Valentino: Hotel des Artistes, 1 West 67th Street at Central Park West (Map 4 West/2B)

Dave Van Ronk: 190 Waverly Place between West 10th and Charles Streets (Map 2 West/1B)

Staten Island
Born or lived in Staten Island:
Edward Platt
("Chief" on Get Smart)
Christine Aguilera
Steve Augeri
Joan Baez
Robin Quivers

Staten Island

4 **6A**

Upper Manhattan
Count Basie
Coleman Hawkins
Lena Horne

The Bronx

Harlem
Duke Ellington
Billie Holiday
Ed Sullivan

Manhattan

The Bronx
Born or lived in the Bronx:
Woody Allen
Lauren Bacall
Anne Bancroft
Mary J. Blige
Bobby Darin
Grandmaster Flash
Billy Joel
Ralph Lauren
Jennifer Lopez
Laura Nyro
Al Pacino
Chazz Palminteri
Regis Philbin
Big Pun
Gil Scott-Heron
Steven Tyler
Kerry Washington

Queens
Born or lived in Queens:
Louis Armstrong
Adrien Brody
Jon Favreau
Art Garfunkel
Paul Simon
Judd Apatow
Tony Bennet
Fran Drescher
50 Cent
Cyndi Lauper
John Leguizamo
LL Cool J
Michael Landon
Lucy Liu
Nicki Minaj
Ray Romano
Susan Sarandon
Martin Scorsese
Howard Stern
Christopher Walken

Brooklyn
Born or lived in Brooklyn:
Emily Blunt
Steve Buscemi
Rose Byrne
Bobby Cannavale
Lena Dunham
Paul Giamatti
Maggie Gyllenhaal
Anne Hathaway
Ethan Hawke
Norah Jones
John Krasinski
Emily Mortimer
Kerri Russell
Peter Sarsgaard
Patrick Stewart
John Turturro
Michelle Williams

Brooklyn

4 6B

"Miami" Steven Van Zandt: 135 West 4th Street between 6th Avenue and MacDougal Street (Map 2 West/2B)

Sid Vicious: The Chelsea Hotel, 222 West 23rd Street between 7th and 8th Avenues (Map 3 West/2D)

Meredith Vieira: 300 Central Park West between 90th and 91st Streets (Map 5 West/2C)

Rufus Wainwright: London Terrace, between 9th and 10 Avenues and 23rd and 24th Streets (Map 3 West/1D)

Rufus Wainwright: 38 Gramercy Park North at Third Avenue (Map 3 East/4D)

Christopher Walken: Born in Astoria, Queens (Map 6 East/Queens)

Warwick Hotel: 65 West 54th Street at Sixth Avenue. Elvis and The Beatles stayed here. (Map 4 East/3D)

Denzel Washington: 15 Central Park West between 61st and 62nd Streets (Map 4 West/2C)

Kerry Washington: Born in the Bronx (Map 6 East/Bronx)

Sigourney Weaver: 12 West 72nd Street between Columbus and Central Park West (Map 4 West/2B)

Kanye West: 225 Lafayette Street at Spring Street (Map 2 West/2D)

Michelle Williams: 126 Hoyt Street, Boerum Hill, Brooklyn (Map 6 East/Brooklyn)

Bruce Willis: 300 Central Park West between 90th and 91st Streets (Map 5 West/2C)

Anna Wintour: 172 Sullivan Street between West Houston and Bleecker Streets (Map 2 West/2B)

Stevie Wonder: 325 East 18th Street between 2nd and 3rd Avenues (Map 2 East/3A)

Lester Young: Alvin Hotel, 223 West 52nd at Broadway (Map 4 West/2D)

NUMERAL–NAMED APARTMENT BUILDINGS OF CENTRAL PARK WEST

15 Central Park West: 15 Central Park West between 61st and 62nd Streets (Map 4 West/2C)

75 Central Park West: 75 Central Park West at 67th Street (Map 4 West/2B)

101 Central Park West: 101 Central Park West between 70th and 71st Streets (Map 4 West/2B)

241 Central Park West: 241 Central Park West at 84th Street (Map 5 West/2D)

271 Central Park West: 271 Central Park West at 87th Street (Map 5 West/1B)

275 Central Park West: 275 Central Park West at 88th Street (Map 5 West/1B)

5
LITERARY LANDMARKS AND NEW YORK NOVELS BY NEIGHBORHOOD

NEW YORK NOVELS

HERE ARE OVER FIFTY ICONIC NEW YORK CITY NOVELS—highbrow, low-brow, and in between—that illustrate the kaleidoscope of city life, along with the locations mentioned in the books, listed in order of year of publication.

Washington Square by Henry James (1880): In the book, Dr. Sloper moves to Washington Square in 1835. James' grandmother grew up at 18 Washington Square North. James grew up on Washington Place, east of the park; the building that replaced his house was the location of the Triangle Shirtwaist Fire. Greenwich Village.

Maggie: A Girl of the Streets by Stephen Crane (1893): The Bowery. Lower East Side.

The House of Mirth by Edith Wharton (1905): Begins in 1870 at the Academy of Music, Bryant Park. Wharton lived on Park Avenue when she wrote it. Upper East Side.

The Age of Innocence by Edith Wharton (1920): New York Opera House, Metropolitan Museum. Midtown.

The Great Gatsby by F. Scott Fitzgerald (1922): Queensboro Bridge, Penn Station, Yale Club, Metropole Hotel on 43rd Street, The Plaza, Central Park. Midtown.

Call It Sleep by Henry Roth (1934): 9th Street and Avenue D. East Village.

The Thin Man by Dashiell Hammett (1934): Midtown speakeasies, Saks, The Little Theater (240 West 44th Street), Hotel Normandie (38th and Broadway; gone). Midtown.

The League of Frightened Men by Rex Stout (1935): Detective Nero Wolfe's three-floor brownstone is on the "south side of West 35th Street," which would put it between 5th Avenue and the West Side Highway. Chelsea.

A Tree Grows in Brooklyn by Betty Smith (1943): Williamsburg, Brooklyn.

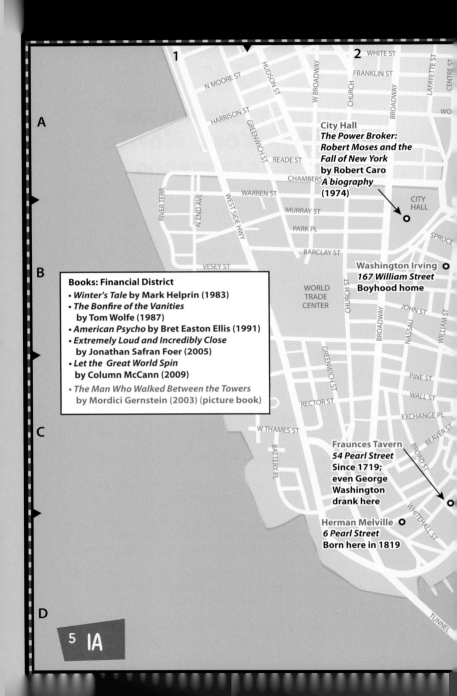

1

N MOORE ST
HUDSON ST
W BROADWAY
CHURCH
BROADWAY

2 WHITE ST
FRANKLIN ST
LAFAYETTE ST
CENTRE ST

HARRISON ST
GREENWICH ST
READE ST

A
WO

City Hall
The Power Broker:
Robert Moses and the
Fall of New York
by Robert Caro
A biography
(1974)

CHAMBERS ST

WARREN ST

CITY
HALL

RIVER TERR.
N END AVE
WEST SIDE HWY

MURRAY ST

PARK PL

SPRUCE

BARCLAY ST

VESEY ST

B

Washington Irving O
167 William Street
Boyhood home

Books: Financial District
- *Winter's Tale* by Mark Helprin (1983)
- *The Bonfire of the Vanities*
  by Tom Wolfe (1987)
- *American Psycho* by Bret Easton Ellis (1991)
- *Extremely Loud and Incredibly Close*
  by Jonathan Safran Foer (2005)
- *Let the Great World Spin*
  by Column McCann (2009)
- *The Man Who Walked Between the Towers*
  by Mordici Gernstein (2003) (picture book)

WORLD
TRADE
CENTER

CHURCH ST
BROADWAY
NASSAU
JOHN ST
WILLIAM ST

GREENWICH ST

PINE ST
WALL ST

RECTOR ST

EXCHANGE PL

C

W THAMES ST

BATTERY PL

BEAVER ST
BROAD ST

Fraunces Tavern
54 Pearl Street
Since 1719;
even George
Washington
drank here

WHITEHALL ST

Herman Melville O
6 Pearl Street
Born here in 1819

D

TUNNEL

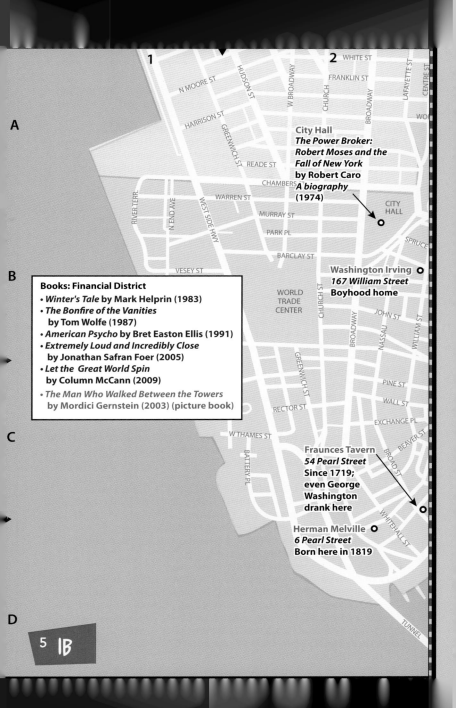

1   2   WHITE ST

N MOORE ST   HUDSON ST   W BROADWAY   CHURCH   FRANKLIN ST   BROADWAY   LAFAYETTE ST   CENTRE ST

HARRISON ST   GREENWICH ST   WO

A

READE ST

City Hall
*The Power Broker:
Robert Moses and the
Fall of New York*
by Robert Caro
A biography
(1974)

CHAMBERS
CITY HALL

WARREN ST

RIVER TERR.   N END AVE   WEST SIDE HWY

MURRAY ST
PARK PL

SPRUCE

BARCLAY ST

VESEY ST

B

Washington Irving ○
167 William Street
Boyhood home

Books: Financial District
- *Winter's Tale* **by Mark Helprin (1983)**
- *The Bonfire of the Vanities*
 by Tom Wolfe (1987)
- *American Psycho* **by Bret Easton Ellis (1991)**
- *Extremely Loud and Incredibly Close*
 by Jonathan Safran Foer (2005)
- *Let the Great World Spin*
 by Column McCann (2009)
- *The Man Who Walked Between the Towers*
 by Mordici Gernstein (2003) (picture book)

WORLD
TRADE
CENTER

CHURCH ST   JOHN ST   BROADWAY   NASSAU ST   WILLIAM ST

GREENWICH ST

PINE ST

WALL ST

RECTOR ST

EXCHANGE PL

C

W THAMES ST

BATTERY PL

Fraunces Tavern
54 Pearl Street
**Since 1719;
even George
Washington
drank here**

BROAD ST   BEAVER ST

WHITEHALL ST

○

Herman Melville ○
6 Pearl Street
Born here in 1819

D

TUNNEL

***The Fountainhead* by Ayn Rand (1943):** Ayn Rand lived at 139 East 35th at Lexington Avenue when she wrote the book from 1941 to 1942. Murray Hill.

***Death of a Salesman* (play) by Arthur Miller (1949):** Brooklyn.

***I, the Jury* by Micky Spillane (1947):** Mike Hammer's Hammer Investigative Agency was in "a two-room suite at the Hackard Building," Room 808. Velda, his secretary and associate PI, worked in the other room. Midtown.

***Here Is New York* (non-fiction) by E.B. White (1949):** Turtle Bay Gardens. Midtown.

***The Catcher in the Rye* by J.D. Salinger (1951):** Fictional Edmont Hotel, the Carousel in Central Park, Ernie's Jazz Club in the Village, Biltmore Hotel, "Radio City skating rink," The Pond in Central Park, Grand Central, the clock at the Biltmore, McBurney School. Midtown.

***On the Road* by Jack Kerouac (1951):** Kerouac wrote it at 450 West 20th Street; at the end of the novel Dean parts from Sal to go to Penn Station at 20th Street and 7th Avenue. Chelsea.

***Howl* (poem) by Allen Ginsberg (1956):** Bowery, the Bronx, Harlem, Brooklyn Bridge, Empire State Building. East Village.

***Invisible Man* by Ralph Ellison (1952):** Harlem.

***Go Tell It on the Mountain* by James Baldwin (1953):** Lemon Avenue, Harlem, in the 1930s. Harlem.

***Go* by John Clennon Holmes (1952):** The first "beat" novel. Times Square dives. Times Square.

***Breakfast at Tiffany's* by Truman Capote (1958):** A "brownstone on the Upper East Side" (in the movie, 169 East 71st Street), Tiffany's. Upper East Side.

***Runyon on Broadway* (collected short stories) by Damon Runyon (1950):** Many of his stories start outside Mindy's Restaurant (in real life, Lindy's) at Broadway and West 51st Street just above Times Square. *Guys and Dolls* is based on his characters. Times Square.

***Franny and Zooey* by J.D. Salinger (1961):** East 70s. Upper East Side.

***The Group* by Mary McCarthy (1963):** Follows the lives of nine 1933 Vassar classmates, most in New York. The Vassar Club was at 138 East 48th Street. Inspired *Sex and the City*. Upper East Side.

***The Bell Jar* by Sylvia Plath (1963):** Fictional *Ladies Day* magazine; fictional Amazon Hotel for women. Midtown.

***City of Night* by John Rechy (1963):** Times Square.

***Last Exit to Brooklyn* by Hubert Selby Jr. (1964):** Sunset Park. Brooklyn.

***From the Mixed-Up Files of Mrs. Basil E. Frankweiler* by E.L. Konigsburg (1967):** Metropolitan Museum of Art, Grand Central, New York Public Library, Donnell Library, Automat, Chock Full o'Nuts. Upper East Side.

***The Chosen* by Chaim Potok (1967):** Williamsburg. Brooklyn.

***Down These Mean Streets* by Piri Thomas (1967):** El Barrio, aka Spanish Harlem. Harlem.

Rosemary's Baby by Ira Levin (1967): The book is set in the Bramford on the Upper East Side near 6th Avenue and 55th Street. The Dakota (Upper West Side) famously played the Bramford in the movie. Upper East Side.

The Godfather, by Mario Puzo (1969): Don Corleone's mansion is in Long Beach, Long Island, next to Queens. Queens.

Time and Again, by Jack Finney (1970): Dakota Hotel, 19 Gramercy Park, Madison Square Park. Upper West Side.

The Power Broker: Robert Moses and the Fall of New York (non-fiction) by Robert Caro (1974): His later childhood was at East 46th Street near Fifth Avenue. City Hall.

Ragtime by E.L. Doctorow (1975): New Rochelle; Lower East Side. Lower East Side.

Winter's Tale by Mark Helprin (1983): Ellis Island, all over. Financial District.

Bright Lights, Big City by Jay McInerney (1984): Fictionalized *New Yorker* offices on 25 West 43rd Street, Odeon Restaurant, 145 West Broadway (on cover). Midtown.

The New York Trilogy by Paul Auster (1985, 1986, 1986): Orange Street, Brooklyn Heights. Brooklyn

Slaves of New York by Tama Janowitz (1986): Downtown New York, East Village.

The Bonfire of the Vanities by Tom Wolfe (1987): The Bronx, Wall Street. Financial District.

Billy Bathgate by E.L. Doctorow (1989): The Bronx.

American Psycho by Bret Easton Ellis (1991): Wall Street. Financial District.

Jazz by Toni Morrison (1992): Harlem.

The Alienist by Caleb Carr (1994): Police headquarters on Mulberry Street. Lower East Side.

Angela's Ashes by Frank McCourt (1996): Brooklyn.

Underworld by Don DeLillo (1997): Polo Grounds, 1951; Arthur Avenue in the Bronx. The Bronx.

Motherless Brooklyn by Jonathan Lethem (1999): Brooklyn.

'Tis by Frank McCourt (1999): Biltmore Hotel, NYU, Staten Island, Stuyvesant High School at 345 East 15th Street. Gramercy.

The Amazing Adventures of Kavalier & Clay by Michael Chabon (2000): Brooklyn, sleeps in the Empire State Building. Brooklyn.

The Nanny Diaries (#1) by Emma McLaughlin (2002): Park Avenue. Upper East Side.

The Devil Wears Prada by Lauren Weisberger (2003): *Runway* magazine. Midtown.

The Fortress of Solitude by Jonathan Lethem (2003): Brooklyn.

Extremely Loud and Incredibly Close by Jonathan Safran Foer (2005): World Trade Center. Financial District.

North River by Pete Hamill (2007): Winter Garden Theater, Lower West Side, Times Square, Washington Square Park. Midtown.

Lush Life by Richard Price (2008): Lower East Side.

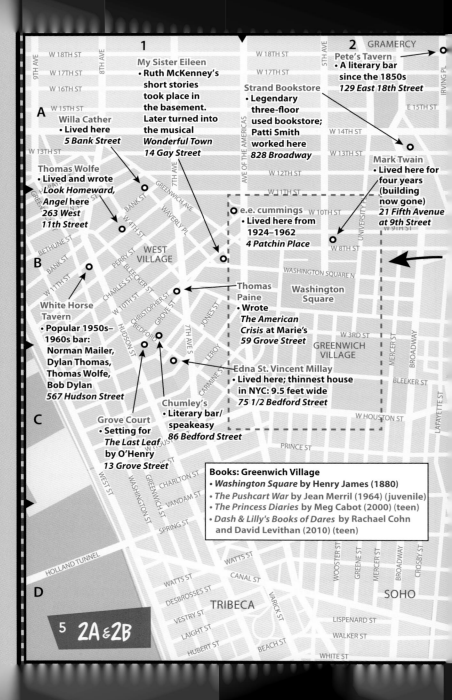

W 18TH ST
W 17TH ST
W 16TH ST
W 15TH ST

9TH AVE
8TH AVE

W 18TH ST
W 17TH ST

5TH AVE

IRVING PL

A

Willa Cather
• Lived here
5 Bank Street

W 13TH ST

My Sister Eileen
• Ruth McKenney's short stories took place in the basement. Later turned into the musical *Wonderful Town*
14 Gay Street

Strand Bookstore
• Legendary three-floor used bookstore; Patti Smith worked here
828 Broadway

Pete's Tavern
• A literary bar since the 1850s
129 East 18th Street

E 15TH ST

W 14TH ST

AVE OF THE AMERICAS

W 13TH ST

Thomas Wolfe
• Lived and wrote *Look Homeward, Angel* here
263 West 11th Street

GREENWICH ST
BANK ST
W 4TH ST

W 12TH ST
W 11TH ST

7TH AVE
WAVERLY PL

Mark Twain
• Lived here for four years (building now gone)
21 Fifth Avenue at 9th Street

BETHUNE ST

e.e. cummings
• Lived here from 1924–1962
4 Patchin Place

W 10TH ST

UNIVERSITY

W 9TH ST
W 8TH ST

B

BANK ST
W 11TH ST

PERRY ST
BLEECKER ST
CHARLES ST
W 10TH ST

WEST VILLAGE

GROVE ST
CHRISTOPHER ST
JONES ST

WASHINGTON SQUARE N

Washington Square

White Horse Tavern
• Popular 1950s–1960s bar: Norman Mailer, Dylan Thomas, Thomas Wolfe, Bob Dylan
567 Hudson Street

HUDSON ST
BEDFORD ST
7TH AVE S
LEROY

Thomas Paine
• Wrote *The American Crisis* at Marie's
59 Grove Street

W 3RD ST

GREENWICH VILLAGE

MERCER ST
BROADWAY

Edna St. Vincent Millay
• Lived here; thinnest house in NYC: 9.5 feet wide
75 1/2 Bedford Street

BLEECKER ST

LAFAYETTE ST

C

CARMINE ST

Grove Court
• Setting for *The Last Leaf* by O'Henry
13 Grove Street

Chumley's
• Literary bar/speakeasy
86 Bedford Street

W HOUSTON ST

PRINCE ST

WEST ST
WASHINGTON ST
GREENWICH ST

CHARLTON ST
VANDAM ST
SPRING ST

Books: Greenwich Village
• *Washington Square* by Henry James (1880)
• *The Pushcart War* by Jean Merril (1964) (juvenile)
• *The Princess Diaries* by Meg Cabot (2000) (teen)
• *Dash & Lilly's Books of Dares* by Rachael Cohn and David Levithan (2010) (teen)

WOOSTER ST
GREENE ST
MERCER ST
BROADWAY
CROSBY ST

SOHO

HOLLAND TUNNEL

WATTS ST

CANAL ST

VARICK ST

D

DESBROSSES ST

TRIBECA

LISPENARD ST

WALKER ST

VESTRY ST

LAIGHT ST

HUBERT ST

BEACH ST

WHITE ST

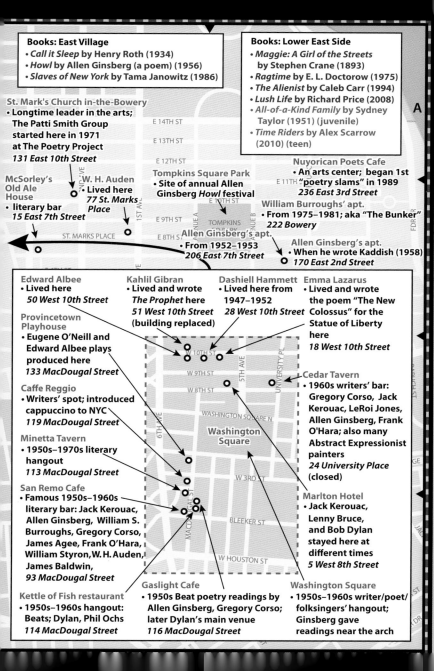

Books: East Village
- *Call it Sleep* by Henry Roth (1934)
- *Howl* by Allen Ginsberg (a poem) (1956)
- *Slaves of New York* by Tama Janowitz (1986)

Books: Lower East Side
- *Maggie: A Girl of the Streets* by Stephen Crane (1893)
- *Ragtime* by E. L. Doctorow (1975)
- *The Alienist* by Caleb Carr (1994)
- *Lush Life* by Richard Price (2008)
- *All-of-a-Kind Family* by Sydney Taylor (1951) (juvenile)
- *Time Riders* by Alex Scarrow (2010) (teen)

A

St. Mark's Church in-the-Bowery
- Longtime leader in the arts; The Patti Smith Group started here in 1971 at The Poetry Project
131 East 10th Street

Nuyorican Poets Cafe
- An arts center; began 1st "poetry slams" in 1989
236 East 3rd Street

McSorley's Old Ale House
- literary bar
15 East 7th Street

W. H. Auden
- Lived here
77 St. Marks Place

Tompkins Square Park
- Site of annual Allen Ginsberg *Howl* festival

William Burroughs' apt.
- From 1975–1981; aka "The Bunker"
222 Bowery

Allen Ginsberg's apt.
- From 1952–1953
206 East 7th Street

Allen Ginsberg's apt.
- When he wrote Kaddish (1958)
170 East 2nd Street

Edward Albee
- Lived here
50 West 10th Street

Provincetown Playhouse
- Eugene O'Neill and Edward Albee plays produced here
133 MacDougal Street

Caffe Reggio
- Writers' spot; introduced cappuccino to NYC
119 MacDougal Street

Minetta Tavern
- 1950s–1970s literary hangout
113 MacDougal Street

San Remo Cafe
- Famous 1950s–1960s literary bar: Jack Kerouac, Allen Ginsberg, William S. Burroughs, Gregory Corso, James Agee, Frank O'Hara, William Styron, W. H. Auden, James Baldwin,
93 MacDougal Street

Kettle of Fish restaurant
- 1950s–1960s hangout: Beats; Dylan, Phil Ochs
114 MacDougal Street

Kahlil Gibran
- Lived and wrote *The Prophet* here
51 West 10th Street (building replaced)

Dashiell Hammett
- Lived here from 1947–1952
28 West 10th Street

Emma Lazarus
- Lived and wrote the poem "The New Colossus" for the Statue of Liberty here
18 West 10th Street

Cedar Tavern
- 1960s writers' bar: Gregory Corso, Jack Kerouac, LeRoi Jones, Allen Ginsberg, Frank O'Hara; also many Abstract Expressionist painters
24 University Place (closed)

Marlton Hotel
- Jack Kerouac, Lenny Bruce, and Bob Dylan stayed here at different times
5 West 8th Street

Gaslight Cafe
- 1950s Beat poetry readings by Allen Ginsberg, Gregory Corso; later Dylan's main venue
116 MacDougal Street

Washington Square
- 1950s–1960s writer/poet/folksingers' hangout; Ginsberg gave readings near the arch

Washington Square

***Let the Great World Spin* by Colum McCann (2009):** 100 Centre Street, the DA's office, World Trade Center. Financial District.

***Girl in Translation* by Jean Kwok (2010):** Lives in Brooklyn, works in Chinatown. Chinatown.

***Open City* by Teju Cole (2012):** Ground Zero, Harlem, Columbia University, Carnegie Hall. Midtown.

***The Goldfinch* by Donna Tartt (2013):** Metropolitan Museum of Art, Park Avenue apartment. Upper East Side.

CLASSIC AND CONTEMPORARY JUVENILE AND YOUNG ADULT BOOKS SET IN NEW YORK CITY, AND THE AREAS MENTIONED

The Diviners by Libba Bray (1926): Chinatown.

***Tar Beach* by Faith Ringgold (1939):** Harlem rooftop. Harlem.

***Stuart Little* by E.B. White (1945):** Central Park model boat pond. Central Park.

***All-of-a-Kind Family* by Sydney Taylor (1951):** Lower East Side tenements. Lower East Side.

***The Cricket in Times Square* by George Selden (1960):** Newsstand in a Times Square subway station, Nedick's lunch counter, Chinatown, Washington Square Park. Midtown.

***It's Like This Cat* by Emily Cheney Neville (1963):** Coney Island, Fulton Fish Market, Bronx Zoo. Brooklyn.

***The Genie of Sutton Place* by George Selden (1973):** Sutton Place. Upper East Side.

***Harriet the Spy* by Louise Fitzhugh (1964):** Her house is near Carl Schultz Park on East 87th Street. Also Lexington Candy Shop. Upper East Side.

***The Pushcart War* by Jean Merrill (1964):** Based on the author's experience growing up. Greenwich Village.

***The Jazz Man* by Mary Hays Weik (1966):** Harlem.

***From the Mixed-Up Files of Mrs. Basil E. Frankweiler* by E.L. Konigsburg (1967):** The Met, Grand Central, New York Public Library, Donnell Library, The UN. Upper East Side.

***The Young Unicorns* by Madeline L'Engle (1968):** Cathedral of St. John the Divine. Upper West Side.

***The Pigman and Me* by Paul Zindel (1991):** Staten Island.

***Tales of a Fourth Grade Nothing* by Judy Blume (1972):** 25 West 68th Street, her apartment, Huckster Playground, Bloomingdale's. Upper West Side.

***The Princess Diaries* by Meg Cabot (2000):** Greenwich Village, Plaza Hotel. Greenwich Village.

***Gossip Girl* by Cecily von Ziegesar (2002):** based on the Nightingale-Bamford School, Central Park. Upper East Side.

***City of Bones* by Cassandra Clare (2005):** Brooklyn.

***Percy Jackson & the Olympians: #1: The Lightning Thief* by Rick Riordan (2005):** Metropolitan Museum of Art. Upper East Side.

***The Night Tourist* by Katherine Marsh (2008):** Grand Central Whisper Gallery, White Horse Tavern, Bethesda Fountain, Chumley's, 79th Street Boat Basin, New York Public Library. Midtown.

***When You Reach Me* by Rebecca Stead (2009):** Upper West Side.

***Dash & Lilly's Books of Dares* by Rachel Cohn and David Levithan (2010):** The Strand, Max Brenner's, Dyker Heights, FAO Schwartz. Greenwich Village.

***Time Riders* by Alex Scarrow (2010):** Williamsburg Bridge. Lower East Side.

***Better Nate Than Ever* by Tim Federle (2013):** Times Square, Port Authority, Madison Square Garden. Times Square.

***Under the Egg* by Laura Marx Fitzgerald (2014):** The Metropolitan Museum of Art. Upper East Side.

***At Your Service* by Jen Malone (2014):** The fictional Hotel Street Michele, Serendipity 3, Roosevelt Island Tram, FAO Schwartz, Apple Store, many other places. Midtown.

***Shadowshaper* by Daniel Jose Older (2015):** Brooklyn.

TEN OF THE MOST FAMOUS CHILDREN'S PICTURE BOOKS SET IN NEW YORK CITY

Listed by year of publication.

***The Little Red Lighthouse and the Great Gray Bridge* by Hildegarde H. Swift (1942):** The lighthouse is on the Hudson River under the "great gray" George Washington Bridge in Fort Washington. Upper Manhattan.

***Eloise* by Kay Thompson (1955):** The Plaza Hotel. Midtown.

***This Is New York* by M. (Miroslav) Sasek (1960):** All over Manhattan. Midtown.

***Lyle, Lyle, Crocodile* by Bernard Wager (1965):** Lyle lives on a house on East 88th Street. Upper East Side.

***How Pizza Came to Queens* by Dayal Kaur Khalsa (1989):** Queens.

***The Adventures of Taxi Dog* by Debra Barracca (1990):** All over. Manhattan.

***Next Stop Grand Central* by Maira Kalman (1999):** Grand Central Terminal. Midtown.

***Curious George in the Big City* by Margret and H.A. Rey (2001):** Macy's, Empire State Building, Radio City Music Hall, The Guggenheim. Midtown.

***They Came from the Bronx: How the Buffalo Were Saved from Extinction* by Neil Waldman (2001):** The Bronx Zoo. The Bronx

***The Man Who Walked Between the Towers* by Mordicai Gerstein (2003):** World Trade Center towers. Financial District.

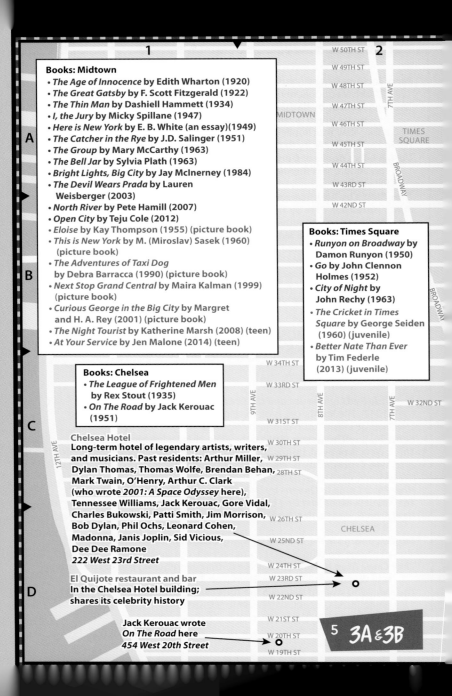

1

2

W 50TH ST
W 49TH ST
W 48TH ST
W 47TH ST
W 46TH ST
W 45TH ST
W 44TH ST
W 43RD ST
W 42ND ST

7TH AVE

MIDTOWN

TIMES SQUARE

BROADWAY

Books: Midtown
- *The Age of Innocence* by Edith Wharton (1920)
- *The Great Gatsby* by F. Scott Fitzgerald (1922)
- *The Thin Man* by Dashiell Hammett (1934)
- *I, the Jury* by Micky Spillane (1947)
- *Here is New York* by E. B. White (an essay)(1949)
- *The Catcher in the Rye* by J.D. Salinger (1951)
- *The Group* by Mary McCarthy (1963)
- *The Bell Jar* by Sylvia Plath (1963)
- *Bright Lights, Big City* by Jay McInerney (1984)
- *The Devil Wears Prada* by Lauren Weisberger (2003)
- *North River* by Pete Hamill (2007)
- *Open City* by Teju Cole (2012)
- *Eloise* by Kay Thompson (1955) (picture book)
- *This is New York* by M. (Miroslav) Sasek (1960) (picture book)
- *The Adventures of Taxi Dog* by Debra Barracca (1990) (picture book)
- *Next Stop Grand Central* by Maira Kalman (1999) (picture book)
- *Curious George in the Big City* by Margret and H. A. Rey (2001) (picture book)
- *The Night Tourist* by Katherine Marsh (2008) (teen)
- *At Your Service* by Jen Malone (2014) (teen)

A

B

Books: Times Square
- *Runyon on Broadway* by Damon Runyon (1950)
- *Go* by John Clennon Holmes (1952)
- *City of Night* by John Rechy (1963)
- *The Cricket in Times Square* by George Seiden (1960) (juvenile)
- *Better Nate Than Ever* by Tim Federle (2013) (juvenile)

BROADWAY

Books: Chelsea
- *The League of Frightened Men* by Rex Stout (1935)
- *On The Road* by Jack Kerouac (1951)

W 34TH ST
W 33RD ST
W 32ND ST
W 31ST ST
W 30TH ST
W 29TH ST
W 28TH ST
W 26TH ST
W 25ND ST
W 24TH ST
W 23RD ST
W 22ND ST
W 21ST ST
W 20TH ST
W 19TH ST

9TH AVE
8TH AVE
7TH AVE
12TH AVE

C

Chelsea Hotel
Long-term hotel of legendary artists, writers, and musicians. Past residents: Arthur Miller, Dylan Thomas, Thomas Wolfe, Brendan Behan, Mark Twain, O'Henry, Arthur C. Clark (who wrote *2001: A Space Odyssey* here), Tennessee Williams, Jack Kerouac, Gore Vidal, Charles Bukowski, Patti Smith, Jim Morrison, Bob Dylan, Phil Ochs, Leonard Cohen, Madonna, Janis Joplin, Sid Vicious, Dee Dee Ramone
222 West 23rd Street

CHELSEA

D

El Quijote restaurant and bar
In the Chelsea Hotel building; shares its celebrity history

Jack Kerouac wrote
On The Road here
454 West 20th Street

5 **3A & 3B**

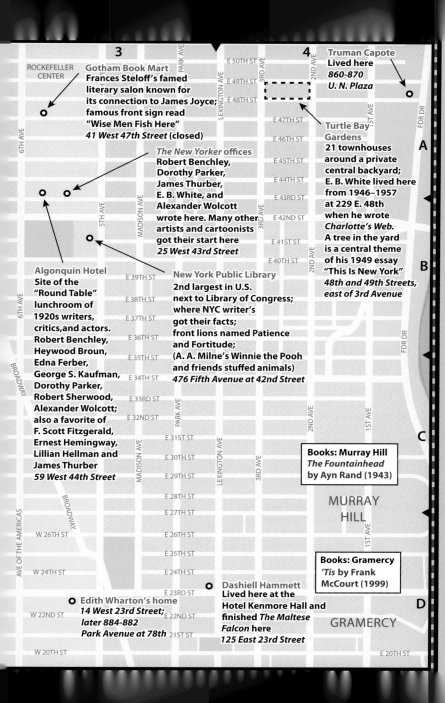

3

ROCKEFELLER CENTER

Gotham Book Mart
Frances Steloff's famed
literary salon known for
its connection to James Joyce;
famous front sign read
"Wise Men Fish Here"
41 West 47th Street (closed)

The New Yorker offices
**Robert Benchley,
Dorothy Parker,
James Thurber,
E. B. White, and
Alexander Wolcott**
wrote here. Many other
artists and cartoonists
got their start here
25 West 43rd Street

Algonquin Hotel
Site of the
"Round Table"
lunchroom of
1920s writers,
critics, and actors.
**Robert Benchley,
Heywood Broun,
Edna Ferber,
George S. Kaufman,
Dorothy Parker,
Robert Sherwood,
Alexander Wolcott;**
also a favorite of
**F. Scott Fitzgerald,
Ernest Hemingway,
Lillian Hellman** and
James Thurber
59 West 44th Street

New York Public Library
2nd largest in U.S.
next to Library of Congress;
where NYC writer's
got their facts;
front lions named Patience
and Fortitude;
(A. A. Milne's Winnie the Pooh
and friends stuffed animals)
476 Fifth Avenue at 42nd Street

4

Truman Capote
Lived here
*860-870
U. N. Plaza*

**Turtle Bay
Gardens**
21 townhouses
around a private
central backyard;
E. B. White lived here
from 1946–1957
at 229 E. 48th
when he wrote
Charlotte's Web.
A tree in the yard
is a central theme
of his 1949 essay
"This Is New York"
*48th and 49th Streets,
east of 3rd Avenue*

Books: Murray Hill
The Fountainhead
by Ayn Rand (1943)

MURRAY HILL

Books: Gramercy
'Tis by Frank
McCourt (1999)

Edith Wharton's home
*14 West 23rd Street;
later 884-882
Park Avenue at 78th*

Dashiell Hammett
Lived here at the
Hotel Kenmore Hall and
finished *The Maltese
Falcon* here
125 East 23rd Street

GRAMERCY

BOOKSTORES

Large chain bookstores: Manhattan

Barnes and Noble, Upper West Side: 2289 Broadway at 82nd Street, Upper West Side. barnesandnoble.com

Barnes and Noble, Upper East Side: 150 East 86th Street near Lexington Avenue, Upper East Side

Barnes and Noble, Citigroup: 160 East 54th Street at 3rd Avenue, Midtown East

Barnes and Noble, Fifth Avenue: 555 Fifth Avenue at 46th Street, Midtown East

Barnes and Noble, Tribeca: 97 Warren Street at Greenwich Avenue, Tribeca

Barnes and Noble, Union Square: 33 East 17th Street near Broadway, Flatiron

Barnes and Noble, Columbia University Bookstore: 2922 Broadway at 116th Street, Upper West Side

Amazon Bookstore: Time Warner Center, 10 Columbus Circle at 59th Street and Broadway, Upper West Side

Amazon Bookstore: 7 West 34th Street between 5th and 6th Avenues, Midtown South

Independent, General Book Stores: Manhattan

Book Culture: 536 West 112th Street near Broadway, Upper West Side (Morningside Heights). bookculture.com. Main store. General and scholarly books. New and used. Some textbooks. Near Columbia University.

Book Culture: 2915 Broadway at West 114th Street, Upper West Side (Morningside Heights). Neighborhood store. General books and gifts.

Book Culture on Columbus: 450 Columbus Avenue near 82nd Street, Upper West Side. General books and gifts.

Bookbook: 266 Bleecker Street near Morton Street, Greenwich Village. bookbooknyc.com. General book shop, emphasis on fiction/literature.

The Corner Bookstore: 1313 Madison Avenue at 93rd Street, Upper East Side. cornerbookstorenyc.com. Specializes in bestsellers, children's, and travel books.

Crawford Doyle Booksellers: 1082 Madison Avenue at 81st Street, Upper East Side. crawforddoyle.com

McNally Jackson: 52 Prince Street near Mulberry Street, Soho. mcnallyjackson.com. Coffee, new releases, book printing machine for books on demand.

New York University Bookstore: 726 Broadway at Waverly Place, East Village. bookstores.nyu.edu. General books, textbooks, and gifts.

Posman Books in Chelsea Market: 75 Ninth Avenue, Chelsea. posmanbooks.com. General neighborhood-style bookstore.

Posman Books in Rockefeller Center: 30 Rockefeller Plaza (concourse) near West 50th Street, Midtown West. posmanbooks.com. General neighborhood-style bookstore.

Rizzoli Bookstore: 1133 Broadway at West 26th Street, Flatiron District. rizzoliusa.com. General bookstore plus illustrated art, design, and fashion books.

Shakespeare & Co.: 939 Lexington Avenue near 69th Street, Upper East Side. shakeandco.com. General bookstore plus textbooks for Hunter and Marymount colleges. Book printing machine.

Three Lives & Co.: 154 West 10th Street at Waverly Place, Greenwich Village. threelives.com. Local community bookstore since 1968. All types of books.

Unoppressive Non-Imperialist Bargain Books: 34 Carmine Street near Bleecker Street, West Village. unoppressivebooks.blogspot.com. Small bookstore with all discounted books: music, art, philosophy, literature. Shares the space with Carmine Street Comics.

Used Books (also Out-of-Print and Rare Books): Manhattan and Brooklyn
Manhattan

Alabaster Bookshop: 122 Fourth Avenue at 12th Street, East Village

Argosy Book Store: 116 East 59th Street near Park Avenue, Midtown East. argosybooks.com. Elegant, old-school six-story bookstore since 1925. Used and rare books.

Book-Off: 49 West 45th Street between 5th and 6th Avenues, Midtown. (212) 685-1410. bookoffusa.com. Used books, CDs, video games, manga, movies, home objects, and electronics.

Codex: 1 Bleecker Street at Bowery, East Village. Has an emphasis on literary fiction and art books.

East Village Books: 99 St. Mark's Place, East Village. buyusedbooksnewyork.com. Small but hip basement-level used book and record store with emphasis on literature and the arts.

Housing Works Bookstore Cafe: 126 Crosby Street near East Houston Street, Soho. housingworks.org/bookstore. A volunteer-run nonprofit. All type of books, including rare and out-of-print, especially the arts. Writing workshops.

Mast Books: 66 Avenue A near East 4th Street, East Village. mastbooks.com. Sells used and rare volumes on a variety of topics. Hip and edgy independent West Village bookstore.

Mercer Street Books & Records: 206 Mercer Street at Bleecker Street, West Village. mercerstreetbooks.com. Basement-level used books. Hipster.

Strand Bookstore ("The Strand"): 828 Broadway at 12th Street, East Village. (212) 473-1452. strandbooks.com. Legendary New York used bookstore (since 1927), and the largest. All type of books plus a floor of rare books. Eighteen miles of books.

Westsider Rare and Used Books: 2246 Broadway near 80th Street, Upper West Side. (212) 362-0706. westsiderbooks.com. Used general books, records, and DVDs. Seen in the John Turturro film *Fading Gigolo* starring Woody Allen, as a bookstore called "M. Schwartz and Sons: Rare & Used Books."

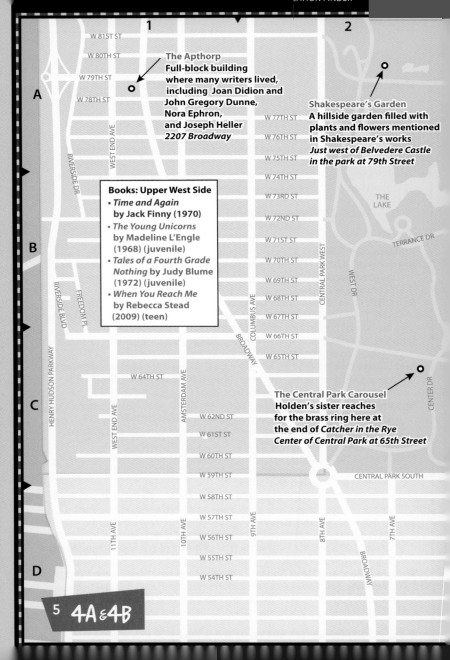

1

W 81ST ST
W 80TH ST
W 79TH ST
W 78TH ST

A

The Apthorp
Full-block building
where many writers lived,
including Joan Didion and
John Gregory Dunne,
Nora Ephron,
and Joseph Heller
2207 Broadway

2

Shakespeare's Garden
A hillside garden filled with
plants and flowers mentioned
in Shakespeare's works
Just west of Belvedere Castle
in the park at 79th Street

W 77TH ST
W 76TH ST
W 75TH ST
W 74TH ST
W 73RD ST
W 72ND ST
W 71ST ST
W 70TH ST
W 69TH ST
W 68TH ST
W 67TH ST
W 66TH ST
W 65TH ST

THE
LAKE

TERRANCE DR

RIVERSIDE DR
WEST END AVE

Books: Upper West Side
- *Time and Again*
  by Jack Finny (1970)
- *The Young Unicorns*
  by Madeline L'Engle
  (1968) (juvenile)
- *Tales of a Fourth Grade*
  Nothing by Judy Blume
  (1972) (juvenile)
- *When You Reach Me*
  by Rebecca Stead
  (2009) (teen)

B

RIVERSIDE BLVD
FREEDOM PL
HENRY HUDSON PARKWAY

COLUMBUS AVE
BROADWAY
CENTRAL PARK WEST
WEST DR

CENTER DR

C

W 64TH ST

WEST END AVE
AMSTERDAM AVE

W 62ND ST
W 61ST ST
W 60TH ST
W 59TH ST
W 58TH ST
W 57TH ST
W 56TH ST
W 55TH ST
W 54TH ST

The Central Park Carousel
Holden's sister reaches
for the brass ring here at
the end of *Catcher in the Rye*
Center of Central Park at 65th Street

CENTRAL PARK SOUTH

11TH AVE
10TH AVE
9TH AVE
8TH AVE
7TH AVE
BROADWAY

D

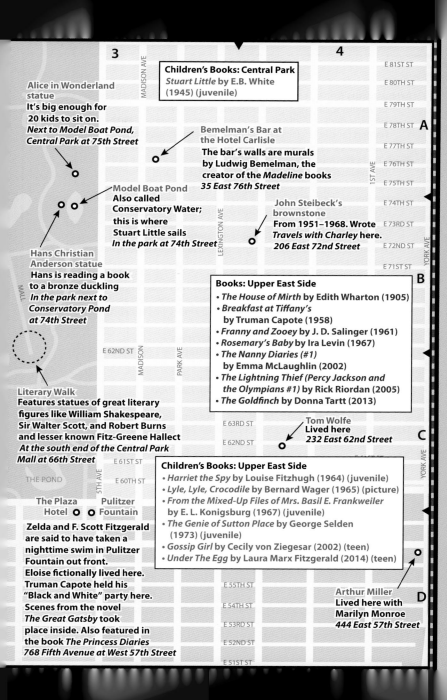

3 **4**

MADISON AVE · 1ST AVE · LEXINGTON AVE · YORK AVE · PARK AVE · 5TH AVE · MALL · THE POND

E 81ST ST
E 80TH ST
E 79TH ST
E 78TH ST — **A**
E 77TH ST
E 76TH ST
E 75TH ST
E 74TH ST
E 73RD ST
E 72ND ST
E 71ST ST — **B**
E 62ND ST
E 63RD ST
E 62ND ST — **C**
E 61ST ST
E 60TH ST
E 55TH ST
E 54TH ST — **D**
E 53RD ST
E 52ND ST
E 51ST ST
E 66TH ST

Children's Books: Central Park
Stuart Little by E.B. White
(1945) (juvenile)

Alice in Wonderland statue
It's big enough for 20 kids to sit on.
Next to Model Boat Pond, Central Park at 75th Street

Bemelman's Bar at the Hotel Carlisle
The bar's walls are murals by Ludwig Bemelman, the creator of the *Madeline* books
35 East 76th Street

Model Boat Pond
Also called Conservatory Water; this is where Stuart Little sails
In the park at 74th Street

John Steibeck's brownstone
From 1951–1968. Wrote *Travels with Charley* here.
206 East 72nd Street

Hans Christian Anderson statue
Hans is reading a book to a bronze duckling
In the park next to Conservatory Pond at 74th Street

Books: Upper East Side
• *The House of Mirth* by Edith Wharton (1905)
• *Breakfast at Tiffany's* by Truman Capote (1958)
• *Franny and Zooey* by J. D. Salinger (1961)
• *Rosemary's Baby* by Ira Levin (1967)
• *The Nanny Diaries (#1)* by Emma McLaughlin (2002)
• *The Lightning Thief (Percy Jackson and the Olympians #1)* by Rick Riordan (2005)
• *The Goldfinch* by Donna Tartt (2013)

Literary Walk
Features statues of great literary figures like William Shakespeare, Sir Walter Scott, and Robert Burns and lesser known Fitz-Greene Hallect
At the south end of the Central Park Mall at 66th Street

Tom Wolfe
Lived here
232 East 62nd Street

Children's Books: Upper East Side
• *Harriet the Spy* by Louise Fitzhugh (1964) (juvenile)
• *Lyle, Lyle, Crocodile* by Bernard Wager (1965) (picture)
• *From the Mixed-Up Files of Mrs. Basil E. Frankweiler* by E. L. Konigsburg (1967) (juvenile)
• *The Genie of Sutton Place* by George Selden (1973) (juvenile)
• *Gossip Girl* by Cecily von Ziegesar (2002) (teen)
• *Under The Egg* by Laura Marx Fitzgerald (2014) (teen)

The Plaza Hotel   **Pulitzer Fountain**
Zelda and F. Scott Fitzgerald are said to have taken a nighttime swim in Pulitzer Fountain out front. Eloise fictionally lived here. Truman Capote held his "Black and White" party here. Scenes from the novel *The Great Gatsby* took place inside. Also featured in the book *The Princess Diaries*
768 Fifth Avenue at West 57th Street

Arthur Miller
Lived here with Marilyn Monroe
444 East 57th Street

Brooklyn

Archestratus Books + Foods: 160 Huron Street near Manhattan Avenue, Greenpoint, Brooklyn. archestrat.us. One of New York's newest bookstores is dedicated to all things delicious and literary. Archestratus, named for the ancient Greek poet and food lover, carries cookbooks, food memoirs, vintage culinary collections, and more. It also has a cafe.

Book Thug Nation: 100 North 3rd Street near Berry Street, Williamsburg, Brooklyn. bookthugnation.com. A bookstore and community space. Specializes in used literary fiction, poetry, and pulps.

Human Relations: 1067 Flushing Avenue near Knickerbocker Avenue, East Williamsburg, Bushwick, Brooklyn. humanrelationsbooks.com

Unnameable Books: 600 Vanderbilt Avenue, Project Heights, Brooklyn. (718) 789-1534. unnameablebooks.blogspot.com. A new and used bookstore and community space. Specializes in used literary fiction, poetry, and pulps.

Specialty Bookstores: Manhattan

Most museums like the Met and MoMa have large bookstores with books of the museums' specialties. There is a list of specialty museums later in the book.

African–American

Sister's Uptown Bookstore & Cultural Center: 1942 Amsterdam Avenue, Harlem. sistersuptownbookstore.com

Art/Photography/Fashion

Printed Matter: 231 11th Avenue at 26th Street, Chelsea. printedmatter.org. A nonprofit book center that sells books made and distributed by artists.

Dashwood Books: 33 Bond Street between Lafayette Street and Bowery. New, used, and rare photography books.

Karma: 21 Downing Street between Bedford and Bleecker Streets. Bookstore and gallery featuring new, used, and rare artists' publications.

Morrison Hotel Gallery: 116 Prince Street, second floor, between Wooster and Greene Streets. Rock music photo gallery with many oversize rock 'n' roll photography books.

Taschen Store New York: 107 Greene Street near Prince. taschen.com

Ursus Books: 981 Madison Avenue between 76th and 77th Streets, Upper East Side. ursusbooks.com. Rare and out-of-print art and photography books.

Bookmarc: 400 Bleecker Street at West 11th Street. A small, eclectic selection of art books in this Marc Jacobs store.

Chess

Chess Forum: 219 Thompson Street near West 3rd Street, Greenwich Village. chessforum.com. All things chess.

Fred Wilson Chess Books: 80 East 11th Street, upstairs, Greenwich Village. fredwilsonchess.com

Comic Books

JHU Comic Books: 481 Third Avenue at East 33rd Street

Cookbooks

Bonnie Slotnick Cookbooks: 28 East Second Street, East Village. (212) 989-8962. bonnieslotnickcookbooks.com. Relocated from its original West Village location, Bonnie Slotnick Cookbooks displays and sells vintage, rare, and international cookbooks.

Kitchen Arts & Letters: 1435 Lexington Avenue near 93rd Street, Upper East Side. kitchenartsandletters.com. "The country's largest store devoted to books on food and wine." Over 700 cooking titles.

Drama: Theater

The Drama Book Shop: 250 West 40th Street near 8th Avenue, Midtown West. (212) 944-0595. dramabookshop.com. The Tony Award–winning Drama Book Shop, now celebrating its one hundredth anniversary. Theater, plays, musicals, gifts.

Theatre Circle bookstore: 268 West 44th Street #1, Times Square. (212) 391-7075. Theater books and gifts.

Fashion Magazines

Around the World: 28 West 40th Street. Fashion magazines.

Foreign Language
French

Albertine: 927 5th Avenue at 79th Street, Upper East Side. albertine.com. Offers over 14,000 titles from French-speaking countries.

Israeli

Sefer Israel: 213 West 35th Street #302a, between 7th and 8th Avenues

Japanese

Kinokuniya Bookstores: 1073 6th Avenue, Theater District, Midtown West. (212) 869-1700. kinokuniya.com

Korean

Koryo Books: 35 West 32nd Street between 5th and 6th Avenues. koryobooks.com

Chinese

Oriental Culture Enterprises: 13-17 Elizabeth Street between Canal and Bayard Streets. oceweb.com

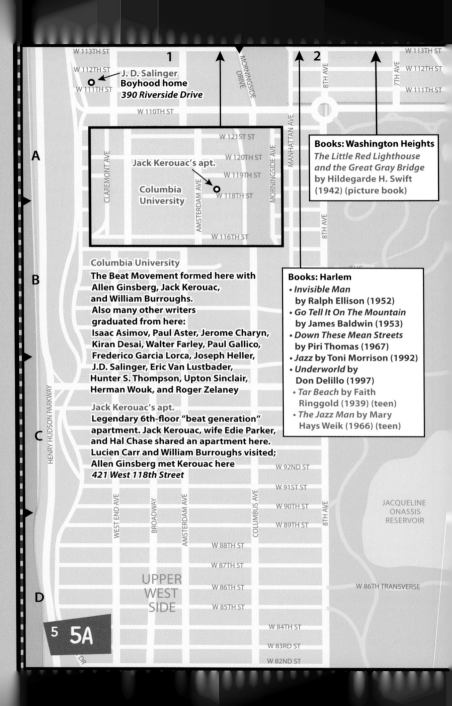

W 113TH ST
W 112TH ST
W 111TH ST

1

MORNINGSIDE DRIVE

2

8TH AVE
7TH AVE

W 113TH ST
W 112TH ST
W 111TH ST

J. D. Salinger
Boyhood home
390 Riverside Drive

W 110TH ST

W 121ST ST

MANHATTAN AVE

Books: Washington Heights
*The Little Red Lighthouse
and the Great Gray Bridge*
by Hildegarde H. Swift
(1942) (picture book)

A

CLAREMONT AVE

Jack Kerouac's apt.

**Columbia
University**

AMSTERDAM AVE

MORNINGSIDE AVE

W 120TH ST
W 119TH ST
W 118TH ST

W 116TH ST

8TH AVE

B

Columbia University
**The Beat Movement formed here with
Allen Ginsberg, Jack Kerouac,
and William Burroughs.
Also many other writers
graduated from here:
Isaac Asimov, Paul Aster, Jerome Charyn,
Kiran Desai, Walter Farley, Paul Gallico,
Frederico Garcia Lorca, Joseph Heller,
J.D. Salinger, Eric Van Lustbader,
Hunter S. Thompson, Upton Sinclair,
Herman Wouk, and Roger Zelaney**

Books: Harlem
• *Invisible Man*
  by Ralph Ellison (1952)
• *Go Tell It On The Mountain*
  by James Baldwin (1953)
• *Down These Mean Streets*
  by Piri Thomas (1967)
• *Jazz* by Toni Morrison (1992)
• *Underworld* by
  Don Delillo (1997)
• *Tar Beach* by Faith
  Ringgold (1939) (teen)
• *The Jazz Man* by Mary
  Hays Weik (1966) (teen)

Jack Kerouac's apt.
**Legendary 6th-floor "beat generation"
apartment. Jack Kerouac, wife Edie Parker,
and Hal Chase shared an apartment here.
Lucien Carr and William Burroughs visited;
Allen Ginsberg met Kerouac here**
421 West 118th Street

HENRY HUDSON PARKWAY

C

W 92ND ST
W 91ST ST
W 90TH ST
W 89TH ST

WEST END AVE
BROADWAY
AMSTERDAM AVE
COLUMBUS AVE
8TH AVE

JACQUELINE
ONASSIS
RESERVOIR

W 88TH ST
W 87TH ST

**UPPER
WEST
SIDE**

W 86TH ST
W 85TH ST

W 86TH TRANSVERSE

D

W 84TH ST
W 83RD ST
W 82ND ST

DR

5 5A

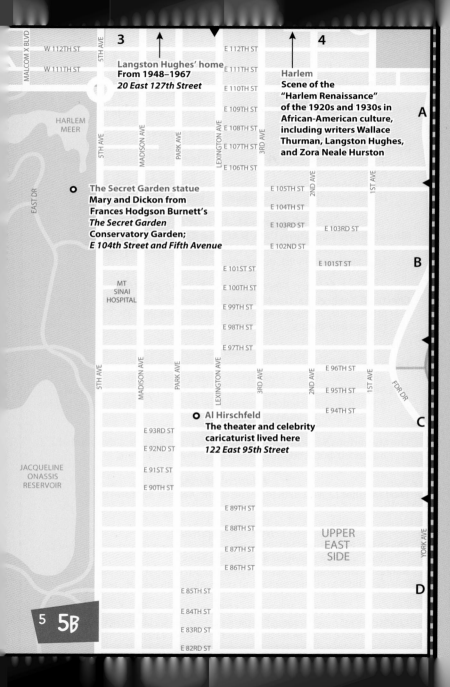

3

4

W 112TH ST
W 111TH ST

E 112TH ST
E 111TH ST
E 110TH ST
E 109TH ST

Langston Hughes' home
From 1948–1967
20 East 127th Street

Harlem
Scene of the
"Harlem Renaissance"
of the 1920s and 1930s in
African-American culture,
including writers Wallace
Thurman, Langston Hughes,
and Zora Neale Hurston

A

MALCOM X BLVD
5TH AVE

HARLEM
MEER

5TH AVE
MADISON AVE
PARK AVE
LEXINGTON AVE
3RD AVE
2ND AVE
1ST AVE

E 108TH ST
E 107TH ST
E 106TH ST

EAST DR

○ The Secret Garden statue
Mary and Dickon from
Frances Hodgson Burnett's
The Secret Garden
Conservatory Garden;
E 104th Street and Fifth Avenue

E 105TH ST
E 104TH ST
E 103RD ST
E 102ND ST

E 103RD ST

E 101ST ST

B

MT
SINAI
HOSPITAL

E 101ST ST
E 100TH ST
E 99TH ST
E 98TH ST
E 97TH ST

5TH AVE
MADISON AVE
PARK AVE
LEXINGTON AVE
3RD AVE
2ND AVE
1ST AVE

E 96TH ST
E 95TH ST
E 94TH ST

FDR DR

C

○ Al Hirschfeld
The theater and celebrity
caricaturist lived here
122 East 95th Street

E 93RD ST
E 92ND ST
E 91ST ST
E 90TH ST

JACQUELINE
ONASSIS
RESERVOIR

E 89TH ST
E 88TH ST
E 87TH ST
E 86TH ST

UPPER
EAST
SIDE

YORK AVE

D

E 85TH ST
E 84TH ST
E 83RD ST
E 82RD ST

Judaica

J. Levine Books and Judaica: 5 West 30th Street near Fifth Avenue, Chelsea.
    levinejudaica.com

West Side Judaica & Bookstore: 2412 Broadway, Upper West Side

Juvenile (Children's Books)

Bank Street Book Store: 2780 Broadway at 107th Street, Upper West Side.
    bankstreetbooks.com. Large children's bookstore. Books for "children,
    parents, and teachers."

Books of Wonder: 18 West 18th Street near 5th Avenue, Chelsea.
    booksofwonder.com. Large children's bookstore.

LGBTQ, Feminist, Activist (see Politics)

Bluestockings Bookstore, Cafe, & Activist Center: 172 Allen Street at
    Stanton Street, Lower East Side. (212) 777-6028. bluestockings.com.
    Specializes in feminist, queer, and activist.

Military First Editions/Winston Churchill

Chartwell Booksellers/The Military Bookman: 55 East 52nd Street near
    5th Avenue, Midtown East. churchillbooks.com. Winston Churchill; rare
    military and literary.

Music

The Julliard Store: 144 West 66th Street near Broadway, Upper West Side.
    thejulliardstore.com. Sheet music, scores, classical music.

Jazz Record Center: 236 West 26th Street between 7th and 8th Avenues,
    Room 804. jazzrecordcenter.com. New and used jazz records and books.

Mystery

The Mysterious Bookshop: 58 Warren Street near West Broadway, Tribeca.
    mysteriousbookshop.com. A mecca for mystery readers.

Nautical/Marine

West Marine: 12 West 37th Street near Fifth Avenue, Midtown West.
    westmarine.com

New Age/Spiritual

The Quest Bookshop: 240 East 53rd Street, Midtown East. questbookshop.
    com. New age, spiritual, and esoteric books.

Namaste Bookshop: 2 West 14th Street at 5th Avenue, Greenwich Village.
    Sells books on philosophy and spirituality; also crystals, jewelry.

New York City (Official Publications)

CityStore: 1 Centre Street at Chambers Street, Financial District. nyc.gov/
    citystore. Official publications and NYC memorabilia.

Political

Revolution Books: 437 Malcolm X Boulevard (Lenox Avenue) at 132nd Street, Harlem. revolutionbooksnyc.org. "The center of a movement for revolution."

Rare Books

J.N. Bartfield Galleries and Fine & Rare Books: 30 West 57th Street, 3rd floor. bartfield.com. Rare books, first editions, American West art.

Bauman Rare Books: 535 Madison Avenue near 54th Street. baumanrarebooks.com. Rare books and autographs.

Imperial Fine Art Books: 790 Madison Avenue #200, near 67th Street. imperialfinebooks.com. Leatherbound books and those with fine bindings.

Religious Books

Logos Bookstore: 1575 York Avenue, Upper East Side. logosbookstorenyc. com. Judeo-Christian books.

Science Fiction/Fantasy

Forbidden Planet: 832 Broadway near 12th Street, East Village. fpnyc.com. Science fiction, comics, anime.

Travel

Idlewild Books: 170 Seventh Avenue South at Perry Street, Greenwich Village. Specializing in travel books in different languages, and language lessons.

General Bookshops: Brooklyn Bookstores

Barnes & Noble: 106 Court Street between State and Schermerhorn Streets, Brooklyn Heights, Brooklyn. barnesandnoble.com

Barnes & Noble: 267 7th Avenue between 6th Street and 5th Avenue, Park Slope, Brooklyn. barnesandnoble.com

Book Culture: 26-09 Jackson Avenue, Long Island City, Queens. bookculture. com

Bookmark Shoppe: 8415 3rd Avenue between 84th and 85th Streets, Bay Ridge, Brooklyn. bookmarkshoppe.com

Books Are Magic: 225 Smith Street at Butler Street, Cobble Hill, Brooklyn. booksaremagic.net

Boulevard Books & Cafe: 7518 13th Avenue between Bay Ridge Parkway and 76th Street, Bensonhurst, Brooklyn

Community Bookstore: 143 7th Avenue between Garfield Place and Carroll Street, Park Slope, Brooklyn. communitybookstore.net

Greenlight Bookstore: 686 Fulton Street at South Portland Avenue, Fort Greene, Brooklyn. greenlightbookstore.com

Greenlight Bookstore: 632 Flatbush Avenue between Hawthorne and Fenimore Streets, Prospect Lefferts Gardens, Brooklyn. greenlightbookstore. com

Books: Brooklyn
- *A Tree Grows in Brooklyn* by Betty Smith (1943)
- *Death of a Salesman* by Arthur Miller (1949) (Play)
- *Last Exit to Brooklyn* by Hubert Selby Jr. (1964)
- *The Chosen* by Chaim Potok (1967)
- *The New York Trilogy* by Paul Auster
  (1985, 1986, 1986)
- *Angela's Ashes* by Frank McCourt (1996)
- *Motherless Brooklyn* by Jonathan Lethem (1999)
- *The Amazing Adventures of Kavalier & Clay*
  by Michael Chabon (2000)
- *The Fortress of Solitude* by Jonathan Lethem (2003)
- *It's Like This Cat* by Emily Cheny Neville
  (1963) (juvenile)
- *City of Bones* by Cassandra Clare (2005) (teen)
- *Shadowshaper* by Daniel Jose Older (2015) (teen)

Manhattan

Truman Capote's house
70 Willow Street,
Brooklyn Heights

Norman Mailer
Lived here on the 4th floor
142 Columbia Heights (street)
in Brooklyn Heights

Books: Staten Island
The Pigman by Paul Zindel
(1968) (young adult)

Staten Island

5 **6A**

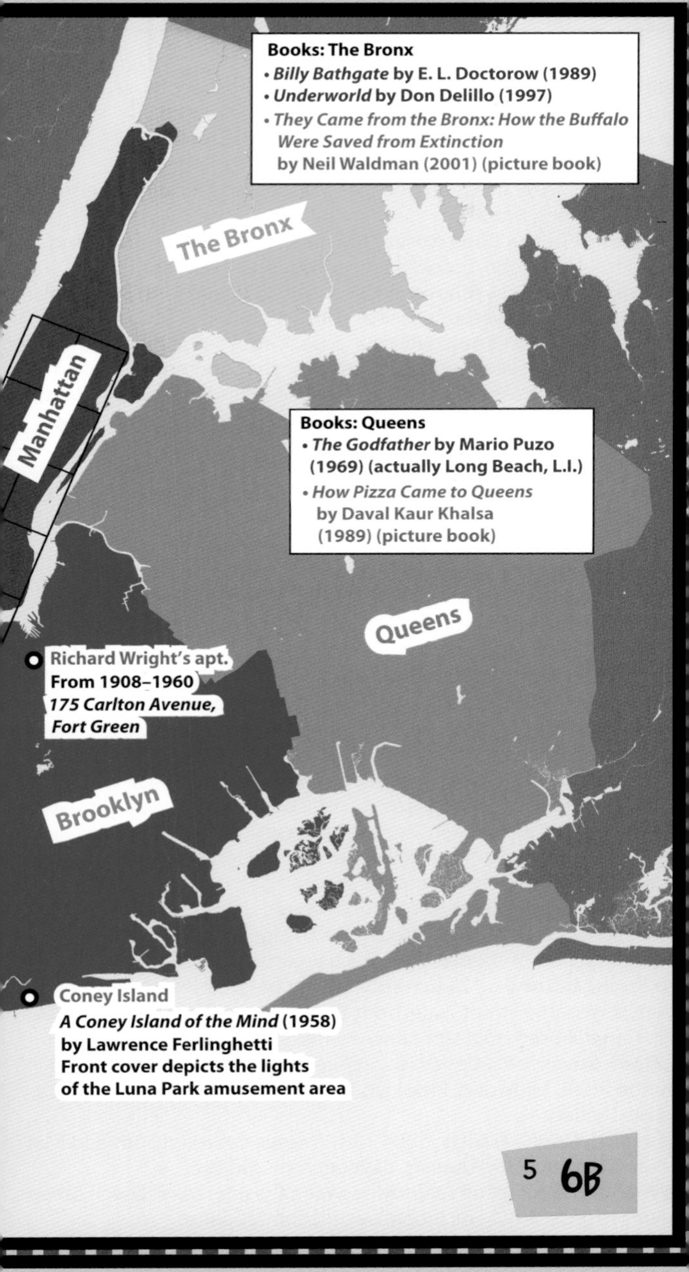

Books: The Bronx
- *Billy Bathgate* by E. L. Doctorow (1989)
- *Underworld* by Don Delillo (1997)
- *They Came from the Bronx: How the Buffalo Were Saved from Extinction* by Neil Waldman (2001) (picture book)

The Bronx

Manhattan

Books: Queens
- *The Godfather* by Mario Puzo (1969) (actually Long Beach, L.I.)
- *How Pizza Came to Queens* by Daval Kaur Khalsa (1989) (picture book)

Queens

○ **Richard Wright's apt. From 1908–1960** *175 Carlton Avenue, Fort Green*

Brooklyn

○ Coney Island
A Coney Island of the Mind (1958) by Lawrence Ferlinghetti Front cover depicts the lights of the Luna Park amusement area

5 **6B**

Hullabaloo Books: 658 Franklin Avenue between Prospect Place and St. Mark's Avenue, Crown Heights, Brooklyn. New and used.

McNally Jackson: 76 North 4th Street, WIlliamsburg, Brooklyn. mcnallyjackson.com

Molasses Books: 770 Hart Street between Wilson and Knickerbocker Avenues, Bushwick, Brooklyn

The Powerhouse Arena Bookstore: 37 Main Street, between Front and Water Streets, Dumbo, Brooklyn. powerhousearena.com

Powerhouse on 8th: 1111 8th Avenue between 12th and 11th Streets, Park Slope, Brooklyn. powerhouseon8th.com

Spoonbill & Sugartown Booksellers: 218 Bedford Avenue between 4th and 5th Streets, Williamsburg's North Side, Brooklyn. spoonbillbooks.com

Terrace Books: 242 Prospect Park West between Windsor Place and Prospect Avenue, Windsor Terrace, Brooklyn. communitybookstore.net/terrace-books

Word Bookstore: 126 Franklin Street at Milton Street between Noble Street and Greenpoint Avenue, Greenpoint, Brooklyn. wordbookstores.com

Specialty Bookstores: Brooklyn

Archipelago Books: 232 3rd Street Suite A-111 at 4th Avenue, Gowanus, Brooklyn. archipelagobooks.org. Specializing in books in translation.

Berl's Brooklyn Poetry Shop: 141 Front Street, Dumbo, Brooklyn. berlspoetry.com

Better Read Than Dead: 867 Broadway between Belvidere Street and Lewis Avenue, Bushwick, Brooklyn. Used books, part of a flea market.

Black Sea Bookstore: 3175 Coney Island Avenue at Brighton Beach Avenue, Coney Island, Brooklyn. Russian books.

Book Maze: 1122 Coney Island Avenue between Glenwood Road and Avenue H, Flatbush, Brooklyn. bookmazecity.com. Books for a Russian audience.

Desert Island: 540 Metropolitan Avenue between Lorimer Street and Union Avenue, Williamsburg North Side, Brooklyn. desertislandbrooklyn.com. Comics, graphic novels, art, etc.

Edamama Cute Cuts & More: 568 Union Avenue, Unit B, between Richardson and Frost Streets, Williamsburg North Side, Brooklyn. edamama.com. A selection of children's books, haircutting.

Freebird Books & Goods: 123 Columbia Street between Kane and Irving Streets, Columbia Street Waterfront District, Brooklyn. freebirdbooks.com. General used bookstore and events.

Here's a Book Store: 1964 Coney Island Avenue between Avenue P and Quentin Road, Midwood, Brooklyn. New and used children's, Judaica, and best sellers.

Eichler's Jewish Books & Gifts: 5004 13th Avenue between 50th and 51st Streets, Borough Park, Queens. eichlers.com. Judaica.

Judaica World: 329 Kingston Avenue between President and Union Streets, Crown Heights, Brooklyn. judaica-world.com. Judaica.

Maktaba Dar-Us-Salam: 486 Atlantic Avenue between 3rd Avenue and Nevins Street, Boerum Hill, Brooklyn. darussalamny.com. Specializes in Islamic books.

Melville House: 46 John Street, Dumbo, Brooklyn. mhpbooks.com. Publishing house bookshop.

Pioneer Books: 289 Van Brunt Street, Red Hook, Brooklyn. pioneerworks.org. Bookstore.

PopFuzz: 123 Wythe Avenue between 9th and 10th Streets, Williamsburg North Side, Brooklyn. popfuzz.net. Specializing in pop culture books, videos, and toys.

Quimby's Bookstore NYC: 536 Metropolitan Avenue between Union Avenue and Lorimer Street, Williamsburg, Brooklyn. Specializing in zines.

Singularity & Co.: 18 Bridge Street between Plymouth and John Streets, Vinegar Hill, Brooklyn. Specializing in sci-fi.

Stories Bookshop + Storytelling Lab: 458 Bergen Street between 5th and Flatbush Avenues, Park Slope, Brooklyn. storiesbk.com. Children's books and storytelling.

Umbrage Editions: 111 Front Street, suite 208, between Washington and Adams Streets, Dumbo, Brooklyn. umbragebooks.com. Art books, art gallery, and art book publisher.

Z Berman Books: 1586 Coney Island Avenue between Locust Avenue and Avenue L, Midwood, Brooklyn. zbermanbooks.com. Judaica.

Queens General Interest Bookstores

The Astoria Bookshop: 31–29 31st Street between Broadway and 31st Avenue, Astoria, Queens. astoriabookshop.com

Austin Bookshop: 10429 Jamaica Avenue, Richmond Hill, Queens. Sixty years old.

Kew & Willow Books: 81-63 Lefferts Boulevard., Kew Gardens, Queens. thequeensbookshop.com

Topos Bookstore Cafe: 788 Woodward Avenue between Madison Street and Putnam Avenue, Ridgewood, Queens. toposbookstore.com. General bookstore and coffee shop.

Queens Used Bookstores

Turn the Page . . . Again: 39–15 Bell Boulevard between 39th and 40th Avenues, Bayside, Queens. turnthepageagain.com. General used books, run by a non-profit. Most books under $5.

Staten Island Bookstores

Barnes and Noble: 2245 Richmond Avenue, Heartland Village, Staten Island

Everything Goes Book Cafe and Neighborhood Stage: 208 Bay Street, Tompkinsville, Staten Island

New York City Superheroes and Comic Book Stores

NEW YORK CITY SUPERHERO LOCATIONS

NEW YORK IS A SUPER CITY made for superheroes and supervillains. Its big buildings and big spaces make for big battles. Many Marvel comics make New York City their base, including Spider-Man, The Fantastic Four, Daredevil, and the Avengers. New York is also the thinly disguised Gotham City of Batman and Superman's Metropolis. Here are some locations from superhero comics.

COMIC BOOK STORES
Manhattan

Alex's MVP Cards: 1577 York Avenue, Upper East Side. cardsandcomics.com

Carmine Street Comics: 34 Carmine Street near Bleecker Street, Greenwich Village. carminestreetcomics.com

Chameleon Comics: 3 Maiden Lane at Broadway, Financial District. chameleoncomics.com

Forbidden Planet: 832 Broadway at 13th Street, East Village. fpnyc.com

JHU Comic Books: 32 East 32nd Street near Fifth Avenue, Murray Hill; and 299B New Dorp Lane, Staten Island. jhucomicbooks.com. Formerly Jim Hanley's Universe.

Kinokuniya: 1073 6th Avenue, top floor, near 41st Street, Midtown West. kinokuniya.com

Metropolis Comics and Collectibles: 36 West 37th Street, 6th floor, near 6th Avenue, Midtown West. metropoliscomics.com. Gallery by appointment.

Midtown Comics: 200 West 40th Street, Midtown West; 459 Lexington Avenue at 45th Street, Midtown East; 64 Fulton Street at Gold Street, Financial District. midtowncomics.com

Mysterious Time Machine: 418 6th Avenue at 9th Street (basement level), Greenwich Village. facebook.com/mysterioustimemachine

St. Mark's Comics: 11 St. Mark's Place, Greenwich Village; and 148 Montague Street, Brooklyn. facebook.com/stmarkscomicsny

Montasy Comics: 431 Fifth Avenue, second floor, near 38th Street; and 70–17 Austin, second floor, Forest Hills, Queens. montasycomics.com

Strand Book Store: 828 Broadway at 12th Street, Greenwich Village. strandbooks.com

1   WHITE ST   **2**

LAFAYETTE ST

CENTRE ST

NKLIN ST

Timely Plaza (fictional)
- Outside of She-Hulk Jennifer Walter's office, "near the New York Supreme Court Building"
- Named after Timely Productions, the original name of Marvel Comics

WO

A

W BRO

CHURCH

BROADWAY

Foley Square
Centre St. and Pearl Street
Spider-Man 3: Just as Gwen kisses Spider-Man and the celebration for him starts, Sandman arrives and Spider-Man has to stop him from robbing an armored car

RIVER TERR.

N END AVE

City Hall
Broadway at Park Row
- *Spiderman:* Peter Parker marries Mary Jane Watson
- *Spider-Man 2:* Spider-Man drops off Aunt May after rescuing her

SPRUC

VESEY ST

B

ANN ST

World Trade Center (original Twin Towers)
- Featured in many superhero comics
- Superman flies Lois over them in *Superman*

Ground Zero
Post-9/11, several superheroes pay tribute here

BROADWAY

NASSAU

WILLIAM ST

BATTERY PARK CITY

LIBERTY ST

PINE ST

GREENWICH ST

WALL ST

RECTOR ST

EXCHANGE PL

The New York Stock Exchange
Wall Street and Broad Street
In *The Dark Knight Rises*, Bane and his men take over the Stock Exchange; then Bane battles Batman and the police outside in the streets

BEAVER ST

C

BROAD ST

WHITEHALL ST

FINANCIAL DISTRICT

Ellis Island
In the first X-Men movie, the X-men battle Magento here and on Liberty Island

TUNNEL

Statue of Liberty
On Liberty Island
In 1960s comics, Spider-Man and the Human Torch used to meet secretly in the torch

D

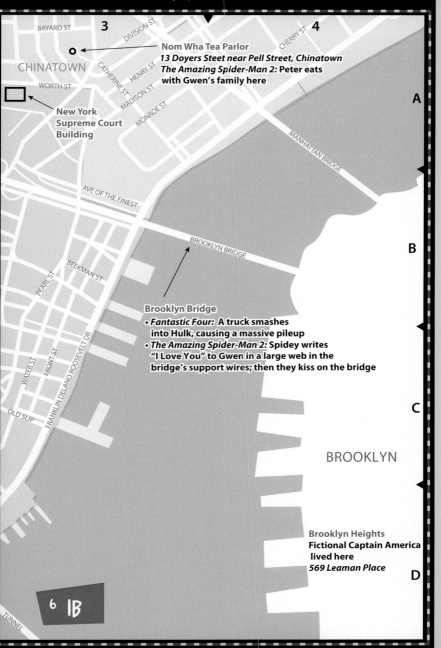

3   BAYARD ST   DIVISION ST   CHERRY ST   **4**

CHINATOWN

CATHERINE ST   HENRY ST   MADISON ST   MONROE ST

WORTH ST

Nom Wha Tea Parlor
13 Doyers Steet near Pell Street, Chinatown
The Amazing Spider-Man 2: Peter eats
with Gwen's family here

A

MANHATTAN BRIDGE

New York
Supreme Court
Building

AVE OF THE FINEST

BROOKLYN BRIDGE

B

BEEKMAN ST

PEARL ST

Brooklyn Bridge
• *Fantastic Four:* A truck smashes
  into Hulk, causing a massive pileup
• *The Amazing Spider-Man 2:* Spidey writes
  "I Love You" to Gwen in a large web in the
  bridge's support wires; then they kiss on the bridge

WATER ST   FRONT ST   FRANKLIN DELANO ROOSEVELT DR

OLD SLIP

C

BROOKLYN

Brooklyn Heights
Fictional Captain America
lived here
569 Leaman Place

D

6 1B

TUNNEL

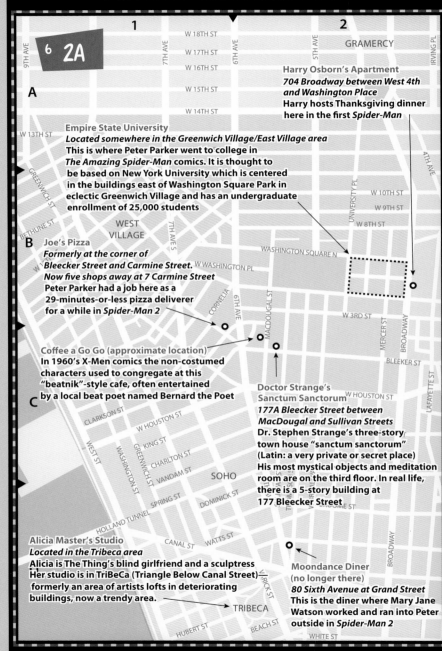

6 2A

1   **2**

W 18TH ST
W 17TH ST
W 16TH ST
W 15TH ST
W 14TH ST
W 13TH ST

GRAMERCY

A

Harry Osborn's Apartment
704 Broadway between West 4th and Washington Place
Harry hosts Thanksgiving dinner here in the first *Spider-Man*

Empire State University
Located somewhere in the Greenwich Village/East Village area
This is where Peter Parker went to college in *The Amazing Spider-Man* comics. It is thought to be based on New York University which is centered in the buildings east of Washington Square Park in eclectic Greenwich Village and has an undergraduate enrollment of 25,000 students

W 10TH ST
W 9TH ST
W 8TH ST

WEST VILLAGE

B

Joe's Pizza
Formerly at the corner of Bleecker Street and Carmine Street. Now five shops away at 7 Carmine Street
Peter Parker had a job here as a 29-minutes-or-less pizza deliverer for a while in *Spider-Man 2*

WASHINGTON SQUARE N

WASHINGTON PL

W 3RD ST

BLEEKER ST

Coffee a Go Go (approximate location)
In 1960's X-Men comics the non-costumed characters used to congregate at this "beatnik"-style cafe, often entertained by a local beat poet named Bernard the Poet

C

Doctor Strange's Sanctum Sanctorum
W HOUSTON ST
177A Bleecker Street between MacDougal and Sullivan Streets
Dr. Stephen Strange's three-story town house "sanctum sanctorum" (Latin: a very private or secret place) His most mystical objects and meditation room are on the third floor. In real life, there is a 5-story building at 177 Bleecker Street

CLARKSON ST
W HOUSTON ST
KING ST
CHARLTON ST
VANDAM ST
SPRING ST
DOMINICK ST
SOHO

Alicia Master's Studio
Located in the Tribeca area
Alicia is The Thing's blind girlfriend and a sculptress Her studio is in TriBeCa (Triangle Below Canal Street) formerly an area of artists lofts in deteriorating buildings, now a trendy area.

HOLLAND TUNNEL
CANAL ST   WATTS ST

Moondance Diner
(no longer there)
80 Sixth Avenue at Grand Street
This is the diner where Mary Jane Watson worked and ran into Peter outside in *Spider-Man 2*

TRIBECA
HUBERT ST   BEACH ST
WHITE ST

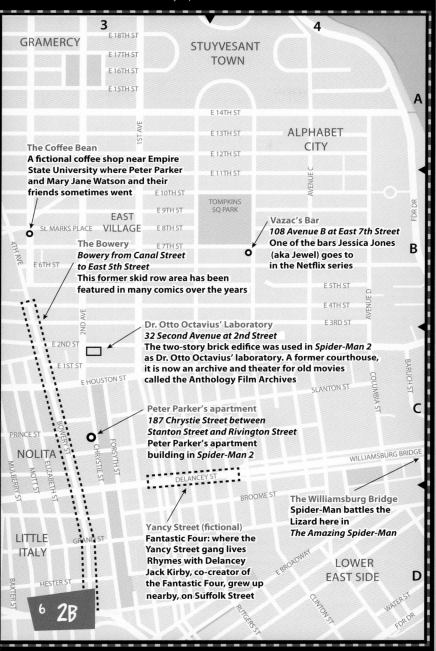

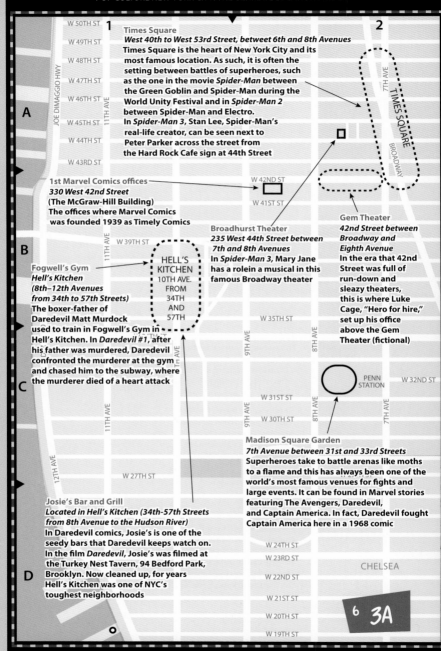

1

2

Times Square
West 40th to West 53rd Street, betweet 6th and 8th Avenues
Times Square is the heart of New York City and its
most famous location. As such, it is often the
setting between battles of superheroes, such
as the one in the movie *Spider-Man* between
the Green Goblin and Spider-Man during the
World Unity Festival and in *Spider-Man 2*
between Spider-Man and Electro.
In *Spider-Man 3*, Stan Lee, Spider-Man's
real-life creator, can be seen next to
Peter Parker across the street from
the Hard Rock Cafe sign at 44th Street

A

1st Marvel Comics offices
330 West 42nd Street
(The McGraw-Hill Building)
The offices where Marvel Comics
was founded 1939 as Timely Comics

Gem Theater
*42nd Street between
Broadway and
Eighth Avenue*
In the era that 42nd
Street was full of
run-down and
sleazy theaters,
this is where Luke
Cage, "Hero for hire,"
set up his office
above the Gem
Theater (fictional)

Broadhurst Theater
*235 West 44th Street between
7th and 8th Avenues*
In *Spider-Man 3*, Mary Jane
has a rolein a musical in this
famous Broadway theater

B

Fogwell's Gym
*Hell's Kitchen
(8th–12th Avenues
from 34th to 57th Streets)*
The boxer-father of
Daredevil Matt Murdock
used to train in Fogwell's Gym in
Hell's Kitchen. In *Daredevil #1*, after
his father was murdered, Daredevil
confronted the murderer at the gym and
chased him to the subway, where
the murderer died of a heart attack

HELL'S
KITCHEN
10TH AVE.
FROM
34TH
AND
57TH

C

Madison Square Garden
7th Avenue between 31st and 33rd Streets
Superheroes take to battle arenas like moths
to a flame and this has always been one of the
world's most famous venues for fights and
large events. It can be found in Marvel stories
featuring The Avengers, Daredevil,
and Captain America. In fact, Daredevil fought
Captain America here in a 1968 comic

Josie's Bar and Grill
*Located in Hell's Kitchen (34th-57th Streets
from 8th Avenue to the Hudson River)*
In Daredevil comics, Josie's is one of the
seedy bars that Daredevil keeps watch on.
In the film *Daredevil*, Josie's was filmed at
the Turkey Nest Tavern, 94 Bedford Park,
Brooklyn. Now cleaned up, for years
Hell's Kitchen was one of NYC's
toughest neighborhoods

D

CHELSEA

6 **3A**

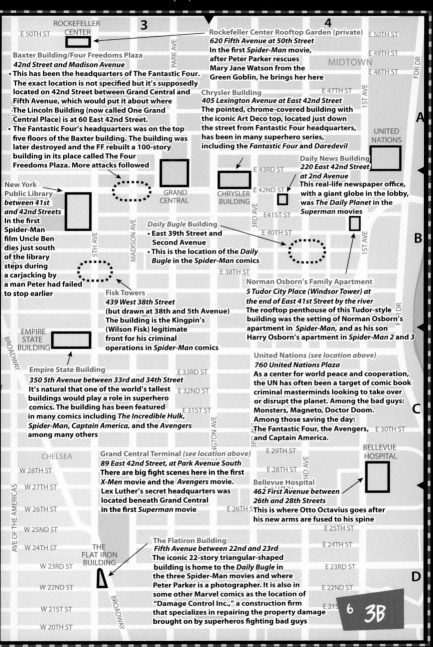

3

Baxter Building/Four Freedoms Plaza
42nd Street and Madison Avenue
• This has been the headquarters of The Fantastic Four.
The exact location is not specified but it's supposedly
located on 42nd Street between Grand Central and
Fifth Avenue, which would put it about where
The Lincoln Building (now called One Grand
Central Place) is at 60 East 42nd Street.
• The Fantastic Four's headquarters was on the top
five floors of the Baxter building. The building was
later destroyed and the FF rebuilt a 100-story
building in its place called The Four
Freedoms Plaza. More attacks followed

**New York
Public Library**
*between 41st
and 42nd Streets*
In the first
Spider-Man
film Uncle Ben
dies just south
of the library
steps during
a carjacking by
a man Peter had failed
to stop earlier

Fisk Towers
*439 West 38th Street
(but drawn at 38th and 5th Avenue)*
The building is the Kingpin's
(Wilson Fisk) legitimate
front for his criminal
operations in *Spider-Man* comics

Empire State Building
350 5th Avenue between 33rd and 34th Street
It's natural that one of the world's tallest
buildings would play a role in superhero
comics. The building has been featured
in many comics including *The Incredible Hulk,
Spider-Man, Captain America,* and the *Avengers*
among many others

Grand Central Terminal *(see location above)*
89 East 42nd Street, at Park Avenue South
There are big fight scenes here in the first
X-Men movie and the *Avengers* movie.
Lex Luther's secret headquarters was
located beneath Grand Central
in the first *Superman* movie

The Flatiron Building
Fifth Avenue between 22nd and 23rd
The iconic 22-story triangular-shaped
building is home to the *Daily Bugle* in
the three Spider-Man movies and where
Peter Parker is a photographer. It is also in
some other Marvel comics as the location of
"Damage Control Inc.," a construction firm
that specializes in repairing the property damage
brought on by superheros fighting bad guys

4

Rockefeller Center Rooftop Garden (private)
620 Fifth Avenue at 50th Street
In the first *Spider-Man* movie,
after Peter Parker rescues
Mary Jane Watson from the
Green Goblin, he brings her here

Chrysler Building
405 Lexington Avenue at East 42nd Street
The pointed, chrome-covered building with
the iconic Art Deco top, located just down
the street from Fantastic Four headquarters,
has been in many superhero series,
including the *Fantastic Four* and *Daredevil*

Daily News Building
*220 East 42nd Street,
at 2nd Avenue*
This real-life newspaper office,
with a giant globe in the lobby,
was *The Daily Planet* in the
Superman movies

Daily Bugle Building
• East 39th Street and
Second Avenue
• This is the location of the *Daily
Bugle* in the *Spider-Man* comics

Norman Osborn's Family Apartment
*5 Tudor City Place (Windsor Tower) at
the end of East 41st Street by the river*
The rooftop penthouse of this Tudor-style
building was the setting of Norman Osborn's
apartment in *Spider-Man,* and as his son
Harry Osborn's apartment in *Spider-Man 2* and *3*

United Nations *(see location above)*
760 United Nations Plaza
As a center for world peace and cooperation,
the UN has often been a target of comic book
criminal masterminds looking to take over
or disrupt the planet. Among the bad guys:
Monsters, Magneto, Doctor Doom.
Among those saving the day:
The Fantastic Four, the Avengers,
and Captain America.

Bellevue Hospital
*462 First Avenue between
26th and 28th Streets*
This is where Otto Octavius goes after
his new arms are fused to his spine

6 3B

145

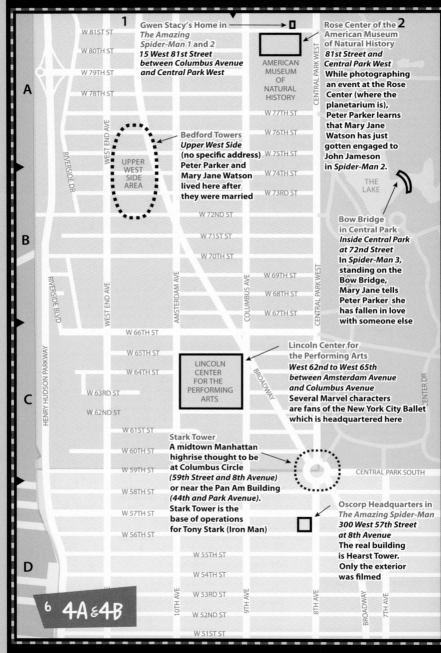

Gwen Stacy's Home in *The Amazing Spider-Man 1 and 2*
15 West 81st Street between Columbus Avenue and Central Park West

Rose Center of the American Museum of Natural History
81st Street and Central Park West
While photographing an event at the Rose Center (where the planetarium is), Peter Parker learns that Mary Jane Watson has just gotten engaged to John Jameson in *Spider-Man 2*.

Bedford Towers
Upper West Side
(no specific address)
Peter Parker and Mary Jane Watson lived here after they were married

Bow Bridge
in Central Park
Inside Central Park at 72nd Street
In *Spider-Man 3*, standing on the Bow Bridge, Mary Jane tells Peter Parker she has fallen in love with someone else

Lincoln Center for the Performing Arts
West 62nd to West 65th between Amsterdam Avenue and Columbus Avenue
Several Marvel characters are fans of the New York City Ballet which is headquartered here

Stark Tower
A midtown Manhattan highrise thought to be at Columbus Circle *(59th Street and 8th Avenue)* or near the Pan Am Building *(44th and Park Avenue)*.
Stark Tower is the base of operations for Tony Stark (Iron Man)

Oscorp Headquarters in *The Amazing Spider-Man*
300 West 57th Street at 8th Avenue
The real building is Hearst Tower. Only the exterior was filmed

6 4A &4B

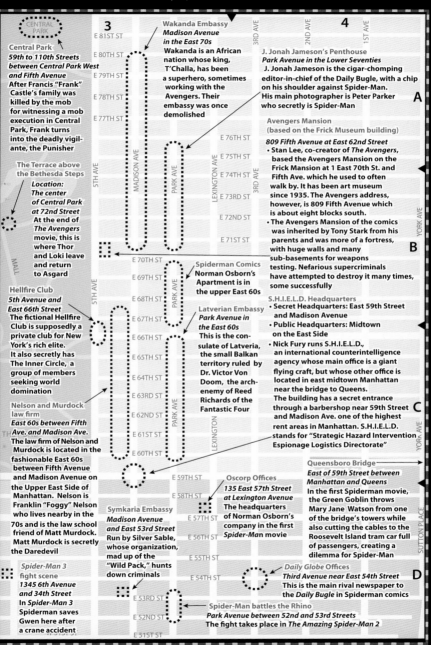

3

E 81ST ST
E 80TH ST
E 79TH ST
E 78TH ST
E 77TH ST
E 76TH ST
E 75TH ST
E 74TH ST
E 73RD ST
E 72ND ST
E 71ST ST
E 70TH ST
E 69TH ST
E 68TH ST
E 67TH ST
E 66TH ST
E 65TH ST
E 64TH ST
E 63RD ST
E 62ND ST
E 61ST ST
E 60TH ST
E 59TH ST
E 58TH ST
E 57TH ST
E 56TH ST
E 55TH ST
E 54TH ST
E 53RD ST
E 52ND ST
E 51ST ST

4

3RD AVE · 2ND AVE · 1ST AVE · YORK AVE · SUTTON PLACE · LEXINGTON AVE · PARK AVE · MADISON AVE · 5TH AVE · MALL

CENTRAL PARK

Central Park
59th to 110th Streets between Central Park West and Fifth Avenue
After Francis "Frank" Castle's family was killed by the mob for witnessing a mob execution in Central Park, Frank turns into the deadly vigilante, the Punisher

The Terrace above the Bethesda Steps
Location:
The center of Central Park at 72nd Street
At the end of *The Avengers* movie, this is where Thor and Loki leave and return to Asgard

Hellfire Club
5th Avenue and East 66th Street
The fictional Hellfire Club is supposedly a private club for New York's rich elite. It also secretly has The Inner Circle, a group of members seeking world domination

Nelson and Murdock law firm
East 60s between Fifth Ave. and Madison Ave.
The law firm of Nelson and Murdock is located in the fashionable East 60s between Fifth Avenue and Madison Avenue on the Upper East Side of Manhattan. Nelson is Franklin "Foggy" Nelson who lives nearby in the 70s and is the law school friend of Matt Murdock. Matt Murdock is secretly the Daredevil

Spider-Man 3 **fight scene**
1345 6th Avenue and 34th Street
In *Spider-Man 3* Spiderman saves Gwen here after a crane accident

Wakanda Embassy
Madison Avenue in the East 70s
Wakanda is an African nation whose king, T'Challa, has been a superhero, sometimes working with the Avengers. Their embassy was once demolished

Spiderman Comics
Norman Osborn's Apartment is in the upper East 60s

Latverian Embassy
Park Avenue in the East 60s
This is the consulate of Latveria, the small Balkan territory ruled by Dr. Victor Von Doom, the arch-enemy of Reed Richards of the Fantastic Four

Symkaria Embassy
Madison Avenue and East 53rd Street
Run by Silver Sable, whose organization, mad up of the "Wild Pack," hunts down criminals

Oscorp Offices
135 East 57th Street at Lexington Avenue
The headquarters of Norman Osborn's company in the first *Spider-Man* movie

J. Jonah Jameson's Penthouse
Park Avenue in the Lower Seventies
J. Jonah Jameson is the cigar-chomping editor-in-chief of the Daily Bugle, with a chip on his shoulder against Spider-Man. His main photographer is Peter Parker who secretly is Spider-Man

Avengers Mansion (based on the Frick Museum building)
809 Fifth Avenue at East 62nd Street
• Stan Lee, co-creator of *The Avengers*, based the Avengers Mansion on the Frick Mansion at 1 East 70th St. and Fifth Ave. which he used to often walk by. It has been art museum since 1935. The Avengers address, however, is 809 Fifth Avenue which is about eight blocks south.
• The Avengers Mansion of the comics was inherited by Tony Stark from his parents and was more of a fortress, with huge walls and many sub-basements for weapons testing. Nefarious supercriminals have attempted to destroy it many times, some successfully

S.H.I.E.L.D. Headquarters
• Secret Headquarters: East 59th Street and Madison Avenue
• Public Headquarters: Midtown on the East Side
• Nick Fury runs S.H.I.E.L.D., an international counterintelligence agency whose main office is a giant flying craft, but whose other office is located in east midtown Manhattan near the bridge to Queens. The building has a secret entrance through a barbershop near 59th Street and Madison Ave. one of the highest rent areas in Manhattan. S.H.I.E.L.D. stands for "Strategic Hazard Intervention Espionage Logistics Directorate"

Queensboro Bridge
East of 59th Street between Manhattan and Queens
In the first Spiderman movie, the Green Goblin throws Mary Jane Watson from one of the bridge's towers while also cutting the cables to the Roosevelt Island tram car full of passengers, creating a dilemma for Spider-Man

Daily Globe Offices
Third Avenue near East 54th Street
This is the main rival newspaper to the *Daily Bugle* in Spiderman comics

Spider-Man battles the Rhino
Park Avenue between 52nd and 53rd Streets
The fight takes place in *The Amazing Spider-Man 2*

A
B
C
D

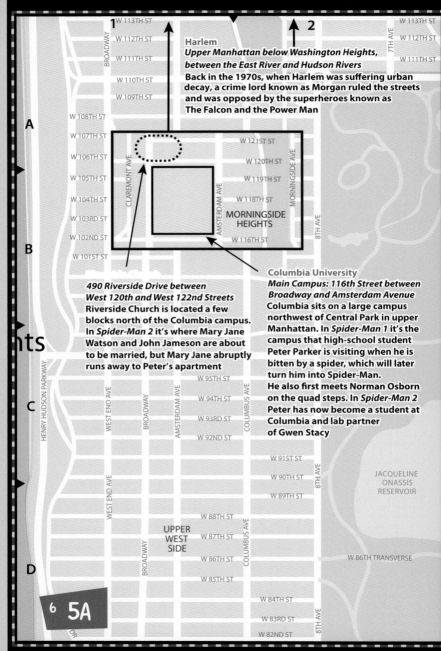

1

Harlem
Upper Manhattan below Washington Heights,
between the East River and Hudson Rivers
Back in the 1970s, when Harlem was suffering urban decay, a crime lord known as Morgan ruled the streets and was opposed by the superheroes known as The Falcon and the Power Man

2

MORNINGSIDE HEIGHTS

490 Riverside Drive between West 120th and West 122nd Streets
Riverside Church is located a few blocks north of the Columbia campus. In *Spider-Man 2* it's where Mary Jane Watson and John Jameson are about to be married, but Mary Jane abruptly runs away to Peter's apartment

Columbia University
Main Campus: 116th Street between Broadway and Amsterdam Avenue
Columbia sits on a large campus northwest of Central Park in upper Manhattan. In *Spider-Man 1* it's the campus that high-school student Peter Parker is visiting when he is bitten by a spider, which will later turn him into Spider-Man.
He also first meets Norman Osborn on the quad steps. In *Spider-Man 2* Peter has now become a student at Columbia and lab partner of Gwen Stacy

UPPER WEST SIDE

JACQUELINE ONASSIS RESERVOIR

6 5A

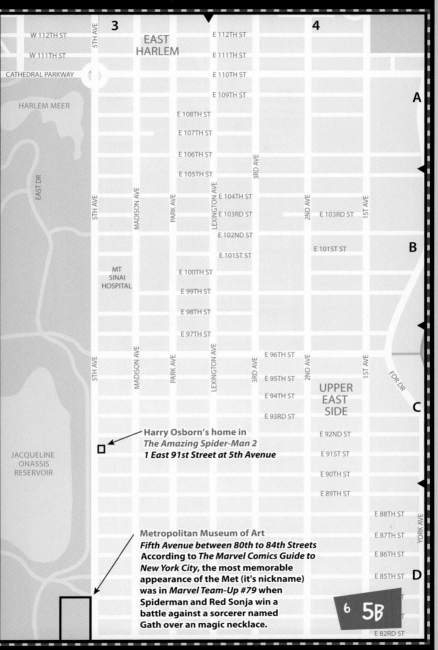

3

W 112TH ST

W 111TH ST

5TH AVE

EAST HARLEM

CATHEDRAL PARKWAY

HARLEM MEER

EAST DR

5TH AVE

MADISON AVE

PARK AVE

4

E 112TH ST

E 111TH ST

E 110TH ST

E 109TH ST

E 108TH ST

E 107TH ST

E 106TH ST

E 105TH ST

3RD AVE

LEXINGTON AVE

E 104TH ST

E 103RD ST

E 102ND ST

E 101ST ST

MT SINAI HOSPITAL

E 100TH ST

E 99TH ST

E 98TH ST

E 97TH ST

MADISON AVE

PARK AVE

LEXINGTON AVE

2ND AVE

E 103RD ST

1ST AVE

E 101ST ST

A

B

3RD AVE

2ND AVE

E 96TH ST

E 95TH ST

E 94TH ST

E 93RD ST

1ST AVE

UPPER EAST SIDE

FDR DR

C

JACQUELINE ONASSIS RESERVOIR

5TH AVE

Harry Osborn's home in
The Amazing Spider-Man 2
1 East 91st Street at 5th Avenue

E 92ND ST

E 91ST ST

E 90TH ST

E 89TH ST

E 88TH ST

E 87TH ST

E 86TH ST

E 85TH ST

YORK AVE

D

Metropolitan Museum of Art
Fifth Avenue between 80th to 84th Streets
According to *The Marvel Comics Guide to New York City*, **the most memorable appearance of the Met (it's nickname) was in** *Marvel Team-Up #79* **when Spiderman and Red Sonja win a battle against a sorcerer named Gath over an magic necklace.**

6 **5B**

E 82RD ST

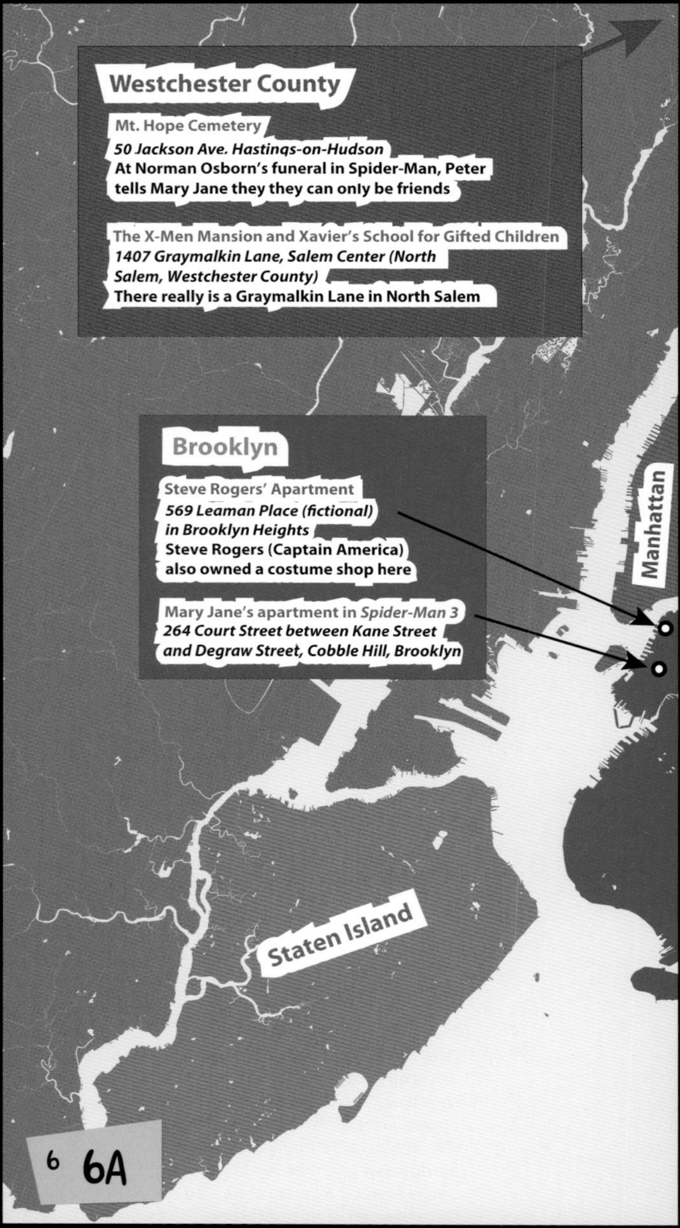

Westchester County

Mt. Hope Cemetery
50 Jackson Ave. Hastings-on-Hudson
At Norman Osborn's funeral in Spider-Man, Peter tells Mary Jane they they can only be friends

The X-Men Mansion and Xavier's School for Gifted Children
1407 Graymalkin Lane, Salem Center (North Salem, Westchester County)
There really is a Graymalkin Lane in North Salem

Brooklyn

Steve Rogers' Apartment
569 Leaman Place (fictional) in Brooklyn Heights
Steve Rogers (Captain America) also owned a costume shop here

Mary Jane's apartment in *Spider-Man 3*
264 Court Street between Kane Street and Degraw Street, Cobble Hill, Brooklyn

Manhattan

Staten Island

6 **6A**

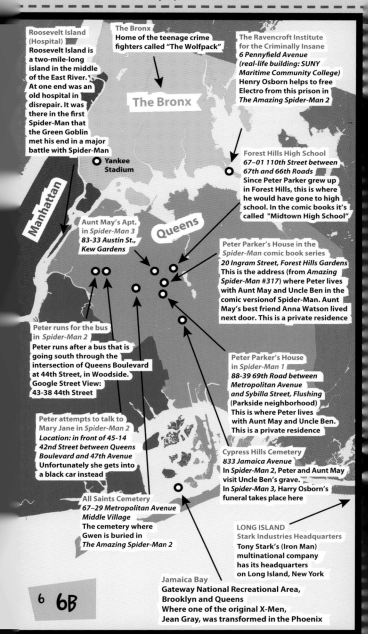

Roosevelt Island (Hospital)
Roosevelt Island is a two-mile-long island in the middle of the East River. At one end was an old hospital in disrepair. It was there in the first Spider-Man that the Green Goblin met his end in a major battle with Spider-Man

The Bronx
Home of the teenage crime fighters called "The Wolfpack"

The Ravencroft Institute for the Criminally Insane
6 Pennyfield Avenue (real-life building: SUNY Maritime Community College) Henry Osborn helps to free Electro from this prison in *The Amazing Spider-Man 2*

The Bronx

○ Yankee Stadium

Manhattan

Forest Hills High School
67–01 110th Street between 67th and 66th Roads
Since Peter Parker grew up in Forest Hills, this is where he would have gone to high school. In the comic books it's called "Midtown High School"

Queens

Aunt May's Apt. in *Spider-Man 3*
83-33 Austin St., Kew Gardens

Peter Parker's House in the *Spider-Man* comic book series
20 Ingram Street, Forest Hills Gardens
This is the address (from *Amazing Spider-Man #317*) where Peter lives with Aunt May and Uncle Ben in the comic version of Spider-Man. Aunt May's best friend Anna Watson lived next door. This is a private residence

Peter runs for the bus in *Spider-Man 2*
Peter runs after a bus that is going south through the intersection of Queens Boulevard at 44th Street, in Woodside. Google Street View: 43-38 44th Street

Peter Parker's House in *Spider-Man 1*
88-39 69th Road between Metropolitan Avenue and Sybilla Street, Flushing
(Parkside neighborhood) This is where Peter lives with Aunt May and Uncle Ben. This is a private residence

Peter attempts to talk to Mary Jane in *Spider-Man 2*
Location: in front of 45-14 42nd Street between Queens Boulevard and 47th Avenue
Unfortunately she gets into a black car instead

Cypress Hills Cemetery
833 Jamaica Avenue
In *Spider-Man 2*, Peter and Aunt May visit Uncle Ben's grave. In *Spider-Man 3*, Harry Osborn's funeral takes place here

All Saints Cemetery
67–29 Metropolitan Avenue Middle Village
The cemetery where Gwen is buried in *The Amazing Spider-Man 2*

LONG ISLAND
Stark Industries Headquarters
Tony Stark's (Iron Man) multinational company has its headquarters on Long Island, New York

Jamaica Bay
Gateway National Recreational Area, Brooklyn and Queens Where one of the original X-Men, Jean Gray, was transformed in the Phoenix

6 6B

Brooklyn

Desert Island Comics: 540 Metropolitan Avenue, Williamsburg, Brooklyn. desertislandbrooklyn.com

Mama Says Comics Rock: 306 Court Street, Cobble Hill, Brooklyn. mamasayscomicsrock.com

Joseph Koch Comics Warehouse: 206 41st Street, Sunset Park, Brooklyn. kochcomics.com

Bulletproof Comics and Games: 2178 Nostrand Avenue, Flatbush, Brooklyn. bulletproofcomix.com

Bronx

The Lair: 1808 Colden Avenue, Bronx. laironline.net

Fordham Comics: 390 East Fordham Road, Bronx. facebook.com/fordham-comics

Queens

Royal Collectibles: 96–01 Metropolitan Avenue, Forest Hills, Queens. royalcomicsnyc.com

Anime Castle: 35–32 Union Street, Flushing, Queens. animecastle.com

Iconic Buildings, Bridges, and Sculptures

BUILDINGS AND BRIDGES

American Museum of Natural History: Central Park West between 77th and 81st Streets) (Map 4A/Grid 2A)

The Ansonia: 2109 Broadway between 73rd and 74th Streets (Map 4A/Grid 1B)

The Apollo Theater: 253 West 125th Street between Frederick Douglass and A.C. Powell Boulevards, Harlem (Map 6/Manhattan)

Apple Store (Apple Fifth Avenue): 767 5th Avenue and East 58th Street (Map 4B/Grid 3D)

Barclays Center: 620 Atlantic Avenue at Flatbush Avenue. Large rust-colored sports arena with huge overhang entrance. (Map 6/Brooklyn)

Belvedere Castle: Inside Central Park at 79th Street (Map 4A/Grid 2A)

Bloomberg Tower (and Beacon Court): 731 Lexington Avenue between East 58th and East 59th Streets (Map 4B/Grid 3D)

Bloomingdale's: 160 East 60th Street at Lexington Avenue (Map 4B/Grid 3C)

Bronx Zoo: 2300 Southern Boulevard. The original domed elephant building has concrete elephant heads over the columns (Map 6/Bronx)

Brooklyn Bridge: East River, east of City Hall. Over 125 years old. Fun to walk/bike over to Brooklyn Heights and back. (Map 1B/Grid 3B)

Carnegie Hall: 881 7th Avenue at West 57th Street (Map 4A/Grid 2D)

Castle Clinton: In Battery Park, near Battery Place (Map 1A/Grid 2D)

Cathedral of St. John the Divine: 1047 Amsterdam Avenue at 112th Street, Morningside Heights (Map 6/Grid 2B)

Chelsea Piers: West Side Highway and 17th–22nd Streets. Sports piers. Originally a passenger ship terminal for the *Lusitania* and the ill-fated *Titanic*. (Map 2A/Grid 1D)

Chrysler Building: 405 Lexington Avenue and 42nd Street (Map 3B/Grid 3B)

Citi Field: Flushing Meadows, Corona Park (Map 6/Queens)

Citigroup Center: 601 Lexington Avenue between 53rd and 54th Streets (Map 4B/Grid 4D)

City Hall: City Hall Park; Broadway and Park Row (Map 1A/Grid 2B)

The Cloisters: 99 Margaret Corbin Drive, Inwood (Map 6/Manhattan)

Columbia University: 116th Street and Broadway, Morningside Heights (Map 5/Grid 2B)

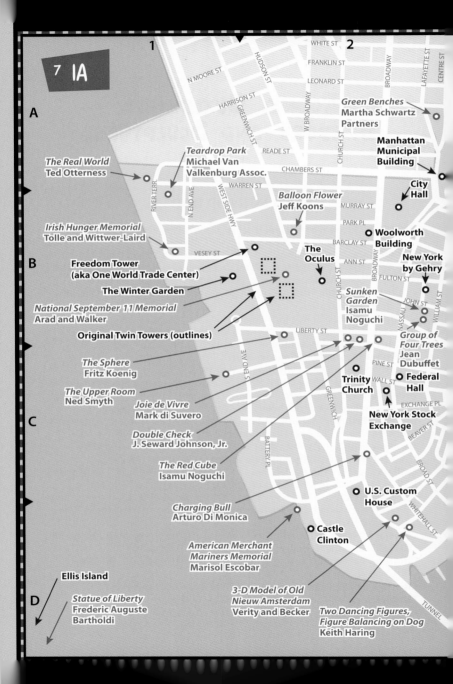

Green Benches
Martha Schwartz
Partners

**Manhattan
Municipal
Building**

Teardrop Park
Michael Van
Valkenburg Assoc.

**City
Hall**

The Real World
Ted Otterness

Balloon Flower
Jeff Koons

**Woolworth
Building**

Irish Hunger Memorial
Tolle and Wittwer-Laird

**The
Oculus**

**New York
by Gehry**

**Freedom Tower
(aka One World Trade Center)**

*Sunken
Garden*
Isamu
Noguchi

The Winter Garden

National September 11 Memorial
Arad and Walker

*Group of
Four Trees*
Jean
Dubuffet

Original Twin Towers (outlines)

The Sphere
Fritz Koenig

Joie de Vivre
Mark di Suvero

**Trinity
Church**

**Federal
Hall**

The Upper Room
Ned Smyth

Double Check
J. Seward Johnson, Jr.

**New York Stock
Exchange**

The Red Cube
Isamu Noguchi

**U.S. Custom
House**

Charging Bull
Arturo Di Monica

**O Castle
Clinton**

*American Merchant
Mariners Memorial*
Marisol Escobar

Ellis Island

*3-D Model of Old
Nieuw Amsterdam*
Verity and Becker

Statue of Liberty
Frederic Auguste
Bartholdi

*Two Dancing Figures,
Figure Balancing on Dog*
Keith Haring

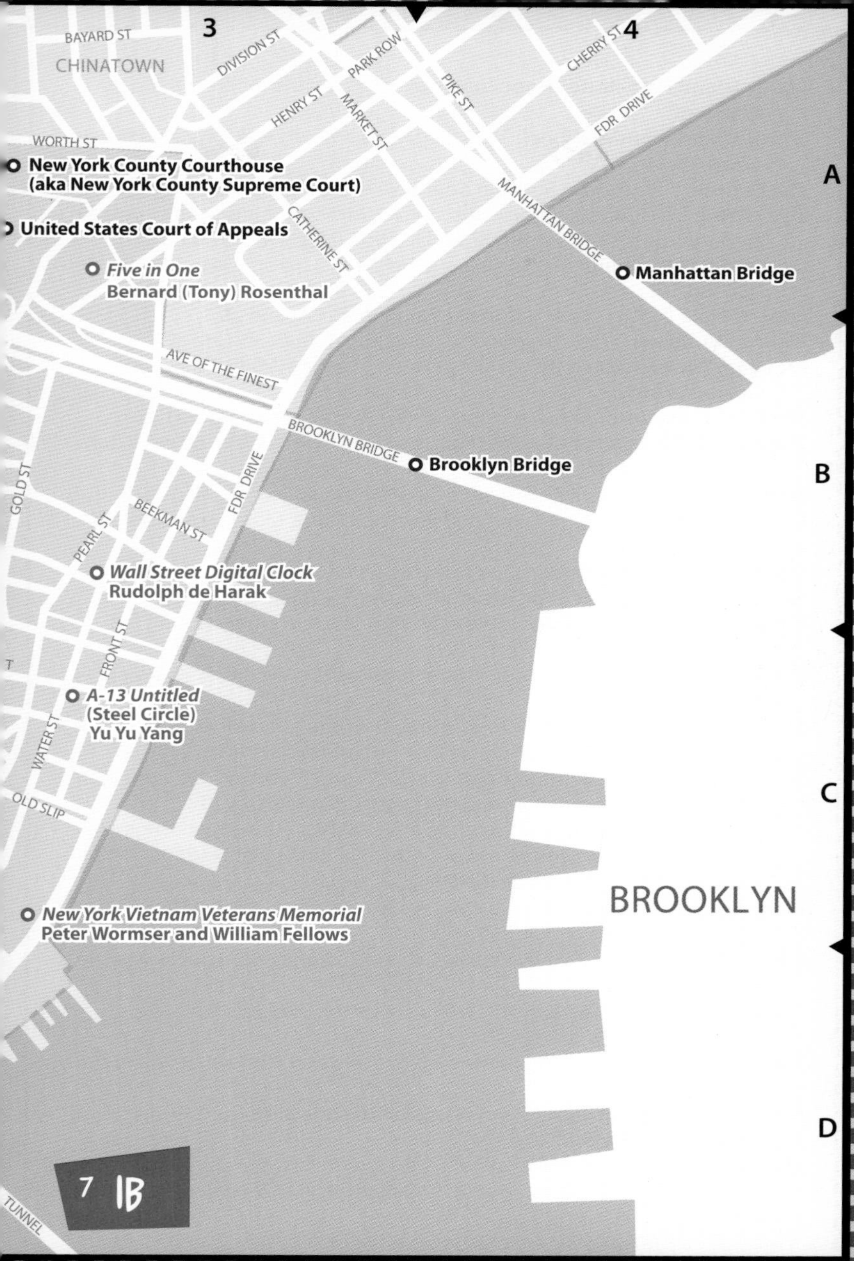

BAYARD ST

CHINATOWN

DIVISION ST

PARK ROW

CHERRY ST

HENRY ST

MARKET ST

PIKE ST

FDR DRIVE

WORTH ST

O New York County Courthouse
(aka New York County Supreme Court)

MANHATTAN BRIDGE

A

> United States Court of Appeals

CATHERINE ST

O Five in One
Bernard (Tony) Rosenthal

O Manhattan Bridge

AVE OF THE FINEST

BROOKLYN BRIDGE

GOLD ST

FDR DRIVE

O Brooklyn Bridge

B

BEEKMAN ST

PEARL ST

O Wall Street Digital Clock
Rudolph de Harak

FRONT ST

T

O A-13 Untitled
(Steel Circle)
Yu Yu Yang

WATER ST

OLD SLIP

C

BROOKLYN

O New York Vietnam Veterans Memorial
Peter Wormser and William Fellows

D

TUNNEL

Coney Island Parachute Drop: Boardwalk near West 16th Street (Map 6/Brooklyn)

Coney Island Wonder Wheel: 1025 Riegelmann Boardwalk, Brooklyn (Map 6/Brooklyn)

The Dakota: 1 West 72nd Street at Central Park West (Map 4A/Grid 2B)

Ellis Island: Ellis Island is in the Hudson River. Millions of immigrants passed through these buildings in the early 1900s. (Map 1A/Grid 1D)

Empire State Building: 350 5th Avenue between 33rd and 34th Streets (Map 3B/Grid 3C)

Federal Hall: 26 Wall Street at Nassau Street (Map 1A/Grid 2C)

Flatiron Building: 175 Fifth Avenue at 23rd Street (Map 3B/Grid 3D)

Freedom Tower: West Street at Vesey Street. AKA One World Trade Center. (Map 1A/Grid 2B).

The Frick Museum: 1 East 70th Street at 5th Avenue (Map 4B/Grid 3B)

The George Washington Bridge: Hudson River west of 179th Street, Washington Heights (Map 6/Bronx)

Grand Central Terminal: 89 East 42nd Street and Park Avenue (Map 3B/Grid 3B)

Grant's Tomb: West 122nd Street and Riverside Drive, Morningside Heights (Map 6/Grid 1A)

Hayden Planetarium: Central Park West and 81st Street (Map 4A/Grid 2A)

Hearst Tower: 300 West 57th Street at 8th Avenue (Map 4A/Grid 2D)

The High Line: Little West 12th Street to 34th Street, roughly along 10th Avenue (Map 2A/Grid 1A)

Hook & Ladder 8: 14 North Moore Street at Varick Street. FDNY Ladder 8. (Map 2A/Grid 2D)

IAC Building: 555 West 18th Street. InterActiveCorp's headquarters by Frank Gehry is sheathed in white glass that resembles sails. (Map 2A/Grid 1A)

The Jacob Javits Convention Center: 11th Avenue between 34th and 38th Streets. NYC's biggest convention center. (Map 3A/Grid 1B)

Jefferson Market Library: 425 Sixth Avenue at West 10th Street. Originally a courthouse, this High Victorian Gothic building once held the trial of Mae West in 1927. (Map 2A/Grid 1B)

Lever House: 390 Park Avenue between 53rd and 54th Streets (Map 4B/Grid 3D)

Lincoln Center: Columbus Avenue between 62nd and 65th Streets (Map 4A/Grid 2C)

"The Lipstick Building": 885 3rd Avenue between 53rd and 54th Streets (Map 4B/Grid 4D)

Macy's: 151 West 34th Street between Broadway and 7th Avenue (Map 3A/Grid 2C)

Madison Square Garden: 4 Penn Plaza, 8th Avenue between 31st and 32nd Streets (Map 3B/Grid 2C)

Manhattan Bridge: East River, off of South Street. A suspension bridge (new for its time in 1909) that connects Manhattan with Brooklyn. (Map 1B/Grid 4A)

Manhattan Municipal Building: 1 Centre Street at Chambers Street. Massive government building used as City Hall in *Ghostbusters*. (Map 1A/Grid 2A)

The Met Breuer: 945 Madison Avenue at East 75th Street. Formerly the Whitney Museum. (Map 4B/Grid 3A)

Met Life Building: 200 Park Avenue at 44th Street. Has a rooftop heliport. Formerly the Pan Am building. (Map 3B/Grid 3A)

Metropolitan Life Insurance Building: 1 Madison Avenue at 23rd Street. Modelled after the Campanile in Venice, Italy. (Map 3B/Grid 3D)

The Metropolitan Museum of Art: 1000 5th Avenue at 82nd Street (Map 5B/Grid 3D)

MoMA (Museum of Modern Art): 11 West 53rd Street between 5th and 6th Avenues (Map 4A/Grid 3D)

The Morgan Library & Museum: 225 Madison Avenue between 36th and 37th Streets (Map 3B/Grid 3B)

Museum of the City of New York: 1220 5th Avenue between 103rd and 104th Streets (Map 5B/Grid 3B)

New York by Gehry: 8 Spruce Street at William Street. Seventy six–story residential skyscraper with an undulating steel façade. (Map 1B/Grid 1A)

New York Chinese Scholar's Garden: 1000 Richmond Terrace, Staten Island. Snug Harbor Cultural Center. (Map 6/Staten Island)

New York County Courthouse: 60 Centre Street at Pearl Street. AKA the New York State Supreme Court Building. Large traditional courthouse used in dozens of movies like *Legal Eagles*. (Map 1A/Grid 3A)

New York Historical Society: 170 Central Park West between 76th and 77th Streets (Map 4B/Grid 2A)

New York Public Library: 476 5th Avenue between 40th and 42nd Streets (Map 3B/Grid 3B)

New York Stock Exchange: Broad Street at White Street (Map 1A/Grid 2C)

The New York Times Building: 242 West 41st Street at 8th Avenue (Map 3A/Grid 2B)

The Oculus: Church and Dey Streets (Map 1A/Grid 1A)

The Original Twin Towers (World Trade Center): Greenwich and Fulton Streets (Map 1A/Grid 2B)

The Paramount Building: 1501 Broadway between 43rd and 44th Streets (Map 3A/Grid 2A)

Plaza Hotel: 768 5th Avenue between 58th and 59th Streets (Map 4B/Grid 3D)

Radio City Music Hall: 1260 6th Avenue and West 50th Street (Map 3A/Grid 3A)

St. Patrick's Cathedral: 5th Avenue between 50th and 51st Streets (Map 4B/Grid 3A)

San Remo: 145 Central Park West between 74th and 75th Streets (Map 4A/Grid 2A)

Seagram Building: 375 Park Avenue between 52nd and 53rd Streets (Map 4B/Grid 3D)

Shea Stadium: Flushing Meadows, Corona Park. Demolished. (Map 6/Queens)

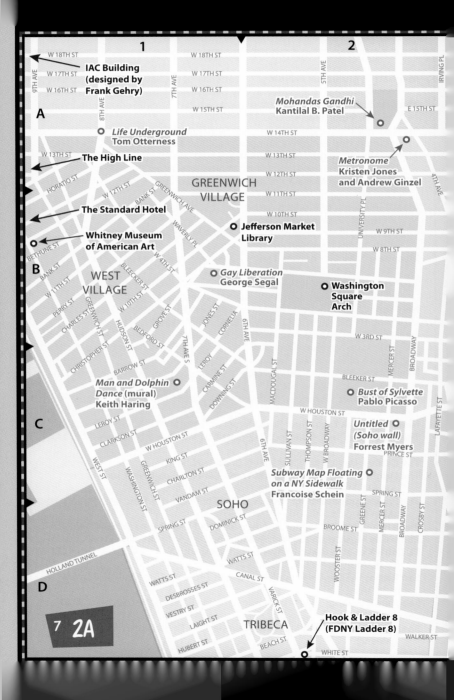

W 18TH ST
W 17TH ST
W 16TH ST

1

W 18TH ST
W 17TH ST
W 16TH ST
W 15TH ST

2

9TH AVE
8TH AVE
7TH AVE
5TH AVE
IRVING PL

IAC Building (designed by Frank Gehry)

Mohandas Gandhi Kantilal B. Patel

E 15TH ST

A

Life Underground **Tom Otterness**

W 14TH ST

W 13TH ST

The High Line

HORATIO ST

W 12TH ST
BANK ST
GREENWICH AVE

GREENWICH VILLAGE

W 13TH ST
W 12TH ST
W 11TH ST
W 10TH ST

Metronome **Kristen Jones and Andrew Ginzel**

UNIVERSITY PL
4TH AVE

The Standard Hotel

WAVERLY PL

Jefferson Market Library

W 9TH ST
W 8TH ST

Whitney Museum of American Art

BETHUNE ST

B

WEST VILLAGE

BANK ST
W 11TH ST
BLEECKER ST
W 4TH ST
PERRY ST
CHARLES ST
GREENWICH ST
W 10TH ST
HUDSON ST
BEDFORD ST
GROVE ST
JONES ST
CORNELIA
6TH AVE

Gay Liberation **George Segal**

Washington Square Arch

W 3RD ST

MERCER ST
BROADWAY

CHRISTOPHER ST
BARROW ST

7TH AVE S
LEROY ST
CARMINE ST
DOWNING ST

BLEEKER ST

Man and Dolphin Dance (mural) **Keith Haring**

LEROY ST
CLARKSON ST
W HOUSTON ST

MACDOUGAL ST
SULLIVAN ST
THOMPSON ST
W BROADWAY

Bust of Sylvette **Pablo Picasso**

LAFAYETTE ST

C

WEST ST
WASHINGTON ST
GREENWICH ST

KING ST
CHARLTON ST
VANDAM ST

6TH AVE

Untitled **(Soho wall) Forrest Myers**

PRINCE ST

Subway Map Floating on a NY Sidewalk **Francoise Schein**

GREENE ST
MERCER ST
BROADWAY
CROSBY ST

SOHO

SPRING ST
DOMINICK ST

SPRING ST

BROOME ST

WOOSTER ST

HOLLAND TUNNEL

WATTS ST
CANAL ST

D

WATTS ST
DESBROSSES ST
VESTRY ST
LAIGHT ST
HUBERT ST

VARICK ST
BEACH ST

TRIBECA

Hook & Ladder 8 (FDNY Ladder 8)

WHITE ST
WALKER ST

7 **2A**

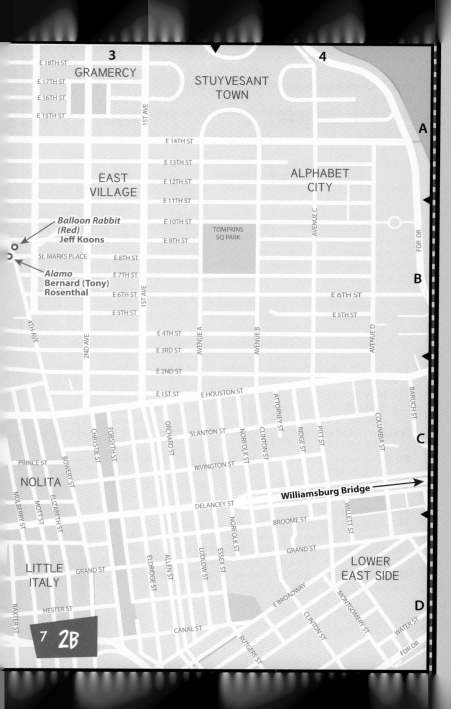

Sherry-Netherland Hotel: 781 Fifth Avenue at East 59th Street (Map 4B/Grid 3C)

The Solomon Guggenheim Museum: 1071 5th Avenue between 88th and 89th Streets (Map 5B/Grid 3A)

Sony Building: 550 Madison Avenue between 55th and 56th Streets. A Philip Johnson building. (Map 4B/Grid 3D)

The Standard, High Line: 848 Washington Street at West 13th Street. Hotel that uniquely straddles the High Line. (Map 2A/Grid 1B)

Statue of Liberty: Liberty Island is in the Hudson River. The famous gift from France with the poem by Emma Lazarus: "Give us your tired, your poor. . . ." (Map 1A/Grid 1D)

Tiffany and Company: 727 5th Avenue at East 57th Street (Map 4B/Grid 3D)

Time Warner Center: 10 Columbus Circle at 59th Street (Map 4A/Grid 2C)

Trinity Church: 75 Broadway at Wall Street (Map 1A/Grid 2C)

Trump Tower: 725 5th Avenue at East 56th Street (Map 4B/Grid 3D)

TWA Terminal at JFK: JFK International Airport. Jet Blue Terminal 5. (Map 6/Queens)

The Unisphere: Flushing Meadows, Corona Park (Map 6/Queens)

The United Nations: 1st Avenue between 42nd and 48th Streets. A Le Corbusier building. (Map 3B/Grid 3B)

United States Court of Appeals: 40 Foley Square at Pearl Street. Columned courthouse used in *Night Court*. (Map 1A/Grid 3A)

U.S. Custom House/National Museum of the American Indian: 1 Bowling Green At Broadway. Built over the center of the original settlement of New Amsterdam; was an art museum in *Ghostbusters*. (Map 1A/Grid 2C)

U.S. Post Office: 8th Avenue between 31st and 32nd Streets. The James A. Farley Post Office Building. (Map 3B/Grid 2C)

Waldorf Astoria: 301 Park Avenue between 49th and 50th Streets (Map 3B/Grid 4A)

Washington Square Arch: Washington Square North and 5th Avenue (Map 2A/Grid 2B)

Whitney Museum of American Art: 99 Gansevoort Street at Washington Street (Map 2A/Grid 1B)

Williamsburg Bridge: East River, east of Delancey Street (Map 2A/Grid 4C)

Williamsburg Savings Bank Tower: One Hanson Place at Ashland Place. Old-school tower that once dominated the skyline. (Map 6/Brooklyn)

The Winter Garden: West Street at Vestry Street, in 3 World Trade Center. Year-round indoor space with tall palm trees. (Map 1A/Grid 1B)

Woolworth Building: 233 Broadway at Barclay Street (Map 1A/Grid 1A)

Yankee Stadium: 1 East 161st Street at River Avenue (Map 6/Bronx)

Numbers

1 Times Square: 42nd Street and 7th Avenue. Where the New Year's ball drops. (Map 3A/Grid 2A)

30 Rockefeller Center: 6th Avenue between 50th and 51st Streets (Map 4A/Grid 3A)

59th Street Bridge: East River and 59th Street. Ed Koch Queensboro Bridge. (Map 4B/Grid 3C)

432 Park Avenue: Just west of Park Avenue on East 57th Street (Map 4B/Grid 3D)

PUBLIC SCULPTURES THAT POP CULTURE LOVERS LOVE IN NYC

***A-13 Untitled (Steel Circle),* Yu Yu Yang (1973):** 88 Pine Street at Water Street (Map 1B/Grid 3C)

***Adam & Eve,* Fernando Botero:** Time-Warner Center Lobby, 59th and Broadway. Two twelve-foot tall sculptures. (Map 4A/Grid 2C)

***Alamo,* Bernard (Tony) Rosenthal (1967):** Astor Place, 8th Street and 4th Avenue (Map 2B/Grid 3B)

***Alice in Wonderland,* Jos**é **de Creeft (1959)**: Central Park, next to Conservancy Pond, 74th Street (Map 4B/Grid 3A)

***Alice in Wonderland (Sophie Irene Loeb Fountain),* Frederick George Richard Roth (1936):** Central Park/Levin Playground at 77th Street (Map 4B/Grid 3A)

***Alma Mater,* Daniel Chester French (1900–1903):** Columbia University, on steps of Low Library, near 116th and Broadway. Look for an owl in the robe folds. (Map 5A/Grid 2B)

***American Merchant Mariners Memorial,* Marisol Escobar (1991):** Off Battery Park, south of Battery Place (Map 1A/Grid 2D)

***Angel of the Waters in Bethesda Fountain,* Emma Stebbins (1868):** Central Park/Bethesda Terrace (Map 4B/Grid 2B)

***Atlas,* Lee Lawrie and Rene Paul Chambellan (1937):** 630 5th Avenue between 50th and 51st Streets. In Greek mythology, Atlas has to hold up the sky for eternity. No shrugging! (Map 3B/Grid 3A)

***Balloon Flower,* Jeff Koons (1995–2000):** West Broadway and Greenwich Street (Map 1A/Grid 2B)

***Balloon Rabbit (Red),* Jeff Koons (2005–2010):** IBM Building window, 4th Avenue between 8th and 9th Streets (Map 2B/Grid 3B)

***Balto,* Frederick George Richard Roth (1925):** Central Park, East Drive at 66th Street (Map 4B/Grid 3B)

***Bartman,* Nancy Cartwright (2015):** 1211 6th Avenue between 47th and 48th Streets. Bronze head of Bart Simpson by the actress who does his voice on *The Simpsons*. (Map 3B/Grid 3A)

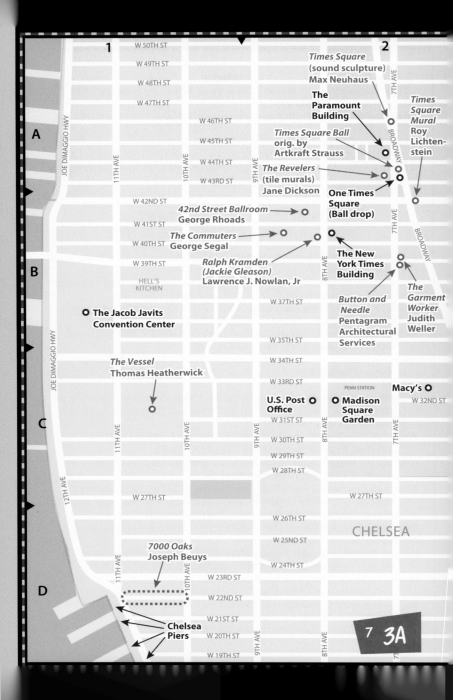

1

W 50TH ST
W 49TH ST
W 48TH ST
W 47TH ST

W 46TH ST
W 45TH ST
W 44TH ST
W 43RD ST

W 42ND ST
W 41ST ST
W 40TH ST
W 39TH ST

HELL'S KITCHEN

2

*Times Square
(sound sculpture)*
Max Neuhaus

**The
Paramount
Building**

*Times
Square
Mural*
Roy
Lichten-
stein

Times Square Ball
orig. by
Artkraft Strauss

The Revelers
(tile murals)
Jane Dickson

**One Times
Square**
(Ball drop)

42nd Street Ballroom
George Rhoads

The Commuters
George Segal

*Ralph Kramden
(Jackie Gleason)*
Lawrence J. Nowlan, Jr

**The New
York Times
Building**

*Button and
Needle*
Pentagram
Architectural
Services

**The
Garment
Worker**
Judith
Weller

**O The Jacob Javits
Convention Center**

The Vessel
Thomas Heatherwick

W 37TH ST

W 35TH ST

W 34TH ST

W 33RD ST

PENN STATION

Macy's O

W 32ND ST

**U.S. Post O
Office**

**O Madison
Square
Garden**

W 31ST ST
W 30TH ST
W 29TH ST
W 28TH ST

W 27TH ST

W 27TH ST

W 26TH ST

W 25ND ST

CHELSEA

7000 Oaks
Joseph Beuys

W 24TH ST

W 23RD ST
W 22ND ST

D

A

B

C

JOE DIMAGGIO HWY

11TH AVE

10TH AVE

9TH AVE

8TH AVE

7TH AVE

BROADWAY

12TH AVE

W 21ST ST
W 20TH ST
W 19TH ST

**Chelsea
Piers**

7 **3A**

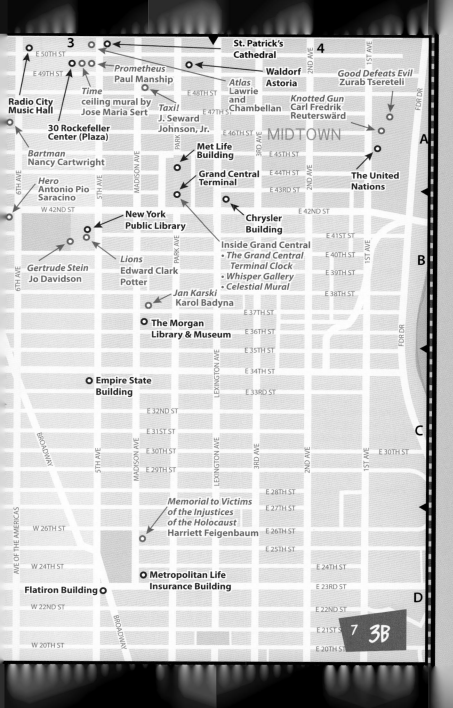

3

E 50TH ST

E 49TH ST

St. Patrick's Cathedral

4

2ND AVE

1ST AVE

FDR DR

Prometheus
Paul Manship

Waldorf Astoria

Good Defeats Evil
Zurab Tsereteli

Atlas
Lawrie and
Chambellan

E 48TH ST

Time
ceiling mural by
Jose Maria Sert

Knotted Gun
Carl Fredrik
Reuterswärd

Radio City Music Hall

Taxi!
J. Seward
Johnson, Jr.

E 47TH ST

30 Rockefeller Center (Plaza)

E 46TH ST

3RD AVE

MIDTOWN

A

Bartman
Nancy Cartwright

Met Life Building

E 45TH ST

2ND AVE

6TH AVE

MADISON AVE

5TH AVE

Hero
Antonio Pio
Saracino

Grand Central Terminal

E 44TH ST

E 43RD ST

The United Nations

W 42ND ST

Chrysler Building

E 42ND ST

New York Public Library

E 41ST ST

B

PARK AVE

Inside Grand Central
• *The Grand Central*
Terminal Clock
• *Whisper Gallery*
• *Celestial Mural*

E 40TH ST

1ST AVE

6TH AVE

Gertrude Stein
Jo Davidson

Lions
Edward Clark
Potter

E 39TH ST

E 38TH ST

Jan Karski
Karol Badyna

E 37TH ST

The Morgan Library & Museum

E 36TH ST

E 35TH ST

LEXINGTON AVE

E 34TH ST

E 33RD ST

Empire State Building

E 32ND ST

E 31ST ST

MADISON AVE

E 30TH ST

LEXINGTON AVE

3RD AVE

2ND AVE

1ST AVE

C

E 30TH ST

E 29TH ST

BROADWAY

E 28TH ST

Memorial to Victims of the Injustices of the Holocaust
Harriett Feigenbaum

E 27TH ST

E 26TH ST

W 26TH ST

E 25TH ST

FDR DR

AVE OF THE AMERICAS

W 24TH ST

E 24TH ST

Metropolitan Life Insurance Building

E 23RD ST

Flatiron Building

D

W 22ND ST

E 22ND ST

BROADWAY

W 20TH ST

E 21ST ST

E 20TH ST

7 **3B**

***Bellerophon Taming Pegasus,* Jacques Lipchitz (1964–1967):** Columbia University, Above 117th and Amsterdam Avenue (Map 5A/Grid 2B)

***Bust of Sylvette,* Pablo Picasso (1968):** Washington Square South Towers, near Bleecker Street and University Place (Map 2A/Grid 2C)

***Button and Needle,* Pentagram Architectural Services (1996):** 555 7th Avenue and 39th Street (Map 3A/Grid 2B)

***Celestial Mural,* J. Monroe Hewlett and four others (1913):** East 42nd Street and Park Avenue. Grand Central Terminal ceiling. (Map 3B/Grid 3B)

***Charging Bull,* Arturo Di Monica (1989):** Broadway near Morris Street (Map 1A/Grid 2C)

***Colgate Clock,* originally by Seth Thomas Clock Co. (1924):** Exchange Place, Jersey City, New Jersey. A replacement. (Map 6A/New Jersey)

***The Commuters,* George Segal (1980):** Port Authority Bus Terminal, South Wing, 40th Street and 8th Avenue (Map 3A/Grid 2B)

***Crack is Wack* mural, Keith Haring (1986):** 128th Street and 2nd Avenue (Map 6B/Manhattan)

***Cyclone* Roller Coaster, Vernon Keenan (1927):** Surf and West 10th Streets, Coney Island (Map 6B/Brooklyn)

***The Delacorte Clock,* Andrea Spadini (1964–1965):** Central Park, Central Park Zoo, 5th Avenue and 64th Street (Map 4B/Grid 3C)

***Double Check,* J. Seward Johnson, Jr. (1982):** Zuccotti Park, Liberty Street and Trinity Place (Map 1A/Grid 2B)

***Double Dutch* (Intervale Avenue at Kelly Street) and *Life on Dawson Street* (Dawson Street at Longwood Avenue), John Ahearn & Rigoberto Torres:** South Bronx wall sculptures. (Map 6B/Bronx)

***Duke Ellington,* Robert Graham (1997):** 110th Street and Fifth Avenue (Map 5B/Grid 3A)

***East River Roundabout,* Alice Aycock (1995):** York Avenue and East 60th Street (Map 4B/Grid 4C)

Egyptian Obelisk ("Cleopatra's Needle") (circa 16th century B.C.): Central Park, behind the Met at 82nd Street (Map 4B/Grid 3A)

***Five in One,* Bernard (Tony) Rosenthal (1971–1974):** Police Plaza, behind the Municipal Building near Madison Street. The sculpture represents the five boroughs of New York City. (Map 1B/Grid 3A)

***The Garment Worker,* Judith Weller (1984):** 555 7th Avenue at 39th Street (Map 3A/Grid 2B)

***Gay Liberation,* George Segal (1992):** Christopher Park, across from 51–53 Christopher Street (Map 2A/Grid 1B)

***Gertrude Stein,* Jo Davidson (1923):** In Bryant Park behind the library (Map 3B/Grid 3B)

***Good Defeats Evil,* Zurab Tsereteli (1990):** The UN, 46th Street and 1st Avenue. St. George, on horseback, slays a winged dragon made of missile parts. Presented by the Soviet Union. (Map 3B/Grid 4A)

***The Grand Central Terminal Clock,* Seth Thomas Clock Company (1913):**
Grand Central, atop the information booth, Main Concourse (Map 3B/
Grid 3B)

***Grant's Tomb,* John Duncan (1897):** Riverside Drive at West 122nd Street
(Map 5A/Grid 1A)

***Green Benches,* Martha Schwartz Partners (1997):** Jacob Javits Plaza/Fed-
eral Plaza, Lafayette and Worth Streets (Map1A/2A)

***Group of Four Threes,* Jean Dubuffet (1972):** 1 Chase Manhattan Plaza, near
Pine and William Streets (Map 1A/Grid 2B)

***Hans Christian Andersen,* Georg John Lober (1956):** Central Park, next to
the Conservancy Pond, 74th Street (Map 4B/Grid 3B)

***Hare on Bell,* Barry Flanagan (1983):** In the small park between East 51st
and 52 Streets and 6th and 7th Avenues (Map 4A/Grid 2D)

***Hero,* Antonio Pio Saracino (2014):** In a small park on 42nd Street, west of
6th Avenue (Map 3A/Grid 3B)

***Higher Ground: The Adam Clayton Powell, Jr. Memorial,* Branly Cadet
(2005):** 125th Street and Adam Clayton Powell, Jr. Boulevard, Harlem
(Map 6B/Manhattan)

***Hope (Red/Blue),* Robert Indiana (2009):** Corner of West 53rd Street and 7th
Avenue (Map 4A/Grid 2D)

***Imagine* Mosaic (1985):** Strawberry Fields, Central Park, near West 72nd
Street. Made in Naples, Italy. (Map 4B/Grid 2B)

***Invisible Man: A Memorial to Ralph Ellison,* Elizabeth Catlett (2003)**: River-
side Park at 150th Street (Map 6B/Manhattan)

***Irish Hunger Memorial,* Brian Tolle, Gail Wittwer-Laird, and 1100 Architect
(firm) (2002):** Vesey Street and North End Avenue (Map 1A/Grid 1B)

***Jan Karski,* Karol Badyna (2002):** 233 Madison Avenue at East 37th Street. In
front of the Polish Consulate mansion, Karski, a Polish WW2 hero, seems
to invite you play chess with him. (Map 3B/Grid 3B)

***Joie de Vivre,* Mark di Suvero (1996):** Zuccotti Park, Broadway and Cedar
Street (Map 1A/Grid 2B)

***Knotted Gun,* Carl Fredrik Reuterswärd (1985):** The UN, 46th Street and 1st
Avenue, at the Visitor's Plaza. Made in response to the shooting of John
Lennon. (Map 3B/Grid 4A)

***Lapstrake,* Jesús Bautista Moroles (1987):** Plaza next to 31 West 52nd
Street between 5th and 6th Avenues (Map 4B/Grid 3D)

***Le Guichet (The Ticket Window),* Alexander Calder (1963):** Lincoln Center,
near the Reflecting Pool (Map 4A/Grid 1C)

***Life Underground,* Tom Otterness (2004):** 14th Street and 8th Avenue (in
subway) (Map 2A/Grid 1A)

***Lincoln Center Reclining Figure,* Henry Moore (1965):** Lincoln Center, in the
Reflecting Pool (Map 4A/Grid 1C)

***Love,* Robert Indiana (1970):** Corner of West 55th Street and 6th Avenue
(Map 4B/Grid 3D)

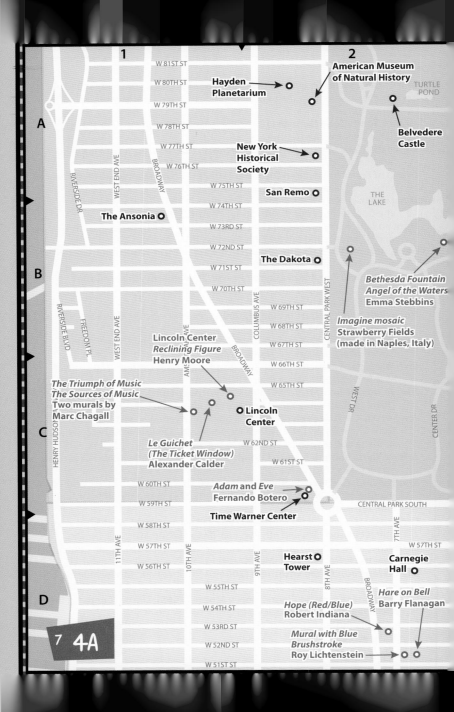

1

W 81ST ST

W 80TH ST

Hayden → ○
Planetarium

W 79TH ST

2

American Museum
of Natural History

TURTLE
POND

A

W 78TH ST

W 77TH ST

W 76TH ST

New York → ○
Historical
Society

Belvedere
Castle

RIVERSIDE DR

WEST END AVE

BROADWAY

W 75TH ST

San Remo ○

THE
LAKE

W 74TH ST

The Ansonia ○

W 73RD ST

W 72ND ST

B

W 71ST ST

The Dakota ○

W 70TH ST

COLUMBUS AVE

CENTRAL PARK WEST

Bethesda Fountain
Angel of the Waters
Emma Stebbins

RIVERSIDE BLVD

FREEDOM PL

WEST END AVE

W 69TH ST

W 68TH ST

Lincoln Center
Reclining Figure
Henry Moore

AMSTERDAM AVE

W 67TH ST

BROADWAY

W 66TH ST

Imagine mosaic
Strawberry Fields
(made in Naples, Italy)

W 65TH ST

The Triumph of Music
The Sources of Music
Two murals by
Marc Chagall

HENRY HUDSON

○   ○
↗
○ **Lincoln**
Center

WEST DR

CENTER DR

C

Le Guichet
(The Ticket Window)
Alexander Calder

W 62ND ST

W 61ST ST

W 60TH ST

W 59TH ST

Adam **and** *Eve* → ○
Fernando Botero   ○

CENTRAL PARK SOUTH

Time Warner Center

W 58TH ST

11TH AVE

10TH AVE

9TH AVE

7TH AVE

W 57TH ST

W 56TH ST

Hearst ○
Tower

8TH AVE

W 57TH ST

Carnegie
Hall ○

W 55TH ST

BROADWAY

Hare on Bell
Barry Flanagan

D

W 54TH ST

Hope (Red/Blue)
Robert Indiana

W 53RD ST

7 **4A**

W 52ND ST

Mural with Blue
Brushstroke
Roy Lichtenstein → ○ ○

○

W 51ST ST

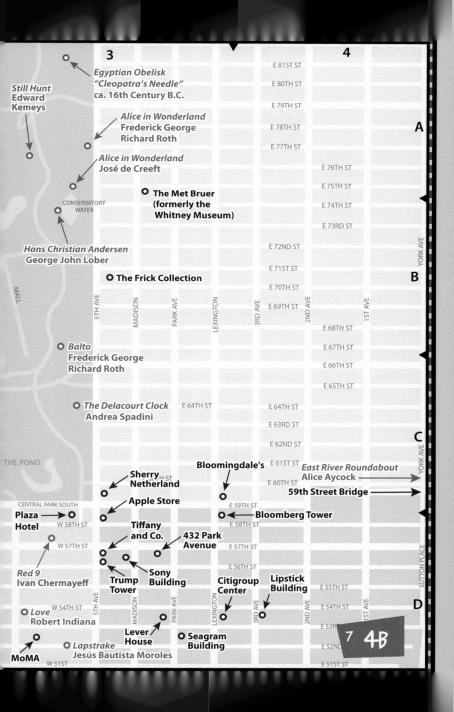

3
4

E 81ST ST
E 80TH ST
E 79TH ST
E 78TH ST
E 77TH ST
E 76TH ST
E 75TH ST
E 74TH ST
E 73RD ST
E 72ND ST
E 71ST ST
E 70TH ST
E 69TH ST
E 68TH ST
E 67TH ST
E 66TH ST
E 65TH ST
E 64TH ST
E 63RD ST
E 62ND ST
E 61ST ST
E 60TH ST
E 59TH ST
E 58TH ST
E 57TH ST
E 56TH ST
E 55TH ST
E 54TH ST
E 53R
E 52N
E 51ST ST

W 58TH ST
W 57TH ST
W 54TH ST
W 51ST

A
B
C
D

Egyptian Obelisk
"Cleopatra's Needle"
ca. 16th Century B.C.

Still Hunt
Edward
Kemeys

Alice in Wonderland
Frederick George
Richard Roth

Alice in Wonderland
José de Creeft

CONSERVATORY
WATER

○ **The Met Bruer**
(formerly the
Whitney Museum)

Hans Christian Andersen
George John Lober

○ **The Frick Collection**

MALL

○ *Balto*
Frederick George
Richard Roth

○ *The Delacourt Clock*
Andrea Spadini

THE POND

5TH AVE
MADISON
PARK AVE
LEXINGTON
3RD AVE
2ND AVE
1ST AVE
YORK AVE
YORK AVE
SUTTON PLACE

Bloomingdale's

East River Roundabout
Alice Aycock ⟶

Sherry
Netherland

59th Street Bridge ⟶

Apple Store

Plaza
Hotel ⟶

○ ⟵ **Bloomberg Tower**

Tiffany
and Co.

432 Park
Avenue

Red 9
Ivan Chermayeff

Sony
Building

Trump
Tower

Citigroup
Center

Lipstick
Building

○ *Love*
Robert Indiana

Lever
House

○ **Seagram**
Building

○ *Lapstrake*
Jesús Bautista Moroles

MoMA

7 **4B**

Lions, **Edward Clark Potter (1911):** On the New York Public Library steps, 5th Avenue and 41st Street. Nicknamed "Patience" and "Fortitude." (Map 3B/Grid 3B)

Man and Dolphin Dance, **Keith Haring (1987**): Carmine Street swimming pool mural, Clarkson Street and 7th Avenue South (Map 2A/Grid 1C)

Memorial to Victims of the Injustices of the Holocaust, **Harriet Feigenbaum (1990):** New York Appellate Court Building, 27 Madison Avenue between East 25th and East 26th Streets (Map 3B/Grid 3D)

Metronome, **Kristen Jones and Andrew Ginzel (1999):** 58–60 East 14th Street between Broadway and 4th Avenue, Union Square (Map 2A/Grid 2A)

Mohandas Gandhi, **Kantilal B. Patel (1986):** Union Square West and 15th Street (Map 2A/Grid 2A)

Mother Goose, **Frederick George Richard Roth (1938):** Central Park, near East Drive at 72nd Street (Map 4B/Grid 3A)

Mural with Blue Brushstroke, **Roy Lichtenstein (1986):** AXA Equitable Center lobby, 787 7th Avenue between West 51st and 52nd Streets (Map 3A/Grid 2D)

National September 11 Memorial, **Michael Arad (design) and Peter Walker + Partners (landscape) (2011):** 180 Greenwich Street between Fulton Street and Liberty Street (Map 1A/Grid 2B)

New York Vietnam Veterans Memorial, **Peter Wormser and William Fellows (1985):** 55 Water Street near Coenties Slip (Map 1B/Grid 3C)

OY/YO sculpture, **Deborah Kass (2015):** Brooklyn Bridge Park, Dumbo (Map 6B/Brooklyn)

Parachute Jump, **James H. Strong and Stanley Switlik (1939):** Coney Island. Not in service. (Map 6B/Brooklyn)

Peace Fountain, **Greg Wyatt (1984–1985):** Next to the Cathedral of St. John the Divine, Amsterdam Avenue at West 111th Street (Map 5A/Grid 2B)

Pepsi-Cola Sign, **Artkraft Strauss Sign Corporation (1936):** Gantry Plaza State Park, Hunter's Point, Queens. (Map 6B/Queens)

Peter Pan, **Charles Andrew Hafner (1928):** Carl Schulz Park, East End Avenue at 86th Street. Originally created for the lobby of the Paramount Theater in Times Square. (Map 5B/Grid 4D).

Postcards, **Masayuki Sono (2004):** St. George Esplanade near Hamilton Avenue. The Staten Island September 11 memorial. (Map 6A/Staten Island)

Prometheus, **Paul Manship (1934):** The Rink at 30 Rockefeller Plaza, 5th Avenue between West 49th and West 50th Streets (Map 3A/Grid 3A)

Ralph Kramden (Jackie Gleason), **Lawrence J. Nowlan, Jr. (2000):** 40th Street and 8th Avenue, Port Authority Bus Terminal, south building (Map 3A/Grid 2B)

The Real World, **Ted Otterness (1992):** River Terrace and Warren Street (Map 1A/Grid 1A)

The Red Cube, **Isamu Noguchi (1967):** 140 Broadway at Liberty Street (Map 1A/Grid 2B)

***Red 9* sculpture, Ivan Chermayeff (1972):** 9 West 57th Street (Solow Building) near Fifth Avenue (Map 4B/Grid 3D)

***The Revelers* (tile murals), Jane Dickson (2008):** 42nd Street and 7th Avenue, Times Square Subway. There are many tile artworks on other Manhattan subway platforms. (Map 3A/Grid 2A)

***The Seat,* David Saunders (1987):** Owen Dolan Park, Westchester Square, Bronx (Map 6B/Bronx)

***Sphere,* Fritz Koenig:** Mount Sinai Hospital, 1184 Fifth Avenue at 100th Street. View through fence. (Map 5B/Grid 3B)

***Sphere for Plaza Fountain,* Fritz Koenig (1968–1971):** Liberty Park, near West Street at Liberty Street (Map 1A/Grid B2)

***Statue of Liberty,* Frederic Auguste Bartholdi (design), Gustave Eiffel (builder) (1886):** Liberty Island, New York Harbor (Map 1A/Grid 1D)

***Statue of Shinran Shonin,* sculptor unknown:** 331 Riverside Drive between 105th and 106th Streets (Map 5A/Grid 1A)

***Still Hunt,* Edward Kemeys (1883):** Central Park, East Drive at 76th Street (Map 4B/Grid 3A)

***Subway Map Floating on a NY Sidewalk,* Francoise Schein (1985):** 110 Greene Street between Prince and Spring Streets (Map 2A/Grid 2C)

***Sunken Garden, Chase Manhattan Bank Plaza,* Isamu Noguchi (1961–1964):** 1 Chase Manhattan Plaza, near Pine and William Streets (Map 1A/Grid 2B)

***Taxi!,* J. Seward Johnson, Jr. (1983):** Southeast corner of Park Avenue and East 48th Street (Map 3B/Grid3A)

***Teardrop Park,* Michael Van Valkenburgh Associates (1999–2006):** Warren Street and River Terrace (Map 1A)

***The Thinker (Le Penseur),* Auguste Rodin (1880):** Columbia University, Philosophy Building courtyard near 117th and Amsterdam (Map 5A/Grid 2A)

***Time,* Jose Maria Sert (1941):** Ceiling mural in main lobby, 30 Rockefeller Plaza, 5th Avenue between West 49th and 50th Streets (Map 3A/Grid 3A)

***Times Square,* Max Neuhaus (1977):** Broadway at 7th Avenue and 46th Street, vent shaft on traffic island. Sound sculpture. (Map 3A/Grid 2A)

***Times Square Ball,* originally by Artkraft Strauss (1907):** Atop One Times Square at 42nd Street and Broadway (Map 3A/Grid 2A)

***Times Square Mural,* Roy Lichtenstein (1994):** Times Square, 42nd Street subway near the 7 shuttle (Map 4A/Grid 2B)

***The Triumph of Music* (left) and *The Sources of Music* (right), Marc Chagall (1966):** Two murals at the Metropolitan Opera House, Lincoln Center, Broadway at 63rd Street (Map 4A/Grid 1C)

***(Untitled) Two Dancing Figures* (1989) and *(Untitled) Figure Balancing on Dog* (1986), Keith Haring:** Two sculptures at 17 State Street between Pearl and Walker Streets (Map 1A/Grid 2D)

***The Unisphere,* Gilmore D. Clarke (1964):** Flushing Meadows, Corona Park (Map 6B/Queens)

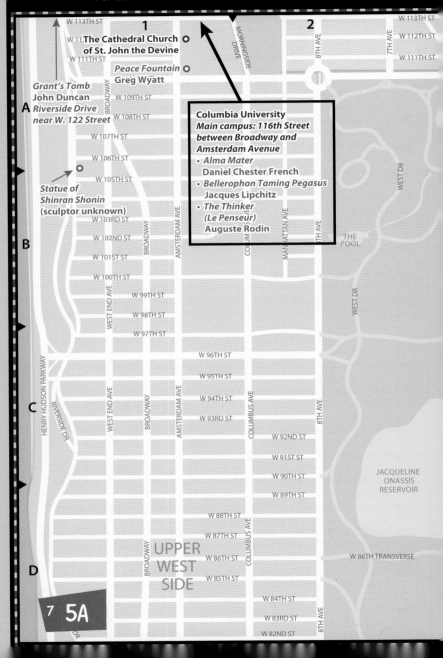

1

W 113TH ST
W 112TH ST

The Cathedral Church of St. John the Devine ○

W 111TH ST

Peace Fountain ○
Greg Wyatt

Grant's Tomb
John Duncan
Riverside Drive
near W. 122 Street

W 109TH ST
W 108TH ST
W 107TH ST
W 106TH ST
W 105TH ST

Statue of
Shinran Shonin
(sculptor unknown)

W 103RD ST
W 102ND ST
W 101ST ST
W 100TH ST
W 99TH ST
W 98TH ST
W 97TH ST
W 96TH ST
W 95TH ST
W 94TH ST
W 93RD ST
W 92ND ST
W 91ST ST
W 90TH ST
W 89TH ST
W 88TH ST
W 87TH ST
W 86TH ST
W 85TH ST
W 84TH ST
W 83RD ST
W 82ND ST

Columbia University
Main campus: 116th Street
between Broadway and
Amsterdam Avenue
- *Alma Mater*
  Daniel Chester French
- *Bellerophon Taming Pegasus*
  Jacques Lipchitz
- *The Thinker*
  (Le Penseur)
  Auguste Rodin

2

W 113TH ST
W 112TH ST
W 111TH ST

THE POOL

WEST DR

JACQUELINE ONASSIS RESERVOIR

W 86TH TRANSVERSE

UPPER WEST SIDE

A
B
C
D

MORNINGSIDE DRIVE
8TH AVE
7TH AVE
BROADWAY
AMSTERDAM AVE
COLUMBUS AVE
MANHATTAN AVE
WEST END AVE
HENRY HUDSON PARKWAY
RIVERSIDE DR

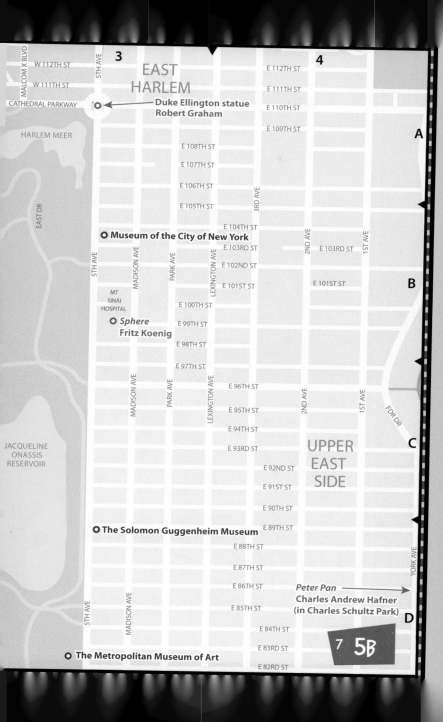

3

W 112TH ST

5TH AVE

EAST
HARLEM

E 112TH ST

4

W 111TH ST

E 111TH ST

MALCOM X BLVD

CATHEDRAL PARKWAY

E 110TH ST

Duke Ellington statue
Robert Graham

E 109TH ST

A

HARLEM MEER

E 108TH ST

E 107TH ST

E 106TH ST

EAST DR

3RD AVE

E 105TH ST

E 104TH ST

Museum of the City of New York

E 103RD ST

2ND AVE

1ST AVE

E 103RD ST

MADISON AVE

PARK AVE

LEXINGTON AVE

E 102ND ST

5TH AVE

E 101ST ST

E 101ST ST

B

MT
SINAI
HOSPITAL

E 100TH ST

Sphere
Fritz Koenig

E 99TH ST

E 98TH ST

E 97TH ST

MADISON AVE

PARK AVE

LEXINGTON AVE

E 96TH ST

2ND AVE

1ST AVE

E 95TH ST

E 94TH ST

FDR DR

JACQUELINE
ONASSIS
RESERVOIR

E 93RD ST

C

E 92ND ST

UPPER
EAST
SIDE

E 91ST ST

E 90TH ST

E 89TH ST

The Solomon Guggenheim Museum

E 88TH ST

E 87TH ST

E 86TH ST

YORK AVE

Peter Pan
**Charles Andrew Hafner
(in Charles Schultz Park)**

5TH AVE

MADISON AVE

E 85TH ST

D

E 84TH ST

E 83RD ST

⁷ **5B**

The Metropolitan Museum of Art

E 82RD ST

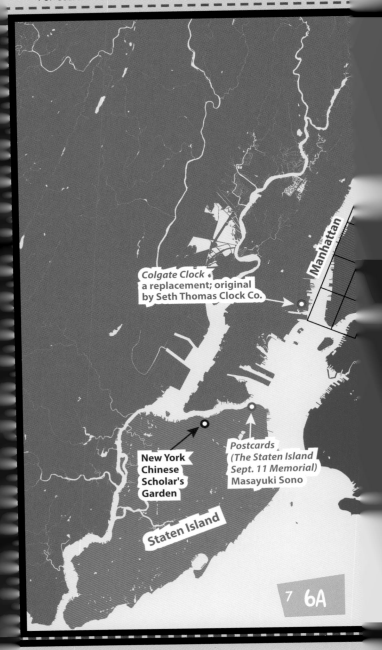

Colgate Clock
a replacement; original
by Seth Thomas Clock Co.

Manhattan

**New York
Chinese
Scholar's
Garden**

*Postcards
(The Staten Island
Sept. 11 Memorial)*
Masayuki Sono

Staten Island

7 **6A**

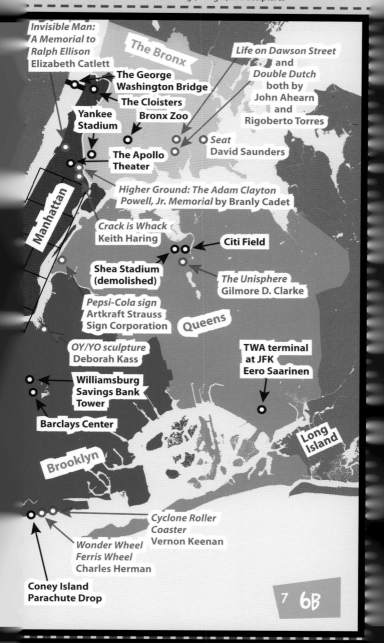

Invisible Man: A Memorial to Ralph Ellison Elizabeth Catlett

The Bronx

Life on Dawson Street and **Double Dutch** both by John Ahearn and Rigoberto Torres

The George Washington Bridge

The Cloisters

Yankee Stadium

Bronx Zoo

Seat David Saunders

The Apollo Theater

Manhattan

Higher Ground: The Adam Clayton Powell, Jr. Memorial by Branly Cadet

Crack is Whack Keith Haring

Citi Field

Shea Stadium (demolished)

The Unisphere Gilmore D. Clarke

Pepsi-Cola sign Artkraft Strauss Sign Corporation

Queens

OY/YO sculpture Deborah Kass

TWA terminal at JFK Eero Saarinen

Williamsburg Savings Bank Tower

Barclays Center

Long Island

Brooklyn

Cyclone Roller Coaster Vernon Keenan

Wonder Wheel Ferris Wheel Charles Herman

Coney Island Parachute Drop

7 6B

Untitled, **Forrest Myers (1973):** 599 Broadway at Houston Street (Soho wall) (Map 2A/Grid 2C)

The Upper Room, **Ned Smyth (1984–1987):** Battery Park City on Albany Street at the Esplanade (Map 1A/Grid 1C)

The Vessel, **Thomas Heatherwick** (2018): Between 10th and 11th Avenues and 31st to 32nd Streets (Map 3B/C1)

Wall Street Digital Clock, **Rudolph de Harak (1971):** 200 Water Street at John Street (Map 1B/Grid 3B)

Whisper Gallery **(1903):** Outside Oyster Bar, Grand Central Terminal, East 42nd Street and Park Avenue (Map 3B/Grid 3B)

Wonder Wheel, **Charles Herman (1918–1920):** Coney Island ferris wheel (Map 6B/Brooklyn)

Numbers

3D Model of Old Nieuw Amsterdam: 1660, **Simon Verity and Martha Becker (2011):** In the park outside the Staten Island Ferry (Map 1A/Grid 2D)

42nd Street Ballroom, **George Rhoads (1983):** Port Authority Bus Terminal North Wing, 42nd Street and 8th Avenue (Map 3A/Grid 2B)

7000 Oaks, **Joseph Beuys (1982):** West 22nd Street between 10th and 11th Avenues (Map 3A/Grid 1D)

NEW YORK CITY HISTORY

FAMOUS NYC MOB LOCATIONS

Where They Lived

Al Capone (as a youth): 21 Garfield Place between 4th and 5th Avenues, Park Slope, Brooklyn

Frank Costello: The Majestic, 115 Central Park West at 72nd Street

Vincent "The Chin" Gigante: 225 Sullivan Street between Bleecker and West 3rd Streets

Meyer Lansky: 40 Central Park South between Fifth and Sixth Avenues

Lucky Luciano: The Majestic, 115 Central Park West at 72nd Street

Benjamin "Bugsy" Siegel: Waldorf-Astoria, 100 East 50th Street at Park Avenue

The Mob's Greatest Hits: Where They Got Rubbed Out

Herman Rosenthal (1912): Hotel Metropole, 147 West 43rd Street. Sidewalk.

Arnold "The Brain" Rothstein (1928): Park Central Hotel, 870 7th Avenue at 55th Street. Suite.

Vincent "Mad Dog" Coll (1931): 314 West 23rd Street. Drugstore phone booth.

Abe "Kid Twist" Reles (1941): Half Moon Hotel, Coney Island. Out a window.

Albert Anastasia (1957): Park Sheraton, now Park Central, 870 Seventh Avenue at 56th Street. Barbershop.

Joe Colombo (1971): Columbus Circle. Standing, at a rally.

"Crazy Joe" Gallo (1972): Umberto's Clam house; then at 129 Mulberry Street at Hester Street. Dining.

Carmine Galante (1979): Joe & Mary's Italian Restaurant, 205 Knickerbocker Avenue, Bushwick, Brooklyn. Backyard.

Big Paul Castellano (1985): Sparks Steak House, 210 East 46th Street. Entering car.

Social Clubs

Ravenite Social Club (John Gotti): 247 Mulberry Street, south of Prince Street. Now a shoe store.

Triangle Civic Improvement Association (Vincent "The Chin" Gigante): 208 Sullivan Street. Now a tea store.

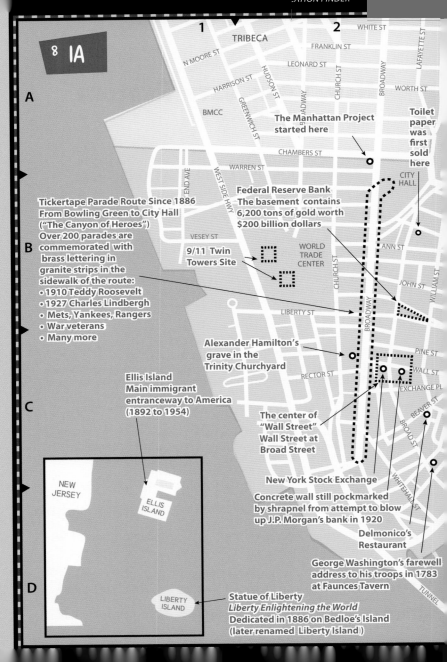

8 1A

TRIBECA

WHITE ST

FRANKLIN ST

LEONARD ST

N' MOORE ST

HARRISON ST

HUDSON ST

BROADWAY

CHURCH ST

WORTH ST

LAFAYETTE ST

BROADWAY

A

BMCC

GREENWICH ST

The Manhattan Project started here

CHAMBERS ST

WARREN ST

Toilet paper was first sold here

CITY HALL

ANN ST

Federal Reserve Bank
The basement contains 6,200 tons of gold worth $200 billion dollars

END AVE

WEST SIDE HWY

VESEY ST

Tickertape Parade Route Since 1886 From Bowling Green to City Hall ("The Canyon of Heroes") Over 200 parades are commemorated with brass lettering in granite strips in the sidewalk of the route:
• **1910 Teddy Roosevelt**
• **1927 Charles Lindbergh**
• **Mets, Yankees, Rangers**
• **War veterans**
• **Many more**

9/11 Twin Towers Site

WORLD TRADE CENTER

CHURCH ST

JOHN ST

WILLIAM ST

B

LIBERTY ST

BROADWAY

PINE ST

Alexander Hamilton's grave in the Trinity Churchyard

WALL ST

RECTOR ST

EXCHANGE PL

Ellis Island Main immigrant entranceway to America (1892 to 1954)

BEAVER ST

The center of "Wall Street" Wall Street at Broad Street

C

New York Stock Exchange

BROAD ST

WHITEHALL ST

Concrete wall still pockmarked by shrapnel from attempt to blow up J.P. Morgan's bank in 1920

Delmonico's Restaurant

NEW JERSEY

ELLIS ISLAND

George Washington's farewell address to his troops in 1783 at Faunces Tavern

TUNNEL

D

LIBERTY ISLAND

Statue of Liberty *Liberty Enlightening the World* **Dedicated in 1886 on Bedloe's Island (later renamed Liberty Island)**

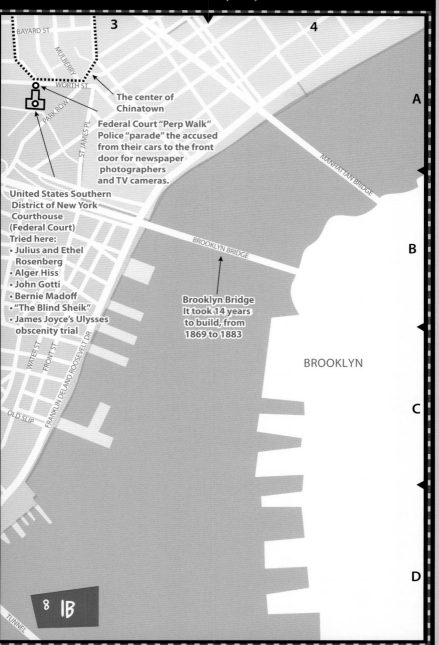

3

BAYARD ST.

MULBERRY

WORTH ST.

PARK ROW

ST JAMES PL.

4

MANHATTAN BRIDGE

A

The center of
Chinatown

Federal Court "Perp Walk"
Police "parade" the accused
from their cars to the front
door for newspaper
photographers
and TV cameras.

BROOKLYN BRIDGE

B

United States Southern
District of New York
Courthouse
(Federal Court)
Tried here:
• Julius and Ethel
  Rosenberg
• Alger Hiss
• John Gotti
• Bernie Madoff
• "The Blind Sheik"
• James Joyce's Ulysses
  obscenity trial

Brooklyn Bridge
It took 14 years
to build, from
1869 to 1883

WATER ST.

FRONT ST.

FRANKLIN DELANO ROOSEVELT DR

BROOKLYN

C

OLD SLIP

D

8 1B

TUNNEL

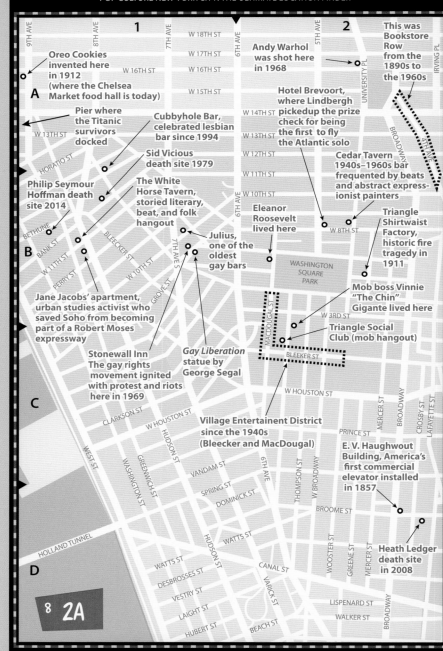

1

2

W 18TH ST
W 17TH ST
W 16TH ST
W 15TH ST
W 14TH ST
W 13TH ST
W 12TH ST
W 11TH ST
W 10TH ST

Oreo Cookies invented here in 1912 (where the Chelsea Market food hall is today)

A

Andy Warhol was shot here in 1968

This was Bookstore Row from the 1890s to the 1960s

Pier where the Titanic survivors docked

Cubbyhole Bar, celebrated lesbian bar since 1994

Sid Vicious death site 1979

Hotel Brevoort, where Lindbergh pickedup the prize check for being the first to fly the Atlantic solo

Philip Seymour Hoffman death site 2014

The White Horse Tavern, storied literary, beat, and folk hangout

Cedar Tavern 1940s–1960s bar frequented by beats and abstract expressionist painters

Triangle Shirtwaist Factory, historic fire tragedy in 1911

Eleanor Roosevelt lived here

Julius, one of the oldest gay bars

B

Jane Jacobs' apartment, urban studies activist who saved Soho from becoming part of a Robert Moses expressway

WASHINGTON SQUARE PARK

Mob boss Vinnie "The Chin" Gigante lived here

W 3RD ST

Triangle Social Club (mob hangout)

BLEEKER ST

Stonewall Inn The gay rights movement ignited with protest and riots here in 1969

Gay Liberation statue by George Segal

W HOUSTON ST

C

CLARKSON ST
W HOUSTON ST

Village Entertainment District since the 1940s (Bleecker and MacDougal)

PRINCE ST

E. V. Haughwout Building, America's first commercial elevator installed in 1857

VANDAM ST
SPRING ST
DOMINICK ST

BROOME ST

HOLLAND TUNNEL

WATTS ST

Heath Ledger death site in 2008

D

WATTS ST
DESBROSSES ST
VESTRY ST
LAIGHT ST
HUBERT ST

CANAL ST

LISPENARD ST
WALKER ST

8 2A

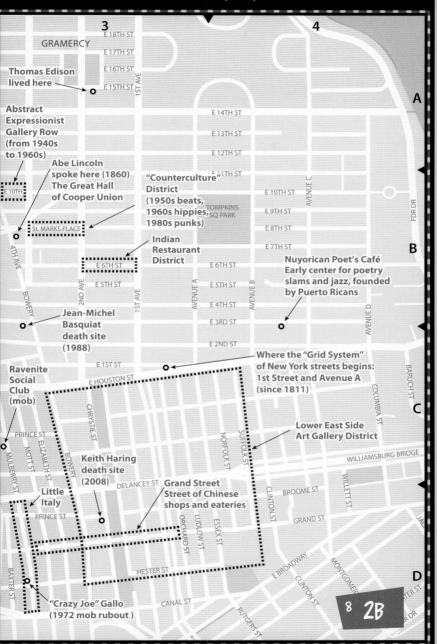

GRAMERCY

E 18TH ST
E 17TH ST
E 16TH ST
E 15TH ST

Thomas Edison lived here

Abstract Expressionist Gallery Row (from 1940s to 1960s)

E 10TH

Abe Lincoln spoke here (1860) The Great Hall of Cooper Union

St. MARKS PLACE

"Counterculture" District (1950s beats, 1960s hippies, 1980s punks)

E 14TH ST
E 13TH ST
E 12TH ST
E 11TH ST
E 10TH ST
E 9TH ST
E 8TH ST
E 7TH ST

TOMPKINS SQ PARK

AVENUE C

FDR DR

A

Indian Restaurant District

E 6TH ST

Nuyorican Poet's Café Early center for poetry slams and jazz, founded by Puerto Ricans

E 6TH ST
E 5TH ST
E 4TH ST
E 3RD ST
E 2ND ST

4TH AVE

BOWERY

2ND AVE

1ST AVE

E 5TH ST

AVENUE A

AVENUE B

AVENUE D

B

Jean-Michel Basquiat death site (1988)

Where the "Grid System" of New York streets begins: 1st Street and Avenue A (since 1811)

E 1ST ST
E HOUSTON ST

Ravenite Social Club (mob)

PRINCE ST

MULBERRY ST

MOTT ST

ELIZABETH ST

BOWERY

CHRYSTIE ST

Keith Haring death site (2008)

DELANCEY ST

Little Italy

PRINCE ST

Grand Street Street of Chinese shops and eateries

NORFOLK ST

SUFFOLK ST

CLINTON ST

Lower East Side Art Gallery District

BARUCH ST

COLUMBIA ST

WILLIAMSBURG BRIDGE

C

BROOME ST

GRAND ST

ORCHARD ST

LUDLOW ST

ESSEX ST

WILLETT ST

"Crazy Joe" Gallo (1972 mob rubout)

BAXTER ST

HESTER ST

CANAL ST

E BROADWAY

CLINTON ST

RUTGERS ST

MONTGOMERY

FDR DR

D

8 **2B**

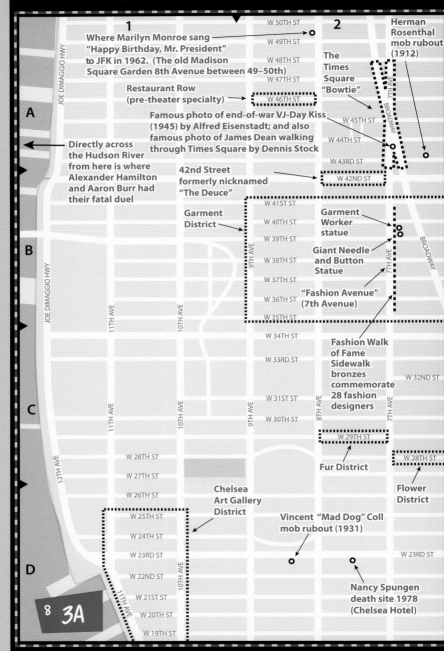

1

W 50TH ST
W 49TH ST

Where Marilyn Monroe sang "Happy Birthday, Mr. President" to JFK in 1962. (The old Madison Square Garden 8th Avenue between 49–50th)

W 48TH ST
W 47TH ST

Restaurant Row (pre-theater specialty)

W 46TH ST

Famous photo of end-of-war VJ-Day Kiss (1945) by Alfred Eisenstadt; and also famous photo of James Dean walking through Times Square by Dennis Stock

A

Directly across the Hudson River from here is where Alexander Hamilton and Aaron Burr had their fatal duel

42nd Street formerly nicknamed "The Deuce"

Garment District

W 45TH ST
W 44TH ST
W 43RD ST
W 42ND ST
W 41ST ST
W 40TH ST
W 39TH ST
W 38TH ST
W 37TH ST
W 36TH ST
W 35TH ST
W 34TH ST
W 33RD ST
W 32ND ST
W 31ST ST
W 30TH ST
W 29TH ST
W 28TH ST
W 27TH ST
W 26TH ST
W 25TH ST
W 24TH ST
W 23RD ST
W 22ND ST
W 21ST ST
W 20TH ST
W 19TH ST

2

Herman Rosenthal mob rubout (1912)

The Times Square "Bowtie"

B

Garment Worker statue

Giant Needle and Button Statue

"Fashion Avenue" (7th Avenue)

Fashion Walk of Fame Sidewalk bronzes commemorate 28 fashion designers

C

Fur District

Flower District

Chelsea Art Gallery District

Vincent "Mad Dog" Coll mob rubout (1931)

D

Nancy Spungen death site 1978 (Chelsea Hotel)

JOE DIMAGGIO HWY
12TH AVE
11TH AVE
10TH AVE
9TH AVE
8TH AVE
7TH AVE
BROADWAY

8 3A

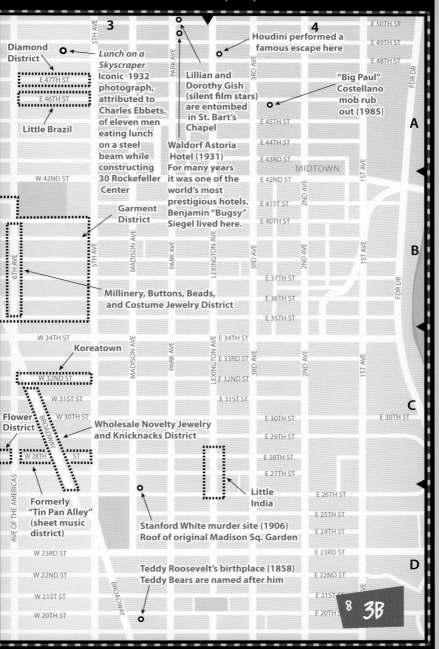

3

4

Diamond District

Lunch on a Skyscraper Iconic 1932 photograph, attributed to Charles Ebbets, of eleven men eating lunch on a steel beam while constructing 30 Rockefeller Center

Lillian and Dorothy Gish (silent film stars) are entombed in St. Bart's Chapel

Houdini performed a famous escape here

"Big Paul" Costellano mob rub out (1985)

A

Little Brazil

Waldorf Astoria Hotel (1931) For many years it was one of the world's most prestigious hotels. Benjamin "Bugsy" Siegel lived here.

W 42ND ST

E 45TH ST

E 44TH ST

E 43RD ST

E 42ND ST

E 41ST ST

E 40TH ST

MIDTOWN

Garment District

B

Millinery, Buttons, Beads, and Costume Jewelry District

E 37TH ST

E 36TH ST

E 35TH ST

W 34TH ST

Koreatown

E 34TH ST

E 33RD ST

E 32ND ST

E 31ST ST

W 32ND ST

W 31ST ST

W 30TH ST

C

Flower District

Wholesale Novelty Jewelry and Knicknacks District

E 30TH ST

E 30TH ST

E 29TH ST

W 28TH ST

E 28TH ST

E 27TH ST

Little India

E 26TH ST

Formerly "Tin Pan Alley" (sheet music district)

E 25TH ST

E 24TH ST

Stanford White murder site (1906) Roof of original Madison Sq. Garden

W 23RD ST

E 23RD ST

D

W 22ND ST

Teddy Roosevelt's birthplace (1858) Teddy Bears are named after him

E 22ND ST

W 21ST ST

E 21ST ST

W 20TH ST

E 20TH ST

8 3B

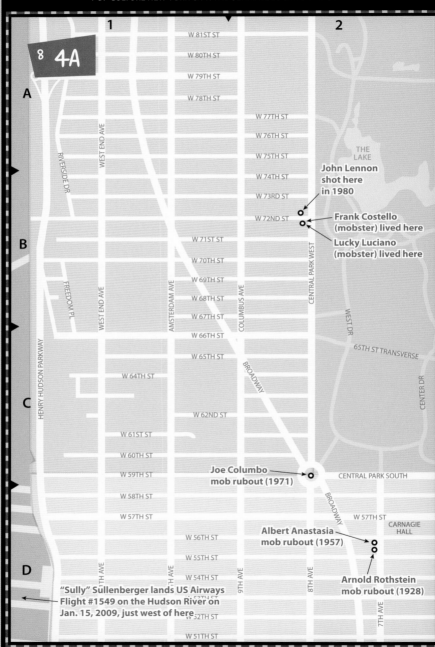

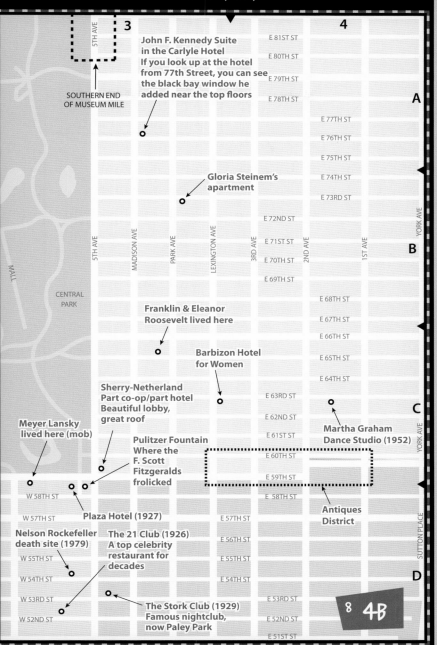

3

4

John F. Kennedy Suite in the Carlyle Hotel
If you look up at the hotel from 77th Street, you can see the black bay window he added near the top floors

5TH AVE

E 81ST ST
E 80TH ST
E 79TH ST
E 78TH ST

SOUTHERN END OF MUSEUM MILE

A

E 77TH ST
E 76TH ST
E 75TH ST

Gloria Steinem's apartment

E 74TH ST
E 73RD ST

E 72ND ST

5TH AVE   MADISON AVE   PARK AVE   LEXINGTON AVE   3RD AVE   2ND AVE   1ST AVE   YORK AVE

B

E 71ST ST
E 70TH ST
E 69TH ST

CENTRAL PARK

MALL

Franklin & Eleanor Roosevelt lived here

E 68TH ST
E 67TH ST
E 66TH ST
E 65TH ST
E 64TH ST

Barbizon Hotel for Women

Sherry-Netherland
Part co-op/part hotel
Beautiful lobby, great roof

E 63RD ST
E 62ND ST
E 61ST ST

Martha Graham Dance Studio (1952)

C

YORK AVE

Meyer Lansky lived here (mob)

Pulitzer Fountain
Where the F. Scott Fitzgeralds frolicked

E 60TH ST
E 59TH ST
E 58TH ST

Antiques District

W 58TH ST
W 57TH ST

Plaza Hotel (1927)

E 57TH ST
E 56TH ST
E 55TH ST
E 54TH ST

SUTTON PLACE

D

Nelson Rockefeller death site (1979)

The 21 Club (1926)
A top celebrity restaurant for decades

W 55TH ST
W 54TH ST
W 53RD ST
W 52ND ST

The Stork Club (1929)
Famous nightclub, now Paley Park

E 53RD ST
E 52ND ST
E 51ST ST

8 4B

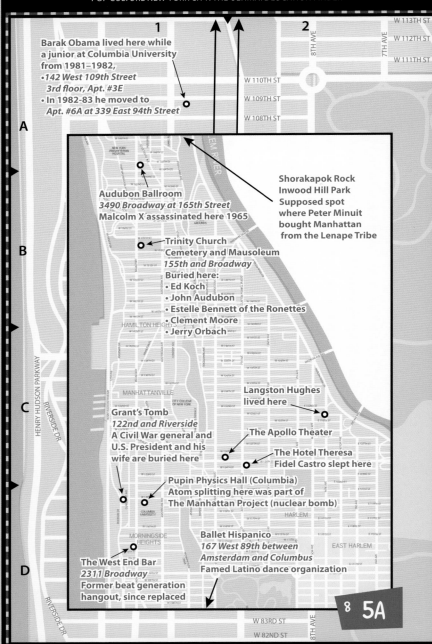

Barak Obama lived here while a junior at Columbia University from 1981–1982,
•*142 West 109th Street 3rd floor, Apt. #3E*
• *In 1982-83 he moved to Apt. #6A at 339 East 94th Street*

Shorakapok Rock Inwood Hill Park Supposed spot where Peter Minuit bought Manhattan from the Lenape Tribe

Audubon Ballroom
3490 Broadway at 165th Street
Malcolm X assassinated here 1965

Trinity Church Cemetery and Mausoleum
155th and Broadway
Buried here:
• Ed Koch
• John Audubon
• Estelle Bennett of the Ronettes
• Clement Moore
• Jerry Orbach

Langston Hughes lived here

Grant's Tomb
122nd and Riverside
A Civil War general and U.S. President and his wife are buried here

The Apollo Theater

The Hotel Theresa
Fidel Castro slept here

Pupin Physics Hall (Columbia)
Atom splitting here was part of The Manhattan Project (nuclear bomb)

Ballet Hispanico
167 West 89th between Amsterdam and Columbus
Famed Latino dance organization

The West End Bar
2311 Broadway
Former beat generation hangout, since replaced

8 **5A**

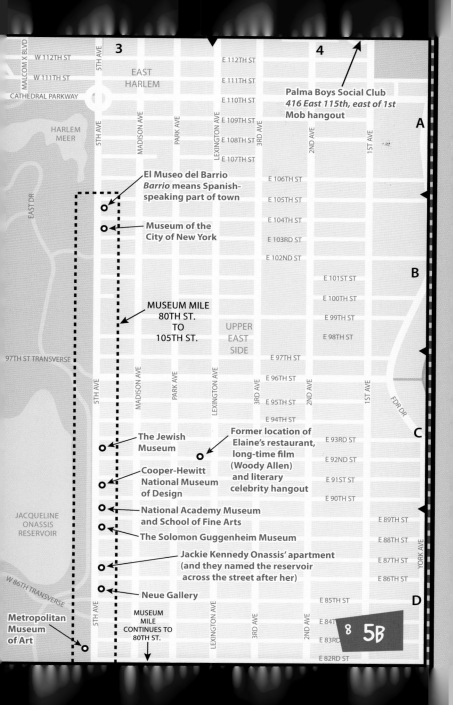

W 112TH ST

MALCOM X BLVD

W 111TH ST

5TH AVE

EAST
HARLEM

E 112TH ST

E 111TH ST

Palma Boys Social Club
416 East 115th, east of 1st
Mob hangout

CATHEDRAL PARKWAY

E 110TH ST

E 109TH ST

A

HARLEM
MEER

MADISON AVE

PARK AVE

LEXINGTON AVE

3RD AVE

2ND AVE

1ST AVE

E 108TH ST

E 107TH ST

5TH AVE

El Museo del Barrio
Barrio means Spanish-
speaking part of town

E 106TH ST

E 105TH ST

Museum of the
City of New York

E 104TH ST

E 103RD ST

E 102ND ST

B

E 101ST ST

E 100TH ST

MUSEUM MILE
80TH ST.
TO
105TH ST.

UPPER
EAST
SIDE

E 99TH ST

E 98TH ST

97TH ST TRANSVERSE

E 97TH ST

MADISON AVE

PARK AVE

LEXINGTON AVE

3RD AVE

E 96TH ST

2ND AVE

1ST AVE

FDR DR

5TH AVE

E 95TH ST

E 94TH ST

C

The Jewish
Museum

Former location of
Elaine's restaurant,
long-time film
(Woody Allen)
and literary
celebrity hangout

E 93RD ST

E 92ND ST

Cooper-Hewitt
National Museum
of Design

E 91ST ST

E 90TH ST

JACQUELINE
ONASSIS
RESERVOIR

National Academy Museum
and School of Fine Arts

E 89TH ST

The Solomon Guggenheim Museum

E 88TH ST

YORK AVE

Jackie Kennedy Onassis' apartment
(and they named the reservoir
across the street after her)

E 87TH ST

E 86TH ST

W 86TH TRANSVERSE

Neue Gallery

E 85TH ST

D

**Metropolitan
Museum
of Art**

5TH AVE

MUSEUM
MILE
CONTINUES TO
80TH ST.

LEXINGTON AVE

3RD AVE

2ND AVE

E 84TH ST

E 83RD ST

8 **5B**

E 82RD ST

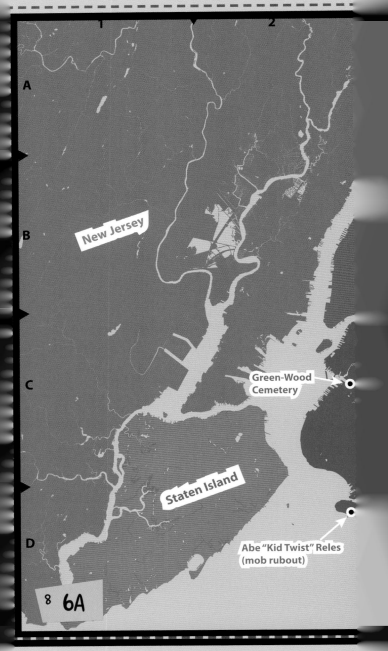

1 2

A

B

New Jersey

C

Green-Wood Cemetery

Staten Island

D

Abe "Kid Twist" Reles
(mob rubout)

8 6A

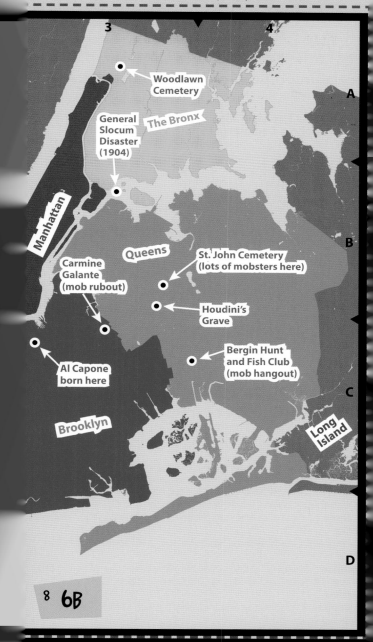

3

4

Woodlawn
Cemetery

A

General
Slocum
Disaster
(1904)

The Bronx

Manhattan

B

Queens

St. John Cemetery
(lots of mobsters here)

Carmine
Galante
(mob rubout)

Houdini's
Grave

Al Capone
born here

Bergin Hunt
and Fish Club
(mob hangout)

C

Brooklyn

Long
Island

D

8 6B

Palma Boys Social Club (Anthony "Fat Tony" Salerno): 416 East 115th Street
Bergin Hunt and Fish Club (John Gotti): 98–04 101st Avenue, Ozone Park, Queens. Now a pet grooming business.

The Main Mob Burial Ground:
St. John's Cemetery, Middle Village, Queens

Joe Colombo
Carmine Galante
Carlo Gambino
Vito Genovese
John Gotti
Charles "Lucky" Luciano
Joe Profaci
Salvatore Maranzano
Frank Costello

WHERE FAMOUS NEW YORK ARTISTS
AND PHOTOGRAPHERS LIVED OR WORKED

Alice Austen: 2 Hylan Boulevard, Rosebank, Staten Island
Diane Arbus: 71 Washington Place between 6th Avenue and Washington Square West, 121 1/2 Charles Street between Greenwich Street and Hudson Street
Jean-Michael Basquiat: 57 Great Jones Street between Bowery and Lafayette Street
Marc Chagall: 4 East 74th between 5th and Madison Avenues, 75 Riverside Drive between 79th and 80th Streets
Howard Chandler Christy: 1 West 67th Street between Central Park West and Columbus Avenue
Chuck Close: 20 Bond Street at Lafayette Street
William de Kooning: 88 East 10th Street between 3rd and 4th Avenues; 831 Broadway between 12th and 13th Streets, top floor
Marcel Duchamp: 28 West 10th Street between 5th and 6th Avenues
Milton Glaser: 27 West 67th Street between Central Park West and Columbus Avenue
Keith Haring: 676 Broadway between Bond and Great Jones Streets, 5th floor
Hans Hoffman: His school was at 52 West 8th Street between 5th and 6th Avenues. He later lived at 88 East 10th Street between 3rd and 4th Avenues.
Edward Hopper: 3 Washington Square North between 5th Avenue and University Place, fourth floor

NYC Tech Companies

Jasper Johns: 278 Pearl Street between Fulton and Beekman Streets. Since demolished.

Andre Kertesz: 2 Fifth Avenue at 8th Street between Washington Square North and 8th Street

Franz Klein: 52 East Ninth Street between University Place and Broadway

Jeff Koons: 11 East 67th Street between 5th and Madison Avenues

Lee Krasner: 46 East 8th Street at Greene Street

Stan Lee: 220 East 63rd Street between 2nd and 3rd Avenues

Fernand Leger: 222 Bowery between Prince and String Streets. His studio, 1940–1941.

Annie Leibovitz: 307 West 11th Street at Greenwich Street; London Terrace Gardens, 400 block of West 23rd Street

Jay Maisel: 190 Bowery at Spring Street

Piet Mondrian: 345 East 56th Street at 1st Avenue

Georgia O'Keefe: Shelton Hotel, 525 Lexington between 48th and 49th Streets, 30th floor (1925–1937)

Maxfield Parrish: 49 East 63rd Street between Madison and Park Avenues

Jackson Pollock: 446 East 8th Street at Greene Street (one of many)

Robert Rauschenberg: 278 Pearl Street between Fulton and Beekman Streets, since demolished

Mark Rothko: 157 East 69th Street between Lexington and Third Avenues

Julien Schnabel: 360 West 11th Street between Washington Street and West Street. Called the "Palazzo Chupi."

Alfred Stieglitz: Hotel Shelton, 525 Lexington Avenue between 48th and 49th Streets

Andy Warhol: 242 Lexington Avenue at 34th Street (before 1960), 1342 Lexington between 89th and 90th Streets (from 1960–1974), 57 East 66th between Madison and Park Avenues (from 1974–1987)

FAMOUS ARTIST BARS

The Cedar Tavern: 24 University Place between 8th and 9th Streets. Since replaced.

Chumley's: 86 Bedford Street at Barrow Street

The Lion's Head: 59 Christopher Street at 7th Avenue South. Now the Kettle of Fish.

The San Remo: 93 MacDougal Street at Bleecker Street. Closed.

Slugs' Saloon: 242 East 3rd Street between Avenues B and C. Closed.

Stanley's: 12th Street and Avenue B. Closed.

New York City Sports History Sites

LEGENDARY NEW YORK SPORTS FIGURES: RESIDENCES AND HANGOUTS

New York Sports Legends: Residences

Tiki Barber: 515 East 72nd Street between York Avenue and FDR Drive. Giants football.

Yogi Berra: 19 Highland Avenue, Montclair, New Jersey, for 40 years. Yankees baseball.

Tom Brady: Time Warner Center, 10 Columbus Circle, 59th and Broadway. New England Patriots football.

Bob Costas: 15 Central Park West between 61st and 62nd Streets. Sports announcer.

Jack Dempsey: The Ritz Carlton Hotel (1934–1935), 112 Central Park South between 6th and 7th Avenues. Boxer, restaurateur.

Joe DiMaggio: 400 West End Avenue between 79th and 80th Streets during his 56-game streak (1941). Hotel Elysee, 60 East 54th Street between Madison and Park Avenues (early 50s). Lexington Hotel, 511 Lexington Avenue at 48th Street, Suite 1806, during his marriage to Marilyn Monroe (1954–1955). Lexington Hotel (1957–1962). Yankees baseball.

Patrick Ewing: 174 Vaccaro Drive, Cresskill, New Jersey. Knicks basketball.

Walt Frazier: 381 Lenox Avenue at West 129th Street, Upper East Side. Knicks basketball.

Lou Gehrig: 9 Meadow Lane, New Rochelle, New York; 5204 Delafield Avenue, Riverdale, New York. Yankees baseball.

Frank Gifford: 322 East 57th Street between 1st and 2nd Avenues. Giants football, sports announcer.

Derek Jeter: 845 UN Plaza (Trump Tower), 1st Avenue between 47th and 48th Streets. Yankees baseball.

Billie Jean King: 101 West 79th Street at Columbus Avenue. Tennis player.

Joe Lewis: Park Central Hotel, 870 Seventh Avenue between 55th and 56th Streets (1960s). Boxer.

Patrick McEnroe: 285 Lafayette Street at Jersey Street. Tennis player.

Don Mattingly: 230 Engle Street, Tenafly, New Jersey. Yankees baseball.

Mickey Mantle: Concourse Plaza Hotel, 900 Grand Concourse at 161st Street, Bronx, near Yankee Stadium. Apartment over Stage Deli, 834 7th Avenue between 53rd and 54th Streets (1950s). St. Moritz Hotel, 50 Central Park South at 59th Street. Jackson Heights, Queens with Roger Maris and Bob Cerv (1961). Yankees baseball.

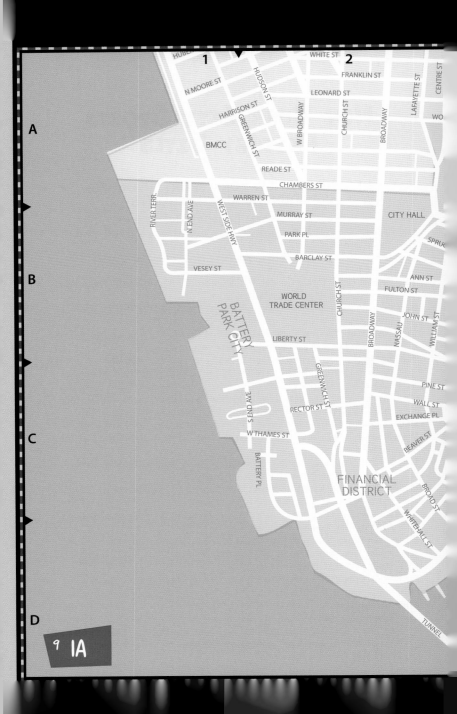

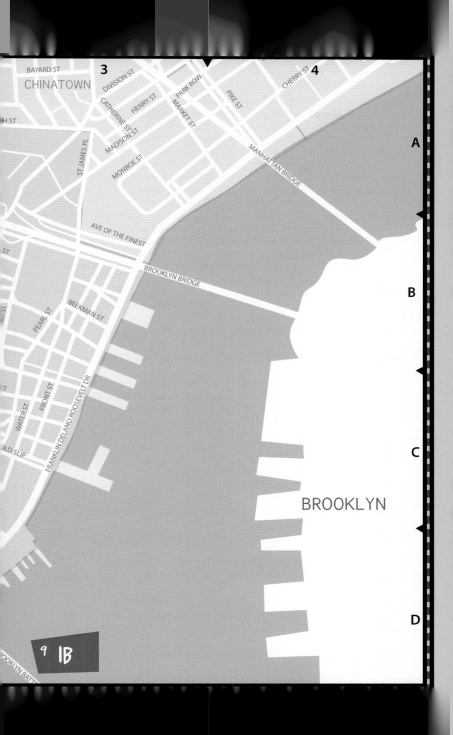

Willy Mays: 80 St. Nicholas Place, first floor, near 153rd and 155th Streets, Harlem. San Francisco Giants, Mets baseball.

Mark Messier: The Osborne, 205 West 57th Street (one-room apartment); 29 West 85th Street, Unit 3, brownstone (2006). Rangers hockey.

Joe Namath: 370 East 76th Street near East End (late 1960s); The Dakota, 1 West 72nd Street at Central Park West. Jets football.

Mike Piazza: 161 Hudson Street at Laight Street. Mets baseball.

Willis Reed: 61-35 98th Street in Park City Estates, Rego Park, Queens; Apartment in Kip Bay (after 1977). Knicks basketball.

Phil Rizzuto: 241 Windsor Way, Hillside, New Jersey (near Newark); 912 Westminster Avenue in Hillside, New Jersey. Yankees baseball.

Jackie Robinson: 5224 Tilden Street, Brooklyn. A National Historic Landmark. (1947–1949). 112–40 177th Street, Addisleigh Park, Queens (1949–1955). Broke the color barrier and was the first African-American in major league baseball. Dodgers baseball.

Sugar Ray Robinson: 940 St. Nicholas Avenue at West 157th Street (mother's apartment). Sugar Ray's, 2074 7th Avenue between 123rd and 124 Streets (replaced). Moved to L.A. (1960s). Boxer.

Andy Roddick: 205 East 22nd street between 2nd and 3rd Avenues. Tennis player.

Alex Rodriguez: 15 Central Park West between 61st and 62nd Streets. Yankees baseball.

Babe Ruth: Concourse Plaza Hotel, 900 Grand Concourse at 161st Street, Bronx; Ansonia Hotel, 2107 Broadway between West 73rd and 74th Streets (1920–1929); 345 West 88th Street between Riverside Drive and West End Avenue (1929–1942); 173 Riverside Drive at 89th Street; 110 Riverside Drive at 83rd Street (last residence). Yankees baseball.

Daryl Strawberry: 312 11th Avenue at 30th Street. Mets, Yankees baseball.

Lawrence Taylor: LT's Restaurant and Sports Bar, Route 17 South, East Rutherford, New Jersey. Closed. Giants football.

Serena Williams: 28 West 38th Street between 5th and 6th Avenues. Tennis player.

Venus Williams: 28 West 38th Street between 5th and 6th Avenues. Tennis player.

Tiger Woods: 421 Hudson Street between Clarkson and Leroy Streets. Golfer.

Legendary Sports Hangouts (All Closed)

Toots Shor's: 51 West 51st Street between 5th and 6th Avenues (1940s–1950s)

Jack Dempsey's: 1619 Broadway between 49th and 50th Streets

Mickey Mantle's: 42 Central Park South between 5th and 6th Avenues

Lindy's Restaurant: 1655 Broadway between 51st and 52nd Streets. Replaced.

Sugar Ray's: 2074 7th Avenue between 123rd and 124th Streets. Sugar Ray Robinson's Harlem nightclub.

FAMOUS NYC–AREA SPORTS ARENAS, PAST AND PRESENT LOCATIONS

Manhattan
Hockey, Basketball

Madison Square Garden #4 (1968–present): 7th Avenue and 32nd Street, Chelsea. New York Rangers hockey, New York Knicks basketball, New York Liberty basketball. Capacity 19,763.

Madison Square Garden #3 (1925–1968): 8th Avenue between 49th and 50th Streets, Hell's Kitchen. Capacity 18,500.

Madison Square Garden #1 and #2 (1879–1890; 1890–1925): Madison Avenue and 25th Street, Flatiron. Capacity 10,000.

Baseball

The Polo Grounds (#4) (1911–1963): 157th Street and 8th Avenue, Washington Heights. New York Giants baseball (1911–1957); team moved and became the San Francisco Giants in 1958. New York Yankees baseball (1913–1922). New York Mets baseball (1962–1963). Demolished 1964. Capacity 55,000.

Hilltop Park (1903–1914): Between Broadway and Fort Washington Avenue and 165th and 168th Street, Washington Heights. New York Yankees (1903–1912) when they were known as "The Highlanders." AKA American League Park. Capacity 16,000.

Lewisohn Stadium (1915–1973): City College of New York, 136th to 138th Streets and Convent Avenue, Harlem. Semi-circular outdoor stadium; seen in *Serpico* where Al Pacino meets Tony Roberts. Capacity 8,000.

Icahn Stadium (2005–Present): Randall's Island. Track and field events and music concerts. Capacity 5,000.

Baker Athletics Complex: Columbia University, 533 West 218th Street at Park Terrace West. Baker Field (1928–1982): Capacity 32,000. Lawrence Wein Stadium (1984–present): Capacity 17,100

The Bronx
Baseball, Soccer

Original Yankee Stadium (1923–1973, 1976–2008): 1 East 161st Street, Bronx. New York Yankees baseball (1923–1973, 1976–2008); New York Giants football (1956–1973). Capacity between 57,000 and 67,000.

Yankee Stadium (2009–present): 1 East 161st Street, Bronx. New York Yankees baseball, New York City FC soccer. Capacity 54,251.

Queens
Baseball

Citi Field (2009–present): 123–01 Roosevelt Avenue, Flushing Meadows, Corona Park, Queens. New York Mets baseball. Capacity approximately 41,922.

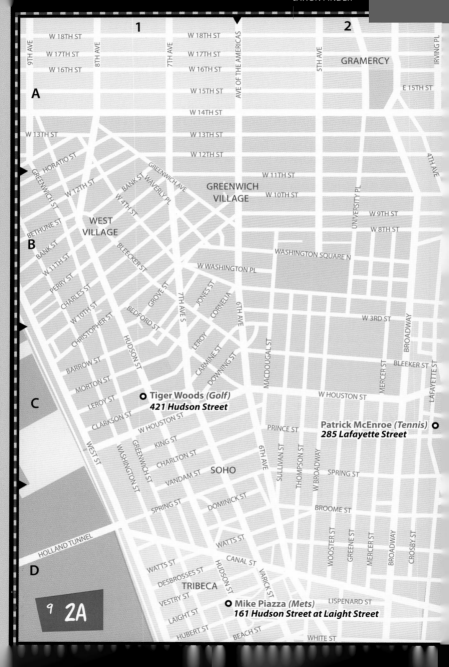

Shea Stadium (1964–2008): 123–01 Roosevelt Avenue, Flushing-Meadows-Corona Park, Queens. New York Mets baseball. Held the first stadium rock concert, The Beatles (1965, 55,000 sellout). Capacity approximately 45,000.

Tennis

USTA Billie Jean King National Tennis Center (1978–present): Flushing Meadows, Corona Park, Queens. Formerly the USTA National Tennis Center (until 2006). Has held the US Open Grand Slam since 1978. Capacity, Arthur Ashe Stadium 22,000.

Brooklyn
Basketball, Hockey

Barclays Center (2012–present): 620 Atlantic Avenue, Brooklyn. Brooklyn Nets basketball, New York Islanders hockey. Capacity 18,103.

Baseball

Ebbets Field (1913–1957; demolished 1960): 55 Sullivan Place at Bedford Avenue, Flatbush, Brooklyn. Brooklyn Dodgers baseball. Capacity 32,000.

MCU Park (2001–present): 1904 Surf Avenue, Brooklyn. Formerly KeySpan Park. Brooklyn Cyclones minor league baseball. Capacity 7,000 plus 2,000 standing.

Staten Island

Richmond County Bank Ballpark (2001–present): 75 Richmond Terrace, St. George, Staten Island. Staten Island Yankees minor league baseball. Capacity 7,171.

Long Island
Hockey

Nassau Coliseum (1972–present): 1255 Hempstead Turnpike, Uniondale, Town of Hempstead. New York Islanders hockey (1972–2015). New York Nets basketball (1972–1977). Capacity: 17,686.

New Jersey
Football

MetLife Stadium (2010–present): 1 MetLife Stadium Drive, East Rutherford, New Jersey. New York Giants football, New York Jets football. Capacity 82,500.

Giants Stadium (1976–2010): 50 New Jersey Route 120, East Rutherford, New Jersey. New York Giants (1976–2010), New York Jets (1984–2010). AKA "The Meadowlands." Capacity 80,242.

Basketball, Hockey

Meadowlands Arena (1981–present, under various names): 50 New Jersey Route 120, East Rutherford, New Jersey. New York Nets basketball, New Jersey Devils hockey. Formerly Continental Airlines Arena (1996–2007), Brendan Byrne Arena (1981–1996), Izod Center (2007–2016). Capacity 20,000.

Prudential Arena (2007–present): 25 Lafayette Street, Newark, New Jersey. New Jersey Devils hockey. AKA "The Rock." Capacity 18,711.

Soccer

Red Bull Arena (2009–present): 600 Cape May Street, Harrison, New Jersey. New York Red Bulls soccer. Capacity 25,000.

NEW YORK CITY SPECTATOR SPORTS

Major League Baseball

New York Mets: Citi Field, Queens
New York Yankees: Yankee Stadium, Bronx

Minor League Baseball

Brooklyn Cyclones: MCU Park, Brooklyn
Staten Island Yankees: Richmond County Bank Ballpark, Staten Island

Basketball

Brooklyn Nets: Barclay Stadium, Brooklyn
New York Knicks: Madison Square Garden, Manhattan
New York Liberty (WNBA): Madison Square Garden, Manhattan

Boxing

Madison Square Garden: Manhattan. Various bouts are held throughout the year.
Golden Gloves: An amateur boxing tournament that the *New York Daily News* sponsors annually.

Football

New York Giants: MetLife Stadium, New Jersey
New York Jets: MetLife Stadium, New Jersey

Hockey

New York Islanders: Barclay Center, Long Island
New York Rangers: Madison Square Garden, Manhattan
New Jersey Devils: Prudential Center, Newark, New Jersey

Jack Dempsey's Broadway Restaurant
1619 Broadway

○ **Daryl Strawberry** *(Mets, Yankees)*
312 Eleventh Avenue

HELL'S KITCHEN

CHELSEA

PENN STATION

JOE DIMAGGIO HWY

BROADWAY

1 2

A

B

C

D

W 50TH ST
W 49TH ST
W 48TH ST
W 47TH ST
W 46TH ST
W 45TH ST
W 44TH ST
W 43RD ST
W 42ND ST
W 41ST ST
W 40TH ST
W 39TH ST
W 38TH ST
W 37TH ST
W 36TH ST
W 35TH ST
W 34TH ST
W 33RD ST
W 32ND ST
W 31ST ST
W 30TH ST
W 29TH ST
W 28TH ST
W 27TH ST
W 26TH ST
W 25ND ST
W 24TH ST
W 23RD ST
W 22ND ST
W 21ST ST
W 20TH ST
W 19TH ST

11TH AVE
10TH AVE
9TH AVE
8TH AVE
7TH AVE
12TH AVE

9 3A

Horse Racing (Harness)
Yonkers Raceway: 810 Yonkers Avenue, Yonkers, New York. Half-mile harness racetrack and a casino with slot machines.
Meadowlands Racetrack: 1 Racetrack Drive, East Rutherford, New Jersey

Horse Racing (Thoroughbred)
Aqueduct Racetrack: 110-00 Rockaway Boulevard, South Ozone Park, Queens (May to October)
Belmont Park: 2150 Hempstead Turnpike, Belmont, Nassau County. Annual site of the Belmont Stakes Triple Crown championship, as well as seasonal thoroughbred horse races.
Meadowlands Racetrack: 1 Racetrack Drive, East Rutherford, New Jersey

Soccer
New York City Football Club: Yankee Stadium, Bronx
New York Red Bulls: Red Bull Arena, Harrison, New Jersey

Tennis
U.S. Open: USTA Billie Jean King National Tennis Center, Flushing Meadows, Corona Park, Queens (August)

Track and Field
Millrose Games: New Balance Track and Field Center at the Armory, 216 Fort Washington Avenue at 168th Street, Washington Heights. (February)

Professional Wrestling (WWE)
World Wrestling Entertainment: Events are held at Madison Square Garden, Manhattan, and MetLife Stadium, East Rutherford, New Jersey.

SPORTS STORES SELLING
OFFICIAL NYC TEAM CLOTHING

General (All Sports)
Modell's Sporting Goods: 234 West 42nd Street between 7th and 8th Avenues, and seven other locations in Manhattan.

Baseball
The New York Yankees Clubhouse Shop: 295 West 42nd Street between 7th and 8th Avenues, and four other locations
The New York Mets Clubhouse Shop: 11 West 42nd Street between 5th and 6th Avenues

Basketball
NBA Store: 545 Fifth Avenue at West 45th Street

Football
Official New York Jets Store: 44 East 50th Street, near Madison Avenue

Hockey
NHL Store Powered by Reebok: 1185 Sixth Avenue at 47th Street. Merchandise from all thirty NHL teams.

PARTICIPATORY SPORTS

Arcade Games/Pinball
Modern Pinball: 362 3rd Avenue between East 26th and 27th Streets, Kips Bay
Two Bit's Retro Arcade: 153 Essex Street at Stanton Street, Lower East Side
Chinatown's Fair Family Fun Center: 8 Mott Street between Worth and Pell Streets, Chinatown
Barcade: 148 West 25th Street between 6th and 7th Avenues, Chelsea
Dave and Buster's: 234 West 42nd Street between 7th and 8th Avenues, Times Square

Bicycling
There are many places to rent bikes in different neighborhoods. Download a map of the best bicycling routes in NYC free from the Department of Transportation: google "DOT NYC Bike Map." These are some of the easiest places to ride:

Manhattan Waterfront Greenway: A bike path along the rivers on almost the entire east and west sides of Manhattan.
Central Park: Manhattan
Riverside Park: Upper West Side of Manhattan
Prospect Park: Brooklyn

Billiards
Amsterdam Billiard Club: 110 East 11th Street at 4th Avenue, East Village
Fat Cat: 75 Christopher Street at 7th Avenue South, West Village
Eastside Billiards: 163 East 86th Street between Lexington and 3rd Avenues

Bocce
Union Hall: 702 Union Street at 5th Avenue, Park Slope, Brooklyn. A bar with two bocce courts.
Floyd NY: 131 Atlantic Avenue between Henry and Clinton Streets, Cobble Hill. A bar with one court.

Boating (Manhattan)
Loeb Boathouse: The Lake off East Drive at 74th Street, Central Park. One hundred rowboats for rent for $15/hour, cash only, seasonal and weather permitting. Gondola rides are $30 an hour.

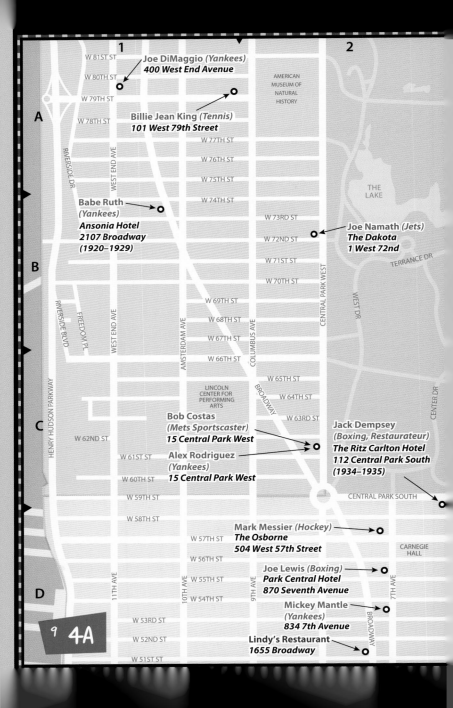

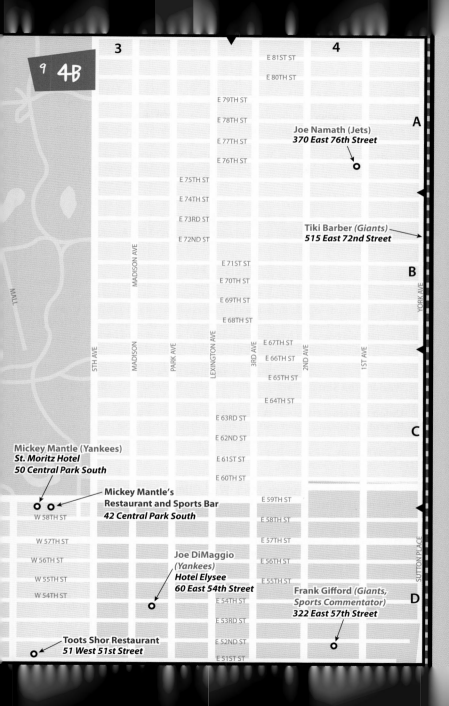

3

4

E 81ST ST

E 80TH ST

E 79TH ST

E 78TH ST

A

Joe Namath (Jets)
370 East 76th Street

E 77TH ST

E 76TH ST

E 75TH ST

E 74TH ST

E 73RD ST

Tiki Barber (Giants)
515 East 72nd Street

E 72ND ST

MADISON AVE

E 71ST ST

E 70TH ST

B

E 69TH ST

E 68TH ST

YORK AVE

MALL

5TH AVE

MADISON

PARK AVE

LEXINGTON AVE

3RD AVE

E 67TH ST

2ND AVE

E 66TH ST

1ST AVE

E 65TH ST

E 64TH ST

E 63RD ST

C

E 62ND ST

E 61ST ST

Mickey Mantle (Yankees)
St. Moritz Hotel
50 Central Park South

E 60TH ST

E 59TH ST

Mickey Mantle's
Restaurant and Sports Bar
42 Central Park South

W 58TH ST

E 58TH ST

SUTTON PLACE

W 57TH ST

E 57TH ST

W 56TH ST

Joe DiMaggio
(Yankees)
Hotel Elysee
60 East 54th Street

E 56TH ST

W 55TH ST

E 55TH ST

W 54TH ST

Frank Gifford (Giants,
Sports Commentator)
322 East 57th Street

D

E 54TH ST

E 53RD ST

Toots Shor Restaurant
51 West 51st Street

E 52ND ST

E 51ST ST

Bowling

Bowlmor Chelsea Piers: Pier 60, 23rd Street at the West Side Highway
Bowlmor Times Square: 222 West 44th, between 7th and 8th Avenues
Lucky Strike NYC: 624-660 West 42nd Street at 12th Avenue
Frames Bowling Lounge: 550 9th Avenue at 40th Street, in the Port Authority
Brooklyn Bowl: 61 Wythe Avenue at North 12th Street, Brooklyn. Combination bar and concert space with sixteen lanes. Doors open 6:00 p.m. Must be twenty-one to enter, but children allowed Saturday and Sunday 12 p.m.–5 p.m.

Bull Riding, Mechanical

Johnny Utah's: 25 West 51st Street between 5th and 6th Avenues. Barbecue restaurant.

Chelsea Piers

Chelsea Piers: New York's largest sports complex, encompassing three piers just west of 22nd street. There are facilities for a myriad of sports: gymnastics, basketball, indoor soccer, baseball batting cages, a rock climbing wall, a bowling center, a three-story golf driving range, ice rinks for skating and hockey, a health club, a spa, and a skateboard park. The Sky Rink is the only year-round ice skating rink in Manhattan.

Chess and Checkers

Washington Square Park: (on the west side). Try your best against chess sharks where they filmed *Searching for Bobby Fischer*.
Union Square: 14th Street and Broadway. Free to the public.
Bryant Park: 42nd Street and 6th Avenue. free to the public.
The Chess and Checkers Building: Center of Central Park near 65th street
Chess Forum: 219 Thompson between West 3rd and Bleecker Streets. Pickup games for $5 an hour.

Climbing, Indoor Rock Wall Climbing (Day Passes)

The Sports Center at Chelsea Piers: 23rd Street and West Side Highway
Brooklyn Boulders: 575 Degraw Street at 3rd Avenue, Gowanus, Brooklyn
The Cliffs at LIC: 11–11 44th Drive at 11th Street, Long Island City
The Climbing Gym at Manhattan Plaza Health Club: 482 West 43rd Street at 10th Avenue
Steep Rock Bouldering: 1506 Lexington Avenue at 97th Street

Climbing, Outdoor (Day Passes)

DUMBO Boulders: 99 Plymouth Street at Washington Street, Dumbo, Brooklyn

Croquet

Central Park: Behind the Mineral Springs Cafe, north of Sheep Meadow at about 69th Street. Watch the New York Croquet club play. Free Monday evening clinics for the public, May to October.

Fishing, Deep Sea

Sheepshead Bay: Brooklyn. There are many deep-sea day boats out of Sheepshead Bay near Coney Island. Most will provide a rod and reel. Google "Deep Sea Fishing NYC."

Golf (Driving Ranges)

The Golf Club at Chelsea Piers: 23rd Street and West Side Highway. Three-story driving range. Year-round, two hundred–yard fairway.

Golf Manhattan: 108 West 39th Street between 6th Avenue and Broadway. Golf simulator.

Premier Indoor Golf: 1 East 28th Street at Fifth Avenue, 3rd floor. Golf simulator.

Golf, Miniature

Pier 25 Mini Golf: 225 West Street (West Side Highway) at North Moore Street. Seasonal from April.

Brooklyn Crab: 24 Reed Street between Conover and Van Brunt Streets. On the roof.

Shipwrecked Miniature Golf: 621 Court Street at Bay Street, Red Hook. Year-round indoor mini-golf with fluorescent décor and black lights.

Horseback Riding

New York City Riding Academy: Harlem River Path Way, Randall's Island

Chateau Stables: 608 West 48th Street between 11th and 12th Avenues. Offers rides in Central Park.

Bronx Equestrian Center: 9 Shore Road, Bronx

Kensington Stables: 51 Caton Place, Flatbush, Brooklyn. Offers rides in Prospect Park.

Jamaica Bay Riding Academy: 7000 Shore Parkway, Bergen Beach, Brooklyn. Woods and beach trails.

Ice Skating

All are winter-only except the year-round Sky Rink.

Ice Rink at Rockefeller Center: 49–50th Streets, between Fifth and Sixth Avenues

Winter Village in Bryant Park: 6th Avenue and 42nd Street

Lasker Ice Skating Rink: Central Park, enter at 110th Street and Lenox Avenue

The Rink at Riverbank State Park: 679 Riverside Drive at 145th Street. Roller skating during warm weather.

Sky Rink at Chelsea Piers: Pier 61, entrance at 23rd Street and the West Side Highway. Year-round.

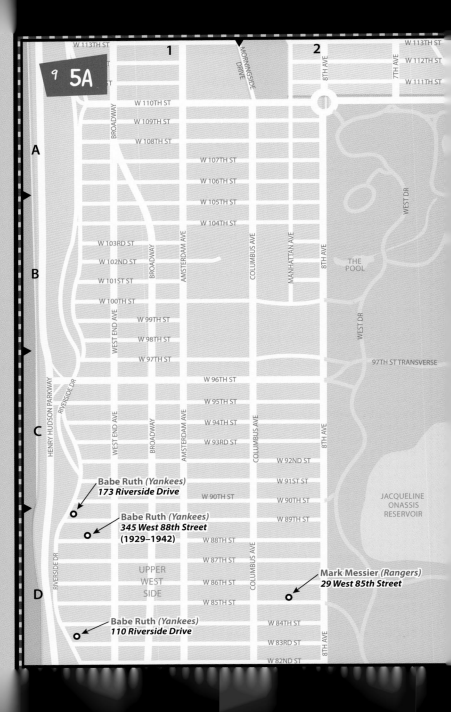

1

2

W 113TH ST

MORNINGSIDE DRIVE

8TH AVE

7TH AVE

W 113TH ST

W 112TH ST

W 111TH ST

W 110TH ST

W 109TH ST

W 108TH ST

BROADWAY

A

W 107TH ST

W 106TH ST

W 105TH ST

W 104TH ST

AMSTERDAM AVE

COLUMBUS AVE

MANHATTAN AVE

8TH AVE

WEST DR

W 103RD ST

W 102ND ST

BROADWAY

THE POOL

B

W 101ST ST

W 100TH ST

WEST END AVE

W 99TH ST

W 98TH ST

W 97TH ST

WEST DR

HENRY HUDSON PARKWAY

RIVERSIDE DR

97TH ST TRANSVERSE

W 96TH ST

W 95TH ST

WEST END AVE

BROADWAY

AMSTERDAM AVE

W 94TH ST

W 93RD ST

COLUMBUS AVE

C

8TH AVE

W 92ND ST

Babe Ruth *(Yankees)*
173 Riverside Drive

W 91ST ST

W 90TH ST

JACQUELINE
ONASSIS
RESERVOIR

Babe Ruth *(Yankees)*
345 West 88th Street
(1929–1942)

W 90TH ST

W 89TH ST

W 88TH ST

W 87TH ST

COLUMBUS AVE

UPPER
WEST
SIDE

W 86TH ST

Mark Messier *(Rangers)*
29 West 85th Street

RIVERSIDE DR

D

W 85TH ST

Babe Ruth *(Yankees)*
110 Riverside Drive

W 84TH ST

W 83RD ST

8TH AVE

W 82ND ST

3   **4**

MALCOM X BLVD

W 112TH ST

W 111TH ST

CATHEDRAL PARKWAY

5TH AVE

EAST HARLEM

E 112TH ST

E 111TH ST

E 110TH ST

E 109TH ST

E 108TH ST

E 107TH ST

E 106TH ST

E 105TH ST

3RD AVE

A

HARLEM MEER

EAST DR

5TH AVE

MADISON AVE

PARK AVE

LEXINGTON AVE

E 104TH ST

E 103RD ST

E 102ND ST

E 101ST ST

E 100TH ST

E 99TH ST

E 98TH ST

E 97TH ST

E 96TH ST

E 95TH ST

E 94TH ST

E 93RD ST

2ND AVE

1ST AVE

B

MT SINAI HOSPITAL

MADISON AVE

PARK AVE

LEXINGTON AVE

2ND AVE

1ST AVE

FDR DR

C

JACQUELINE ONASSIS RESERVOIR

E 92ND ST

E 91ST ST

E 90TH ST

E 89TH ST

UPPER EAST SIDE

E 88TH ST

E 87TH ST

E 86TH ST

E 85TH ST

YORK AVE

D

5TH AVE

MADISON AVE

E 84TH ST

E 83RD ST

E 82RD ST

⁹ **5B**

Wollman Rink: Central Park, enter at West 59th and Sixth Avenue
Lefrak Center: 171 East Drive, Prospect Park, Brooklyn
World Ice Arena: 12540 Roosevelt Avenue at 126th Street, Queens

Kayaking

Kayaking at Pier 26 and Governor's Island: Seasonal, free. Google "kayak NYC."
New York Kayak Company: Pier 40, Hudson River Park, West Side Highway at Houston Street
Manhattan Kayak: Pier 84 Boathouse, 555 12th Avenue at West 44th Street. Seasonal.

New York City Marathon

New York City Marathon: The largest marathon in the world, with over 50,000 runners and 98,000 applicants to the race lottery. Held on the first Sunday in November since 1970, it goes through five boroughs, starting on the Verrazano Bridge and ending in Central Park.

Ping Pong

Fat Cat: 75 Christopher Street at 7th Avenue South (basement). Also has other games and features jazz music.
Spin New York: 48 East 23rd Street between Park and Madison Avenues, basement. Bar and restaurant co-owned by Susan Sarandon.

Roller Derby

The Gotham Girls: You can view the teams of this NYC organization between March and August, most often at the John Jay College of Criminal Justice gymnasium at 524 West 59th Street at 11th Avenue.

Running: Top Scenic Running Routes in Manhattan

Central Park Outer Park Drive: 6.1 miles
Central Park Reservoir Loop: 1.5 miles
Hudson River Greenway: Battery Park to West 59th Street. 6 miles.
Hudson River Greenway: West 50th to West 125th Streets. 3.7 miles.
Hudson River Greenway: 125th Street to George Washington Bridge. 2.6 miles.
East River: Battery Park to 125th Street. 7 miles.
Manhattan Bridge: 1.6 miles
Williamsburg Bridge: 1.6 miles
Roosevelt Island Loop: 3.6 miles

Shuffleboard

The Royal Palms Shuffleboard Club: 514 Union Street, Gowanus, Brooklyn. Ten courts.

Skee–Ball

Full Circle Bar: 318 Grand Street at Havermeyer Street, Williamsburg, Brooklyn

Barcade: 148 West 24th Street between 6th and 7th Avenues, Chelsea

Ace Bar: 531 East 5th Street between Avenues A and B, East Village

Swimming (Beaches)

Robert Moses State Park: Long Island. Transportation: LIRR and bus.

Orchard Beach: Bronx. Transportation: 6 train to bus. The water is murky.

Coney Island: Brooklyn. Transportation: subway to Coney Island stop.

Brighton Beach: Brooklyn. Transportation: subway to Brighton Beach.

Rockaway Beach: Queens. Transportation: subway to Rockaway Beach, or ferry from Wall Street.

South Beach: Staten Island. Transportation: Staten Island Ferry and bus.

Swimming (Indoor)

The Sports Center at Chelsea Piers: 23rd Street and West Side Highway, Chelsea **Chelsea Recreation Center:** 430 West 25th Street between 9th and 10th Avenues **McBurney Branch YMCA:** 125 West 14th Street between 6th and 7th Avenues **Sportspark:** 250 Main Street at North Loop Road, Roosevelt Island

Tennis

USTA Billie Jean King National Tennis Center: Flushing Meadows, Corona Park, Queens. World's largest public tennis facility. Forty-two courts.

Hudson River Park: Along the river, just north of Spring Street, there are three free courts. Otherwise you need a permit to play on city courts.

Trapeze

Trapeze School New York: Pier 40, Houston Street and the West Side Highway. Outdoors May to October.

Trapeze School New York: 467 Marcy Avenue, Williamsburg, Brooklyn; enter at 30 Tompkins Avenue. Indoors, year-round.

GREAT POP CULTURE MOMENTS IN NYC SPORTS HISTORY

Baseball
Lou Gehrig's Retirement Speech (July 4, 1939)

Lou Gehrig, "The Iron Horse," had played 2,130 consecutive games for the Yankees but on May 2, 1939, had to give up baseball because he was suffering from ALS, later to be called Lou Gehrig disease. He would be dead two years later at age thirty-seven. On July 4, 1939, between games of a doubleheader and in front of 62,000 people, baseball held Lou Gehrig Appreciation

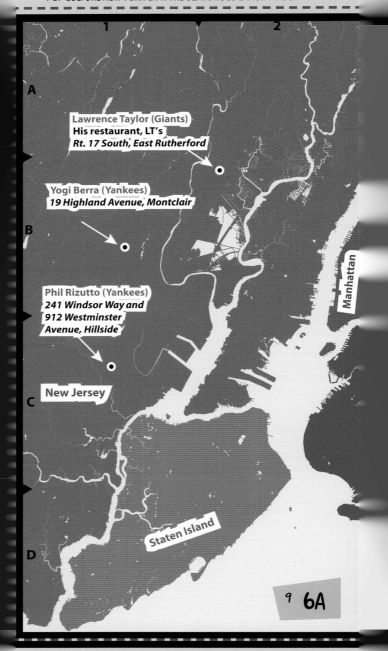

Lawrence Taylor (Giants)
His restaurant, LT's
Rt. 17 South, East Rutherford

Yogi Berra (Yankees)
19 Highland Avenue, Montclair

Phil Rizutto (Yankees)
*241 Windsor Way and
912 Westminster
Avenue, Hillside*

New Jersey

Manhattan

Staten Island

9 6A

3

Don Mattingly *(Yankees)*
230 Engle Street, Tenafly

4 **Lou Gherig** *(Yankees)*
**9 Meadow Lane,
New Rochelle**

Patrick Ewing *(Knicks)*
174 Vaccaro Drive, Cresskill

Lou Gherig *(Yankees)*
**5204 Delefield Avenue,
Riverdale**

The Bronx

Mickey Mantle *(Yankees)*
Babe Ruth *(Yankees)*
**Concourse Plaza Hotel
900 Grand Concourse
at 161st Street**

Sugar Ray Robinson *(Boxer)*
80 St. Nicholas Place, Harlem

Willy Mays *(Giants, Mets)*
80 St. Nicholas Place, Harlem

Manhattan

Walt Frazier *(Knicks)*
**381 Lenox Avenue at
West 129th Street**

Mickey Mantle *(Yankees)*
Jackson Heights
**Lived with Roger Maris
and Bob Cerv during
the 1961 season**

Sugar Ray's
Sugar Ray Robinson's
**Harlem Nightclub
2074 7th Avenue**

Queens

Willis Reed *(Knicks)*
**61–35 98th Street
in Park City Estates,
Rego Park**

Brooklyn

Jackie Robinson *(Dodgers)*
**112–40 177th Street,
Addisleigh Park**

Jackie Robinson *(Dodgers)*
5224 Tilden Street, Brooklyn

A

B

C

D

9 **6B**

day, where he was given gifts and toasts. His own speech, about getting "a bad break" but talking about the "privilege" of having played baseball, is said to be one of the most quoted in American history: and also filmed in *The Pride of the Yankees* with Gary Cooper.

The Photo of Babe Ruth Bowing Out (June 13, 1948)

One of the most iconic images in baseball history was taken of Babe Ruth by photographer Nat Fein on June 13, 1948 at Yankee Stadium, the day Ruth's number was retired. He had played for twenty-two seasons, from 1914 to 1935, but as he aged, baseball decided to honor him by retiring his number. Most great photos are of a person's face, but Fein stood in back of Ruth so he could record the number 3 on his shirt. His photo, *The Babe Bows Out*, of the bent but heroic Ruth taking in the love of his fans, won him a Pulitzer Prize, the first for a sports photographer.

The 1969 "Miracle of the Mets"

For most of their first eight years, the Mets were the Rodney Dangerfield of professional baseball: no gave them any respect. But in 1969, in a miraculous turnaround, they became known America-wide as "The Amazin' Mets," not only making it into the World Series, but beating the Baltimore Orioles to win the championship.

The Dodgers and Giants Leave New York for California in 1957

When two beloved National League Baseball teams decided to move to the West Coast at the same time in 1957, it was a crushing blow for New York City sports fans. But L.A. offered to build the Dodgers a new stadium, and New York wouldn't. And Giants attendance was down and it was thought a move would fill seats. So they left, leaving Brooklyn teamless and only the Yankees in the Bronx to cheer for until the arrival of the Mets in 1962 in the Polo Grounds.

Simon & Garfunkel Ask the Question: "Where Did You Go, Joe DiMaggio?" (1968)

They called him "Joltin' Joe" and "The Yankee Clipper," partly for his fifty six–game hitting streak from May 15 to July 16, 1941. An American hero, he eloped with America's #1 female movie star in San Francisco. But the marriage didn't last, and Paul Simon turned his lament for the "short supply" of "true American heroes" into the 1968 hit song, "Mrs. Robinson."

Roger Maris Breaks Babe Ruth's Record (1961)

Babe Ruth's record of sixty home runs in the 1927 season held for thirty-four years. But on October 1, 1961, Yankee Roger Maris slammed his sixty-first home run against the Red Sox in the very last game of the season. All season, Maris had been in a back-and-forth race for home runs with Mickey Mantle, his friend and roommate in Queens, but a hip infection put Mantle in the hospital, allowing Maris to go after Ruth's record alone. Ruth hit his homers in a season of fewer games, thus the (*) asterisk that sometimes appears next to Maris' name in the record books.

Don Larsen's Perfect Game
in the 1956 World Series (1956)

A perfect game is when a pitcher pitches a nine-inning game and not one of the opposing players ever reaches a base. It's happened only twenty-three times, and only once in a World Series game. That was Yankee Don Larsen's perfect game against the Dodgers in Game Five of the World Series on October 8, 1956. At the game's close, catcher Yogi Berra leapt into Larsen's arms: an iconic moment in sports photo history.

Jackie Robinson Breaks the Color Barrier
in Professional Baseball (1947)

When Jackie Robinson stepped onto Ebbets Field for the Brooklyn Dodgers on April 15, 1947, he became the first African-America player in Major League Baseball, heralding a new wave of integration of American sports and American society. Robinson went on to become a member of baseball's Hall of Fame. And his Brooklyn home from 1947 to 1949, at 5224 Tilden Avenue, was declared a National Historic Landmark in 1976.

Jerry Seinfeld's Second Thoughts on his Friendship
with Keith Hernandez on Seinfeld (1992)

One of New York baseball fandom's greatest moments came in an 1992 episode of *Seinfeld* when Jerry makes a friend of Yankee baseball legend Keith Hernandez, and then gets jealous where Elaine starts dating him. When Hernandez then asks Jerry to help him move his furniture, Jerry thinks Hernandez is abusing the friendship and breaks it off. Meanwhile, Hernandez has to defend himself to Kramer and Newman, who say he spit on them after a game. The incident is acted in slow motion like the Zapruder film of the Kennedy assassination.

"The Shot Heard 'Round the World":
Bobby Thompson's Pennant–Winning Homer (1951)

At then end of 1951, two National League teams were tied with 96–58 records: cross-town rivals the New York Giants (of Manhattan) and the Brooklyn Dodgers. A three-game playoff would have to determine the league victor. Played at the Polo Grounds and Dodger Stadium, the games evened up at 1–1. In the last and determining game at the Polo Grounds on October 3, 1951, the Giants were down 4 to 2 in the ninth inning with two men on base. That's when third baseman and outfielder Bobby Thompson of the Dodgers hit a game-winning home run to win the game 5–4. That homer became known as "the shot heard round the world" as the gripping game was heard by millions on radio as well as millions more watching on TV in baseball's first nationally televised game.

1 **2**

Izod Center *(1981–Present, under various names)*
- **New York Nets** *(1981–2010)*
- **New Jersey Devils** *(1982–2007)*
Name history:
- **Izod Center** *(2007–Present)*
- **Continental Airlines Arena** *(1996–2007)*
- **Brendan Byrne Arena** *(1981–1996)*

Giants Stadium
(aka "The Meadowlands")
(1976–2010)
- **New York Giants**
(1976–2010)
- **New York Jets**
(1984–2010)

A

MetLife Stadium *(2010–Present)*
- **New York Giants** *(NFL Football)*
- **New York Jets** *(NFL Football)*

Red Bull Arena
(2009–Present)
New York Red Bulls
(MLS Soccer)

Elysian Fields
(Hoboken)
Site of the first
baseball game
(1846)

B

Prudential Center
(2007–Present)
New Jersey Devils
(NHL Ice Hockey)

Madison Square Garden #4
(1968–Present)
- **New York Rangers**
(NHL Hockey)
- **New York Knicks**
(NBA Basketball)
- **New York Liberty**
(WNBA Basketball)

Former site of Madison
Square Garden #3
(1925–1968)

Former site of Madison
Square Garden #1 and #2
(1879–1890; 1890–1925)

C

Brooklyn

Richmond County
Bank Ballpark
(2001–Present)
Staten Island Yankees
(Class A Minor league baseball)

MCU Park
(2001–Present)
Brooklyn Cyclones
(Class A Minor league baseball)
Formerly KeySpan Park
(2001–2010)

D

Staten Island

Five Boroughs:
Sports Stadiums

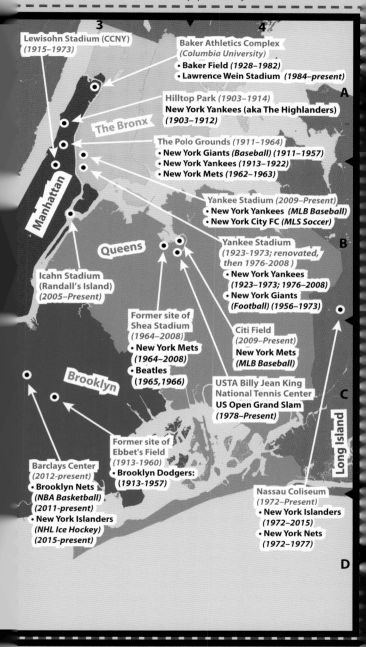

3 **4**

Lewisohn Stadium (CCNY)
(1915–1973)

Baker Athletics Complex
(Columbia University)
• Baker Field *(1928–1982)*
• Lawrence Wein Stadium *(1984–present)*

Hilltop Park *(1903–1914)*
New York Yankees (aka The Highlanders)
(1903–1912)

The Bronx

The Polo Grounds *(1911–1964)*
• New York Giants *(Baseball) (1911–1957)*
• New York Yankees *(1913–1922)*
• New York Mets *(1962–1963)*

Manhattan

Yankee Stadium *(2009–Present)*
• New York Yankees *(MLB Baseball)*
• New York City FC *(MLS Soccer)*

Queens

B

A

Yankee Stadium
*(1923-1973; renovated,
then 1976-2008)*
• New York Yankees
(1923–1973; 1976–2008)
• New York Giants
(Football) (1956–1973)

Icahn Stadium
(Randall's Island)
(2005–Present)

Former site of
Shea Stadium
(1964–2008)
• New York Mets
(1964–2008)
• Beatles
(1965,1966)

Citi Field
(2009–Present)
New York Mets
(MLB Baseball)

USTA Billy Jean King
National Tennis Center
US Open Grand Slam
(1978–Present)

C

Brooklyn

Former site of
Ebbet's Field
(1913-1960)
• Brooklyn Dodgers:
(1913–1957)

Long Island

Barclays Center
(2012-present)
• Brooklyn Nets
(NBA Basketball)
(2011-present)
• New York Islanders
(NHL Ice Hockey)
(2015-present)

Nassau Coliseum
(1972–Present)
• New York Islanders
(1972–2015)
• New York Nets
(1972–1977)

D

Basketball
The Knicks Captain Willis Reed Returns,
though Injured, and Inspires a Big Win (1970)

Sometimes the attempt counts more than the result. When a torn muscle kept team captain Willis Reed out of the sixth game in the 1970 NBA Playoffs in Madison Square Garden, everyone wondered: Would he play in the all-decisive seventh game of the finals? Reed surprised both fans and teammates by hobbling onto the court and starting the first period, causing excited pandemonium. Although he only scored two baskets, his determination to play inspired the team to clinch the league victory against the Lakers 113–99 on May 8, 1970.

Boxing
The Two Joe Louis Versus Max Schmeling
Boxing Matches (1936 and 1938)

There were two matchups in Yankee Stadium between these forces of nature. In the first on June 19, 1936, Schmeling, a German, won by a knockout in round twelve against Joe Louis, an African-American folk hero. In the second, a rematch two years later on June 22, 1938, Joe Louis won by a knockout in round one. About more than just boxing, the fight took on greater symbolism against the larger fight between American democracy and rise of German Nazi fascism in the 1930s. Louis' deciding victory, heard on the radio the world over, would make Louis one of the greatest African-American heroes.

"The Fight of the Century"
between Muhammad Ali and Joe Frazier (1971)

Muhammad Ali had his World Heavyweight Champion title taken away from him in 1967 by boxing authorities for refusing induction into the army. Subsequently, an undefeated "Smokin' Joe" Frazier won the title. So when the two paired off against each other on March 8, 1971, it was truly "The Fight of the Century": Would the brash Ali win his title back? In the end, Frazier won by a unanimous decision in fifteen rounds. In a larger sense the fight was also about Liberals versus Conservatives in America. During this time of the Vietnam war, would left-leaning conscientious objector Ali dominate over Frazier, who somewhat represented the American status quo?

Martin Scorsese's Raging Bull *Elevates the Story of*
Boxer Jake LaMotta into a Film for the Ages

The story of Jake LaMotta, formerly a footnote in boxing history, was not much on its own: some winning bouts and then a fall from grace due to personal problems. But in the hands of Martin Scorsese, it became an epic film of obsession, jealousy, and self-destruction and was often found on lists of the greatest films of all time. In addition to a mostly New York cast, the film was primarily set in the Bronx and Manhattan and featured the Carmine Street Pool (1 Clarkson Street), the Copacabana (then at 10 East 60th Street), and Webster Hall (128 East 11th Street).

Football
"Broadway" Joe Namath's Noxzema Shaving Cream Commercials

Handsome New York Jets superstar "Broadway Joe" Namath was asked to endorse a lot of products in the '70s, but his TV ads for Noxzema have stood out of pop culture time. In the ad, Joe says "I'm so excited I'm gonna get creamed!" Farrah Fawcett then rubs his face with shaving cream while singing "Let Noxzema Cream your Face," to which he responds, "You've got a great set of hands. They don't make 'em like they used to."

Hockey
The Rangers Win the Stanley Cup after Fifty-Four Years (1994)

After a fifty four-year championship drought, it came down to the last game of seven in the 1994 Stanley Cup playoffs at Madison Square Garden. But the New York Rangers came through with a 3–2 win against the Canucks to clinch the title on June 14, 1994. It was the Rangers' first Cup victory since 1940, when they defeated Toronto.

Pro Wrestling
The Era of Giant Audiences for Octagon Fighting and Pro-Wrestling Entertainment Begins with Wrestlemania (1985)

Combat sports on cable TV are a billion-dollar industry, with the UFC (Ultimate Fighting Championship) and the WWE (World Wrestling Entertainment) the industry leaders. Though the former is real fighting, and the latter scripted entertainment, they entertain millions around he world. One of the prime events that led the way was *Wrestlemania 1,* a series of nine (scripted) wrestling matches that took place in Madison Square Garden on March 31, 1985. With 19,121 in attendance and over one million viewers watching through closed-circuit television, it began the combat cable revolution. The main event featured Hulk Hogan and Mr. T, who would defeat Roddy Piper and "Mr. Wonderful" Paul Orndorff. To add to the fun, Muhammed Ali was the special outside-ring guest referee and Liberace was the time keeper, with the aid of some Radio City Rockettes.

Sailing
The New York Yacht Club Loses the America's Cup after 132 years (1983)

In 1851 the schooner *America* won a sailing race around the Isle of Wight to claim title to the America's Cup for The New York Yacht Club. The trophy would stay in their clubhouses (including their 37 West 44th Street head-quarters financed by J.P. Morgan in 1899) for a record 132 years, one of the longest winning streaks in the history of sports. Then, in the 1983 competition, an Australian boat, *Australia ii,* in a highly charged seventh race, beat the American boat by forty-one seconds to claim the Cup, ending America's domination of the sport. Soon after, the Cup was placed in a Brink's armored truck to eventually make its way to Perth, Australia.

MUSEUMS AND TOURIST ATTRACTIONS

NYC'S MOST POPULAR LARGE MUSEUMS

Metropolitan Museum of Art (the Met): Fifth Avenue at 82nd Street, Upper East Side. Pay what you wish. 6 million visitors a year.

American Museum of Natural History: Central Park West at 79th Street, Upper West Side. Pay what you wish (planetarium, etc. are extra). 5 million visitors a year.

The Museum of Modern Art (MoMA): 11 West 53rd Street between 5th and 6th Avenues, Midtown West. Free admission Friday nights, 4:00–8:00 p.m. 3 million visitors a year.

National September 11th Memorial and Museum: 180 Greenwich Street at Cortlandt Street, Financial District. Limited free tickets are given out Tuesdays at 4:00 p.m. (see website). 2 million visitors a year.

The Whitney Museum of American Art (The Whitney): 99 Gansevoort Street at Washington Street, Meatpacking District. Pay what you wish on Saturday nights. 1.2 million visitors a year.

Intrepid Sea, Air, and Space Museum: Pier 86, 12th Avenue at 46th Street, Midtown West. No discounted times. 1 million visitors a year.

Solomon R. Guggenheim Museum: 1071 Fifth Avenue between 88th and 89th Streets, Upper East Side. Pay what you wish Saturday night 5:45–7:15 p.m. 800,000 visitors a year.

Brooklyn Museum: 200 Eastern Parkway at Washington Avenue, Prospect Park, Brooklyn. Free admission Thursday 6–10 p.m. and First Saturdays 5–11 p.m. 326,000 visitors a year.

The Frick Collection: 1 East 70th Street at 5th Avenue, Upper East Side. Free admission Wednesdays 2:00–6:00 p.m. 280,000 visitors a year.

New York Historical Society: 170 Central Park West between West 76th and West 77th Streets, Upper West Side. Free admission Friday 6:00–8:00 p.m. 250,000 visitors a year.

Museum of the City of New York: 1220 Fifth Avenue between 103rd and 104th Streets, Upper East Side. Pay what you wish admission, but $18 adult admission suggested. 250,000 visitors a year.

The Morgan Library: 225 Madison Avenue between East 36th and East 37th Streets, Midtown East. Free admission Friday 7:00 p.m. 200,000 visitors a year.

Neue Gallery: 1048 Fifth Avenue between East 85th and 86th Streets, Upper East Side. Free admission First Friday 6:00 p.m.–8:00 p.m. 150,000 visitors a year.

Rubin Museum: 150 West 17th Street, Chelsea. Free Friday 6:00–10:00 p.m. (seasonal). 100,000 visitors a year.

NYC MUSEUMS WITH MODERN AND/OR POP ART

The Metropolitan Museum of Art
The Museum of Modern Art
The Whitney Museum (Soho)
The Met Breuer
Brooklyn Museum
Guggenheim Museum
New Museum of Contemporary Art
Studio Museum of Harlem

NYC SPECIALTY MUSEUMS BY MAIN SUBJECT

9/11: National September 11 Memorial & Museum
Aircraft Carrier: Intrepid Air and Space Museum
Anne Frank: Anne Frank Center
Armstrong, Louis: Louis Armstrong House Museum, Queens
Architecture: Center for Architecture
Army, U.S.: Harbor Defense Museum, Fort Hamilton, Brooklyn
Art, Asian: Rubin Museum of Art, Chelsea
Art, Central Asia: Nicholas Roerich Museum, Upper Manhattan
Art, Japanese: Noguchi Museum, Long Island City, Queens
Art, Contemporary: The New Museum of Contemporary Art
Art, Contemporary: Dia Center for the Arts: The New York Earth Room and The Broken Kilometer
Art, Contemporary: PS 1 Contemporary Art Center, Long Island City, Queens
Art, Psychiatric Patient: The Living Museum at Creedmoor Psychiatric Center
African-American Culture: Schomburg Center for Research in Black Culture, Harlem
Aviation: Intrepid Air and Space Museum
Barge: Waterfront (Barge) Museum, Red Hook, Brooklyn
Boats: South Street Seaport Museum
Books: New York Public Library. Constant exhibits
Carnegie Hall History: Carnegie Hall
Caruso, Enrico: Enrico Caruso Museum
Chinese: Chinese Scholar's Garden, Staten Island

Chinese: Asia Society
Chinese, House: Chinese Scholar's Garden, Staten Island
Chinese: Museum of the Chinese in America, LES/Chinatown
Comic Art: Museum of Comic and Cartoon Art
Coney Island: Coney Island Museum; Nathan's Famous Hot Dog Eating Wall of Fame
Fashion: Museum at FIT, Chelsea
Finance: Museum of American Finance, Lower Manhattan
Firefighters: New York City Fire Museum, West Soho
Garibaldi: Garibaldi-Meucci Museum, Staten Island
Hispanic: Hispanic Society of America, Upper Manhattan
Illustration: Museum of American Illustration
Italian: Italian-American Museum, Little Italy
Japan: Japan Society, Midtown Manhattan
Jazz: National Jazz Museum, Harlem
Jewish: Museum at Eldridge Street, Lower East Side
Judaica: Herbert and Eileen Bernard Museum of Judaica at Temple Emanuel
Judaica: Museum of the Hebrew Home for the Aged, Riverdale
Maritime: Maritime Industry Museum at Fort Schuyler, SUNY Maritime College
Masonic Temple: Masonic Hall and Chancellor Robert R. Livingston Masonic Library and Museum of the Grand Lodge
Maps: Map Room of the New York Public Library, Midtown Manhattan
Medicine: New York Academy of Medicine, Upper Manhattan
Money: American Numismatic Society, New York Federal Reserve Bank, Museum of American Finance
Music: Carnegie Hall; Library for the Performing Arts, Lincoln Center; Louis Armstrong House Museum, Queens
Native American: Museum of the American Indian, Smithsonian National
New York: Museum of the City of New York, Upper Manhattan
Photography: International Center of Photography, Bowery
Police: New York City Police Museum
Planetarium: Natural History Museum
Publishing: Grolier Club, Midtown Manhattan
Poetry: Poets House, Lower Manhattan
Roosevelt, Teddy: Theodore Roosevelt's birthplace
Scandinavia: Scandinavia House, Midtown Manhattan
Sex: Museum of Sex
Skyscrapers: The Skyscraper Museum, Lower Manhattan
Staten Island: Staten Island Museum. Arts and science exhibits.
Subways, Buses: New York City Transit Museum, downtown Brooklyn
Space Shuttle: Intrepid Air and Space Museum
Submarines: Intrepid Air and Space Museum
Tenement Life: Lower East Side Tenement Museum
Theater: New York Library for the Performing Arts, Lincoln Center. Constant exhibitions.

Track and Field: National Track and Field Hall of Fame in the Armory, Washington Heights
Ukrainian: Ukrainian Museum
U.S. History: Fraunces Tavern Museum
Washington, George: Fraunces Tavern Museum. Including Washington's teeth and hair.

OTHER MUSEUMS

Restored Houses

Alice Austen House Museum: Staten Island
Dyckman Farmhouse: Upper Manhattan
Merchant's House Museum: East Village
Mt. Vernon Hotel Museum and Garden: Midtown East
Edgar Allen Poe Cottage: Bronx
Queens County Farm Museum: Queens

NYC ZOOS BY SIZE

Bronx Zoo: 265 acres
Prospect Park Zoo: 12 acres
Staten Island Zoo: 8 acres
Central Park Zoo: 6.5 acre
Queens Zoo: 5 acres

AQUARIUM

Coney Island: 14 acres

BOTANICAL GARDENS

Bronx Botanical Garden: 250 acres
Brooklyn Botanical Garden: 52 acres. Has cool Japanese garden and pond.
Queens Botanical Garden: 39 acres
Staten Island Botanical Garden: 83 acres. Has various gardens scattered throughout, including ten acres of wetlands. Also has cool New York Chinese Scholar's Garden, a replica of a large Chinese house with pond. AKA Snug Harbor Botanical Garden.

NYC ISLANDS TO VISIT

Roosevelt Island: Gondola to get there, several parks, restaurants
Governor's Island: Fort, biking, playgrounds

LIGHTHOUSES

Little Red Lighthouse: Fort Washington Park
Roosevelt Island Lighthouse: Lighthouse Park

UNIQUE SPACES TO VISIT

Brooklyn Botanical Garden: Japanese garden
Staten Island: Chinese Scholar's House and Gardens
Met Museum: Astor Court. Indoor Chinese house garden.
Met Museum: Temple of Dendur
Central Park: Belvedere Castle

OVER FIFTY OF THE MOST POPULAR POP CULTURE SIGHTS IN MANHATTAN FOR POP CULTURE FANS
Most of these are neighborhoods or buildings that you can experience for free.

Uptown (59th–125th Streets)
The Must–Sees
Central Park: The Lake, The Mall, Bethesda Fountain
The Dakota/Strawberry Fields: *Imagine* mosaic, the John Lennon memorial
The Metropolitan Museum of Art
The Guggenheim Museum: You can just walk inside to see the spiral; you
    don't have to see an exhibit.
The Plaza Hotel
The Apple Store

Also Pop–Culturally Cool
Bloomingdale's
The Apollo Theater/Harlem
Columbia University Campus
Grant's Tomb
Cathedral of St. John the Divine
American Museum of Natural History

Midtown (34th–59th Streets)
The Must-Sees

Times Square, 42nd Street: The New Year's Ball, the red steps, the costumed characters.
The Broadway Theater Area
Rockefeller Center: The skating rink and Christmas tree (in winter).
St. Patrick's Cathedral
Fifth Avenue Stores: From Rockefeller Center to 59th Street.
The New York Public Library: Lions out front, Winnie the Pooh inside, and main reading room.
Grand Central Station: The clock and the Whisper Gallery.
The Empire State Building

Also Pop-Culturally Cool

The Chrysler Building
Bryant Park
Lincoln Center: The fountain and Henry Moore sculpture.
Macy's
The UN
The Diamond District
Roosevelt Island Tramway

Lower Midtown, Between the Village and Midtown (17th–34th Streets)
The Must-Sees

The Flatiron Building: 23rd Street
The High Line

Also Pop-Culturally Cool

Chelsea Market: 16th Street and Ninth Avenue
Little India: Around 28th Street and Lexington Avenue
Koreatown: West 32nd Street between Broadway and Fifth Avenue

Greenwich Village, the East Village, and Soho
The Must-Sees

Washington Square Park
MacDougal Street
Union Square
East Village: St. Mark's Place and Astor Place.
Soho: Prince Street, Spring Street, and Broadway from Canal to Houston.

Also Pop-Culturally Cool

The Meatpacking District: Gansevoort Street, The Standard Hotel.
The Far West Village: Commerce Street, Grove Street, Bedford Street, Perry Street (*Friends* and *Sex and the City*).

Sheridan Square: Christopher Park, the Stonewall Inn.
The Whitney Museum

Downtown: Below Canal Street to the Battery
The Must–Sees
Chinatown: Mulberry, Mott, Bayard, and Doyers Streets.
Little Italy: Mulberry from Canal to Spring.
National September 11th Memorial
The Oculus: Huge bird-shaped transit center.
The World Financial Center: Palm Trees, Yacht Basic, two food courts.
The Statue of Liberty: Viewed from Battery Park or the Staten Island Ferry.
The Wall Street Bull Sculpture

Also Pop–Culturally Cool
View of the Brooklyn Bridge from the South Street Seaport
Walking across Brooklyn Bridge
South Street Seaport
Staten Island Ferry

Uptown and the Boroughs
Uptown Manhattan: The Cloisters
Brooklyn: Brooklyn Heights Promenade, Coney Island, Japanese Garden in Prospect Park.
Queens: The Unisphere in Flushing Meadows, Corona Park.
The Bronx: The Bronx Zoo, The Bronx Botanical Garden, Arthur Avenue (Little Italy).
Staten Island: Staten Island Ferry, Chinese Scholar's House: Sailor's Snug Harbor.

ATTRACTIONS, THEME STORES, RESTAURANTS, AND SPECIALTY MUSEUMS
NYC's Top Pop Culture Tourist Attractions with Admission Charges (by Neighborhood)
Times Square, 42nd Street
Madame Tussauds New York: 234 West 42nd Street
Ripley's Believe It or Not: Times Square
The Ride: Times Square
Citywide Bus Tours: Various companies

West of Times Square: Hudson River at 42nd Street
Circle Line Boat Tours
The Intrepid Sea, Air, & Space Museum

East of Times Square: East River at 42nd Street
United Nations Tour

Empire State Building, 34th Street and Fifth Avenue
Empire State Building Observatory
New York Skyride: In the Empire State Building.

Rockefeller Center, 50th Street and Fifth Avenue
Top of the Rock Observatory
Radio City Music Hall Tour
NBC Studios Tour

Downtown by the World Trade Center
One World Observatory, One World Trade Center
9/11 Memorial Museum
The Tiger: Boat ride downtown.
Statue of Liberty Ferries
Ellis Island Boats

Top Theme Stores (NYC Visitor–Oriented)
Times Square
The Disney Store: 1540 Broadway between 45th and 46th Street, in Times Square. Three escalated floors of all things Disney.
Hershey's Chocolate World: 1593 Broadway at 48th Street. Immerse yourself in candy, clothes, and collectibles all related to Hershey's chocolate.
M&M World New York: 1600 Broadway at 48th Street
The Hard Rock Cafe: 1501 Broadway at 43rd Street. Rock 'n' roll–oriented clothing and gifts. Restaurant and displays downstairs.
HBO Store: One block east of Times Square
NBA Store: On Fifth Avenue west of Tines Square

Rockefeller Center
Nintendo New York: 10 Rockefeller Plaza at West 48th Street. Nintendo software and merchandise with interactive gaming stations.
The NBC Store
Lego Store: 620 Fifth Avenue, in Rockefeller Center; 200 5th Avenue at 23rd Street. Lego products and huge sculptures made of Lego.
Top of the Rock

Twenty–Four–Hour Shopping in Times Square

H+M	Old Navy/Gap
Sephora	Sketchers
Swatch	American Apparel
Forever 21	US Polo
Disney	

Theme and Family–Oriented Restaurants: Times Square and 42nd Street
Times Square

Bubba Gump Shrimp Co.
Hard Rock Cafe: Store/restaurant with rock and roll memorabilia décor.
Buca Di Beppo: Chain with family-style Italian food.
John's of Times Square: Pizza
Carmine's: Upscale Italian
Planet Hollywood: Restaurant with movie memorabilia décor.
B.B. King's
Virgil's Real Barbeque
Junior's Restaurant and Bakery: Famous for cheesecake.
Olive Garden
Ellen's Stardust Restaurant
Brooklyn Diner: West 43rd Street
HB Burger: West 43rd Street

42nd Street and Below

Dave and Buster's
Red Lobster
Ruby Tuesday
Heartland Brewery and Chophouse: West 43rd Street
Applebee's: 42nd Street and West 50th Street
Chevy's
Dallas BBQ
Schnippers

Odds and Ends and Offbeat New York Places

ANNUAL NYC EVENTS WITH A POP ATTITUDE
Top Pop Annual Events by Month: Plan Your Costume Now!

January
No Pants Subway Ride: People calmly go to work in their underpants.

February
Empire State Building Run-Up: Early February. A timed race up 102 floors.
Fashion Week: Activities all over the city, but many in the Village.
Chinese New Year: Late January/early February. Celebrated on Canal Street near Mott Street with fireworks and dancing dragons.
Westminster Dog Show: Madison Square Garden. Many breeds vying for "Best in Show."

March
Saint Patrick's Day Parade: March 17th. Approximately 44th to 86th Streets on Fifth Avenue. Bagpipes, shamrocks, and lots of green . . . and politicians.

April
Tribeca Film Festival: Downtown's answer to uptown's New York Film Festival. Started after 9/11 by Robert DeNiro.
Easter Parade: Sunday in late March or early April. People in extravagantly decorated hats promenade on Fifth Avenue in the 50s.

May
Manhattanhenge: This is when the sun sets in alignment with New York's east-west streets. Cool to see from the middle of the street.
Shakespeare in the Park: Begins its season in Central Park's Delacorte Theater. It runs May to August.

June

River to River Festival: Music, dance, and more from the Hudson east to the East River in downtown Manhattan below Canal Street.

Coney Island Mermaid Parade: Mid-June. The route starts at Surf Avenue at West 10th Street, Coney Island. Body-painted mermaids and local floats, usually with a celebrity King and Queen.

NYC Pride Parade (Gay Pride Parade): Down 5th Avenue from 23rd Street to Washington Square Park, then west to Sheridan Square.

Victorian Gardens: Amusement rides open for the season in Central Park. (June to September)

Museum Mile Festival: Second Tuesday of the month. Fifth Avenue between 82nd and 105th Streets. Seven museums are open free.

Puerto Rican Day Parade: Early June. Salsa dancing and lots of Puerto Rican flags.

July

Macy's Fourth of July Fireworks: Hudson or East River, usually between 14th and 50th Streets. The Big Kahuna.

Nathan's Hot Dog Eating Contest: July 4th. Coney Island, outside of Nathan's Hot Dogs. Latest record: seventy-two hot dogs in ten minutes.

Giglio Festival: Our Lady of Mt. Carmel Church, 275 North 8th Street at Havermeyer Street, Williamsburg, Brooklyn. Annual Italian street celebration since 1903. A four-ton, five-story papier-mâché Giglio tower is paraded through the streets, carried by 125 men.

August

Hong Kong Dragon Boat Festival: Flushing Meadows, Corona Park, Queens. Each boat usually has 20 paddlers, a drummer, and a steerperson. Mid-August.

U.S. Open Tennis Tournament Begins: The Grand Slam is one of the big four tournaments: the others are Wimbledon, The Australian Open, and the French Open. August–September.

September

Fashion Week: Various events all over, many in the Village.

Feast of San Gennaro: Italian feast with lots of food, drink, and games of skill takes place on Mulberry Street from Prince to Bayard Streets. Since 1926.

Atlantic Antic Street Fair: Atlantic Avenue, Brooklyn. Forty-three-year-old annual street fair, the largest in Brooklyn.

New York Film Festival: Produced by the Film Society of Lincoln Center since 1963.

West Indian Day Parade: Crown Heights. A street carnival/parade celebrating Caribbean culture in costume, music, and food. Columbus Day Weekend, early October.

Tribute in Light: At sunset each year on 9/11, a light installation of twin beams of light are cast four miles into the sky from a site near the original World Trade Center towers to honor the victims. Can be seen for miles around.

October

Open House New York: Mid-October. Tours of usually private sites all over the city.

Greenwich Village Halloween Parade: October 31st. Begins at Canal Street, runs up 6th Avenue to 23rd Street. Over a million people watch and over 50,000 people parade in costume.

Tompkins Square Halloween Dog Parade: Around Tompkins Square Park, for almost 30 years. Hundreds of cute, costumed dogs, often with an eccentric East Village flair.

Columbus Day Parade: Second Monday. Fifth Avenue from 44th to 86th Streets. A parade with an Italian accent.

The Blessing of the Animals: Cathedral of St. John the Divine. Hundreds of animals from alpaca and parrots to kangaroos and camels have been blessed each year.

New York Comic Con: Early October. Jacob Javits Center, 655 West 11th Street at 11th Avenue. Giant pop-cultural event with costumed participants, attracting over 150,000 fans.

Bryant Park Winter Skating Opens: Features skate rentals and music. Skating under the lights.

Central Park Winter Skating Opens: In the south section of the park, easily reached.

November

New York City Marathon: Early November. The route is 26.2 miles, through all five boroughs.

Macy's Thanksgiving Day Parade: Fourth Thursday of November. You can also see the balloons get blown up the night before on the street next to the Museum of Natural History; go early.

Holiday Markets: Union Square, Bryant Park. Over one hundred small gift shops.

Rockefeller Center Tree Lighting: Ice rink opens; semi-official beginning of the NYC holiday season.

Radio City Music Hall Christmas Show Begins: Starring the Rockettes.

December

SantaCon: Early December. Mass barhopping in Santa and elf outfits; the route is online.

Tuba Christmas: Tubas and euphoniums played en masse in Rockefeller Center.

New Year's Eve: December 31st. Times Square ball dropping. Revelers are separated into "pens" eight hours before the start, so don't drink too many fluids!

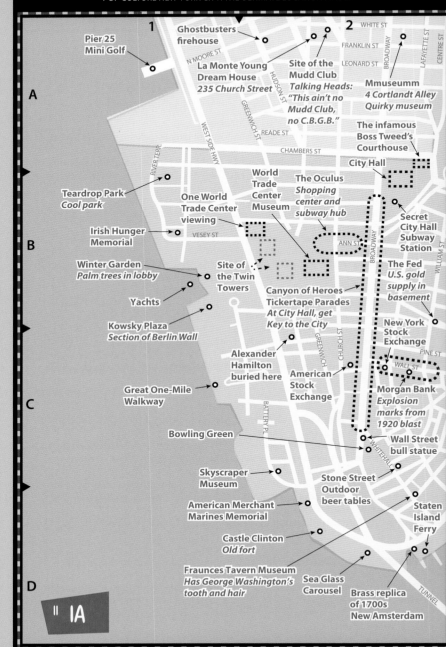

1

Pier 25 Mini Golf

Ghostbusters firehouse

N MOORE ST

La Monte Young Dream House
235 Church Street

Site of the Mudd Club
Talking Heads: "This ain't no Mudd Club, no C.B.G.B."

2 WHITE ST

FRANKLIN ST

LEONARD ST

BROADWAY

LAFAYETTE ST

CENTRE ST

Mmuseumm
4 Cortlandt Alley Quirky museum

HUDSON ST

GREENWICH ST

READE ST

CHAMBERS ST

The infamous Boss Tweed's Courthouse

City Hall

RIVER TERR.

WEST SIDE HWY

Teardrop Park
Cool park

One World Trade Center viewing

World Trade Center Museum

The Oculus
Shopping center and subway hub

Secret City Hall Subway Station

Irish Hunger Memorial

VESEY ST

ANN ST

BROADWAY

WILLIAM ST

B

The Fed
U.S. gold supply in basement

Winter Garden
Palm trees in lobby

Site of the Twin Towers

Yachts

Canyon of Heroes
Tickertape Parades At City Hall, get Key to the City

New York Stock Exchange

PINE ST

Kowsky Plaza
Section of Berlin Wall

GREENWICH ST

CHURCH ST

WALL ST

Alexander Hamilton buried here

American Stock Exchange

Morgan Bank
Explosion marks from 1920 blast

C

Great One-Mile Walkway

BATTERY PL.

Bowling Green

WHITEHALL

Wall Street bull statue

Skyscraper Museum

Stone Street Outdoor beer tables

Staten Island Ferry

American Merchant Marines Memorial

Castle Clinton
Old fort

Fraunces Tavern Museum
Has George Washington's tooth and hair

Sea Glass Carousel

Brass replica of 1700s New Amsterdam

TUNNEL

D

A

IA

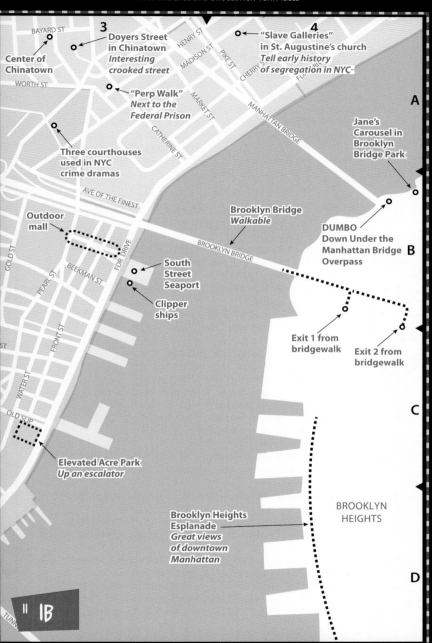

3

BAYARD ST

Center of Chinatown

Doyers Street in Chinatown
Interesting crooked street

HENRY ST

MADISON ST

WORTH ST

"Perp Walk"
Next to the Federal Prison

MARKET ST

PIKE ST

CHERRY ST

4

"Slave Galleries" in St. Augustine's church
Tell early history of segregation in NYC

FL...

MANHATTAN BRIDGE

A

CATHERINE ST

Three courthouses used in NYC crime dramas

AVE OF THE FINEST

Outdoor mall

FDR DRIVE

Brooklyn Bridge
Walkable

BROOKLYN BRIDGE

Jane's Carousel in Brooklyn Bridge Park

DUMBO
Down Under the Manhattan Bridge Overpass

B

GOLD ST

BEEKMAN ST

PEARL ST

South Street Seaport

Clipper ships

FRONT ST

Exit 1 from bridgewalk

Exit 2 from bridgewalk

WATER ST

...ST

OLD SLIP

C

Elevated Acre Park
Up an escalator

Brooklyn Heights Esplanade
Great views of downtown Manhattan

BROOKLYN HEIGHTS

D

TUN...

II **IB**

Tickertape Parades (Occasional)

Since the first tickertape parade in 1886 for the dedication of the Statue of Liberty, New Yorkers have celebrated national and international heroes, foreign dignitaries, astronauts, and champion sports teams with tickertape parades on what is called "the Canyon of Heroes": lower Broadway from the Battery up to City Hall, where sometimes the honoree is given the key to the city. Actual tickertape used to be used, but that has been replaced by shredded paper and confetti brought in by companies along the parade route. If you walk along lower Broadway, the honorees and dates of many of the parades are embedded in the sidewalk all along the Canyon of Heroes.

UNIQUE, OFF-BEAT, OR OLD SCHOOL RESTAURANTS, BARS, AND FOOD STORES

African-American "Soul Food" Restaurants

Amy Ruth's: 113 West 116th Street between Adam Clayton Powell and Malcom X. Boulevards. Since 1999.

Miss Mamie's Spoonbread Too: 366 West 110th Street near Manhattan Avenue. 1950s diner décor.

Sylvia's Restaurant: 328 Malcolm X Boulevard between 126th and 127th Streets. A Harlem landmark since 1962.

Appetizing Stores

"Appetizing stores" sell Jewish food, like lox, that one eats with bagels. The name, from the 1930s–1940s, is fading from use.

Russ and Daughters: 179 East Houston Street between Allen and Orchard Streets. High-end smoked fish and Jewish specialty food since 1914.

Barney Greengrass: 541 Amsterdam Avenue between 86th and 87th Streets. Smoked fish and more since 1908. Cash only.

Old Historic Neighborhood Bars, Still Going Strong

Arthur's Tavern (1937): 57 Grove Street west of 7th Avenue South, West Village

Kenn's Broome Street Bar (1972): 363 West Broadway at Broome Street, Soho

Corner Bistro (1920s): 331 West 4th Street at Jane Street, West Village

Ear Inn (1817): 326 Spring Street between Washington and Greenwich Streets, West Soho

El Quijote (1930): 226 West 23rd Street between 7th and 8th Avenues, Chelsea

Fanelli Cafe (1847): 94 Prince Street at Mercer Street, Soho

Jeremy's Ale House (1974): 288 Front Street between Beekman Street and Peck Slip. Ceiling decorated with hanging bras.

Landmark Tavern (1868): 626 11th Avenue at West 46th Street, Midtown West

Marie's Crisis Cafe (1929): 59 Grove Street west of 7th Avenue South, West Village. Piano bar.

McSorley's Old Ale House (1854): 15 East 7th Street between 2nd and 3rd Avenues, East Village

Mulberry Street Bar (1908): 176 Mulberry Street at Broome Street, Little Italy

Old Town Bar (1882): 45 East 18th Street between Broadway and Park Avenue South, Union Square. Was in the opening credits of David Letterman's show.

Peter McManus Cafe (1911): 152 7th Avenue at 19th Street, Chelsea

P.J. Clarke's (1884): 915 3rd Avenue at East 55th Street, Midtown East

Pete's Tavern (1864): 129 East 18th Street at Irving Place, Union Square

Walker's (1980s): 16 North Moore Street at Varick Street, Tribeca

White Horse Tavern (1880): 567 Hudson Street at West 11th Street, West Village

Bars on Boats

Frying Pan: 207 12th Avenue at 26th Street on Pier 66. May to October.

Grand Banks: Hudson River Park, Pier 25 west of North Moore Street

Bars, Revolving: Times Square

The View at the New York Marriott Marquis: 1535 Broadway between 46th and 48th Streets. Bar/restaurant on the 48th floor revolves 360 degrees every hour.

Bars with a Secret Entrance
(Modern–Day Speakeasies)

PDT (Please Don't Tell): 113 St. Mark's Place between 1st Avenue and Avenue A, East Village. The entrance is through the Crif Dog hot dog store. Go into the phone booth and dial "1".

La Esquina: 114 Kenmore Street at Lafayette, East Village. There's a basement brasserie through the kitchen; call ahead.

The Blind Barber: 339 East 10th Street, Lower East Side. The entrance is through a working barber shop.

The Back Room: 102 Norfolk Street at Delancey, Lower East Side. Speakeasy vibe: enter through a gate that says Lower East Side Toy Company.

Death and Co.: 433 East 6th Street between 1st Avenue and Avenue A, East Village. Enter off the street; resembles a dark speakeasy inside. Ten years old.

Angel's Share: 6 Stuyvesant Street, east of 3rd Avenue, East Village. Entrance is up the inside steps to a Japanese restaurant called Village Yokocho. Look for an unmarked door.

Bars: Unique

Beauty Bar: 231 East 14th Street between 2nd and 3rd Avenues. Bar and music in a retro beauty shop.

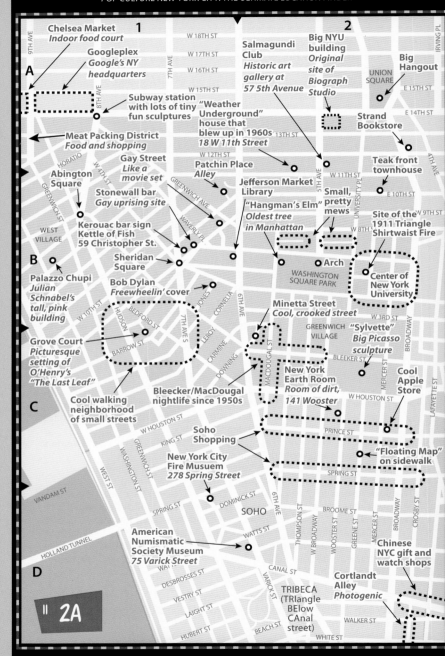

1

W 18TH ST
W 17TH ST
W 16TH ST
W 15TH ST

Chelsea Market
Indoor food court

Googleplex
Google's NY headquarters

A

Subway station with lots of tiny fun sculptures

Meat Packing District
Food and shopping

Gay Street
Like a movie set

Abington Square

Stonewall bar
Gay uprising site

Kerouac bar sign
Kettle of Fish
59 Christopher St.

WEST VILLAGE

Sheridan Square

B

Palazzo Chupi
Julian Schnabel's tall, pink building

Bob Dylan
Freewheelin' cover

Grove Court
Picturesque setting of O'Henry's "The Last Leaf"

Cool walking neighborhood of small streets

C

Soho Shopping

New York City Fire Musuem
278 Spring Street

SOHO

American Numismatic Society Museum
75 Varick Street

D

‖ **2A**

Salmagundi Club
Historic art gallery at 57 5th Avenue

"Weather Underground" house that blew up in 1960s
18 W 11th Street

Patchin Place
Alley

Jefferson Market Library

"Hangman's Elm"
Oldest tree in Manhattan

Minetta Street
Cool, crooked street

Bleecker/MacDougal
nightlife since 1950s

New York Earth Room
Room of dirt, 141 Wooster

2

Big NYU building
Original site of Biograph Studio

UNION SQUARE

Big Hangout

Strand Bookstore

Teak front townhouse

Small, pretty mews

Site of the 1911 Triangle Shirtwaist Fire

Arch

WASHINGTON SQUARE PARK

Center of New York University

GREENWICH VILLAGE

"Sylvette"
Big Picasso sculpture

Cool Apple Store

"Floating Map"
on sidewalk

Chinese NYC gift and watch shops

Cortlandt Alley
Photogenic

TRIBECA
(TRIangle BElow CAnal street)

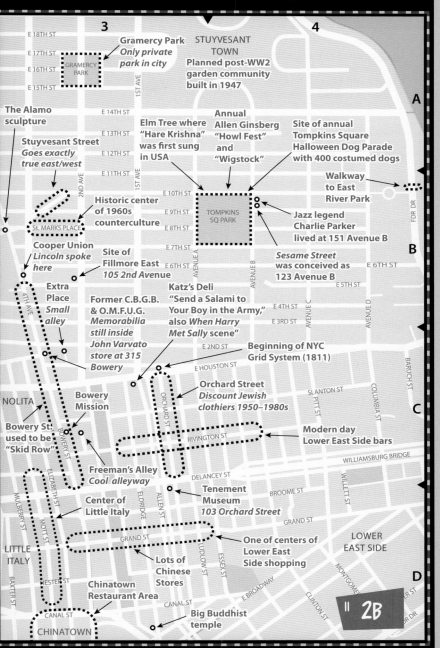

3

Gramercy Park
Only private park in city

GRAMERCY PARK

STUYVESANT TOWN
Planned post-WW2 garden community built in 1947

4

E 18TH ST
E 17TH ST
E 16TH ST
E 15TH ST
E 14TH ST
E 13TH ST
E 12TH ST
E 11TH ST
E 10TH ST
E 9TH ST
E 8TH ST
E 7TH ST

1ST AVE
2ND AVE

A

The Alamo sculpture

Stuyvesant Street
Goes exactly true east/west

Elm Tree where "Hare Krishna" was first sung in USA

Annual Allen Ginsberg "Howl Fest" and "Wigstock"

Site of annual Tompkins Square Halloween Dog Parade with 400 costumed dogs

Walkway to East River Park

FDR DR

Historic center of 1960s counterculture

ST. MARKS PLACE

TOMPKINS SQ PARK

Jazz legend Charlie Parker lived at 151 Avenue B

B

Cooper Union
Lincoln spoke here

Site of Fillmore East
105 2nd Avenue

Sesame Street was conceived as 123 Avenue B

E 6TH ST
E 5TH ST

AVENUE A
AVENUE B
AVENUE C
AVENUE D

4TH AVE

Extra Place
Small alley

Former C.B.G.B. & O.M.F.U.G.
Memorabilia still inside John Varvato store at 315 Bowery

Katz's Deli
"Send a Salami to Your Boy in the Army," also *When Harry Met Sally* scene"

E 4TH ST
E 3RD ST
E 2ND ST
E HOUSTON ST

Beginning of NYC Grid System (1811)

BARUCH ST

NOLITA

Bowery Mission

Orchard Street
Discount Jewish clothiers 1950–1980s

SLANTON ST
PITT ST
COLUMBIA ST

C

Bowery St. used to be "Skid Row"

BOWERY ST
ORCHARD ST

RIVINGTON ST

Modern day Lower East Side bars

WILLIAMSBURG BRIDGE

WILLETT ST

Freeman's Alley
Cool alleyway

ELIZABETH ST
ELDRIDGE ST
ALLEN ST

DELANCEY ST

Tenement Museum
103 Orchard Street

BROOME ST

Center of Little Italy

MULBERRY ST
MOTT ST

GRAND ST

LOWER EAST SIDE

LITTLE ITALY

One of centers of Lower East Side shopping

LUDLOW ST
ESSEX ST

MONTGOMERY ST

D

BAXTER ST

Lots of Chinese Stores

CANAL ST

Chinatown Restaurant Area

CHESTER ST

Big Buddhist temple

E BROADWAY

CLINTON ST

2B

CHINATOWN
CANAL ST

La Caverna: 122 Irvington Street between Essex and Norfolk Streets. Underground cave atmosphere.

Beauty and Essex: 146 Essex Street between Irvington and Stanton Streets. Enter through a small pawn shop.

Beer Halls, Beer Gardens, and Breweries

Brooklyn Brewery: 79 North 11th Street between Wythe and Berry Streets. Watch beer being made, too.

Reichenbach Hall: 5 West 37th Street between 5th and 6th Avenues. Bavarian-style beer hall with giant pretzels and "shot-skis."

Bohemian Hall and Beer Garden: 2919 24th Avenue between 29th and 31st Streets, Astoria, Queens. Large half-block *biergarten* with picnic tables and bratwurst. Since 1910.

Houston Hall: 222 West Houston Street between Varick Street and 6th Avenue. Large downtown indoor beer hall.

Coney Island Brewing Company: 1904 Surf Avenue at West 17th Street, Coney Island. Craft beer and brewery visits.

Cafes: Old School Greenwich Village/East Village

Caffe Reggio (1927): 119 MacDougal Street between West 3rd Street and Minetta Lane

Cafe Dante NYC (1915): 79–81 MacDougal Street between Houston and Bleecker Streets

Veniero's Pasticceria & Caffe (1894): 342 East 11th Street between 1st and 2nd Avenues

Candy

Dylan's Candy Bar: 1011 3rd Avenue at East 60th, Upper East Side. A colorful megastore of all things candy and cupcakes.

Economy Candy: 108 Rivington Street between Ludlow and Essex Streets, Lower East Side. Classic candy bars in an old-school, authentic 1950s-era setting.

M&M's World: 1600 Broadway at 48th Street. Three floors of various M&M goodies and memorabilia in Times Square.

Myzel's Chocolates: 140 West 55th Street between 6th and 7th Avenues. Compact store with over 150 varieties of licorice. Lots of chocolate, of course, too.

The Sweet Life: 63 Hester Street between Essex and Ludlow Streets, Lower East Side. Lots of gourmet candies and chocolates, also dried fruits and gifts. Since 1982.

Cheesecake

Junior's Restaurant and Bakery: 1515 Broadway, enter on 45th Street, Times Square.

Junior's: 386 Flatbush Avenue at DeKalb Avenue, Brooklyn. The original, since 1950.

Eileen's Special Cheesecake: 17 Cleveland Place at Kenmare Street, Nolita. A downtown favorite for 35 years.

Chinese Food in Chinatown (Old School)

Now Wah Tea Parlor: 13 Doyers Street near Pell Street. Dim sum since 1920, as seen in *Spider-Man 2*.

Wo Hop: 17 Mott Street between Worth and Mosco Streets. Cantonese since 1938. Open late.

Golden Unicorn: 18 East Broadway at Catherine Street. Giant Chinese eatery specializing in dim sum.

Great NY Noodletown: 28 Bowery at Bayard Street. Since 1981.

Chocolate Desserts

Max Brenner's Restaurant: 841 Broadway between 13th and 14th Streets. The restaurant specializes in chocolate desserts and gifts.

Coffee Shops: Old Fashioned, Counter

Eisenberg's Sandwich Shop: 174 5th Avenue between 22nd and 23rd Streets. Long counter and all-day breakfast since 1929.

La Bonboniere: 28 8th Avenue between West 12th and Jane Streets. From a bygone era, with sidewalk tables.

Lexington Candy Shop: 1226 Lexington Avenue at 83rd Street. Authentic 1929 burger, soda, and ice cream shop with 1940s decor.

The Donut Pub: 203 West 14th Street at 7th Avenue. Serving cups of joe twenty-four hours a day since 1964.

Pearl Diner: 212 Pearl Street at Fletcher Street. Fifty-year-old stainless steel and Formica diner.

Hector's Cafe & Diner: 44 Little West 12th Street at Washington Street, Meat-packing District. Since 1949.

Twenty-Four-Hour Lower East Side Coffee Shop: 442 East 14th Street near Avenue A. Old-fashioned diner food.

Broadway Restaurant: 2664 Broadway between 101st and 102nd Streets. Complete with U-shaped counter.

Tom's Restaurant: 2880 Broadway at West 112th Street. The exterior was "Monk's" on *Seinfeld*. Sit in similar booths.

B+H Dairy: 127 2nd Avenue between East 7th Street and St. Mark's Place. Tiny, vegetarian, and kosher since about 1940.

Margot Restaurant: 136 West 46th Street between 6th and 7th Avenues. Inexpensive Cubano sandwiches at a small lunch counter off Times Square since 1970.

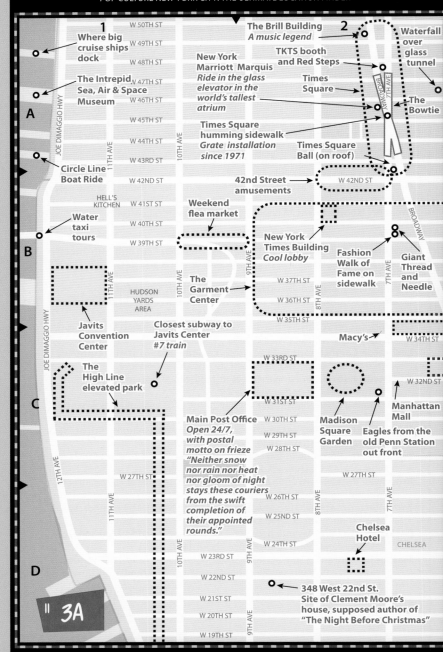

1

Where big cruise ships dock

The Intrepid Sea, Air & Space Museum

A

Circle Line Boat Ride

HELL'S KITCHEN

Water taxi tours

B

HUDSON YARDS AREA

Javits Convention Center

The High Line elevated park

C

The Brill Building *A music legend*

2

Waterfall over glass tunnel

TKTS booth and Red Steps

New York Marriott Marquis *Ride in the glass elevator in the world's tallest atrium*

Times Square

The Bowtie

Times Square humming sidewalk *Grate installation since 1971*

Times Square Ball (on roof)

42nd Street amusements

Weekend flea market

New York Times Building *Cool lobby*

Fashion Walk of Fame on sidewalk

Giant Thread and Needle

The Garment Center

Closest subway to Javits Center #7 train

Macy's

Main Post Office *Open 24/7, with postal motto on frieze "Neither snow nor rain nor heat nor gloom of night stays these couriers from the swift completion of their appointed rounds."*

Madison Square Garden

Eagles from the old Penn Station out front

Manhattan Mall

Chelsea Hotel

CHELSEA

D

348 West 22nd St. Site of Clement Moore's house, supposed author of "The Night Before Christmas"

3A

JOE DIMAGGIO HWY
11TH AVE
10TH AVE
9TH AVE
8TH AVE
7TH AVE
BROADWAY
12TH AVE
11TH AVE
10TH AVE
9TH AVE
8TH AVE
7TH AVE

W 50TH ST
W 49TH ST
W 48TH ST
W 47TH ST
W 46TH ST
W 45TH ST
W 44TH ST
W 43RD ST
W 42ND ST
W 41ST ST
W 40TH ST
W 39TH ST
W 37TH ST
W 36TH ST
W 35TH ST
W 34TH ST
W 33RD ST
W 32ND ST
W 31ST ST
W 30TH ST
W 29TH ST
W 28TH ST
W 27TH ST
W 26TH ST
W 25ND ST
W 24TH ST
W 23RD ST
W 22ND ST
W 21ST ST
W 20TH ST
W 19TH ST

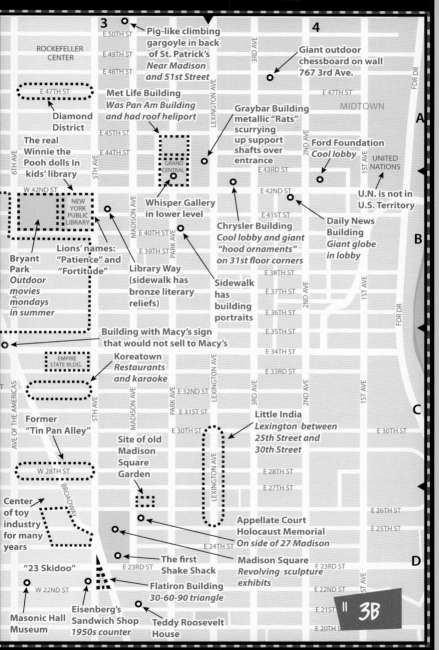

3

ROCKEFELLER CENTER

E 50TH ST
E 49TH ST
E 48TH ST

Pig-like climbing gargoyle in back of St. Patrick's *Near Madison and 51st Street*

4

Giant outdoor chessboard on wall 767 3rd Ave.

3RD AVE

E 47TH ST

MIDTOWN

FDR DR

Met Life Building *Was Pan Am Building and had roof heliport*

E 47TH ST

E 45TH ST

Diamond District

Graybar Building metallic "Rats" scurrying up support shafts over entrance

2ND AVE

Ford Foundation *Cool lobby*

1ST AVE

UNITED NATIONS

A

6TH AVE

5TH AVE

LEXINGTON AVE

E 44TH ST

GRAND CENTRAL

The real Winnie the Pooh dolls In kids' library

E 43RD ST

U.N. is not in U.S. Territory

W 42ND ST

NEW YORK PUBLIC LIBRARY

Whisper Gallery in lower level

E 42ND ST

Daily News Building *Giant globe in lobby*

B

Lions' names: "Patience" and "Fortitude"

MADISON AVE

PARK AVE

E 41ST ST

E 40TH ST

E 39TH ST

Chrysler Building *Cool lobby and giant "hood ornaments" on 31st floor corners*

1ST AVE

Bryant Park *Outdoor movies mondays in summer*

Library Way (sidewalk has bronze literary reliefs)

E 38TH ST

E 37TH ST

2ND AVE

Sidewalk has building portraits

E 36TH ST

E 35TH ST

FDR DR

Building with Macy's sign that would not sell to Macy's

E 34TH ST

EMPIRE STATE BLDG.

Koreatown *Restaurants and karaoke*

E 33RD ST

C

AVE OF THE AMERICAS

MADISON AVE

PARK AVE

LEXINGTON AVE

E 32ND ST

E 31ST ST

3RD AVE

2ND AVE

1ST AVE

Former "Tin Pan Alley"

E 30TH ST

Little India *Lexington between 25th Street and 30th Street*

E 30TH ST

Site of old Madison Square Garden

LEXINGTON AVE

E 28TH ST

E 27TH ST

W 28TH ST

Center of toy industry for many years

BROADWAY

E 26TH ST

E 25TH ST

Appellate Court Holocaust Memorial *On side of 27 Madison*

D

"23 Skidoo"

E 24TH ST

E 23RD ST

The first Shake Shack

Madison Square *Revolving sculpture exhibits*

E 23RD ST

1ST AVE

E 22ND ST

W 22ND ST

Flatiron Building *30-60-90 triangle*

E 21ST ST

II 3B

Masonic Hall Museum

Eisenberg's Sandwich Shop *1950s counter*

Teddy Roosevelt House

E 20TH ST

243

Cupcakes by Sidewalk Vending Machine

Sprinkles: 780 Lexington between East 60th and 61st Streets. Sidewalk ATM stocked 24/7 with Sprinkles cupcakes and cookies.

Deli

Katz's Deli (1888): 205 East Houston Street at Ludlow Street. Giant pricy deli sandwiches and famous hot dogs. Motto: "Send a salami to your boy in the Army!"

Rupert + Jee's Hello Deli: 213 West 53rd between Broadway and 8th Avenue. Made famous on David Letterman's show.

Diners

Standalone old school diners in the shape of railroad cars.

Empire Diner: 210 Tenth Avenue at 22nd Street, Chelsea. Upscale.

Pearl Diner: 212 Pearl Street at Fletcher Street. Fifty-year-old stainless steel and Formica diner.

The Square Diner: 33 Leonard Street at Varick Street. Cash-only train-car diner.

Dining with Dolls

American Girl Place: 609 Fifth Avenue at 49th Street. Dine with your American Girl doll.

Drag Queen Dinner Shows

Diva Royale Drag Queen Show: 512 West 42nd Street between 10th and 11th Avenues. Cabaret-style drag queen show with dinner.

Lips: 227 East 56th Street between 2nd and 3rd Avenues. Drag Queen cabaret and dinner.

Lucky Cheng: 605 West 48th Street between West Street and 11th Avenue. Drag Queen dinner show. As with the others, it's big with bachelorette parties.

Egg Cream

Gem Spa: 132 2nd Avenue at St. Mark's Place. Newsstand that since the 1920s has also sold New York egg cream drinks. A photo of the New York Dolls outside Gem Spa is on the back cover of their first album.

Food Courts, Modern

Stone Street: Between Coenties Alley and William Street. Seasonal. Outdoor picnic tables.

Eataly: 200 Fifth Avenue at 23rd Street. Italian food emporium.

Hudson Eats at Brookfield Place: World Financial Center

Le District at Brookfield place: World Financial Center. French food hall.

The Pennsy: 7th Avenue and West 33rd Street, above Penn Station

Plaza (Hotel) Food Hall: In the basement at 59th Street and Fifth Avenue

Gotham West: 11th Avenue between 44th and 45th Streets. Food hall.
New World Mall: 136–20 Roosevelt Avenue, Flushing, Queens. Large, Asian.
Urbanspace Vanderbilt: Vanderbilt Avenue and 45th Street, near Grand
    Central
Chelsea Market: 75 Ninth Avenue between West 15th and West 16th Streets.
    Block-long indoor mall with various eateries.
Essex Street Market: 120 Essex Street between Delancey and Irvington
    Streets. Seventy-year indoor market with food vendors.

Gay and Lesbian Bars, Long–Established

Julius: 159 West 10th Street at Waverly Place. One of the oldest gay bars in
    NYC. Since the 1950s.
The Monster: 80 Grove Street at Sheridan Square. Large gay bar; music and
    dancing.
The Cubbyhole: 281 West 12th Street near 4th Street. Long-established
    lesbian bar.
Henrietta Hudson: 438 Hudson Street at Morton Street. Lesbian bar open for
    over twenty-five years.

Hamburgers Near Times Square
for Those on a Budget

McDonald's: 220 West 42nd Street between 7th and 8th Avenues, 1560
    Broadway between 46th and 47th Streets. Two of the world's busiest.
Schnippers: 620 Eighth Avenue at 41st Street. Inexpensive hamburgers and
    milkshakes near Times Square.
Steak and Shake: 1695 Broadway between West 53rd and West 54th Streets.
    Part of a chain.

Inexpensive Hamburger Restaurant
with a "Secret" Entrance, Near Central Park

Burger Joint at Le Parker Meridian Hotel: 119 West 56th Street between
    6th and 7th Avenues. An inexpensive old-fashioned burger joint in a
    fancy hotel. Enter through a curtain wall in the lobby.

Hot Dogs (Mostly Long–Time New York Institutions)

Crif Dogs: 113 St. Mark's Place between Avenue A and 1st Avenue. Relatively
    new hot dog shop that uses a fryolator to cook hot dogs.
Gray's Papaya: Broadway at 72nd Street. Since 1973.
Katz's Deli: 205 East Houston Street at Ludlow Street. Since 1888.
Nathan's Famous: 1310 Surf Avenue at Stillwell Avenue, Coney Island,
    Brooklyn. Since 1916. The original.
Nathan's: 761 7th Avenue at 50th Street, other Manhattan locations
Papaya King: 86th Street and Third Avenue. Since 1932.

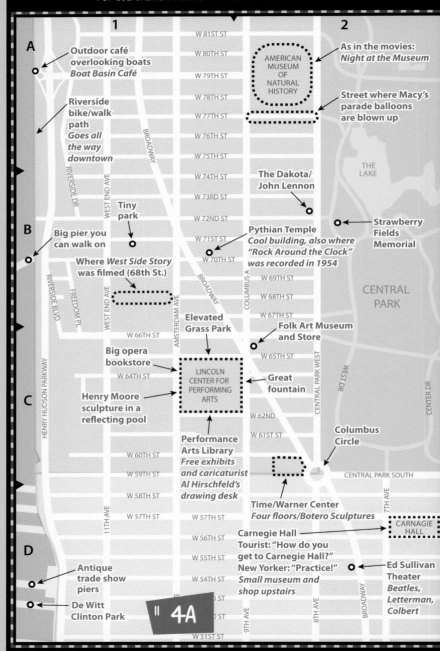

1

2

A

Outdoor café
overlooking boats
Boat Basin Café

Riverside
bike/walk
path
*Goes all
the way
downtown*

AMERICAN
MUSEUM
OF
NATURAL
HISTORY

As in the movies:
Night at the Museum

Street where Macy's
parade balloons
are blown up

THE
LAKE

W 81ST ST
W 80TH ST
W 79TH ST
W 78TH ST
W 77TH ST
W 76TH ST
W 75TH ST
W 74TH ST
W 73RD ST
W 72ND ST

BROADWAY

RIVERSIDE DR

WEST END AVE

The Dakota/
John Lennon

B

Big pier you
can walk on

Tiny
park

Where *West Side Story*
was filmed (68th St.)

Pythian Temple
*Cool building, also where
"Rock Around the Clock"
was recorded in 1954*

Strawberry
Fields
Memorial

CENTRAL
PARK

W 71ST ST
W 70TH ST
W 69TH ST
W 68TH ST
W 67TH ST

RIVERSIDE BLVD

FREEDOM PL

WEST END AVE

AMSTERDAM AVE

BROADWAY

COLUMBUS A

Elevated
Grass Park

Folk Art Museum
and Store

C

Big opera
bookstore

Henry Moore
sculpture in a
reflecting pool

LINCOLN
CENTER FOR
PERFORMING
ARTS

Great
fountain

CENTRAL PARK WEST

WEST DR

CENTER DR

HENRY HUDSON PARKWAY

W 66TH ST
W 64TH ST
W 62ND
W 61ST ST

Performance
Arts Library
*Free exhibits
and caricaturist
Al Hirschfeld's
drawing desk*

Columbus
Circle

Time/Warner Center
Four floors/Botero Sculptures

CENTRAL PARK SOUTH

7TH AVE

11TH AVE

W 60TH ST
W 59TH ST
W 58TH ST
W 57TH ST
W 57TH ST

Carnegie Hall
Tourist: "How do you
get to Carnegie Hall?"
New Yorker: "Practice!"
*Small museum and
shop upstairs*

CARNEGIE
HALL

D

Antique
trade show
piers

De Witt
Clinton Park

W 56TH ST
W 55TH ST
W 54TH ST

Ed Sullivan
Theater
*Beatles,
Letterman,
Colbert*

9TH AVE

8TH AVE

BROADWAY

‖ **4A**

D ST
D ST
W 51ST ST

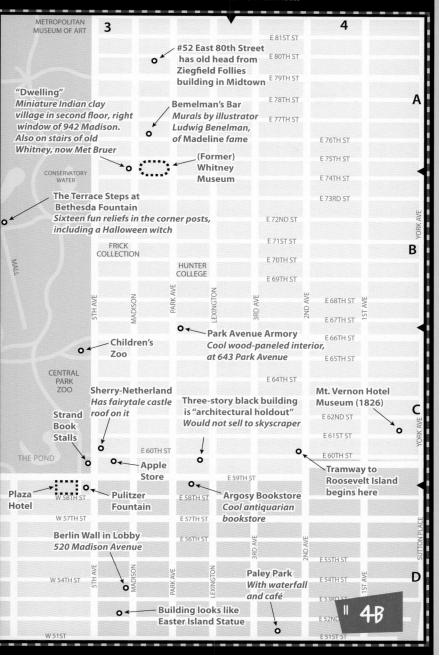

3

METROPOLITAN MUSEUM OF ART

#52 East 80th Street has old head from Ziegfield Follies building in Midtown

"Dwelling"
Miniature Indian clay village in second floor, right window of 942 Madison. Also on stairs of old Whitney, now Met Bruer

Bemelman's Bar
Murals by illustrator Ludwig Benelman, of Madeline fame

(Former) Whitney Museum

CONSERVATORY WATER

The Terrace Steps at Bethesda Fountain
Sixteen fun reliefs in the corner posts, including a Halloween witch

MALL

FRICK COLLECTION

HUNTER COLLEGE

5TH AVE
MADISON
PARK AVE
LEXINGTON
3RD AVE
2ND AVE
1ST AVE

Park Avenue Armory
Cool wood-paneled interior, at 643 Park Avenue

Children's Zoo

CENTRAL PARK ZOO

Sherry-Netherland
Has fairytale castle roof on it

Strand Book Stalls

Three-story black building is "architectural holdout"
Would not sell to skyscraper

Mt. Vernon Hotel Museum (1826)

THE POND

Apple Store

Tramway to Roosevelt Island begins here

Plaza Hotel

Pulitzer Fountain

Argosy Bookstore
Cool antiquarian bookstore

Berlin Wall in Lobby
520 Madison Avenue

3RD AVE
2ND AVE
1ST AVE

Paley Park
With waterfall and café

Building looks like Easter Island Statue

4

E 81ST ST
E 80TH ST
E 79TH ST
E 78TH ST
E 77TH ST
E 76TH ST
E 75TH ST
E 74TH ST
E 73RD ST
E 72ND ST
E 71ST ST
E 70TH ST
E 69TH ST
E 68TH ST
E 67TH ST
E 66TH ST
E 65TH ST
E 64TH ST
E 62ND ST
E 61ST ST
E 60TH ST
E 59TH ST
E 58TH ST
E 57TH ST
E 56TH ST
E 55TH ST
E 54TH ST
E 53RD ST
E 52ND ST
E 51ST ST

W 58TH ST
W 57TH ST
W 54TH ST
W 51ST ST

YORK AVE
YORK AVE
SUTTON PLACE

A
B
C
D

4B

Ice Bar Kept at Minus 5 Degrees Celsius

Minus 5* Ice Bar: New York Hilton, 1335 6th Avenue at West 53rd Street. Like drinking in Siberia. They loan you winter coats.

Ice Cream

Serendipity 3: 225 East 60th Street between 2nd and 3rd Avenues. An Andy Warhol favorite.

Big Gay Ice Cream: 61 Grove Street at 7th Avenue South, other locations

Original Chinatown Ice Cream Factory: 65 Bayard Street between Mott and Elizabeth Streets

Brooklyn Farmacy & Soda Fountain: 513 Henry Street at Sackett Street. Ice cream parlor with a 1920s theme.

Lexington Candy Shop: 1226 Lexington Avenue at 83rd Street. Shakes, sodas, and malts.

Jewish, Kitschy (Old School)

Famous Sammy's Roumanian Restaurant: 157 Christie Street between Delancey and Rivington Streets. Like a bar mitzvah on acid. Schmaltz (pourable chicken fat) at every table, group hora dancing, pricey.

Karaoke

Karaoke Boho: 186 West 4th Street between Barrow and Jones Streets

Karaoke One 17: 29 West 17th Street between 5th and 6th Avenues

Knish

Yonah Schimmel's Knish Bakery: 137 East Houston Street between Forsyth and Eldridge Streets. Old-world Jewish bakery/deli serving knishes, blintzes, and more since 1910.

Lemon Ice

The Lemon Ice King of Corona: 52–02 108th Street at 52nd Avenue, Corona, Queens. The standard of Italian ice since the 1940s, with over forty flavors, from peanut butter to cantaloupe. As seen on the opening credits of *The King of Queens*.

Meatballs in a Cup

Meatball Obsession: Walk-up window at 510 6th Avenue between 13th and 14th Streets. The meatballs come with a small piece of bread and tomato sauce.

Movie Theater Experiences with Bar and Restaurant

Watch the movie and enjoy dinner and have cocktails at your seat.

Alamo Drafthouse Cinema: 445 Albee Square West #4, downtown Brooklyn

iPic Movie theater: 11 Fulton Street at Front Street, South Street Seaport

Nighthawk Cinema: 136 Metropolitan Avenue, Williamsburg, Brooklyn

Pickles

The Pickle Guys: 357 Grand Street at Essex Street. Sells all size cured, kosher pickles from large barrels. "Hey, we got pickles here!"

Pizza: Top–Rated, Stand–Up, Take–Out Pizza by the Slice

Joe's Pizza: 7 Carmine Street between 6th Avenue and Bleecker Street, Greenwich Village. Since 1975.

Sal and Carmine's Pizza: 2671 Broadway between West 101 and West 102 Streets, Upper West Side. Since 1959.

Di Fara Pizza: 1424 Avenue J, Midwood, Brooklyn. Always top-rated $5 slices; open since 1959.

Pizza Suprema: 413 8th Avenue between 30th and 31st Streets, Chelsea, near Madison Square Garden. Since 1964.

Best Pizza: 33 Havemeyer Street between North 7th and 8th Streets, Williamsburg, Brooklyn. Since 2010.

Patsy's Pizzeria: 2287 1st Avenue between 117–118th, East Harlem. Since 1933.

Restaurant with One–Way Mirror in the Bathroom

Peep Restaurant: 177 Prince Street between Sullivan and Thompson Streets. This aptly-named restaurant in Soho has a bathroom in the middle of it with a one-way mirror that you can see out of as you use it.

Rice Pudding

Rice to Riches: 37 Spring Street between Mulberry and Mott Streets. Many flavors, served in space-age Jetson-like decor.

Soup

Grand Central Oyster Bar: 89 East 42nd Street in Grand Central Station's lower level. Famous for red and white clam chowders.

The Original Soupman: 259 West 55th between Broadway and 8th Avenue. Seinfeld's "Soup Nazi" episode was based on this walk-up store.

Veselka: 144 2nd Avenue at East 9th Street, East Village. Twenty-four-hour Ukrainian restaurant. Try the split pea soup.

Spices

Kalustyan's: 123 Lexington Avenue between East 28th and East 29th Streets. Little India spice megastore. Hundreds of varieties.

Tea Ceremony

Urasenke Chanoyu Center: 153 East 69th Street between Lexington and 3rd Avenues. Experience an authentic tea ceremony in a replica Japanese setting in a former East Side stable. Reservations needed far in advance.

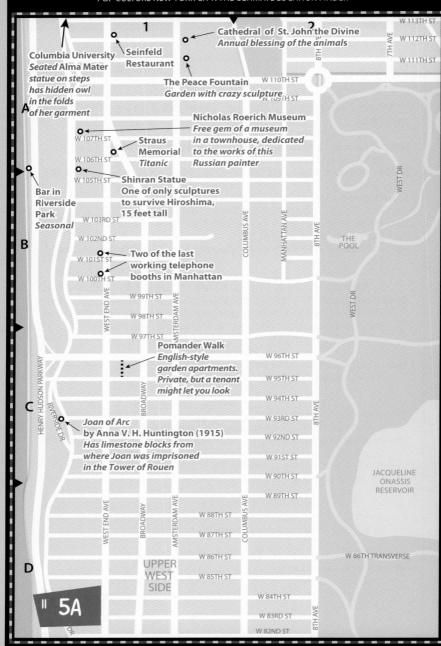

1

Cathedral of St. John the Divine
Annual blessing of the animals

Columbia University
Seated Alma Mater statue on steps has hidden owl in the folds of her garment

Seinfeld Restaurant

The Peace Fountain
Garden with crazy sculpture

A

Nicholas Roerich Museum
Free gem of a museum in a townhouse, dedicated to the works of this Russian painter

Straus Memorial
Titanic

W 107TH ST
W 106TH ST
W 105TH ST

Shinran Statue
One of only sculptures to survive Hiroshima, 15 feet tall

Bar in Riverside Park
Seasonal

W 103RD ST
W 102ND ST

B

W 101ST ST

Two of the last working telephone booths in Manhattan

W 100TH ST

W 99TH ST
W 98TH ST
W 97TH ST

Pomander Walk
English-style garden apartments. Private, but a tenant might let you look

W 96TH ST
W 95TH ST
W 94TH ST

C

W 93RD ST

Joan of Arc
by Anna V. H. Huntington (1915)
Has limestone blocks from where Joan was imprisoned in the Tower of Rouen

W 92ND ST
W 91ST ST
W 90TH ST
W 89TH ST

W 88TH ST
W 87TH ST
W 86TH ST

W 86TH TRANSVERSE

D

UPPER WEST SIDE

W 85TH ST
W 84TH ST
W 83RD ST
W 82ND ST

JACQUELINE ONASSIS RESERVOIR

THE POOL

5A

W 113TH ST
W 112TH ST
W 111TH ST
W 110TH ST

7TH AVE
8TH AVE
COLUMBUS AVE
MANHATTAN AVE
WEST DR
WEST END AVE
AMSTERDAM AVE
BROADWAY
HENRY HUDSON PARKWAY
RIVERSIDE DR

3

EAST HARLEM

4

W 112TH ST
W 111TH ST
CATHEDRAL PARKWAY
HARLEM MEER

5TH AVE
MALCOM X BLVD

MADISON AVE
PARK AVE
LEXINGTON AVE

E 112TH ST
E 111TH ST
E 110TH ST
E 109TH ST
E 108TH ST
E 107TH ST
E 106TH ST
E 105TH ST
E 104TH ST
E 103RD ST
E 102ND ST
E 101ST ST
E 100TH ST
E 99TH ST
E 98TH ST
E 97TH ST
E 96TH ST
E 95TH ST
E 94TH ST
E 93RD ST
E 92ND ST
E 91ST ST
E 90TH ST
E 89TH ST

E 103RD ST
E 101ST ST

3RD AVE
2ND AVE
1ST AVE

A

B

C

D

Andrew Haswell Green Memorial Bench
Big marble bench

New York Academy of Medicine Building
Cool two-tone Byzantine Revival exterior

EAST DR

MT SINAI HOSPITAL

Islamic Cultural Center
Islamic architecture

Old Armory
Looks like medieval castle

MADISON AVE
PARK AVE
LEXINGTON AVE

2ND AVE
1ST AVE

FDR DR

UPPER EAST SIDE

JACQUELINE ONASSIS RESERVOIR

The Solomon Guggenheim Museum

Gracie Mansion ⟶

Carl Schurz Park ⟶
Overlooking the East River

E 88TH ST
E 87TH ST
E 86TH ST
E 85TH ST
E 84TH ST
E 83RD ST
E 82RD ST

5TH AVE
MADISON AVE

YORK AVE

5B
MUSEUM OF ART

Theme/Tourist Restaurants

Bubba Gump Shrimp: 1501 Broadway at West 44th Street. *Forrest Gump.*

Dave and Buster's: 234 West 42nd Street between 7th and 8th Avenues. Arcade games.

Planet Hollywood: 1540 Broadway, enter on 45th Street. Hollywood memorabilia.

Hard Rock Cafe: 1501 Broadway at 43rd Street. Rock memorabilia.

Ninja Restaurant: 25 Hudson Street. Ninjas perform while you eat in an underground "Japanese village."

Ellen's Stardust Diner: 1650 Broadway at West 51st Street. Waitstaff sing on tables; 1950s diner theme.

Brooklyn Diner: 212 West 57th Street between 7th Avenue and Broadway. 1950s diner theme.

Twenty–Four–Hour Restaurants

Veselka: 144 2nd Avenue at East 9th Street, East Village. ($)

L'Express: 249 Park Avenue South at East 20th Street, Gramercy ($$)

Cafeteria: 119 7th Avenue at West 17th Street, Chelsea ($$)

Famous Scenes from Movies Filmed in NYC Restaurants

Bubby's Pie Company: 120 Hudson Street, Tribeca. *The Devil Wears Prada:* Anne Hutchinson gets the boss food.

Buddakan: 75 Ninth Avenue at West 16th Street. *Sex and the City, The Movie:* The rehearsal dinner for Carrie and Mr. Big.

Cafe Lalo: 201 West 83rd Street between Broadway and Amsterdam Avenue. *You've Got Mail:* Tom Hanks sits down with Meg Ryan "'til her fiend arrives."

City Bakery: 3 West 18th Street between 5th and 6th Avenues. *Music and Lyrics:* Hugh Grant and Drew Barrymore are in a scene here.

Joe's Pizza: 7 Carmine Street near 6th Avenue. *Spider-Man 2*: Peter Parker works here delivering pizza. In the movie it was at its old location on the corner of Carmine and Bleecker Streets.

John's of Bleecker Street: 278 Bleecker Street at John Street. Pizza. *Manhattan:* Mariel tells Woody she's going to London.

Katz's Deli: 205 East Houston Street at Ludlow Street. *When Harry Met Sally*: Meg Ryan fakes an orgasm, and a woman says "I'll have what she's having."

Lexington Avenue Candy Shop: 1226 Lexington Avenue at 83rd Street. *Three Days of the Condor:* Robert Redford and Faye Dunaway filmed a scene here.

Magnolia Bakery: 401 Bleecker Street at West 11th Street. *Sex and the City* (TV): Carrie talks to Miranda about a crush over cupcakes.

Russian Tea Room: 150 West 57th Street between 6th and 7th Avenues. *Tootsie:* Dustin Hoffman, as "Dorothy Michaels," fools his agent Sydney Pollack.

Sardi's: 234 West 44th Street between 7th and 8th Avenues. *The Muppets Take Manhattan:* Kermit pretends to be a producer by putting his picture on the wall.

Serendipity 3: 225 East 60th Street between 2nd and 3rd Avenues. *Serendipity*: John Cusack and Kate Beckinsale share hot chocolate.

Tom's Restaurant: 2880 Broadway at West 112th Street. *Seinfeld:* Where the gang talks about nothing over coffee.

21 Club: 21 West 52nd Street between 5th and 6th Avenues. *Wall Street*: Michael Douglas hands Charlie Sheen a million-dollar check.

Veselka: 144 2nd Avenue at East 9th Street. *Nick and Nora's Infinite Playlist:* Michael Cera and Kat Dennings stop off at this twenty-four-hour Ukrainian restaurant on their journey.

UNIQUE OR OFFBEAT STORES THAT ARE LIKE MUSEUMS OF THEIR PRODUCTS

African Handicrafts (Outdoor Market)

Malcolm Shabazz Harlem Market: 52 West 116th Street between 5th and Lenox Avenues. African bazaar with African crafts and textiles under canopied booths.

Antique Oddities

Obscura Antiques & Oddities: 207 Avenue A between East 12th and East 13th Streets. Offbeat antique store with quirky collectibles, including prints, skulls and taxidermy.

Asian Products

Pearl River: 395 Broadway at Walker Street. Food to forks to furnishings, all from Asia. All price levels.

Baking Supplies

New York Cake & Baking Supplies: 56 West 22nd Street between 5th and 6th Avenues. Great one-stop shop for all your baking and decorating needs.

Beads

Toho Shoji New York: 990 6th Avenue between West 36th and West 37th Streets

BeadKraft: 1231 Broadway at West 30th Street

Beads World: 57 West 38th Street between 5th and 6th Avenues

Bead Center: 989 Avenue of the Americas between West 36th and West 37th Streets

Mother Cabrini Shrine
*70 Fort Washington Avenue
You can view her mummified
remains in a glass cabinet
in the church*

The Little Red Lighthouse
*Under the George Washington Bridge
in Fort Washington Park, featured
in the book The Little Red Lighthouse
and The Big Gray Bridge*

The High Bridge (and Tower)
*Newly re-opened tall walkway
Manhattan's oldest bridge*

The Amiable Child Grave
*Across from Grant's Tomb at 123rd
Monument to a five-year-old
boy who died in 1797*

Dyker Heights
*Brooklyn neighborhood
known for its extravagant
holiday light displays*

New York Chinese Scholar's Garden
*A replica of a large 19th century Chinese
house with inner gardens and pond.
Part of the Snug Harbor Cultural Center
42nd Avenue, Staten Island*

Alice Austen House
*A pretty cottage formerly owned
by Alice Austen, a turn-of-the-
century photographer.
2 Hylan Boulevard, Rosebank*

Staten Island

Fort Wadsworth
*If you like old stone forts,
this one's a classic.
The batteries are three
stories high with
vaulted passageways
and spots for 25 cannons.
This is where the annual
New York Marathon
starts, near the Verrazano-
Narrows Bridge*

6A

The Birthplace of Hip Hop
1520 Sedgewick Avenue
DJ Kool Herc threw house parties
here in 1973 while rapping
to the beats

Hall of Fame of Great Americans
Bronx Community College
2155 University Avenue
Semi-circular outdoor
colonnade with bronze
portrait busts of 98 famous
Americans. Designed in
1909 by Stanford White

Our Lady of Lourdes Grotto
(a.k.a. Lourdes of America)
833 Mace Avenue
A 20-foot tall domed wall
of boulders was built in
1939 to resemble the grotto
in France. Piped city water
is said to cure ailments

The Bronx

Garabedian's Christmas House
1605 Pelham Parkway
Over-the-top Christmas lights
in season, like in Dyker Heights

Steinway & Sons
Piano Factory Tour
Steinway Place,
Astoria. See pianos
in the making.
3-hour tour,
Tuesdays only

Panorama of New York
Queens Museum of Art
See a 9,000 square foot
miniature model of
New York City built for
the 1964 World's Fair

Manhattan

Subway Entrance Façade
58 Joralemon Street,
Brooklyn Heights
It looks like a townhouse,
but it's a fake façade,
over an emergency
subway exit

The Ganesh Temple
45-57 Bowne Street, Flushing
A colorful decorative Indian Temple
smack in the middle of Queens

The City Reliquary
370 Metropolitan Avenue, Williamsburg
A smallish non-profit community
museum with quirky exhibits
like World's Fair trinkets,
Statue of Liberty replicas,
and a burlesque exhibit

Queens

Brooklyn

Long Island

Masstransiscope
An art installation that seems
like you're seeing a flickering
movie on the tunnel wall
as your subway car leaves the
northbound platform of
the DeKalb Avenue station.

Coney Island Circus Sideshow
1208 Surf Avenue, Coney Island
A sideshow carrying on the
tradition of "freak, wonders,
and human curiosities"

ll **6B**

Botanica

Original Products Botanica: 2486 Webster Avenue at East 189th Street, Fordham, Bronx. Supermarket-sized religious/Botanica/occult goods store since 1959.

Buttons

Lou Lou Buttons: 71 West 38th Street between 5th and 6th Avenues
M & J Trimmings: 1008 6th Avenue between 58th and 59th Streets
Tender Buttons: 143 East 62nd Street between Lexington and 3rd Avenues

Clothes, Vintage And Used

Buffalo Exchange: 114 West 26th Street, plus other locations in the East Village, Brooklyn, and Queens. Buy, sell, or trade your men's or women's clothes for cash. Great finds!

Reminiscence: 74 Fifth Avenue between 13th and 14th Streets. Antique clothes plus a selection of off-the-wall gifts.

Metropolis Vintage: 43 3rd Avenue between 9th and 10th Streets. Deep East Village selection favored by local stars.

Costumes

Abracadabra Superstore: 19 West 21st Street between 5th and 6th Avenues. Giant store offering all kinds of costumes, accessories, makeup, and magic tricks. Like walking into a circus funhouse.

Halloween Adventures: 104 Fourth Avenue between 11th and 12th Streets. Large store selling huge inventory of Halloween costumes year-round.

Gothic Renaissance: 104 Fourth Avenue between 11th and 12th Streets. Next to Halloween Adventure above. For the goth lover in you.

Dolls

American Girl Place New York: 609 5th Avenue at East 49th Street. Flagship store for the popular doll. Has photo studios and cafes for doll lunches.

Fire Department Clothes and Memorabilia

The FDNY Fire Zone: 34 West 51st Street between 5th and 6th Avenues, Rockefeller Center. Small fire-prevention learning center with New York Fire Department items for sale.

Fishing Tackle

Capitol Fishing Tackle: 132 West 36th Street between 6th and 7th Avenues. America's oldest tackle store. Cool neon sign. Taxidermied fish.

Flea Markets

Grand Bazaar Flea Market: Columbus Avenue at 77th Street. Indoor/outdoor, Sunday year-round 10:00 a.m.–5:30 p.m.

Chelsea Flea Market: 39 West 25th Street between 6th Avenue and Broadway, Flatiron. Saturday and Sunday, $1.00 admission.

Hell's Kitchen Flea Market: West 39th Street between 9 and 10th Avenues. Open Saturdays and Sundays most of the year.

Hester Street Fair: On weekends. Mostly a food fair.

Brooklyn Flea and Smorgasbord: Location varies. Usually Dumbo, Brooklyn. Food vendors.

Fossils

Evolution: 120 Spring Street between Greene and Mercer Streets. Look for the skeleton out front.

Gadgets for Adults

Hammacher Schlemmer: 147 East 57th Street between 3rd and Lexington Avenues. The world's best gadgets are offered by this 169-year-old company to make life easier. Fun to test!

Gambling

Resorts World Casino: 110-00 Rockaway Boulevard South, Ozone Park, Queens, next to Aqueduct Racetrack. New York City's only casino. 18+ only. Slots, video poker, and more.

Empire City Casino at Yonkers Raceway: 810 Yonkers Avenue, Yonkers, just north of New York City. "Guests must be at least 18 years old to play video gaming machines or wager on horses." Bring valid ID.

Games

The Compleat Strategist: 11 East 33rd Street. Headquarters for roleplaying games, strategy games, board games, and miniatures.

Gems

Astro Gallery of Gems: 417 5th Avenue between 37th and 38th Streets. World's largest gallery of gems and minerals in the world. Colorful and cool to see!

Gifts (Offbeat, Fun, Kitschy)

Reminiscence: 74 Fifth Avenue between 13th and 14th Streets

Flying Tiger Copenhagen: 920 Broadway at 21st Street

Gifts (Electronics and Doo–Dads)

AC Gears: 69 East 8th Street between Broadway and Mercer Street

Horse Riding Equipment

Manhattan Saddlery: 117 East 24th Street between Park Avenue South and Lexington Avenue. New York's only equestrian tack shop, selling horseback riding equipment.

Japanese Anime Figures, Toys, and Books

Toy Tokyo: 91 2nd Avenue between 5th and 6th Streets
Forbidden Planet: 832 Broadway between 12th and 13th Streets
Midtown Comics: 200 West 40th Street at 7th Avenue, 2nd floor

Magic

Abracadabra NYC: 19 West 21st Street between 5th and 6th Avenues. Costumes and makeup, too!
Tannen Magic: 45 West 34th Street #608, between 5th and 6th Avenues
Fantasma Magic: 421 7th Avenue at 33rd Street, enter on 33rd. Contains a small Houdini museum.

Musical Instruments, Old

Music Inn: 169 West 4th Street between Cornelia and Jones Streets. Honorary mention.

New York City Official Products

CityStore: 1 Centre Street at Chambers Street. The official New York City government-run store. Sells official NYC souvenirs, books, and memorabilia, some not found elsewhere.

New York City Transit

New York Transit Museum and Exhibit Center): 42nd Street and Vanderbilt Avenue, inside Grand Central. Sells NYC subway, NYC bus, Long Island Rail Road, and Metro North gifts and books. Also has exhibits. A smaller version of the Transit Museum store at the Transit Museum in Brooklyn.

Occult Supplies

Enchantments: 424 East 9th Street between Avenue A and 1st Avenue. Candles, herbs, oils, charms, and more.

Pop Art Gallery

Pop International Galleries: 195 Bowery at Spring Street. Specializes in "Pop art, urban art, and art and photography that is derived from, or influenced by, popular culture."

Science Fiction (Books and Toys)

Forbidden Planet: 840 Broadway at East 13th Street
Image Anime: 242 West 30th Street between 7th and 8th Avenues
Toy Tokyo: 91 Second Avenue between 5th and 6th Streets

Stationers, Old Fashioned

Bowne and Company Stationers: 209–211 Water Street between Fulton and Beekman Streets, South Street Seaport. Watch old-fashioned letterpresses in action; hand-printed cards made on site.

Superhero Supplies

Brooklyn Superhero Supply Company: 372 Fifth Avenue between 5th and 6th Streets, Park Slope, Brooklyn. Sells an array of superhero costumes, gifts, books, and clothes. A fun front for a writing-skills nonprofit program for young students.

Thrift Shops

Housing Works Thrift Shops: 143 West 17th Street between 6th and 7th Avenues, and various other outlets.

Goodwill: 44 West 8th Street between 5th and 6th Avenues. Many other outlets.

East Village Thrift Shop: 186 2nd Avenue between East 11th and East 12th Streets

Vintage Thrift Store: 286 3rd Avenue between 22nd and 23rd Streets

Turkish Bath

The Russian & Turkish Baths: 268 East 10th Street between 1st Street and Avenue A. Authentic 1900s Russian Turkish bathhouse from 1892. Get scrubbed with oak-leaf brooms or get a seaweed salt scrub!

Sexy Stuff

Babeland: 94 Rivington Street between Ludlow and Orchard Streets. Fully stocked sex toy boutique. One of three locations.

The Pleasure Chest: 156 7th Avenue South between Charles and Perry Streets. One of two locations. Adult sex-toy emporium in the West Village since 1972. Featured in a *Sex and the City* episode.

Museum of Sex Store: 23 Fifth Avenue at 27th Street, ground floor. All the kink you never knew you needed: sex toys, games, books. No entrance fee.

SOURCES

MOVIES AND TV

Books

The Movie Lover's Guide to New York, Richard Alleman, Perennial Library, New York, 1988.

Manhattan on Film, Chuck Katz, Hal Leonard Corp., Milwaukee, 1999, rev. 2005.

The Worldwide Guide to Movie Locations, Tony Reeves, Titan Books, London, 2001, rev. 2006.

Celluloid Skyline, James Sanders, Alfred A. Knopf, New York, 2003.

Scenes from the City: Filmmaking in New York, edited by James Sanders, Rizzoli, New York, 2006

On Location NYC: New York City's Top 100 Film and TV Locations, Alex Child, Museyon Guides, New York, 2013.

Ultimate Book of NY Lists, Bert Sugar with C.N. Richardson, Skyhorse Publishing, New York, 2009

Websites

AM New York: Amny.com

On the Set of New York: Otsony.com

Centralparksunsettours.com

"Top 10 Central Park Movies," Centralpark.org

On Location Tours: Onlocationtours.com

I Am Not A Stalker: Iamnotastalker.com

"The Best of New York Filming Locations to Visit," Worldofwanderlust.com

"Lower Manhattan Film and TV Locations," New-york-tours.com

"Staten Island Films," Rob Bailey/Staten Island Advance: http://www.silive.com/entertainment/index.ssf/2016/08/34_movies_you_probably_didnt_know_were_filmed_on_staten_island.html

"Top 20 Movies," Centralparktoursnyc.com

" Lower Manhattan Film and TV Locations," New-york-tours.com

"Visit the Filming Locations of HBO's *Girls*" by Hopper, The Huffington Post, huffingtonpost.com, May 14, 2014.

"Seinfeld Locations": TV Guide

"Take a Walking Tour of NYC based on Mad Men," Timeout.com, August 4, 2009.

LIVE AND TAPED TV SHOWS
NYCgo.com

BROADWAY THEATERS
Playbill.com and *Wikipedia* entries.

JAZZ CLUBS
Books
52nd Street: The Street of Jazz, Arnold Shaw, DaCapo Press, New York, 1971.
Discovering Black New York, Tarrant Reid, Citadel Press, New York, 2001.
Harlem on My Mind, Edited by Allon Schoener, The New Press, New York, 1995.

Websites
"The Rise & Fall of the Original Swing Street," NYPress.com, November 23, 2005.
"Historic Venues," Harlemjazzshrines.org, May 4–9, 2015.

RECORD ALBUM COVER LOCATIONS
Many thanks to Marie Fotini for all her help
in discovering many of these locations.

CELEBRITY ADDRESSES
Books
Literary New York: A History and Guide, Susan Edmonton and Linda D. Cirino,
Houghton Mifflin Company, Boston, 1976.
The Streets Where They Lived: A Walking Guide to the Residences of Famous New Yorkers, Stephen W. Plumb, Marlor Press. St. Paul, Minnesota, 1989.
New York City Starwalks, Larry Wolfe Horowitz, St. Martin's Press, New York, 1993.

Websites
Curbed.com
NewYorkObserver.com
Johnsstarmaps.com
Rightherenyc.com
Infamousnewyork.com
Cityrealty.com

Web Articles
"NYC Celebrity Map," Addressreport.com
"Rentenna's Celebrity Map," NewYorkObserver.com
"Star Maps of New York City: Where to find celebrities in the Big Apple," Matt Young, News.com.au

"Top Ten Celebrity Buildings in NYC," Claire Cooper, Kenner Williams, December 17, 2013.

"Inside New York's Most Expensive Apartment Buildings," Hana R. Alberts, Newyorkpost.com, November 7, 2015.

"Celebrities from Queens," AMNY.com, Dec 8, 2016.

"Brooklyn Star Map: Celebrities are Flocking to New York's Hippest Borough," BusinessInsider.com.

NEW YORK NOVELS

"Tales of New York City," Goodreads.com

"The 16 Best NYC Novels," Rebecca Fishbein, Gothamist.com

"15 Essential Novels of New York City," Qwiklit.com

"The 20 books that will make you fall in love with New York City all over again," Maddie Crum, The Huffington Post

"The 25 Best New York City Novels," Ross Scarano, Brenden Gallagher, and Greg Topscher, Complex.com.

The Best Books About New York City," Matthew Love, *TimeOut New York*, October 14, 2015.

"Ten of the best books set in New York." *The Guardian*, by Malcolm Burgess

"The Best New York City Novels by Neighborhood," Nancy Aravecz, Mid-Manhattan Library.

The Ultimate Book of New York Lists, Bert Sugar with C. N. Richardson, Skyhorse Publishing, New York, 2009.

SUPERHEROES/COMICS
Books

The Marvel Comics Guide to New York City, Peter Sanderson, Pocket Books, Simon & Schuster, New York, 2007.

Websites

"New York Super Hero Tour," Derrick Edwards, Freetoursbyfoot.com, 2017.

"Map of Spider-Man Movie Shooting Locations in New York City," Abraham Riesman, Vulture.com, June 21, 2017.

"The Ultimate Nerd Guide to New York City," Movie-locations.com

"A Guide to Marvel's Manhattan," Jake Rossen and Paul Horn, *Wizard* magazine Issue #199.

"Superheroes of New York," Onthesetognewyork.com

"10 NYC Locations for Sam Raimi's Original *Spider-Man*," Christopher Inoa, Untappedcities.com, May 1, 2014.

"The Superheroes Who Call NYC Home," Vera Panavic, Untappedcities.com, March 2, 2016.

BUILDINGS AND SCULPTURES

*Art in Public Places: Walking New York's Neighborhoods to See the Best Paintings,
Sculptures, Murals, Mosaics, and Mobiles*, David Masello, City & Company,
New York. 1999
*Manhattan's Outdoor Sculpture, the Art Commission and the Municipal Art
Society*, Margot Gayle and Michele Cohen, Prentice Hall Press, New York,
1988.
Unforgotten New York: Legendary Spaces of the Twentieth-Century Avant-Garde,
David Brun-Lambert, John Short, David Tanguy, Munich, New York,
Prestel, 2015.
Gothamist.com

MOB

New York Daily News
The Ultimate Book of New York Lists, Bert Sugar with C. N. Richardson, Skyhorse
Publishing, New York, 2009.

SPORTS
Books
*The Street Where They Lived: A Walking Guide to the Residences of Famous New
Yorkers*, Stephen W. Plumb, Parlor Press, St. Paul, Minnesota, 1989.
The Almanac of New York City, Edited by Kenneth T. Jackson and Fred Kameny,
Columbia University Press, New York, 2008.
"New York Celebrity Map: The Original NYC Star Map," NYCCelebrityMaps.com

Web
"FYI," Katheryn Shattuck, NewYorkTimes.com, April 7, 1996.
NewYorkSonglines.com
"Inside New York's Most Expensive Apartment Buildings," Hana R. Alberts,
Nypost.com, November 7, 2015.
"10 Defining Sports Moments from the Big Apple," Brian Leigh, BleacherRe-
port.com, January 13, 2014.
"The 20 Greatest Moments in New York Sports History," Chris Chase, FoxS-
ports.com, November 11, 2016.
"WFAN'S 25 Top Moments in New York Sports," Newyork.cbslocal.com
"Greatest Moments in New York history," SI.com